REMAKING AMERICA

REMAKING AMERICA

Democracy and Public
Policy in an Age
of Inequality

Joe Soss,
Jacob S. Hacker,
and Suzanne Mettler
Editors

Russell Sage Foundation
New York

The Russell Sage Foundation

The Russell Sage Foundation, one of the oldest of America's general purpose foundations, was established in 1907 by Mrs. Margaret Olivia Sage for "the improvement of social and living conditions in the United States." The Foundation seeks to fulfill this mandate by fostering the development and dissemination of knowledge about the country's political, social, and economic problems. While the Foundation endeavors to assure the accuracy and objectivity of each book it publishes, the conclusions and interpretations in Russell Sage Foundation publications are those of the authors and not of the Foundation, its Trustees, or its staff. Publication by Russell Sage, therefore, does not imply Foundation endorsement.

Library of Congress Cataloging-in-Publication Data

Remaking America : democracy and public policy in an age of inequality / [edited by] Joe Soss, Jacob S. Hacker, Suzanne Mettler.
    p. cm.
  ISBN 978-0-87154-816-0(alk. paper)
  1. Equality—United States. 2. Distributive justice—United States. 3. Public welfare—United States. 4. Marginality, Social—United States. 5. United States—Social policy—1993– I. Soss, Joe, 1967– II. Hacker, Jacob S. III. Mettler, Suzanne.
  HN90.S6R45 2007
  320.60973—dc22

2007015183

The paper used in this publication meets the minimum requirements of American National Standard for Information Sciences—Permanence of Paper for Printed Library Materials. ANSI Z39.48-1992.

Text design by Suzanne Nichols.

RUSSELL SAGE FOUNDATION
112 East 64th Street, New York, New York 10021
10   9   8   7   6   5   4   3   2   1

Contents

About the Authors

JOE SOSS is the Cowles Professor for the Study of Public Service at the Hubert H. Humphrey Institute of Public Affairs, University of Minnesota.

JACOB S. HACKER is a professor of political science at Yale University and a resident fellow of the Institution for Social and Policy Studies.

SUZANNE METTLER is the Clinton Rossiter Professor of American Institutions in the government department at Cornell University.

ANDREA LOUISE CAMPBELL is Alfred Henry and Jean Morrison Hayes Career Development Associate Professor of Political Science at MIT.

RICHARD B. FREEMAN is the Ascherman Professor of Economics and director of the Labor Studies Program at the National Bureau of Economic Research.

JOSHUA GUETZKOW is assistant professor of sociology at the University of Arizona.

JENNIFER HOCHSCHILD is the Henry LaBarre Jayne Professor of Government and a professor of African American studies at Harvard University.

HELEN INGRAM is the Warmington Endowed Chair in the School of Social Ecology and a professor in the departments of political science, planning policy and design, and criminology, law and society at the University of California, Irvine.

LAWRENCE R. JACOBS is the Walter F. and Joan Mondale Chair for Political Studies and director of the Center for the Study of Politics and Governance in the Hubert H. Humphrey Institute and the Department of Political Science at the University of Minnesota.

R. SHEP MELNICK is the Thomas P. O'Neill, Jr. Professor of American Politics at Boston College and co-chair of the Harvard Program on Constitutional Government.

KIMBERLY J. MORGAN is assistant professor of political science and international affairs at the George Washington University.

FRANCES FOX PIVEN is Distinguished Professor of Political Science and Sociology at the Graduate Center of the City University of New York and president of the American Sociology Association.

PAUL PIERSON holds the Avice Saint Chair of Public Policy at the University of California, Berkeley.

JOEL ROGERS is professor of law, political science, and sociology at the University of Wisconsin, Madison.

SANFORD F. SCHRAM teaches social theory and social policy in the Graduate School of Social Work and Social Research at Bryn Mawr College.

DEBORAH STONE is research professor of government at Dartmouth College.

VESLA WEAVER is an assistant professor in the department of government at the University of Virginia.

BRUCE WESTERN is professor of sociology at Harvard University.

Acknowledgments

In assembling this volume, we have accumulated many debts. We are especially grateful to participants in the conference, "Making the Politics of Poverty and Inequality: How Public Policies Are Reshaping American Democracy," held in Madison, Wisconsin, in April 2005. We benefited immensely from the insights provided by all who attended, including those who did not write chapters for this volume: Maria Cancian, Christopher Jencks, Nicole Kazee, Ryan King, Cathie Jo Martin, Marcia Meyers, Erin O'Brien, David Robertson, Virginia Sapiro, Steve Savner, and Timothy Smeeding.

The conference that gave rise to this volume, like this book itself, would not have been possible without the generous support of the Institute for Research on Poverty at the University of Wisconsin-Madison and the Russell Sage Foundation. We are also grateful to Helena Claiborne Lefkow and Kathryn Neumeister at the University of Wisconsin and Matthew Callan at the Russell Sage Foundation for their editorial skill in preparing this book for publication. Finally, we thank the American Political Science Association for permission to reprint revised material from "A Public Transformed? Welfare as Policy Feedback," *American Political Science Review* 101(1): 111–27, © 2007 American Political Science Association, included in Chapter 5 of this volume.

Our spouses, Kira Dahlk, Oona Hathaway, and Wayne Grove, made this volume possible. They each singlehandedly managed busy households of young children while we traveled to the meetings that got the project off the ground. As we proceeded with our work, they offered their support and encouragement, even on those days when we spent more time talking with each other than we did with them. With love and gratitude, we dedicate the volume to them.

Part I

Introduction

Jacob S. Hacker, Suzanne Mettler, and Joe Soss

Chapter 1

The New Politics of Inequality:
A Policy-Centered Perspective

Compared to the generation that grew up in the 1960s and 1970s, Americans coming of age today confront a world of greatly expanded possibilities. The overt forms of discrimination that plagued women and racial minorities since the nation's founding have now been mostly rendered a thing of the past. The American public has become more tolerant of diversity and more comfortable with group differences. And status in American society is now less closely tied to race, gender, religion, and sexual orientation than it was even a few decades ago.

Yet this era of new possibilities has also turned out to be a time of deepening disparities. As older forms of hierarchy have receded, economic inequality has intensified sharply. The equalizing trends that prevailed in the decades after World War II reversed course in the 1970s. Since that time, most Americans have seen their incomes grow only slowly, while the assets and incomes of the very richest have spiraled upward to new heights. Alongside this growing inequality, Americans have also learned to live with greater economic insecurity, as jobs and families have changed in ways that undercut traditional sources of income protection and intensify social risks. Although those disadvantaged by growing inequality and insecurity defy simple characterization, historically marginalized groups remain disproportionately represented among the impoverished and insecure, despite the expansion of civil rights.

Americans today also confront a new world of politics and public policy. Increasingly bitter partisan struggles have produced a broad and deep restructuring of government's role in relation to the economy and society. The welfare reform legislation of 1996, which redefined the purposes of public assistance and ended entitlements for the poorest Americans, is perhaps the most prominent example. Yet it is only the tip of a larger iceberg. Revisions to tax law, labor regulations, and social policies—often made beneath the radar screen of public awareness—have combined to produce changes in nearly every sphere of government action affecting economic inequality and insecurity in the United States. These changes have not had a single or consistent effect. Some have actually increased the generosity of public benefits for the less advantaged and those at risk of economic loss. But, as we shall see, most have reduced government's role as a source of opportunity and security for poor and middle-class Americans, while expanding the scope and size of benefits for the well off.

This book is an attempt to come to grips with these changes—to make sense of them and explore their implications for the future. It is also an effort to put these changes in a larger explanatory context, advancing a new perspective on the transformation of the

American polity and economy that places the evolution of American public policy at the very heart of the story.

The premise of this book is that, in the space of roughly a generation, the role of government in the lives of Americans citizens has changed fundamentally, in ways that are not wholly appreciated in contemporary scholarly and popular commentary. The goal of this book is to unearth this broad restructuring and show how it has both reflected and propelled a major shift in the basic economic and political relationships that connect— and, increasingly, divide—Americans. The aim of *Remaking America*, in short, is to explore how recent political and policy changes affect not just economic inequality and insecurity but also the character of democratic citizenship in the United States today.

To pursue this ambitious goal, this book develops a distinctive perspective on the study of public policy—one that breaks sharply with the two most common approaches to policy development. In the first of these approaches, found in standard political analyses, policies are seen mainly as *outcomes* to be explained. In the second approach, standard in policy analyses, policies are seen as *causes* of social and economic outcomes, the forces that affect societal phenomena such as poverty, income inequality, and the like.

This division of labor between political analysis and policy analysis has value. But it comes at a substantial cost. In particular, the prevailing organization of scholarship has discouraged attention to the *political consequences* of public policy. On both sides of the divide, scholars routinely fail to ask how policies, once established, become part of the political process and transform it by their presence. Thus, in most efforts to understand inequality and democracy in America today, we find little attention paid to the ways in which policies shape the resources and capacities of citizens or affect the content and articulation of public concerns. Policies are seen as the endpoint or starting point of analysis, rather than as a fulcrum connecting changes in American politics to trends in inequality and insecurity. The prevailing division of scholarly labor has thus become a serious obstacle to making sense of what we call "the new politics of inequality" in the United States.

This volume bypasses this common division of labor to advance an alternative approach that we believe yields a clearer picture. We call this approach a "policy-centered perspective" because it places the relationship between policy and politics at the center of analysis and uses this relationship as a lens through which to bring the new politics of inequality into sharper focus. In this perspective, policies are examined as more than just political outcomes or tools of social and economic regulation. They are also strategies for achieving political goals, structures shaping political interchange, and symbolic objects conveying status and identity. Policies, in short, must be grappled with as both products and producers of politics.

The chapters in this volume all take up this challenge. Although they differ in emphasis and topic, every chapter treats public policies as crucial arenas of, tools for, and constraints on political action that in turn create distinctive social and economic consequences. As the chapters unfold, we learn how specific features of American public policies affect opportunities for effective political influence, how they shape the distributions of political resources, how they create (or retard) possibilities for political coalition, and how they influence agendas and ideas for policy reform. In doing so, these explicitly policy-centered analyses not only illuminate our present moment and the path we took to it; they also provide a valuable road map for thinking about how the policy choices that are made today may affect political possibilities in the future.

These chapters also provide a distinctive window into the development and health of American democracy. Public policy and democracy are often considered in isolation from each other—the former is frequently envisioned as the technical resolution of specific public problems; the latter as the larger ideals upheld by a political order. The chapters to come explode this distinction, showing how the character and effect of public policy powerfully shape the quality of democratic institutions and practices. Politics and policy have combined in recent decades to transform basic features of American democratic processes—from the quality of political representation to the depth and distribution of citizen engagement to the capacities of civic groups to participate in the exercise of power. Thus, this book is not just about the politics of inequality in the United States. It is also about the changing nature of American democracy, and the changing meaning of American citizenship.

THE NEW POLITICS OF INEQUALITY AND INSECURITY

The first section of this chapter surveys some of the key changes this book investigates. The second section lays out the policy-centered approach, previewing the chapters to come. Finally, we use this framework to begin to explore the implications of recent policy changes for American democracy.

Rising Economic Inequality and Insecurity

The expression "A rising tide lifts all boats" offers an apt description of how the strong American economy of the mid-twentieth century operated. Earlier in the century, American society had exhibited a pyramid-shaped social structure: a small wealthy elite; a modest-sized middle class; and a large, disadvantaged class of industrial and agricultural workers (Leuchtenburg 1973, 48; Picketty and Saez 2003). Then, throughout the 1950s and 1960s, the ranks of the middle class swelled, changing the social structure from pyramidal to diamond-shaped (Mishel, Bernstein, and Allegretto 2005, 71). Economic historians have described this era as the "great compression"—the most egalitarian, in economic terms, of the twentieth century (Goldin and Katz 1999; Goldin and Margo 1992). White men enjoyed historic rates of upward mobility, landing jobs with significantly higher status than those held by their fathers. Educational attainment increased, and those who attended college gained well-paid positions in the growing ranks of white-collar employment. Those with less education found manufacturing jobs that typically offered strong wages and health and pension benefits, permitting them to enjoy a middle-class lifestyle (Featherman and Hauser 1978, 48).

By the 1960s, the promise of economic progress finally began to extend to African Americans as well. Until then, the persistence of legalized racial segregation and discrimination in labor markets had stymied blacks' opportunities for upward mobility and reinforced a large racial income gap. In the wake of the Civil Rights Act of 1964, that disparity began to diminish rapidly (Mishel, Bernstein, and Allegretto 2005, 49). By the early 1970s, economic opportunity also began to seem within the grasp of women. Thanks in substantial part to legal and policy changes, professions such as law and medicine became more accessible to women, and women in many sectors of the economy realized substantial gains in pay.

Changes to the economic distribution were especially dramatic in the 1960s. In the course of little more than a decade, the ranks of the poor were halved—from around one out of four Americans in 1959 to less than one in eight by 1973 (U.S. Census Bureau 2003). The growth of income and wealth at mid-century was strong at all levels of income, but particularly strong where it had historically been weakest: from the middle to the bottom. Between 1947 and 1973, the real median income of families essentially doubled, and the percentage growth was virtually the same at every point on the income ladder (Mishel, Bernstein, and Allegretto 2005). The standard of living for Americans was fundamentally transformed.

In the mid-1970s, these trends began to slow and, in some cases, reverse. Economic inequality began to increase sharply. Real wages deteriorated in value, particularly among men without a college degree. Deindustrialization and technological change undermined traditional manufacturing employment, with its high wages and good benefits for less-educated workers. Increased workforce participation rates by women helped cushion the resulting loss of family income, but families in the middle and lower ranks of the economy saw meager rates of economic growth over the next few decades. After doubling in just a quarter century, real after-tax income grew by only 21 percent between 1979 and 2004 for the middle 20 percent of American households, and roughly three-quarters of this growth was a result of the increased work hours and earnings of women (see Sherman and Aron-Dine 2007; Bernstein and Kornbluh 2005).

At the same time, the nation's poverty rate, which had been declining, escalated once again. The overall rate peaked at 15 percent during the mid-1980s and again in the early 1990s. The face of poverty changed, too. Poverty among the elderly was greatly reduced, but poverty rose among the most vulnerable of Americans—children. Among those eighteen and under, as many as 23 percent lived in poverty, and nearly 34 percent were either poor or "near-poor" during the 1980s and early 1990s (U.S. Census Bureau 2003; National Center for Children in Poverty 2006)—the highest rate in the advanced industrial world (Smeeding and Rainwater 2003). The strong economy of the late 1990s helped drive down poverty, but in recent years, poverty has been growing again. As of 2005, almost 13 percent of Americans, and almost 18 percent of children, lived in poverty.

Meanwhile, the ranks of affluent Americans ballooned, as highly educated Americans found that the market offered a large and growing premium for their skills. Families with highly educated earners, especially dual-earner professional couples, continued to enjoy strong rates of income growth and pulled further and further away from the median (Burtless and Jencks 2003). Although the booming late-1990s economy improved conditions for low- and middle-income families, these gains proved fleeting, and inequality has continued to grow in the twenty-first century.

The greatest concentration of income has been at the very top. The after-tax income of the top 1 percent of households (with a minimum 2004 income of around a half million dollars for a family of four) rose by 176 percent between 1979 and 2004, compared with 69 percent for the top fifth as a whole and, again, 21 percent for the middle fifth (see Congressional Budget Office 2006). Meanwhile, the share of national pretax income going to the top 1 percent nearly doubled, from 7.5 percent to 14 percent. This is a larger share of pretax income going to the top 1 percent than at any point since 1937, except the peak stock-market years of 1999 and 2000. And income is highly skewed even among the top 1 percent. The share of national pretax income held by the top 0.01 percent (the top tenth of 1 percent)—a group of roughly fourteen thousand households with an average income of more than $14 million—rose from 2.7 percent in 1979 to 8.6 percent in 2004. At the very top, the hundred highest-paid CEOs had an average pay of $18.5 million in 2003, 475 times the average American salary, having increased from 3.6 million in 1979, 105 times the average salary (see Piketty and Saez 2003, appendix tables, accessed at http://emlab.berkeley.edu/users/saez/TabFig2005prel.xls).

As a result of these trends, the United States now exhibits a much wider income distribution, not only in comparison to the United States of the 1970s but also in comparison to other affluent nations. It is tempting to see this change as symptomatic of a general economic deterioration. But although the economy grew more slowly over the post-1973 period than previously, overall economic and productivity growth remained relatively strong, especially in the 1990s. The biggest shift was in who was receiving the gains. Between 1966 and 2001, only the richest 10 percent of earners received wage and salary increases as great as the overall increase in economic productivity, and median earners saw their wage and salary income rise by only 0.3 percent a year over the entire period (Dew-Becker and Gordon 2005). What is more, rising income inequality does not appear to have been accompanied by an increase in income mobility, which might have allowed more Americans at the low end of the economic ladder to climb to its increasingly lofty upper rungs ("Meritocracy in America: Ever Higher Society; Ever Harder to Ascend," *The Economist*, December 29, 2004).

Inequality in wealth tends to be more skewed than inequality in income, and also to be more stable over time and across generations. (Wealth includes property, stocks, retirement savings, mutual funds, and other assets.) As of 2001, the top 1 percent possessed 20 percent of household income but 33.4 percent of net worth and 39.7 percent of net financial assets—in each case, a substantially larger proportion than a generation ago. By contrast, the bottom 90 percent earned 54.8 percent of income and represented only 28.5 percent of net worth and owned 20.2 percent of financial assets (Mishel, Bernstein, and Allegretto 2005, 279).

In short, the United States now possesses a small class of very rich Americans who are much richer than other Americans, than the affluent of other nations, and than American elites in historical perspective.

For the vast majority of Americans, however, income and wealth data alone fail to capture fully the scope of change in their lives. First, families are devoting considerably more hours to paid employment than in the past, and women's increased workforce participation accounts for most of the increased time on the job. Within the middle-income range, for instance, families worked the equivalent of 12.5 more full-time weeks per year in 2000 than in 1979 (Mishel, Bernstein, and Allegretto 2005, 40). This development helps families to maintain or boost income, but it also presents them with the new challenges of what has become familiarly known as the "work-family balance."

For another, Americans today experience greater income volatility—meaning swings in their income—than they did a generation ago (Hacker 2006). Both white-collar and blue-collar workers have been experiencing increasing problems of job displacement, with rates of job loss now essentially what they were in the early 1980s, during the deepest recession since the Great Depression (Farber 2005). Families are more frequently headed by single parents, at least for a period of time, which places obvious strains on family income. But even two-parent families have seen a decline in their economic security. During an era in which the number of Americans filing for bankruptcy has risen from less than 300,000 in 1980 to more than 1.5 million in the early 2000s, married parents are twice as likely to file for bankruptcy as other adults (Warren and Tyagi 2003).

Finally, the United States' employment-based framework of economic security has eroded dramatically (Hacker 2004, 2006). Workers, especially less-educated workers, are less likely to have access to health insurance and company pensions today than was the case just a couple of decades ago. The share of workers covered by employer-sponsored health insurance is down from 69 percent in 1979 to 55.9 percent in 2004 (see Economic Policy Institute 2006), and the number of Americans without health insurance has increased dramatically (U.S. Census 2003). Meanwhile, employers have shifted away from providing a guaranteed income in retirement (so-called defined-benefit pension plans) toward allowing workers to set aside their own money for retirement, perhaps with a company match, in so-called defined-contribution plans, such as 401(k)s. Although defined-contribution plans serve some workers well, they have substantially increased the degree of risk that workers bear in planning for their retirement (Hacker 2006). Careful projections suggest that younger workers are much less likely to enjoy a secure retirement than their parents were (see Center for Retirement Research at Boston College 2006).

In the new era of rising economic inequality and insecurity, the old pecking order in which women and minorities were always on the bottom has been replaced by one in which lines of class and education loom much larger. Racial minorities and women who have become educated professionals have seen major economic gains. Nonetheless, the rise in inequality and insecurity has undermined some of the major gains of the rights revolution, particularly for the poorest members of these groups, who still fare extremely poorly on indicators of economic well-being. In 2003, for example, 29.4 percent of women earned poverty-level wages compared to 19.6 percent of men (Mishel, Bernstein, and Allegretto 2005, 126). Among African Americans, nearly one quarter still live in poverty, and unemployment rates are twice the national average (U.S. Census 2003). In 2004, about 33 percent of black children lived in poverty compared to 10 percent of white children (National Center for Children in Poverty 2006). The racial wealth gap also remains large: the net worth of the typical white family is $81,000, compared to $8,000 for black families (Shapiro 2005, 47). The growth of economic inequality, in short, has not wholly eclipsed old inequalities of race and gender. Rather, it has reintroduced some of these divisions through new mechanisms that divide groups less cleanly than older forms of explicit discrimination did.

The Restructuring of American Public Policy

It is now well accepted that the egalitarian economy of the mid-twentieth century was in important part a product of specific public policies (Hacker, Mettler, and Pinderhughes 2005). A progressive tax system and an array of social and labor policies that had been established during the New Deal, coupled with support for labor unions and the successful implementation of the Fair Labor Standards Act of 1938, with its strong minimum-wage guarantee—all helped spread the gains of economic growth broadly (Mettler 1998; Mettler and Milstein 2007). After World War II, the G.I. Bill granted returning veterans extensive unemployment benefits, low-interest mortgages, and higher education and vocational training at government expense (Behrman, Pollack, and Taubman 1989; Fligstein 1976; Mettler 2006). Support for home ownership and advanced education was extended to the civilian population as well, through the expansion of subsidized mortgages and the creation of new education grants, loans, and work-study programs. The federal government also generously subsidized private employment-based health and pension benefits through the tax code and regulated their operation, encouraging their extension to previously excluded blue-collar workers (Hacker 2002).

To be sure, mid-twentieth-century public policies also exacerbated inequalities. Jim Crow segregation laws persisted, and key New Deal policies continued to exclude most African Americans on the basis of occupational restrictions until the 1950s (Katznelson 2005; Lieberman 1998). As a result, African Americans experienced far fewer of the gains of economic growth than did whites. It is clear that if blacks had achieved civil-rights gains earlier, they would have made greater progress climbing into the middle class before the economic shifts of the 1970s started to reverse positive trends (Mettler 2006).

Nonetheless, New Deal and postwar public policies still played a major role in ensuring that more and more Americans shared in the fruits of a growing economy.

What role has American government played in shaping and responding to more recent economic trends? Inequality of labor earnings and capital income has risen in most Western industrialized economies over this period, though not to the extent that it has in the United States. In most nations, however, government tax and transfer programs have substantially mitigated the increases in inequality these trends have produced (Brandolini and Smeeding 2006; Hacker, Mettler, and Pinderhughes 2005). The United States, by contrast, has done much less, reducing inequality only slightly through policy (Brandolini and Smeeding 2006) and actually redistributing income less than in the past (Hacker 2004).

Indeed, as the economy slowed in the United States in the 1970s, the central focus of American policy changes became the reduction of taxes and government social spending. These efforts have had mixed effects. The components of the welfare state that provide security to senior citizens—notably, Medicare and Social Security—have remained intact and strong, if in places more threadbare. In contrast, the scope and effectiveness of many other components of the American welfare state, and of tax-subsidized private workplace benefits, have deteriorated.

This has happened in part because key social benefits and regulatory policies have not kept pace with the rising cost of critical goods and services. Unlike Social Security, most policies for the disadvantaged increase only if policymakers take action to raise benefits, allowing policymakers to scale programs back simply by failing to take action. As a result of such policy "drift" (Hacker 2004), the value of average benefits has withered to varying degrees in Unemployment Insurance and Food Stamps. Pell Grants for higher education have fallen dramatically as a share of public and private college tuition, as the costs of higher education have skyrocketed. Benefits for Aid to Families with Dependent Children, often known as "welfare," diminished in real terms by more than half between the 1970s and 1990s, and have continued to do so under its successor, Temporary Assistance for Needy Families (Mettler and Milstein 2007). Similarly, lawmakers have permitted the minimum wage to decline from $8.28 in real dollars in 1968 to $5.15 in 2006—the lowest real level in a half decade (though as this volume goes to press Congress is attempting to raise the level to $7.25 over a two-year period).

Some programs have become less inclusive, too. New restrictions on the receipt of cash welfare benefits and unemployment insurance provide one set of examples. Many states have tightened eligibility for unemployment insurance, particularly for low-wage workers, and this is one reason the overall proportion of unemployed workers receiving benefits has declined, dropping a third in recent decades.

Social benefits have also become more restrictive because of shifts in their context, rather than changes in the terms of benefits themselves (Hacker 2004). Although states have trimmed unemployment benefits, the most important reasons why fewer unemployed workers receive benefits are the decline of manufacturing and unionized employment and rise of the service sector and part-time work, and the shift of employment to states with less generous programs.

The same process has played out in many areas, as relatively stable benefit rules interact with a rapidly changing (and increasingly unequal) economy. Tax breaks for employer-provided benefits are now more skewed toward the highly paid, because the likelihood of receiving benefits has fallen most sharply among less-advantaged workers. The G.I. Bill still exists, but its impressive capacity to extend social opportunity to a vast portion of young Americans was undermined when the nation transformed the military into the much smaller, all-volunteer force beginning in 1973. By the same token, the National Labor Relations Act remains intact, but its ability to strengthen workers' leverage has diminished as union membership has substantially declined (Mettler and Milstein 2007). In each of these ways, public social and economic policies have become less visible and consequential in the lives of middle-class and lower-income Americans.

To be sure, there are some significant exceptions to this story, even among programs for the non-elderly. The largest is the Earned Income Tax Credit (EITC), which provides low-wage workers with substantial refundable tax credits and is now the nation's largest antipoverty program. During the 1980s and 1990s, policymakers also acted to expand the benefits and rights of the disabled and to extend Medicaid benefits to pregnant women and children in low-income families. And while the welfare reform law of 1996 imposed strict work requirements and time limits, it also gave states more freedom to provide supplementary services, such as child care and worker training, that had previously been unavailable to most welfare recipients.

These expansions are exceptions to the general pattern, however, and have been swamped by the broader changes in the economy and public policy just described. Most of these policy expansions, moreover, have been at odds with the policy approach of the postwar years. Although they involve significant new commitments of federal spending, they emphasize sharply different principles than programs such as Social Security, Medicare, and the G.I. Bill, which were designed to be broad and inclusive, open to all citizens who qualified regardless of income level. These new initiatives are targeted toward the poor or working poor; they are "means-tested" (limited to those with low incomes and limited assets); and many are structured to limit or direct the behaviors of those they reach—an approach sometimes called "the new paternalism." Finally, many of these initiatives (such as the EITC) are specifically designed to be invisible in the lives of citizens. It is not clear, therefore, whether they foster the same positive images of government and civic capacities among beneficiaries that many New Deal and postwar programs did (Mettler 2006; Campbell 2003; Hacker, Mettler, and Pinderhughes 2005).

Equally important, few of these policy initiatives have responded to the new and intensified social risks that have emerged from social, economic, and demographic changes over the last generation (Hacker 2004). Despite the growth of dual-earner couples and single-parent households, for example, the nation has failed to respond with new policies to help increasingly insecure families balance work and family. While private health coverage has declined, expansions of Medicaid have only covered a small share of those without coverage, and hence the ranks of the uninsured have grown markedly. And even as higher education has become more vital and tuition costs have skyrocketed, policymakers have done little to broaden access to college for less affluent students.

Another exception to the overall story of policy retrenchment (one much less frequently noted than the expansion of the EITC and health benefits for the poor) is the expansion of tax breaks that benefit the privileged. The "hidden welfare state," as such policies have been dubbed by Christopher Howard (1997), permits citizens who meet specific criteria to pay less in taxes than they otherwise would. Perhaps half again as large as direct social spending and growing, the hidden welfare state grants its most lavish rewards to those who receive generous health and pension benefits (an increasingly narrow group) or who own costly homes. Not only do these tax breaks generally bestow their greatest benefits on well-off citizens; they also reduce the amount of revenues the nation can collect for other purposes (Sammartino and Toder 2002; Gitterman and Howard 2003). Despite these drawbacks, tax expenditures have served as the template for nearly all new social policy initiatives in recent years, from child tax credits for families with children to expanded 401(k) retirement plans and Individual Retirement Accounts.

Finally, any effort to understand how public policy affects inequality in America today must come to grips with the stunning recent rise in incarceration. Between 1970 and 2000, the prison population of the United States increased six times over (Western and Pettit 2002). Today, the number of Americans who enter prison for parole violations alone is equal to the total number of prison *admissions* in 1980 (Travis 2005, 40). American incarceration rates are not only much higher than in the recent past; they dwarf levels of incarceration in other affluent democratic nations. This astonishing growth in imprisonment had little to do with changes in crime rates; it was driven almost entirely by changes in criminal justice policies (Travis 2005). Moreover, the effects of rising incarceration have been concentrated among poor blacks and Hispanics (Western 2006). Incarceration rates for blacks are now about eight times that for whites, and by age thirty-five, fully 59 percent of black men without a high school degree can expect to have been imprisoned (Western and Pettit 2005). Even after serving out their punishment, felons are often barred from voting—one in four black men cannot vote because of a felony conviction (Manza and Uggen 2006)—and many find it impossible to gain employment with a criminal record. Because of these deep and pervasive effects, rising incarceration rates have a strong influence on poverty and inequality in the United States today.

In sum, the pattern of policy development over the past three decades has been complex. On the one hand, there has not been a wholesale retrenchment of the welfare state. On the other hand, there has also not been the kind of concerted response to inequality and insecurity seen in other nations—or the United States' own past. American social policies remain generous toward senior citizens (Lynch 2001), but they do comparatively little to reduce poverty and inequality among the non-elderly (Smeeding 2005). A good deal of United States social spending is channeled toward the most advantaged through tax expenditures and private social benefits (Hacker 2002; Howard 1997), and this skew has increased even as the gap between the rich and the rest has widened. The poorest Americans now confront more diverse but also more conditional forms of aid, as their communities grapple with the distinctive burdens arising from mass incarceration. Even as inequality and insecurity have grown, American government has substantially withdrawn from its mid-twentieth-century role of bolstering equality and security among working-age Americans.

The Transformation of American Politics

Rising inequality and insecurity and the policy changes that have contributed to these trends are often viewed in exclusion from politics. Yet both flow directly from a series of fundamental political changes over the last generation.

The most fundamental of these recent shifts is the one that we most frequently take for granted: the rise of an aggressive, well-organized, and politically powerful conservative movement. Conservatism was on the defensive in the 1960s and early 1970s, as vividly confirmed by Barry Goldwater's crushing defeat by Lyndon Johnson in 1964. In the wake of the repudiation of Goldwater, however, conservatives regrouped and refashioned their strategies. Mixing a libertarian emphasis on free markets and limited government with the more authoritarian prescriptions of America's emerging social conservative movement, the Republican Party and its grassroots backers roared back in the late 1970s, particularly in the South, where the national Democratic Party's support for civil rights drove a stake through the heart of its once-dominant one-party regime.

With voting patterns forged during the New Deal finally loosened, Republicans crafted a new electoral and governing coalition that was able to capture the White House in every election but two from 1980 on—and which finally took Congress in 1994.

The essence of this shift is a sharp movement of Republican political elites to the right. Much analysis and commentary calls attention to the "polarization" of American politics, but that term is misleading, inasmuch as it implies that both parties have moved away from the center of American politics at equal speed. In fact, Republicans have moved substantially further to the right of the political spectrum than Democrats have moved to the left (Hacker and Pierson 2005; McCarty, Poole, and Rosenthal 2006). Moreover, the reasons for the shift differ: Republicans have moved right because nearly all Republican politicians are more conservative than Republicans of a generation ago. Among Democrats, most of the shift to the left has occurred because conservative Democrats in the South have lost office to conservative Republicans (Theriault 2006).

The inference most analysts take from this rightward shift is that American voters as a whole have grown more conservative. Popular concerns did indeed spur GOP political gains in the late 1970s. But according to the weight of the evidence, most Americans have not grown more conservative since the early 1980s (Fiorina 2004; Hacker and Pierson 2005). James Stimson (2006), for example, has developed a comprehensive measure that shows that Americans are more *liberal* today than they were in the early 1980s. Given the difficulty of coming up with consistent measures of public opinion that are not simply reactive to present circumstances, these results should be viewed with caution. But they do suggest that the shift of the Republican Party to the right, during an era in which the GOP was the dominant force in American politics, is not driven by a general public shift to the right.

Nor does the rise of a more conservative American political establishment seem to reflect an eclipse of economic concerns by "moral issues"—which might be thought to explain why in an era of rising insecurity and inequality, voters have not turned against the increasingly dominant Republican Party. Instead, voting has become *more* class-stratified—with low-income voters tending to vote Democrat, and high-income voters tending to vote Republican—than it was immediately after World War II (Stonecash 2000; Bartels 2006). At the same time, economic issues appear to have become *more* important in motivating voter choice (Bartels 2006), and a more prominent part of the platform of both parties. In short, the conservative ascendance does not signal that economic issues have faded in importance as a source of partisan conflict or motivator of voter choice.

Indeed, many of the most important changes in American politics have occurred at the level of political organization, rather than that of voter opinions. The decline of organizations that once represented middle- and working-class voters on economic issues, such as unions and fraternal societies (Skocpol 2003), has been accompanied by the rise of a well-networked and politically savvy conservative movement, organized at the grassroots level through churches and local business organizations and at the national level through think tanks, expanded business lobbies, and GOP-affiliated political action committees. With the major exception of Christian conservatives, mass membership organizations with true grassroots presence have atrophied in favor of Washington-based advocacy groups with mailing-list memberships, including so-called "Astroturf" organizations that purport to be broad-based but are run by industry organizations and have few actual members.

These organizational shifts have not pushed consistently in one ideological direction. New "public-interest" organizations, organized around the environment and other single-issue causes that are associated with the left of the political spectrum, have proliferated (Berry 1999). But these groups have neither coordinated their activities as effectively as conservative organizations have, nor focused their attention on the economic issues that have continued to motivate voters and drive party conflict.

Thus, while the net effect of these organizational shifts is not one-dimensional, they have clearly weakened the political voice of ordinary citizens on economic issues. Voting appears to have grown more skewed by income, with declines in voting among lower-income voters driving much of the overall fall in American electoral participation (Freeman 2004). Mass-membership organizations representing the economic interests of voters from the middle to the bottom of the economic ladder, always weak, have atrophied further. Perhaps most important, money has become much more important as a political resource, as the cost of campaigns has skyrocketed and lobbying efforts have grown more extensive and expensive.

Money, of course, has always been the most unequally distributed of political resources. Every American has the vote; many have the time and inclination to participate in collective political activities. But few have the resources to influence today's costly campaigns and lobbyist-dominated policy battles—and politicians know it. In 2000, an eighth of American households had incomes greater than $100,000, yet these fortunate households made up 95 percent of those who gave a thousand dollars or more to a campaign that year (Task Force on Inequality and American Democracy 2004). The parties now contact between a quarter (Democratic Party) and a third (Republican Party) of the wealthiest of Americans directly during campaign seasons, up from less than 15 percent of these high-income voters in the 1950s (Campbell forthcoming).

Thanks to rising gains at the top, moreover, wealthy Americans are more numerous, and much richer, than they used to be. And while they can be found at all points on the political spectrum, they have distinctive policy preferences. Unfortunately, few surveys reach enough truly rich Americans to form reliable inferences about the political preferences of the extremely well off. But what evidence there is suggests that the rich are more conservative economically—less supportive of economic redistribution and measures to provide economic security—and vastly better informed about policy than ordinary Americans. One survey regarding the 2003 tax cuts, for example, found that the wealthiest were both more supportive of and more informed about the dividend and capital gains tax cuts, which primarily benefit upper-income Americans (Hacker and Pierson 2005).

The growing influence of money also has distinctive consequences for the two major parties: It generally reinforces the GOP's low-tax, limited-government message, but it introduces major cross-pressures into the Democratic Party. To appeal to affluent voters and organized groups as sources of campaign money, Democrats have had a strong incentive to reduce their focus on issues of redistribution and economic security.

All these shifts in the American political landscape are closely linked to the changes in policy and society that this chapter has detailed. For the last quarter century, American political debate has been dominated by conservative critiques of government. Conservative elites have sought to privatize existing programs so as to increase personal responsibility and individual exposure to risk. They have emphasized greater control over individual behavior as an alternative to expanded redistribution or insurance. They have argued for a shift away from progressive taxation. Meanwhile, growing partisan conflict over the direction of American policy has reduced the chance that political majorities will come together to support the maintenance or improvement of increasingly threadbare programs, or to fill the growing gaps left by the erosion of private workplace benefits, or to counter the growing concentration of income at the top. Instead, the rising level of disagreement between the parties has led to stalemate in many policy areas, abetting the "drift" of key policies away from their original goals.

It is against this backdrop that our authors have come together to reflect on the state of democracy, inequality, and public policy in America. The aim of this volume is to clarify how the three streams of change that we have just traced—rising economic inequality, the reconfiguration of public policy, and the transformation of American politics—fit together and how they are transforming citizens' lives in America today.

A POLICY-CENTERED PERSPECTIVE

To pursue this project requires an analytic framework—a lens that is capable of linking seemingly unrelated changes and clarifying their connections. The authors in this volume employ a variety of theories and differ in some of their basic assumptions about politics. Yet as a group, the chapters exemplify what we term a "policy-centered perspective" on the politics of inequality and poverty.

The hallmark of this perspective is that it uses public policy as a standpoint for analyzing how political processes operate. In other words, policy serves as the focal point for a broader analysis of how political forces shape governance and how government actions reshape the society and polity.

Policy-centered analyses offer a refreshing counterpoint to the disciplinary divides that typically organize the study of public affairs. Because they do not approach politics from the perspective of any particular actor (such as a legislator, voter, or advocate) or institution (such as a legislature or court), they help to draw connections between the substantive findings and analytic insights generated by different subfields. By treating public policy as an analytic fulcrum, researchers focus attention on the dynamic constellations of social, economic, and political forces that surround specific domains of public action.

There is, of course, a large body of existing scholarship where readers can discover important insights into "the politics of public policy" (see Kingdon 1995; Baumgartner and Jones 1993; Van Horn, Gormley, and Baumer 2001). In most of this literature, however, policies figure primarily as outcomes to be explained. By contrast, our authors begin from the assumption that policies are, not just products of politics, but also active forces in the political transaction itself.

In this regard, the present volume clearly builds on the growing body of research into "policy feedback effects," which emphasizes the potential for policies to play a causal role in politics (see Skocpol 1992; Pierson 1993; Lieberman 1998; Hacker 2002). By introducing the alternative term "policy-centered," we aim to connect this kind of causal analysis to other modes of political scholarship that place an equally strong emphasis on public policy. Thus, policy-centered political analysis can be found not just in causal studies of policy feedback, but also in constructivist analyses that put policy at the center of symbolic political transactions (Schneider and Ingram 1993) and in studies that use policy observations as a basis for interrogating key political concepts such as participation (Fung 2004; Soss 1999), power (Hayward 2000), justice (Shapiro 1999; White 2000), and citizenship (Mettler 1998; Mead and Beem 2005).

Indeed, a key goal of this volume is to highlight the diversity of roles that policies may play in politics and the variety of ways that policy-centered analyses can enhance the study of politics. Consider, for example, Lawrence Jacobs's chapter on Medicare (chapter 4). To build his political analysis, Jacobs wends his way through party politics, legislative dynamics, public opinion processes, interest-group strategies, and a host of other topics usually kept separate in the subfields of political science. Jacobs's analysis, however, does not stop with an explanation of how this rich constellation of factors operates. It pushes further to show how existing policies conditioned reform strategies in the 1960s and how the passage of Medicare ultimately restructured health politics in the United States.

As this example suggests, public policies command attention in this volume partly because they function as structures organizing political action. In any political conflict, some set of policies already exists as historical facts on the ground. Thus, politics unfolds on an existing landscape where policies may already have fostered coalitions, set agendas, defined incentives, given rise to interests, shaped popular understandings, and so on. In this sense, policies can resemble political institutions, structuring social experience, organizing group competition, and channeling political participation. They can structure experience, organize competition, and channel political participation. They can impose obligations, create incentives, and define the paths of action available to governments (Pierson 2004; Hacker 2002). They can supply cognitive categories for interpreting events and populations (Schneider and Ingram 1993) and establish the balance of rhetorical and ideological resources available to political actors.

These sorts of structuring roles are emphasized by a number of authors in the volume. R. Shep Melnick (chapter 3), for example, shows how a categorical social policy regime invited litigation campaigns in the United States after the 1960s and then protected this political strategy during an era in which powerful actors sought to undercut its material and statutory bases. Andrea Louise Campbell (chapter 6) examines this same policy regime, showing how its design differences structure state-citizen relations and influence citizens' interests, beliefs, and patterns of political participation. Likewise, Richard Freeman and Joel Rogers ask how politics is restructured when policies devolve authority to lower levels of government and suggest that such policies may yield surprising new possibilities for egalitarian politics and innovative policymaking.

What the chapters in this volume make clear is that public policies matter not just as structures, but also as tools of agency that actors use to pursue political goals. Whatever their intended effects on social and economic problems, public policies often have secondary functions as instruments of political conflict. As proposals and as accomplishments, policies can be potent tools for mobilizing or placating political constituencies. They can be used to defund opponents and reward allies, to create crises that force difficult policy choices onto the agenda, to obscure which groups are benefiting or being harmed, to change perceptions of who deserves what and who is a member in full standing. In the iterative game of politics, policies are a crucial means for achieving both long-term and short-term strategic goals—in short, for human agency.

Agency is the central theme of Frances Fox Piven's analysis of welfare politics (chapter 7), which offers an illuminating contrast to Campbell's chapter. Piven asks how much policy structures truly constrain innovative political actors, emphasizing instead how policies function as tools used by elites to counter mass unrest, reward powerful political backers, and create the conditions needed to pursue cutbacks in popular social programs. Similar themes are sounded in the pair of chapters by Jacobs (on Medicare) and by Joe Soss and Sanford F. Schram (chapter 5, on welfare reform), which analyze liberal efforts to use policy reform as a springboard for political efforts to aid the disadvantaged and achieve more universal social protections. The authors wrestle with why and how these specific strategies fell short and in the process clarify a number of general dynamics related to the political uses of policy actions.

Thus a policy-centered perspective offers a revised view of both structure and agency in politics. By expanding the analysis of structuring effects beyond formal institutions, it provides greater clarity about when change is possible and what form it will take. Likewise, by alerting us to a broader scope of tools available to actors at a given historical moment, it sharpens our understanding of how political agency works. By bringing policy to the fore, we improve our understandings of the structural constraints on political action and the strategic possibilities at actors' disposal.

Kimberly Morgan (chapter 2) offers a case in point. Morgan shows how highly visible tax policies and low-visibility social-welfare policies combined to create political barriers to social-policy expansion in the United States. Going beyond an analysis of constraint, however, she shows how this combination created opportunities to mobilize a political backlash. The resulting "tax revolt" was organized from above, Morgan contends, but its success depended on the discontent of a public that—because of the structure of tax policy—could see its losses to taxation far more clearly than it could see its gains through social protections. Bringing this analysis full circle, Morgan then shows how tax cutbacks functioned as a tool of political agency in their own right, offering conservatives a way to squeeze the budgets of popular programs and block the development of new protections as a response to changing societal needs.

In addition to themes of structure and agency, this volume also shows how policy-centered political analysis can encompass different yet complementary modes of investigation focused on the material and symbolic dimensions of public policy. More than a decade ago, Paul Pierson (1993)—the author of one of the two integrative essays at the end of this volume (chapter 13)—urged students of politics to remain alert to both the resource and interpretive effects of policy designs. Around the same time, Helen Ingram—the author of the other concluding essay (chapter 12)—and Anne Schneider (1993) argued that policies played a key role in the symbolic construction of social status, political identity, and citizenship. The authors assembled here take both these points to heart. Campbell, for example, in chapter 6 shows how policies that bestow resources on disadvantaged groups can elevate their civic capacity, as in the case of Social Security. Jennifer Hochschild and Vesla Mae Weaver (chapter 8) examine the ongoing interplay of official racial classification policies, patterns of identity, and expressions of political solidarity and demand making. Soss and Schram (chapter 5) use the case of welfare reform to show how a policy's positioning within a broader symbolic landscape can thwart the political strategies of reformers.

As these examples illustrate, a policy-centered analysis does not require scholars to assume that any particular policy has an important political effect. Rather, it encourages scholars to ask whether a given policy plays an influential role in the political process and how, if at all, the policy interacts with other political factors relevant to the phenomenon under investigation. Policies, in this view, are political creations that operate as elements of an ongoing political process.

This, in a nutshell, is what we mean by a "policy-centered analysis" Readers will find in this volume a variety of constructivist and institutionalist arguments, consensus and conflict models, assumptions regarding structure and agency, quantitative and qualitative techniques, and so on. Similarly, while some of our authors conclude that policies functioned as crucial political factors in the areas they examine, others conclude that policies were of limited importance. The thread that connects these diverse chapters is that they are all empirically grounded, theoretically informed analyses that make it a priority to specify how public policies fit into and matter for ongoing political processes.

REORGANIZING DEMOCRACY

Working from a policy-centered perspective, the chapters in this volume invite readers to ask hard questions about how democracy operates in the United States today. They do so not only in the descriptive sense of investigating what is occurring and in the explanatory sense of asking why, but also in the normative sense of contemplating how we should evaluate our polity's current operation in light of aspirations for a just and democratic society. Indeed, this bridging of explanatory and evaluative agendas is the final signature of policy-centered political analysis. Once policy is moved to the analytic foreground, efforts to study the "is" of politics almost inevitably find themselves in close proximity to the "ought" of democratic theory. Moreover, once one acknowledges that policies shape politics, the question of whether particular policies are changing our political lives for good or ill is seldom far behind.

By our lights, this development is felicitous. The joining of empirical and normative investigations should be welcomed, if for no other reason than because so many of our best studies of politics—such as Robert Dahl's 1961 classic *Who Governs?*—have been forged at this intersection. Explanatory analyses tend to yield deeper insights when they are placed in conversation with, but not overwhelmed by, the concepts and concerns of democratic theory. As Harold Lasswell (1956, 1971) argued, political science is at its best when it is also a "policy science for democracy"—concerned with concrete issues of political debate that have substantial implications for the health of democracy.

In the absence of a dialogue between the normative and the positive, political analysis risks becoming nothing more than a technical exercise—a "flight from reality" that evades the pressing questions of the age and the enduring problems of the human condition (Shapiro 2005). The authors in this volume offer a counterpoint to such bloodless social science. Amid rising inequalities and a rapidly changing American polity, they ask how power now operates and what democracy and citizenship have come to mean. Their analyses point readers toward key insights needed to understand, evaluate, and navigate the emerging landscape of democratic governance in America.

At the same time, these essays demonstrate the value of empirical engagement for efforts to reflect on American democracy. A policy-centered perspective encourages scholars to abandon the safe harbor of abstract theorizing for a closer examination of how principles operate in practice. As Lawrence Mead and Christopher Beem note in *Welfare Reform and Political Theory* (2005, 3–5), whereas "conventional policy analysis is [often relentlessly technical and] limited by its concreteness . . . political theory is limited by its frequent abstraction, its separation from the specifics of politics and policy. Theoretical reflection that focuses initially on policy is an improvement on both counts." Indeed, it is no coincidence that when contemporary theorists seek to strengthen the empirical foundation of concepts such as power, justice, citizenship, and democracy, they so often turn to the study of public policy rather than to some other empirical domain of political science (see Gutmann and Thompson 1996; Shapiro 1999; Hayward 2000; White 2000; Fung 2004). Policy designs present us with "operational definitions" of crucial normative concepts (Mead 1986), both creating and revealing the meanings of such concepts in practice.

The core concept whose operational realization is explored in this volume is democratic citizenship. "Democratic citizenship" can be understood as people's abilities to make what they want of their lives by choosing together and by effectively checking arbitrary uses of power (Shapiro 1999, 29–39). But our goal is not to theorize about some idealized form of citizenship. Rather, we aim to explain how American policies have in practice shaped the specific array of rights and obligations and the civic status experienced by members of the polity. The chapters that follow illuminate the lived experience of American citizenship and show how recent changes in American society are reconfiguring that experience.

As these chapters show, democratic citizenship has changed in paradoxical ways.

Since the 1960s Americans have gained greater access than ever before to formal legal and political rights. Yet over the same period, the confident use of these rights to effect political change has withered, particularly among the less-advantaged and the young. Compared to the middle of the twentieth century, Americans have grown much less confident that government is responsive to them and they have much less of a sense of connection to the political system (Hughes and Conway 1997; Orren 1997). Moreover, they are much less interested in and involved in politics (Putnam 2000; Rosenstone and Hansen 1993; Verba, Schlozman, and Brady 1995, 69–74). While affluent and highly educated Americans continue to make their voices heard, the less-advantaged participate far less today than those at the same point in their life cycle and with comparable education and income, even just a few decades ago (Freeman 2004; Zukin et al. 2006).[1] These developments raise the question of how policies have contributed to this atrophying of active citizenship, particularly among those who are most adversely affected by recent economic trends.

To say that policies make politics is to say that policies have the power to enrich or erode the citizen's role, to deepen or warp the workings of democracy. For all their attention to policy, neither political analyses nor policy analyses have told us much about these possibilities. Because politically minded scholars have addressed policies mainly as outputs, they have rarely asked how policies affect the quality of political life (Mettler and Soss 2004).

In this volume, by contrast, public policies emerge as key factors mediating the relationship between economic inequality and democratic citizenship. Chapters such as those by Melnick and Jacobs show how policies created decades ago have structured and constrained contemporary efforts to address rising inequality. The chapter by Campbell, for example, demonstrates how policy designs define civic status and capacity by positioning societal groups in relation to one another and the state. This analysis is complemented by the contributions of Deborah Stone (chapter 9) and by Hochschild and Weaver, who examine how policies affect citizens' identities and public understandings of civic status. Morgan shows how existing policies can limit democratic decisionmaking by foreclosing political options, and Piven elaborates on the strategic use of policies to press unsuspecting citizens toward undesired choices.

As these and the other essays in this volume make clear, recent policy changes are transforming the meaning of American citizenship. Various policy developments elevate participation in the paid workforce as the role most deserving of civic recognition. Meanwhile, as Stone observes, other responsibilities of individuals—namely, caring for children and other family members—are no longer assigned the civic value they once held. Today, workforce participation—a rationale associated primarily with men's social provision in the New Deal—has been extended to women as the primary measure of deservingness for government benefits. More broadly, the contours of recent changes in American social programs, highlighted by Melnick, reveal that the only new policies geared to adults that are *not* justified on the basis of workforce participation are those targeted to the disabled—a group legally defined as unable to work (Stone 1984).

This emphasis on the work role—the citizen as breadwinner and taxpayer—has largely eclipsed an earlier policy emphasis on the citizen as a participating member of the polity. The earliest major forms of social provision in the United States rewarded citizen soldiers for fulfilling their civic obligation through military service; this pattern held through the creation of the G.I. Bill for returning veterans of World War II and its successors (Skocpol 1992; Mettler 2006). This tradition, while still in effect, has receded in significance. Similarly, mothers' pensions, the precursor to welfare, were established in the early twentieth century on the rationale that mothers, in raising their own children, were preparing them to be future citizens (Orloff 1991). Such principles could hardly be further from the logic of contemporary welfare reform. Today, relatively few citizens gain access to generous social provision by honoring ties of mutual obligation and fulfilling duties of citizenship that exist outside the marketplace.

It is not simply that contemporary policies place a higher value on market relations than on bonds of citizenship. It is also that these policies at times actually devalue the civic bonds that support and enable participation in the market. Today, Americans who are neither elderly nor disabled are expected not only to work, but also to ensure the conditions necessary for their labor. As Stone observes, government has largely withdrawn support for the caring functions that families fulfill for newborns, children, and adults. These functions have been relegated to "private life" and thus potential workers must find ways, on their own, to "contract" for such services if they are to participate effectively in the labor market. Moreover, growing percentages of families confront these "private" care obligations given that fewer jobs now offer employment-based health and pension benefits.

Even as the new political order stresses individual liberty, however, government has adopted a more muscular, directive stance toward the poor, particularly the nonwhite poor. For these groups, the American state has become more directive, custodial, and punitive. Low-income women seeking welfare are now subject to stringent behavioral rules, as discussed by both Piven and Stone. At the same time, as Josh Guetzkow and Bruce Western report (chapter 11), less well educated men have become nearly three times as likely to be incarcerated as they were in 1980, and the goal of prison rehabilitation has been replaced by a narrow emphasis on punishment. In the mid-twentieth century, disadvantaged Americans came to experience government as a source of economic security and opportunity. Today, though they continue to have access to many benefits and services, they are far more likely to experience the state through programs that coerce behavior, monitor compliance, and implement punishments.

To the extent that we value democratic citizenship, we should care about how policies are affecting it. Indeed, we see such analysis as a crucial civic activity for an engaged social science. To the extent that a policy has demonstrable positive or negative effects on civic practices, we should work to draw attention to these effects.

To do so, we must first understand how our polity is changing, how these changes relate to growing economic inequalities, and how public policies matter for each. The chapters that follow offer a starting point for this understanding. As editors, we hope the policy-centered perspective developed here offers readers a fresh perspective on democratic citizenship in America. We also hope that it furnishes some of the insights and motivations needed to build a more democratic nation.

NOTES

1. Even in the hotly contested 2004 election, when young people voted at higher rates than they had in years, the turnout gap between eighteen-to-twenty-four-year-olds relative to older voters was still greater than it was in 1972 (19 percent compared to 16 percent). It is also important to note that between 2000 and 2004, the increases in youth voting (ages eighteen to twenty-four) were most impressive among those with some college education, whose turnout increased from 52 to 61 percent, and less so among those without it, whose turnout grew from 27 to 34 percent (Lopez, Kirby, and Sagoff 2005, 10).

REFERENCES

Bartels, Larry M. 2006. "What's the Matter with What's the Matter with Kansas?" *Quarterly Journal of Political Science* 1(2): 201–26.

Baumgartner, Frank R., and Bryan D. Jones. 1993. *Agendas and Instability in American Politics.* Chicago, Ill.: University of Chicago Press.

Behrman, Jere, Robert Pollack, and Paul Taubman. 1989. "Family Resources, Family Size, and Access to Financing for College Education." *Journal of Political Economy* 97(2): 398–419.

Bernstein, Jared, and Karen Kornbluh. 2005. "Running Harder to Stay in Place: The Growth of Family Work Hours and Incomes." Washington: New America Foundation. Accessed at http:// www.newamerica.net/files/archive/Doc_File_2436_1.pdf.

Berry, Jeffrey M. 1999. *The New Liberalism: The Rising Power of Citizen Groups.* Washington: Brookings Institute Press.

Brandolini, Andrea, and Timothy M. Smeeding. 2006. "Patterns of Economic Inequality in Western Democracies: Some Facts on Levels and Trends." *PS: Political Science and Politics* 40(1): 21–26.

Burtless, Gary, and Christopher Jencks. 2003. "American Inequality and Its Consequence." Luxembourg Income Study, working paper series 339. Luxembourg: LIS (March).

Campbell, Andrea Louise. 2003. *How Policies Make Citizens: Senior Political Activism and the American Welfare State.* Princeton, N.J.: Princeton University Press.

———. Forthcoming. "Parties, Electoral Participation, and Shifting Voting Blocs." In *The Transformation of American Politics,* edited by Paul Pierson and Theda Skocpol. Princeton, N.J.: Princeton University Press.

Center for Retirement Research at Boston College. 2006. "Retirements at Risk: A New National Retirement Risk Index." June 2006. Accessed at http://www.bc.edu/centers/crr/issues/ib_48.pdf.

Congressional Budget Office. 2006. "Historical Effective Federal Tax Rates: 1979 to 2004." December 2006. Accessed at http://www.cbo.gov/ftpdocs/77xx/doc7718/EffectiveTaxRates.pdf.

Dahl, Robert A. 1961. *Who Governs? Democracy and Power in the American City.* New Haven, Conn.: Yale University Press.

Dew-Becker, Ian, and Robert Gordon. 2005. "Where Did the Productivity Growth Go? Inflation Dynamics and the Distribution of Income." NBER Working Paper w11482. Cambridge, Mass.: National Bureau of Economic Research (December).

Economic Policy Institute. 2006. "Change in Private Sector Employer-Provided Health Insurance Coverage, 1979-2004." Accessed at http://www.epi.org/datazone/06/health_ins.pdf.

Farber, Henry. 2005. "What Do We Know About Job Loss in the United States?" *Federal Reserve Bank of Chicago Economic Perspectives* 2Q: 13–28.

Featherman, David L., and Robert M. Hauser. 1978. *Opportunity and Change.* New York: Academic Press.

Fiorina, Morris P. 2004. *Culture War? The Myth of a Polarized America.* New York: Longman.

Fligstein, Neil. 1976. "The G.I. Bill: Its Effects on the Educational and Occupational Attainment of U.S. Males, 1940–1973." CDE working paper 76-9. Madison, Wisc.: University of Wisconsin, Center for Demography and Ecology.

Freeman, Richard B. 2004. "What, Me Vote?" In *Social Inequality,* edited by Kathryn Neckerman. New York: Russell Sage Foundation.

Fung, Archon. 2004. *Empowered Participation: Reinventing Urban Democracy.* Princeton, N.J.: Princeton University Press.

Gitterman, Daniel P., and Christopher Howard. 2003. "Tax Credits for Working Families: The New American Social Policy." Discussion paper. Washington: Brookings Institution, Center on Urban and Metropolitan Policy.

Goldin, Claudia, and Lawrence Katz. 1999. "Egalitarianism and the Returns to Education During the Great Transformation of American Education." *Journal of Political Economy* 107: S65–S92.

Goldin, Claudia, and Robert A. Margo. 1992. "The Great Compression: The Wage Structure in the United States at Mid-Century." *The Quarterly Journal of Economics* 107(February): 1–34.

Gutmann, Amy, and Dennis Thompson. 1996. *Democracy and Disagreement.* Cambridge, Mass.: Harvard University Press.

Hacker, Jacob S. 2002. *The Divided American Welfare State: The Battle over Public and Private Social Benefits in the United States.* New York: Cambridge University Press.

———. 2004. "Privatizing Risk Without Privatizing the Welfare State: The Hidden Politics of Social Policy Retrenchment in the United States." *American Political Science Review* 98(2): 243–60.

———. 2006. *The Great Risk Shift: The Assault on American Jobs, Families, Health Care, and Retirement—And How You Can Fight Back.* New York: Oxford University Press.

Hacker, Jacob S., and Paul Pierson. 2005. *Off Center: The Republican Revolution and the Erosion of American Democracy.* New Haven, Conn.: Yale University Press.

Hacker, Jacob S., Suzanne Mettler, and Dianne Pinderhughes. 2005. "Inequality and Public Policy." In *Inequality and American Democracy: What We Know and What We Need to Learn,* edited by Lawrence R. Jacobs and Theda Skocpol. New York: Russell Sage Foundation.

Hayward, Clarissa Rile. 2000. *De-Facing Power.* New York: Cambridge University Press.

Howard, Christopher. 1997. *The Hidden Welfare State: Tax Expenditures and Social Policy in the United States.* Princeton, N.J.: Princeton University Press.

Hughes, John E., and M. Margaret Conway. 1997. "Public Opinion and Political Participation." In *Understanding Public Opinion,* edited by Barbara Norrand and Clyde Wilcox. Washington: Congressional Quarterly Press.

Katznelson, Ira. 2005. *When Affirmative Action Was White: An Untold History of Racial Inequality in Twentieth Century America.* New York: Norton.

Kingdon, John W. 1995. *Agendas, Alternatives, and Public Policies.* 2nd edition. New York: Harper-Collins.

Lasswell, Harold D. 1956. "The Political Science of Science: An Inquiry into the Possible Reconciliation of Mastery and Freedom." *American Political Science Review* 50(December): 961–79.

———. 1971. *A Pre-View of the Policy Sciences.* New York: American Elsevier Publishing.

Leuchtenburg, William E. 1973. *A Troubled Feast: American Society Since 1945.* Boston, Mass.: Little, Brown.

Lieberman, Robert. 1998. *Shifting the Color Line.* Cambridge, Mass.: Harvard University Press.

Lopez, Mark Hugo, Emily Kirby, and Jared Sagoff. 2005. "The Youth Vote 2004: Fact Sheet." CIRCLE. The Center for Information and Research on Civic Learning and Engagement. Accessed at http://www.civicyouth.org/PopUps/FactSheets/FS_Youth_Voting_72-04.pdf.

Lynch, Julia. 2001. "The Age Orientation of Social Policy Regimes in OECD Countries." *Journal of Social Policy* 30(3): 411–36.

Manza, Jeff, and Christopher Uggen. 2006. *Locked Out: Felon Disenfranchisement and American Democracy.* New York: Oxford University Press.

McCarty, Nolan, Keith T. Poole, and Howard Rosenthal. 2006. *Polarized America: The Dance of Ideology and Unequal Riches.* Cambridge, Mass.: MIT Press.

Mead, Lawrence. M. 1986. *Beyond Entitlement: The Social Obligations of Citizenship.* New York: Free Press.

Mead, Lawrence M., and Christopher Beem, editors. 2005. *Welfare Reform and Political Theory.* New York: Russell Sage Foundation.

Mettler, Suzanne. 1998. *Dividing Citizens: Gender and Federalism in New Deal Public Policy.* Ithaca, N.Y.: Cornell University Press.

———. 2006. "Unfinished Work: American Democratization, Citizenship, and Processes of Political Change." Unpublished Paper. Syracuse University.

Mettler, Suzanne, and Andrew Milstein. 2007. "American Political Development from Citizens' Perspective: Tracking Federal Government's Presence in Individual Lives over Time." *Studies in American Political Development* 21(1): 110–30.

Mettler, Suzanne, and Joe Soss. 2004. "The Consequences of Public Policy for Democratic Citizenship: Bridging Policy Studies and Mass Politics." *Perspectives on Politics* 2(1): 55–73.

Mishel, Lawrence, Jared Bernstein, and Sylvia Allegretto. 2005. *The State of Working America 2004/2005*. Ithaca, N.Y.: Cornell University Press/ILR Press.

National Center for Children in Poverty. 2006. "Basic Facts About Low-Income Children: Birth to Age 18." Accessed at http://nccp.org/publications/pdf/text_678.pdf.

Orloff, Ann Shola. 1991. "Gender in Early U.S. Social Policy." *Journal of Policy History* 3(3): 249–81.

Orren, Gary. 1997. "Fall from Grace: The Public's Loss of Faith in Government." In *Why People Don't Trust Government*, edited by Joseph S. Nye, Jr., Philip D. Zelikow, and David C. King. Cambridge, Mass.: Harvard University Press.

Picketty, Thomas, and Emmanuel Saez. 2003. "Income Inequality in the United States, 1913–1998." *Quarterly Journal of Economics* 118(1): 1–39.

Pierson, Paul. 1993. "When Effect Becomes Cause: Policy Feedback and Political Change." *World Politics* 45(July): 595–628.

———. 2004. *Politics in Time: History, Institutions, and Social Analysis*. Princeton, N.J.: Princeton University Press.

Putnam, Robert D. 2000. *Bowling Alone: The Collapse and Revival of American Community*. New York: Simon & Schuster.

Rosenstone, Steven J., and John Mark Hansen. 1993. *Mobilization, Participation, and Democracy in America*. New York: Macmillan.

Sammartino, Frank, and Eric Toder. 2002. *Social Policy and the Tax System*. Washington: Urban Institute.

Schneider, Anne, and Helen Ingram. 1993. "Social Construction of Target Populations: Implications for Politics and Policy." *American Political Science Review* 87(2): 334–47.

Shapiro, Ian. 1999. *Democratic Justice*. New Haven, Conn.: Yale University Press.

———. 2005. *The Flight from Reality in the Human Sciences*. Princeton, N.J.: Princeton University Press.

Sherman, Arloc, and Aviva Aron-Dine. 2007. "New CBO Data Show Income Inequality Continues to Widen." Center on Budget and Policy Priorities. January 23, 2007. Accessed at http://www.cbpp.org/1-23-07inc.htm.

Skocpol, Theda. 1992. *Protecting Soldiers and Mothers: The Political Origins of Social Policy in the United States*. Cambridge, Mass.: Harvard University Press.

———. 2003. *Diminished Democracy: From Membership to Management in American Civil Life*. Norman, Okla.: University of Oklahoma Press.

Smeeding, Timothy M. 2005. "Public Policy, Economic Inequality, and Poverty: The United States in Comparative Perspective." *Social Science Quarterly* 86(5): 955–83.

Smeeding, Timothy M., and Lee Rainwater. 2003. *Poor Kids in a Rich Country: America's Children in Comparative Perspective*. New York: Russell Sage Foundation.

Soss, Joe. 1999. "Lessons of Welfare: Policy Design, Political Learning, and Political Action." *American Political Science Review* 93(2): 363–80.

Stimson, James. 2006. "Public Policy Mood: 1952 to 2004." Graph. In *Public Opinion in America: Moods, Cycles, and Swings*. 2nd edition. Boulder, Colo.: Westview Press. Updated version of graph accessed at http://www.unc.edu/~jstimson/time.html.

Stone, Deborah A. 1984. *The Disabled State*. Philadelphia, Pa.: Temple University Press.

Stonecash, Jeffrey M. 2000. *Class and Party in American Politics*. Boulder, Colo.: Westview Press.

Task Force on Inequality and American Democracy. 2004. *American Democracy in an Age of Rising Inequality*. Washington: American Political Science Association.

Theriault, Sean M. 2006. "Party Polarization in the U.S. Congress: Member Replacement and Member Adaptation." *Pary Politics* 12(4): 483-503.

Travis, Jeremy. 2005. "They All Come Back." Washington: Brookings Institute.

U.S. Census Bureau. 2003. "Poverty in the United States: 2002." Current Population Reports. Accessed at http://www.census.gov/prod/2003pubs/p60-222.pdf.

Van Horn, Carl E., William T. Gormley, Jr., and Donald C. Baumer. 2001. *Politics and Public Policy*. 3rd edition. Washington: Congressional Quarterly Press.

Verba, Sidney, Kay Lehman Schlozman, and Henry Brady. 1995. *Voice and Equality: Civic Voluntarism in American Politics.* Cambridge, Mass.: Harvard University Press.

Warren, Elizabeth, and Amelia Warren Tyagi. 2003. *The Two-Income Trap: Why Middle-Class Mothers and Fathers Are Going Broke.* New York: Basic Books.

Western, Bruce. 2006. *Punishment and Inequality.* New York: Russell Sage Foundation.

Western, Bruce, and Becky Pettit. 2002. "Beyond Crime and Punishment: Prisons and Inequality." *Contexts* 1(3): 37–43.

———. 2005. "Black-White Wage Inequality, Employment Rates, and Incarceration." *American Journal of Sociology*, 111(2): 553-78.

White, Julie Anne. 2000. *Democracy, Justice, and the Welfare State: Reconstructing Public Care.* University Park, Pa.: Pennsylvania State University Press.

Zukin, Cliff, Scott Keeter, Molly Andolina, Krista Jenkins, and Michael X. Delli Carpini. 2006. *A New Engagement: Political Participation, Civic Life, and the Changing American Citizen.* New York: Oxford University Press.

Part II

Policies and Institutions in the New Politics of Inequality

Kimberly J. Morgan

Chapter 2

Constricting the Welfare State: Tax Policy and the Political Movement Against Government

The redistributive programs of the welfare state cannot exist without a politically secure and stable source of finance. All public programs have to be paid for by someone, yet people often want more public spending than they are willing to pay for through taxes. The resulting dilemma for policymakers has been to figure out how to raise the necessary funds to pay for the welfare state without antagonizing the public. Some scholars argue that the form of taxation may affect the ability to raise funds, because some kinds of taxes are less visible or irksome to taxpayers than others. In this view, income and property taxes are highly visible and much resented, particularly by more powerful groups in society, such as the wealthy and the rich. Payroll and sales taxes, by contrast, are either less visible or benefit from greater legitimacy when earmarked for popular social programs, making them a more acceptable source of funding to the public, even though they are less progressive than the income tax. In fact, many countries with large welfare states rely heavily on payroll and value-added taxes to finance them. Thus, different modes of taxation may have feedback effects on the politics of social spending.

This chapter explores this thesis for the American case and finds that there is no inevitable feedback effect of tax systems on social policy outcomes; instead, this relationship is mediated by the behavior of political elites, who choose whether or not to use taxes and other public policies as a resource in their political fights. In the postwar period, the American tax system consisted of steeply progressive income taxes, high taxes on capital and corporate incomes, and a small but growing payroll tax. Yet taxation was not a source of partisan acrimony in this period, nor were there serious disputes about the modestly sized welfare state that was emerging. Political elites were generally in agreement about the size and shape of the welfare state and the way it would be financed, precluding fundamental challenges to either tax or spending policy. Programs such as Social Security had wide support and there were other limited expansions of direct social spending. Otherwise, tax policy was used to encourage the growth of private forms of social provision, such as employer-funded health insurance, thereby bolstering income security for many people but obscuring the role of the federal government in providing this.

By the 1970s, however, bipartisan agreement on fiscal policy began to collapse, and the existing matrix of tax and spending policies offered crucial resources to conservative activists and politicians seeking to build a broad-based political movement against taxation. The combination of a highly visible tax system and a less visible welfare state fueled mass discontent over increasing federal, state, and local tax burdens, particularly in a time of high inflation that increased property assessments and pushed people into higher tax brackets. Rising property and income taxes helped spark tax backlashes and anger at "big government," while the growing tax load seemed not to have brought much return in the form of economic security, especially for non-seniors, who relied heavily on the private sector for their social welfare needs. Conservatives successfully tapped these popular frustrations to build a political movement centered on rolling back the size of government, which put liberals on the defensive. Democrats could shield popular programs, such as Social Security, but could not draw upon evidence of the success of universal programs for the non-elderly to justify high tax rates.

Partisan conflict over taxes and spending has produced a constrained environment for social programs. Conservatives have drawn on popular sympathies for tax cuts as a way to contain federal spending, whereas Democrats have fought to defend existing programs. Not only did deficits grow as a result, but proposed expansions of social programs were repeatedly stymied by the lack of funding and opposition to tax increases. One result has been the continuing transfer of burdens onto states—itself a form of retrenchment as cash-strapped state governments struggle to pay for increasing burdens and responsibilities. Although the tax-cutting drive has reduced tax burdens on the poor, this has neither substantially reduced poverty rates nor mitigated one of the most significant trends since the 1970s—growing income inequality.

PUBLIC POLICY AS A POLITICAL RESOURCE

The idea that politicians employ public policy as a tool in political conflict and debate is hardly new, but often is applied to social-spending programs. Many scholars have argued that universal social programs have different political qualities than means-tested ones; universal programs generate a large constituency of supportive beneficiaries, making it difficult to cut them (Skocpol 1991; Pierson 1993). Universal programs also confer political advantages on those who can claim credit for their creation and defense. Thus, the Democratic Party's "ownership" of Social Security means that the public trusts Democrats when it comes to safeguarding this highly popular program, and that Democrats can assert responsibility for protecting and preserving it (Petrocik 1996). Similar arguments have been made about the welfare state being a "power resource" for left parties in Western Europe (Esping-Andersen 1985). In Sweden, for example, the Social Democratic Party claims credit for fashioning and defending a comprehensive set of universal programs; the welfare state is thus a resource that has helped them maintain political dominance (Blomqvist and Green-Pedersen 2004).

Different forms of taxation may also have distinct political qualities. Some scholars argue that certain taxes are more popular, or less visible, and thus facilitate the expansion of the public sector (Wilensky 2002; Hibbs and Madsen 1981; Steuerle 1992, 7–10; Kato 2003).[1] The Value Added Tax (VAT) and other sales taxes may be less visible to taxpayers because they are included in the price of goods and people rarely calculate how much they have paid in sales taxes over the course of the year (Sausgruber and Tyran 2004). The same may be true of payroll tax contributions, as most people underestimate how much they pay in these taxes (Boeri, Boersch-Supan, and Tabellini 2002). It could also be easier to levy payroll taxes for social insurance programs, which often are labeled "contributions," not taxes, and linked to popular benefits (Hibbs and Madsen 1981, 422–23). Empirically, countries with the largest welfare states generally rely on taxes that may seem the least fair—the payroll and consumption taxes that levy a disproportionate burden on those with lower incomes (see figure 2.1).[2] By contrast, in the United States and most other liberal welfare regimes (Canada, New Zealand, Australia, and the U.K.), in-

FIGURE 2.1   The Tax Mix and Social Spending

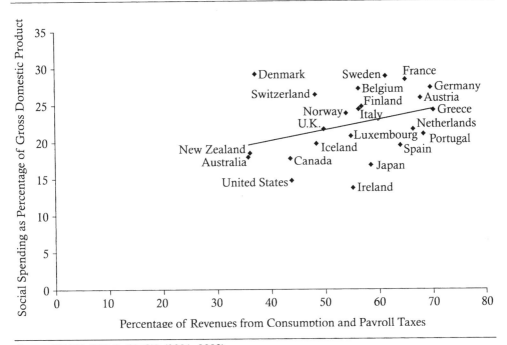

Source: OECD (2004); OECD (2001, 2002).
Note: Spending data are from 2001, and revenues from 2002.

come and profits taxes are the dominant source of revenues, but the overall level of taxation is lower than in much of Western Europe (Lindert 2004, 235–44; Steinmo 1993).[3]

Few have probed the mechanisms that connect tax systems with social spending, though this represents an intriguing correlation. Steep marginal income tax rates may help sustain a citizens' tax revolt, yet taxpayers are a diffuse and heterogeneous group whose members are unlikely to mobilize on their own. It is more likely that narrower subgroups with a strong stake in cutting taxes will take the lead in organizing opposition to these taxes, and could then tap unhappiness in the general population about tax burdens. For that reason, high taxes on capital or corporate incomes may prove the most politically toxic, as they risk arousing the ire of business and richer taxpayers—two traditionally well-organized groups. Indeed, the English-speaking countries have had higher corporate income and property taxes than most Western European countries—particularly before neoconservative political movements took shape during the 1980s, which subsequently lowered these taxes (Peters 1991; see table 2.1).

Another question concerns how to draw the causal arrows between a country's tax mix and its social-spending levels. Certain forms of taxation may facilitate the growth of social programs, but those programs could then create public willingness to pay taxes. Tax and spending systems may thus prove mutually reinforcing. In countries where the welfare state delivers visible and popular benefits to the public, people may be more willing to stomach high tax levels (Hibbs and Madsen 1981). In the liberal regimes, by contrast, the relationship between taxes paid and benefits received is less transparent because

TABLE 2.1   Property and Corporate Income Taxes as a Percentage of
Gross Domestic Product, 1965 to 2004

	1965	1970	1975	1980	1985	1990	1995	2000	2004
Property taxes									
Continental Europe[a]	1.4	1.4	1.3	1.2	1.2	1.5	1.6	1.9	1.9
Scandinavia[b]	1.2	1.1	1.2	1.2	1.4	1.7	1.6	1.6	1.6
Liberal[c]	3.5	3.5	3.1	2.7	2.7	2.7	2.7	2.8	2.9
United States	3.9	3.8	3.6	2.8	2.7	3.1	3.1	3.0	3.1
Corporate income taxes[d]									
Continental Europe[a]	1.7	1.7	1.9	1.8	2.0	2.3	2.1	3.1	2.8
Scandinavia[b]	1.5	1.2	1.3	2.0	2.7	2.0	2.4	4.7	4.3
Liberal[c]	3.3	3.5	2.9	2.7	2.6	2.8	3.3	4.1	3.9
United States	4.0	3.6	2.9	2.8	1.9	2.4	2.9	2.6	2.2

Source: OECD (2006).
a. Continental Europe = Austria, Belgium, France, Germany, Greece, Italy, the Netherlands, Portugal, Spain, and Switzerland.
b. Scandinavia = Denmark, Finland, Iceland, Norway, and Sweden.
c. Liberal = Australia, Canada, Ireland, New Zealand, the United Kingdom, and the United States.
d. Corporate income tax data for Portugal are not available.

private markets and employers provide many social welfare benefits and services (Esping-Andersen 1990, 82–88). Even if employer-provided welfare was heavily subsidized through the tax code or compelled through government mandates (Adema 2001), people would not necessarily see the hand of the state behind these provisions. It was in these countries that antitax or anti-welfare-state movements took shape in the late 1970s—a time when inflation was pushing people into higher income tax brackets—and conservative political forces have played a significant role in these countries ever since (Wilensky 2002).

Close examination of the American case enables us to explore how tax systems, in conjunction with social programs, shape redistributive politics. As we shall see, policies on their own have no inevitable consequences for politics; the key lies in how elites make use of the political opportunities that policies provide them.

FISCAL POLITICS IN THE POSTWAR ERA

The American tax and transfer system that emerged by mid-century combined a relatively visible, and potentially unpopular, tax system with a modestly sized and oft obscured welfare state. Personal and corporate income taxes were the dominant source of revenue at the federal level, having tremendously expanded to pay for American participation in the Second World War. By the end of the conflict, 60 percent of households were paying the federal income tax, and top marginal rates exceeded 90 percent for individuals (Brownlee 2004, 115). Elevated tax rates were largely preserved in the decade following the war, despite public opinion polls revealing the unpopularity of the income tax.[4] Mass opinion was more favorable toward the payroll tax that financed Social Security, Disability Insurance, and, after 1965, Medicare, as people tended to view this as a contribution that entitled them to benefits later on (Campbell and Morgan 2005b, 184). The payroll tax was relatively minor throughout the 1950s and 1960s, however, as personal and corporate income taxes made up the majority of federal revenues.[5]

As for the welfare state, only certain categories of people—the elderly, the poor, the unemployed, the disabled—were entitled beneficiaries of the social programs created in the 1930s and expanded in the decades following the war. People outside these categories were to rely on private forms of social protection: employer-provided pensions and health insurance, home ownership and personal savings, and any services or insurance policies they could purchase in the marketplace (Hacker 2002; Klein 2003). Tax and regulatory policy were critical in enabling the construction of this private "safety net" but often did so in hidden ways (Howard 1997). For example, tax policy had encouraged employer-provided benefits since the 1920s and this practice continued after the Second World War, but it is likely that few workers were aware of this subsidy (Stevens 1988, 128–32; Hacker 2002, 93–95, 239–40). Congress also created numerous tax expenditures that helped individuals cover their own social welfare needs in the private market.[6] By the 1950s, there were tax deductions for exceptional medical expenses, child-care costs, and interest on home mortgages, and Congress continually added more of these exceptions to the tax code (Howard 1997).

Thus, in the decades following the Second World War, the American tax and transfer system consisted of visible and potentially unpopular forms of taxation that financed obscured forms of federal support (Prasad 2006). That neither taxing nor spending became a source of political contention is revealing about the relative consensus among political elites in this period around fiscal policies—a consensus fostered by political, institutional, and economic factors. Politically, divisions within the Democratic and Republican parties on redistributive questions fostered moderate policy stances on taxation and social spending (Stonecash 2000). The Democratic Party was divided between liberal northern Democrats, who favored federal social programs and progressive taxation, and fiscally conservative southerners leery of expanded federal authority and involvement in social affairs. The Republican Party also was divided between more liberal Republicans from the North and Midwest, who were often sympathetic to redistributive legislation, and a more libertarian faction from the West (Rae 1989). The effect of these internal divisions was to dampen partisan conflict over redistributive matters.

Institutional features of Congress reinforced these political tendencies. The two and a half decades following the Second World War were a period of "committee government," when House and Senate committees and their chairmen dominated the legislative process (Rohde 2005). Some of the most powerful committees were the tax and spending committees: House Ways and Means, Senate Finance, and the Appropriations committees and subcommittees. The chairmanships of these committees were largely in the hands of conservative Democrats, often from the South, who favored both a moderate-size government and the distribution of federal resources in ways that reinforced their political power. Tax committees such as Ways and Means and Senate Finance operated largely behind closed doors, as markup sessions were closed to the public, and relied upon nonpartisan staff to guide them in their work (Graetz 1997, 114). More generally, pragmatism rather than partisanship governed tax and spending policy, limiting dramatic expansions of the American welfare state while blunting attacks on it (Zelizer 1998; Taylor 2002; Brownlee 2004, 121–25).

Bipartisanship on tax and spending policy also was facilitated by economic growth, which dampened conflicts over the distribution of federal largesse. Dubbed by some tax scholars the era of "easy finance," the three decades after the Second World War were a time of rapid economic growth, inflation that steadily pushed people into higher tax brackets, and favorable demographics for social insurance programs such as Social Security (Steuerle 1992; Brownlee 2004). All three trends provided the federal government with a pool of resources that could be redirected to constituents through public spending programs or tax breaks. For example, with many more people paying taxes into the Social Security system than were receiving benefits, there were ample revenues to support benefit increases for current retirees. As for the income tax, because tax brackets were not indexed for inflation, people moved into higher brackets as their nominal incomes grew. The result was higher tax revenues for the federal government without legislators having to vote on increasing taxes.

These propitious circumstances began to change in the 1970s, undermining the relative accord among political elites on fiscal policy. Economic downturn put an end to the era of easy finance, creating a more zero-sum budgeting climate that forced explicit trade-offs between taxing and spending priorities (Steuerle 1992). At the same time, the constituencies for the two parties began to shift (Sundquist 1983). The Democratic Party's embrace of civil rights and the war on poverty produced continuing defections of the party's white southern wing, particularly among better-off southerners, and gains among lower-income groups in other parts of the country. The voting base of the Republican Party became more uniformly affluent, in part through an influx of white southern voters (Stonecash 2000). As the class divide sharpened between the two parties, politicians on both sides of the spectrum became more confrontational on redistributive issues (Stonecash and Milstein 2000).

These political shifts brought reinforcing institutional changes in Congress that would further polarize taxing and spending politics. Chafing at the influence of southern Democrats within Congress, northern Democrats pushed through institutional changes that would diminish the southerners' power over fiscal policy. "Sunshine" reforms sought to open up committee decisionmaking and shift some power from committee chairs to subcommittees (Schickler 2001). Henceforth, the closed doors that had shielded tax and spending policy from public scrutiny were open, giving greater access to the media but also to well-organized interest groups. Fiscal policy would no longer be made through backroom, technocratic decisionmaking processes, but could become a source of public and partisan debate (Graetz 1997, 117–18).

Newly mobilized groups sought to fill the opening created by these political and institutional changes. Conservatives hostile to the welfare state and the progressive income tax had never disappeared from the American political system, but had been marginalized during decades of moderate bipartisanship on fiscal policy (Schulman 2001, 193–95). By the 1970s, an elite political movement was gaining strength around a tax-cutting agenda, shaped in part by supply-side economic ideas (Burns and Taylor 2000; Prasad 2006, 48–52). As the Republican Party shifted to the right, the free market values championed by these conservatives gained acceptance. Similarly, a resurgent and politicized business community became more closely allied with the Republican Party than it had been before (Vogel 1989; Martin 1994). Although the tax burden on corporations declined throughout the post-war period, taxation was a source of animus, particularly for the small-business owners subject to personal income taxes. Business groups thus forged closer ties to the Republican Party, began financing free market think tanks, and lobbied members of Congress, particularly through local Chambers of Commerce (Edsall 1984; Vogel 1989).[7]

All of these developments at the elite level were likely to produce a more partisan climate around fiscal policymaking than in the past. Particular targets of conservative elites were the personal income tax and taxes on capital. What gave these elite-level ideas enduring resonance, however, was the electoral success of their advocates, which turned the antitax drive into a broader political movement. In this, the matrix of tax and spending policies would prove critical as the combination of a highly visible tax system and less visible welfare state stoked mass resentment against government.

THE TAX REVOLT AND THE POLITICIZATION OF TAX AND SOCIAL POLICY

Mass discontent with the tax system had a number of sources. One was simply that the burden of taxation had been growing for decades at all levels of government. At the federal level, inflation and real income growth pushed people into higher tax brackets, while the failure to adjust the standard deduction or personal exemption for inflation put more people onto the tax rolls and then moved them into higher brackets (Steuerle 1992). Though tax expenditures compensated some households for these higher tax burdens, these tax breaks tended to benefit upper-income households the most. Already between 1951 and 1962, average income taxes paid by upper-income groups declined—and declined more for those at the highest income levels—while average rates rose for middle-income people (Babilot and Anderson 1967). In the succeeding years, the progressivity of the entire tax system (federal, state, and local) continued to decrease, largely due to the reduced progressivity of federal taxes (Pechman 1985, 70–71).

Increases in state and local revenues also increased the load on taxpayers. The social mobilizations of the 1960s and 1970s brought renewed attention to a host of social questions, including poverty, welfare, and the state of urban areas. Federal responses often employed state or local governments as agents of federal policy, and this was accompanied by federal grants-in-aid and other intergovernmental transfers. Although federal aid rose throughout the 1960s and 1970s, this did not compensate for increasing burdens at the state and local level. Moreover, by the 1970s, unfunded regulatory mandates were increasingly common, particularly given the growing fiscal difficulties of the federal government in the 1970s (Posner 1998).

As a result, taxes and spending at the state and local level continually rose throughout this period, contributing to an ever-increasing tax burden on individuals and families. State and local taxes as a percentage of personal income rose from 7.6 percent in 1953 to 12.1 percent in 1973. Increases were particularly dramatic in states such as California, where state and local taxes reached nearly 14 percent of personal income by the early 1970s (Advisory Commission on Intergovernmental Relations 1975, 23–24). Often, the increase came through highly visible and unpopular property taxes, which rose rapidly in many states and localities as a result of both inflation—which led to higher assessments of property values—and the adoption of more accurate modes of assessment (Martin 2007). When added to rising federal income taxes and Social Security contributions, the tax burden on the "average" family rose over 98 percent between 1953 and 1974 (Advisory Commission on Intergovernmental Relations 1975, 3; see figure 2.2).

Growing income and property tax burdens hit people with some of the most visible and resented forms of taxation. Public opinion data showed that people viewed property and federal income taxes as the least fair and most-hated of all taxes, whereas they found both sales and social security taxes more acceptable. In a 1978 survey, for example, 49

FIGURE 2.2   Federal, Social Security, and State and Local Taxes as
Percentage of Gross Domestic Product, 1929 to 2002[a]

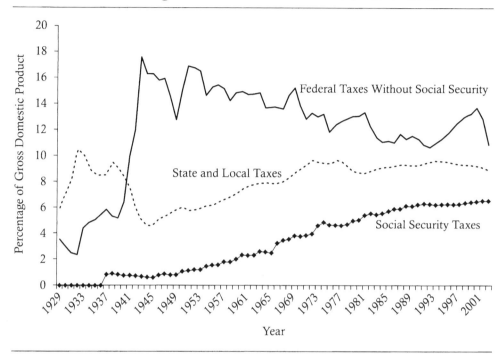

Source: Tax Policy Center (Urban Institute-Brookings).
a. State and local revenues do not include federal grants to states and localities.

percent of people polled cited the personal income tax as the tax most in need of lowering and 33 percent mentioned the property tax. Less visible and more acceptable forms of taxation were better regarded: only 9 percent of respondents said the state sales tax should be lowered, and 8 percent cited social security taxes—this despite the fact that the social security tax burden had significantly increased in the previous two decades (Campbell and Morgan 2005b, 195). With the income tax, what may matter most is the marginal tax rates published in the Internal Revenue Service bulletin, as this is what people actually see. In reality, people's effective tax rates usually are lower, owing to the personal exemption, standard deduction, and whatever other tax credits or deductions they can take, yet many are not aware of this. Especially important is the experience of upper-income people—those mostly likely to vote, donate to campaigns, and become vocal in politics. Between the late 1960s and late 1970s, marginal tax rates on upper-middle class households doubled, reflecting the effects of inflation and the growth of two-earner households (Steuerle 1992, 24–26).

At the same time, many people perceived that they got little in return for many of the taxes that they paid. Surveys during the 1970s showed that fewer than 20 percent of respondents thought they received good value for the federal income taxes they paid, the rest qualifying this as fair or poor. Negative evaluations of the return on federal income taxes spiked at the end of the 1970s.[8] This is hardly surprising given the lack of broad-based social programs for the non-elderly population (Skocpol 2000). The universal Social Security and Medicare programs continued to be favorably regarded, and the taxes paid for them were seen as worth the money. For non-senior-citizens, however, all they saw from the federal government was wasteful spending and abuse of the public purse. Polls showed a major drop in the public's trust in government since the 1960s, as Watergate and the Vietnam War eroded the public's confidence (Ladd et al. 1979).[9] Worse, one of the most visible aspects of the welfare state was the controversial welfare program. The racial associations of this program in the public's eye, and the racialization of poverty in this period (Gilens 1999), fed perceptions that taxpayer dollars were going to welfare cheats who bore children to get larger government checks. To many Americans—and especially white Americans—taxes became a potent symbol of everything that was wrong with government (Sears and Citrin 1982; Ladd et al., 1979).[10]

The critical event that brought mass discontent and elite, antigovernment activism together was the California tax revolt. In 1978, a majority of the state's voters agreed to Proposition 13, an initiative to cap the growth of property taxes. Similar initiatives followed in other states, usually promoted by a mix of home and commercial property owners, antigovernment conservatives, and liberals angry at what they perceived to be a regressive tax (Brownlee 2004, 140; Schulman 2001, 207). For conservative politicians and strategists, these revolts showed the potential of tax issues to mobilize electoral support—particularly given that anti-property-tax sentiment appeared to cross party lines. Concentrating on the most-hated elements of the tax system—income and property taxes—was a way for conservatives to build a larger political movement against taxation and the growth of government.

Ronald Reagan was the first to capitalize on these new possibilities, and he rode a wave of antigovernment sentiment to power in 1981 (Brownlee and Steuerle 2003; Martin 2007). The centerpiece of his domestic agenda was the across-the-board tax cuts that passed in the Omnibus Budget and Reconciliation Act of 1981 (OBRA). There also were a host of favorable tax provisions benefiting business. The effect of these tax cuts, in conjunction with economic downturn and major increases in defense spending, were the largest peacetime budget deficits the country had ever experienced. In response, the Reagan administration agreed to a series of tax *increases* between 1982 and 1984—a move that was supported by some fiscally conservative Republicans in Congress but contested by others as a violation of supply-side ideals. Thus, although the Reagan administration marked the start of the era when the Republican Party embraced a stronger antitax platform, the change was incomplete through the 1980s as Republicans continued to differ on the gravity of budget deficits and necessity of tax increases to combat them.

By the 1990s, however, the party had moved to a more resolutely antitax standpoint and it appeared to yield many political benefits. The tax issue appealed to strong partisans within the party—the activists who are ideologically to the right of the average Republican voter but play a vital role in political campaigns. Opposition to taxes also seemed to appeal to the average voter; the "new conventional wisdom" among politicians and candidates was that the public was hostile to federal taxes (Rivlin 1989, 113). The huge victory of Reagan over Walter Mondale in 1984 was widely interpreted as due, in part, to Mondale's statement that he would raise taxes (LeLoup 2005, 82). The focus on taxes also enabled politicians to tap racial resentments without making overtly racist statements, whether they intended to do so or not (Schulman 2001). Racial sentiments are an important predictor of views on taxes, revealing the power of coded antitax and antiwelfare statements to draw political support from certain segments of the population (Sears and Citrin 1982; Kinder, Burns, and Vieregge 2005).

Another advantage of focusing on taxes is that directly attacking popular social spending programs is politically treacherous. In both the 1980s and 1990s, attempts to cut spending on these programs were political fiascoes for Republicans, as Democrats tagged them with the "grinch" label (Peterson 1998). Moreover, by the 1980s, the intensity of antigovernment feeling had waned, and opinion polls showed people more supportive of paying taxes to support popular social programs (Page and Shapiro 1992, chapter 4). However, people often fail to draw the connection between taxes and social spending, leading them to favor both tax cuts and higher spending (Sears and Citrin 1982; Bartels 2003; Baron and McCaffery 2006). Thus, by appealing to people's willingness to take a tax cut when offered to them, many Republicans have been able to run on a strong anti-tax message rather than challenging social programs directly. The hope, of at least some conservatives, has been that this will restrain the growth of spending without requiring Republicans to directly attack these programs (Friedman 2003; Becker, Lazear, and Murphy 2003).

It is difficult to say how uniformly a "starve-the-beast" strategy has motivated the drive to cut taxes. Reagan publicly likened the federal government to a profligate child whose allowance had to be cut in order to reduce spending, and the administration's 1981 tax cut appeared to be influenced by both supply-side and starve-the-beast motivations (Rauch 2006; Tempelman 2006).[11] Yet, there were divisions among conservatives from the start about this strategy. A former Office of Management and Budget official in the Reagan administration recalls lively debates in the White House about whether "starve-the-beast" or "serve-the-check" would best contain the size of government—the latter matching taxes to spending so that people experience the full cost of government and therefore demand spending restraint (DeMuth 2006). Starve-the-beast goals appeared resurgent in the 1990s, particularly in the push for tax cuts that would dry up the budget surpluses in the late 1990s and in the efforts of the antitax activist Grover Norquist to extract pledges by candidates and elected officials never to vote for a tax increase. Some believe the Bush tax cuts were driven by the desire to drain resources from the federal government; this became evident when President Bush inadvertently heralded the return of budget deficits as putting Congress in a fiscal straitjacket (Brownlee 2004, 221–22; Martin 2007). However, the growth of domestic spending since 2001 has prompted assertions by some conservatives that the starve-the-beast strategy has never been the goal of the Bush administration, and if it has been, then the strategy has failed (Bartlett 2004; Niskanen and Van Doren 2004; Ponnuru 2005).

Regardless of the specific motives (and there usually have been multiple aims), it is clear that by the 1990s, Republicans were increasingly unified in their antitax stance. The majority of Republicans voted against the 1990 budget reconciliation act negotiated between the Bush I White House and the Democratic-controlled Congress that raised taxes as part of a larger deficit-reduction package.[12] Later, conservatives blamed President Bush's failure to win a second term on his having signed this measure and thus violated the "no new taxes" pledge he had made during the 1988 presidential campaign (LeLoup 2005, 155), and tax-cutting goals began to supersede those of deficit reduction for many Republicans. Not a single Republican in the House or Senate voted for the 1993 reconciliation bill that again raised taxes, mostly on higher-income households, in order to reduce the deficit. Republicans then gained control of both the House and Senate in 1994 in an election that they viewed as a repudiation of President Clinton's tax increases and attempt at health-care reform. Believing that the electorate had given them a mandate for smaller government and tax cuts, the House Republicans' "Contract with America" pledged an array of tax reductions, significant cuts in federal spending—especially in programs for the poor, but also for Medicare—a line-item veto, and a constitutional balanced budget amendment. Although Clinton vetoes blocked much of the Republican agenda, he ultimately assented to several of the tax reduction measures.

Significant reductions in federal taxes would have to wait until George W. Bush took office in 2001 with Republican control over both chambers of Congress and a large yet rapidly declining budget surplus. His administration determinedly pursued a series of tax cuts between 2001 and 2006 that cut individual income taxes through rate cuts and expanded tax credits, reduced taxes on dividends and capital gains, granted a number of tax breaks for businesses, and gradually phases out the estate tax by 2010. The total cost of these tax cutting bills over ten years is estimated at $2 trillion, which does not include a remedy for the alternative minimum tax problem (Leiserson and Rohaly 2006).[13] Notable about these tax cuts when compared to those of the Reagan administration is the determination to continue cutting taxes despite the reemergence of budget deficits (Bartlett 2004). After 1981, the Reagan administration agreed to tax increases to redress the deteriorating budgetary situation, but under the Bush II administration, tax cutting has taken priority over deficit reduction. Bush's determination to reduce federal taxes appeared to pay off for him politically: in so doing, he shored up support with his party's base and gained the reputation of being a strong leader who could guide his legislative agenda to victory (Ornstein and Fortier 2002). Although the American public was not strongly clamoring for lower taxes at the time and many hardly noticed the 2001 law, of those who were paying attention the majority supported the cut in their tax bill (Bartels 2003; Kinder, Burns, and Vieregge 2005).

The structure of the American welfare state, with its hidden subsidies and supports for non-elderly Americans, has not provided similar political resources for Democrats. Democrats have successfully defended existing broad-based social programs like Social Security and Medicare, which have a wide constituency and are highly popular. There are no equivalent direct spending programs for the non-elderly population, however, and the role of the federal government in people's lives is obscured by heavy reliance on tax expenditures (Skocpol 2000). Many people do not believe that the government is there to help them, nor do they generally expect help in ensuring basic income security for all families.[14] This makes it difficult for Democrats to justify higher tax rates: no politician has ever called for higher taxes in the name of preserving the tax subsidy for employer-provided health insurance, even though it represents the largest federal subsidy for the health care of non-poor, non-elderly people. The "hidden" nature of tax expenditures may facilitate their creation and expansion, but their invisibility does not enable much political credit claiming (Howard 1997). Efforts to develop new social programs would also be stymied by the difficulty of proposing new tax increases that would quickly be attacked by Republicans and well-organized groups (discussed in the next section).

Failing to gain political traction around the call for new social programs, Democrats have focused their energies on making sure tax reductions benefit people with lower incomes. This set off a contest with Republicans to see who could use the tax code to do more for middle- and low-income people, and in turn shaped Republican strategies. Although Republicans initially focused on cuts in high marginal rates and taxes on capital and corporations, fierce Democratic criticism led Republicans to push for tax benefits for moderate-income people. The growing significance of social conservatives in the Republican Party also influenced this shift, as tax breaks for families with children became a way to satisfy both fiscal conservatives seeking to shrink the size of government and social conservatives eager to direct greater fiscal largesse toward families (Steuerle 1992). The emphasis on tax fairness helped provide broad political support for the Tax Reform

Act of 1986, which included several measures specifically geared toward families, such as an increase in the personal exemption and standard deduction (Steuerle 1992, 121–23). Competition over tax policy also spurred continual expansions of the Earned Income Tax Credit (EITC), a refundable credit on the earnings of low-income people (Howard 1995). The larger consequence has been that both parties endorse the use of tax expenditures as an instrument of social policy, but this tends to shrink the pool of federal resources available for direct social spending.

In sum, features of the American tax and transfer system have impacted fiscal politics by providing disproportionate political resources to those seeking to reduce the size of government. How has the resulting fiscal and political environment affected the politics of social policy and, in particular, the problems of poverty and inequality?

CONSTRICTING THE WELFARE STATE

The constrained fiscal environment since the early 1980s has not led to major cutbacks in the size of the federal government. In fact, one of the main complaints of conservatives in recent years has been that the drive to reduce taxes has not brought a corresponding decline in the size of the public sector, but has instead contributed to large budget deficits (Niskanen and Van Doren 2004). Looking specifically at social spending, OECD (Organization for Economic Cooperation and Development) data show that while spending has fluctuated since the early 1980s, it has not declined overall and has even increased some since the 1990s (figure 2.3). Indeed, Social Security and support for the disabled has become more generous, and Medicaid coverage has grown (Mettler and Milstein 2007; Grogan and Patashnik 2003). As Paul Pierson (1994) and others have observed, popular social programs are politically treacherous to attack head-on, and the desire of many Democrats and Republicans to address social problems through government action remains.

However, a longer perspective on federal spending trends reveals the overall stability of domestic spending since the 1980s, following a rapid increase in the previous decades (figure 2.4). Social spending rose significantly in the 1960s and 1970s, with expansions in Social Security benefits, the creation of Medicare and Medicaid, and increased domestic discretionary spending. Since the 1980s, however, the overall trend has been one of relative stability, with some fluctuations in the 1980s and increased health-care spending in the 1990s, driven in part by medical inflation. Thus, in 1980, the federal government spent the equivalent of 15.4 percent of GDP on domestic discretionary and mandatory (entitlement) spending, and in 2005 the federal government spent nearly the same—15.3 percent of GDP on those two categories (Congressional Budget Office 2007).

In short, although the antitax drive and resulting conditions of fiscal constraint have not starved the federal beast, they have constricted it and prevented much expansion (Pierson 1998, 134). This has occurred through both the adoption of restrictive budget laws and the politicization of taxes. The growth of large budget deficits in the 1980s led to the "fiscalization" of public policy debates, as nearly all proposed or existing spending programs came to be evaluated through the lens of the deficit (Pierson 1998; Patashnik 2005). Accompanying this trend was the development of budget rules that sought to limit the growth of spending, such as the Gramm-Rudman-Hollings Act of 1985, which required mandatory across-the-board spending cuts if deficit targets were not met. Although Gramm-Rudman-Hollings failed to make much of a dent in the deficit during the 1980s, it was followed by a more stringent and effective set of budget rules in 1990: caps on discretionary spending and pay-as-you-go (PAYGO) rules requiring that any increase in entitlement eligibility or reduction in tax revenues be offset by other spending cuts or

FIGURE 2.3   U.S. Public Social Spending as Percentage of Gross Domestic
Product, 1980 to 2003[a]

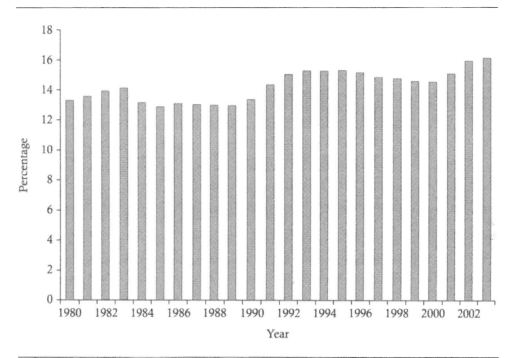

Year

Source: OECD (2004).
a. Social spending includes all direct, public spending on programs such as Old Age Survivors and
Disability Insurance, Medicare and Medicaid, AFDC and TANF, Food Stamps, and other income
supports for the poor. Tax expenditures are excluded, except for cash payments made through the
refundable part of the Earned Income Tax Credit.

higher taxes. In 1993, Clinton signed a deficit reduction bill that extended these caps and
the PAYGO requirement. Both the 1990 and 1993 laws also made cuts in social spending,
with particularly large cuts in Medicare.

This fiscal climate would put a squeeze on domestic spending, producing less visible
but important erosions in the quality and nature of public programs. For example,
Suzanne Mettler and Andrew Milstein (2007) show declines in the real value of Pell
Grants, food stamps, and the average Aid to Families with Dependent Children benefit
since the 1970s, and they show that the value of unemployment insurance also dropped
in real terms. More generally, Jacob S. Hacker (2004) argues that "policy drift" has affected numerous government programs, whereby shortcomings in existing programs, and
the rise of new social needs, are ignored. Of particular importance here is the failure to
deal effectively with medical inflation, which has fueled the growth of Medicare and
Medicaid spending. The rapid growth in these two programs has then squeezed out
spending on other areas. Keeping overall social spending at a constant level in the face of
growing social needs or pressure in other areas of the budget can be a form of welfare
state retrenchment in its own right (Clayton and Pontusson 1998).

FIGURE 2.4   Federal Spending as a Percentage of Gross Domestic
Product, 1962 to 2006

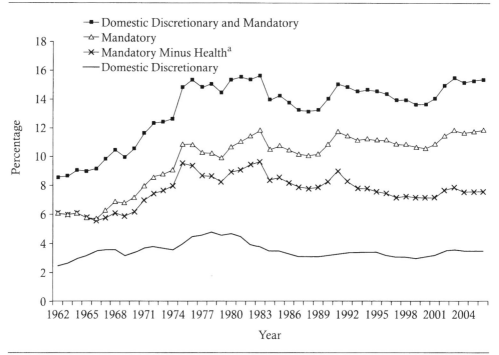

Source: Congressional Budget Office (2007).
a. "Mandatory minus health" means mandatory spending minus Medicare and Medicaid spending.

Budget deficits and the politically toxic environment around tax increases also obstructed efforts to expand social programs. The demise of Medicare Catastrophic Coverage legislation in the late 1980s is illustrative of the political obstacles to financing social programs. The original law, which passed with bipartisan support, added coverage for catastrophic costs and a prescription drug benefit to Medicare, but was financed through higher premiums on senior citizens so as not to worsen existing budget deficits. Although most seniors would pay only a small increase and were happy with the added benefits, the law prompted a vigorous mobilization by wealthier seniors who would have paid substantially higher premiums (Himelfarb 1995). After great hue and cry over the financing of the measure, legislators finally repealed the law. Thereafter, the words "remember catastrophic" were enough to make legislators leery of raising taxes, even if they were to pay for potentially popular social programs (Graetz 1997, 161–62).

Antitax fervor also stymied efforts in the late 1980s to create a federal program of long-term-care insurance. A 1990 bipartisan commission charged with devising a solution to the nation's long-term-care needs deadlocked over the issue of financing: Republicans on the committee refused to countenance any increased taxes to pay for the reform. This effectively put an end to the push for long-term-care reform, despite public opinion polls showing very large support for such a reform (Campbell and Morgan 2005a). The episode also was telling about how the antitax drive had expanded from cutting income and property taxes to limiting all forms of taxation. Public opinion polls in the 1980s showed that payroll taxes were still one of the most acceptable forms of public finance, and a modest payroll tax increase could have financed a social insurance program for long-term care. Despite the political acceptability of these taxes, however, many conservatives were determined to hold the line on any further increases in payroll taxes (Campbell and Morgan 2005b).

Clinton administration officials also struggled with what some labeled "Reagan's revenge"—the fact that tax cuts and budget deficits made it difficult to expand government as they would have liked (Skocpol 1997, 174; Tempelman 2006, 566). Coming into office faced with large budget deficits, the administration first put its energies into a deficit-reduction package that included significant tax increases. This led them away from their core political objective—renewing popular support for activist government through new social programs—as the administration instead lent credence to those arguing for large-scale cuts in government programs (Pierson 1998, 151). The administration then struggled with how to finance its core legislative priority, health care, and present this to the public in a palatable way. Because people were not aware of the tax breaks that subsidize employer-based care, the administration was leery of proposing anything that looked like a tax hike on workers, such as a payroll tax increase (Hacker 2002, 264). Efforts to obscure the fiscal consequences of the reform only undermined the administration's credibility with the general public, however, as most people doubted the Clinton plan could be achieved without further increases in taxes (Blendon, Brodie, and Benson 1995, 16; Skocpol 1997, 174–77). In addition, instead of imposing new payroll contributions—an obvious way to pay for an insurance program—the administration decided to impose employer mandates to provide health coverage. This deeply antagonized the business community, which further undermined the reform effort (Campbell and Morgan 2005b).

With chronic deficits at the federal level, and the lack of action to address other social needs, there has been an accelerated tendency toward burden shifting onto state and local governments. Federal aid to states peaked in 1978 and then declined. At the same time, the number and size of unfunded mandates increased dramatically through the 1980s, and this trend has continued despite the Unfunded Mandates Reform Act of 1995 (Posner 1998). Both Republicans and Democrats have put more unfunded mandates on the states, with President Bush adding more burdens through inadequately funded homeland security mandates, the No Child Left Behind Act, and election reform requirements (Kincaid 2003, 6). Exploding growth in Medicaid also has hurt state budgets, as this program is financed through shared federal-state contributions. In fact, the failure to reform the long-term-care system in the late 1980s has left nursing-home and home-care coverage in Medicaid, adding to the burdens on state governments (Campbell and Morgan 2005a). In addition, federal cuts in income and estate taxes further eroded state-level tax systems, many of which are linked to the federal tax code (Kincaid 2003, 6). This also diminishes progressive sources of revenue at the state level, driving states to increase regressive consumption taxes and user fees to raise the necessary revenues. These have not compensated for decreases in other revenue sources, as state-level tax revenues have leveled off since the late 1970s (see figure 2.2).

The addition of a prescription drug benefit to the Medicare program in 2003 is the exceptional example of program expansion that proves the rule that budgetary constraint obstructs social policy expansion. The push for a prescription drug benefit began in the late 1990s as the budgetary situation improved, and intensified with the emergence of large surpluses in 2000 and 2001. By 2003, tax cuts, recession, and the war on terror had absorbed much of this surplus, but $400 billion could still be set aside for this expansion of Medicare—particularly given that the PAYGO requirements of the 1990s expired in 2002.[15] The drive for reform in 2003 was then critically shaped by a mounting sense that if the benefit was not created in 2003, there would be no budgetary resources in the future to pay for it. In addition, because there was no PAYGO requirement, Republican champions of the reform did not have to propose compensating revenue increases. This meant that legislators could avoid a repeat of the Medicare catastrophic debacle in the late 1980s, in which premium increases to pay for the law became a political lightning rod. Instead, the new program could be created without any immediate or obvious pain for taxpayers. In short, the improved budgetary situation was critical in opening a window of opportunity for this major expansion of the Medicare program (Campbell and Morgan 2006).

The stalled expansion of the American welfare state has had major consequences for poverty and inequality. Progress in the fight against poverty has stagnated since the 1970s, particularly for the non-elderly population, and can be tied to the stunted growth of social programs (Danziger and Danziger 2005). Until the 1970s, poverty rates dropped significantly for senior citizens, adults, and children, but whereas seniors have experienced further declines in poverty, adults and children remain nearly as likely to be poor today as they were three decades ago. These divergent trends can be explained by the failure to expand social programs for the non-elderly population. Nearly the entire drop in elderly poverty since the 1960s can be attributed to spending on Social Security (Engelhardt and Gruber 2004). By the same token, Sheldon Danziger and Sandra K. Danziger (2005) show that, with the exception of the Earned Income Tax Credit, the most effective antipoverty programs continue to be those adopted prior to 1975. In other Western countries, by contrast, direct social spending makes a very large dent in the poverty of adults and children and helps explain their lower poverty rates (Smeeding, Rainwater, and Burtless 2001; Alesina and Glaeser 2004; Smeeding 2004).

The truncated American welfare state also has been unable to counter rising income inequality since the 1970s. Many Western countries have experienced increased inequalities in market-generated incomes over the past few decades, but most reduce this more effectively through public policy than the United States (see figure 2.5) (Smeeding 2004). Moreover, figure 2.4 shows that tax systems reduce the Gini coefficient by only a small amount in most countries; direct transfers play a much more important role. Policymakers in many countries recognize that the tax code is not an effective way to address inequality or poverty, and this helps explain why they are willing to adopt seemingly regressive taxes, like a value added tax, which they use to fund redistributive social programs (Messere, Kam, and Heady 2003; Kato 2003, 63–64). Barring the ability to expand social transfers and services in the United States, American policymakers have sought to cut tax rates on the poor and deliver more tax credits to families with children. As figure 2.4 shows, however, the tax system's redistributive potential is fundamentally limited.

Has the tax-cutting drive since the 1980s contributed to rising inequality? Although the tax system is never particularly effective in redistributing income, the Reagan and Bush II tax cuts have exacerbated this ineffectiveness. One study (Strudler, Petska, and Petska 2004) shows that the tax system had its greatest impact in reducing inequality in the late 1970s, before the OBRA 1981 tax cuts took effect, and during part of the Clinton administration, because of increased taxes on the rich. Both the Reagan and Bush II tax cuts diminished the redistributive potential of the tax system. Although both cut taxes on low- and moderate-income people, the wealthiest members of society gained the most

FIGURE 2.5   The Reduction of Inequality, Measured by the Gini
             Coefficient, by Means of Taxes and Transfers

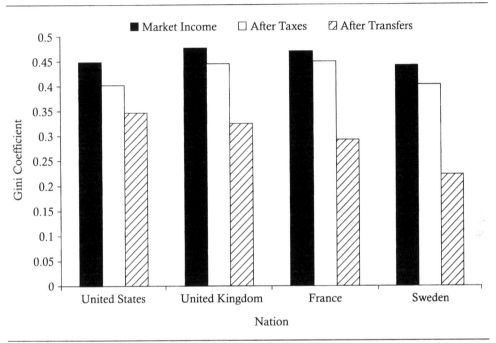

Source: Mahler and Jesuit (2004, 30).

from these tax laws. In the case of the 2001-to-2006 tax cuts, for example, wealthier tax-payers experienced greater gains in their post-tax incomes than did those lower on the income ladder, making these tax cuts regressive in their effects. People in the top income quintile saw a 4.1 percent increase in their incomes, equal to about $5,790, whereas those in the bottom quintile experienced a 0.3 percent increase in income, about $20 on average. Those at the very top of American society, the top one-tenth of one percent of all tax-payers, gained a 6.2 percent increase in income after the tax law changes, worth on average $230,136 (Leiserson and Rohaly 2006). This does not take into account how these tax cuts ultimately will be paid for. Spending reductions generally are regressive, as they usually affect low- and moderate-income people disproportionately (Steuerle 2003). If the 2001-to-2006 tax cuts are paid for largely through cuts in government spending, this will exacerbate the regressivity of the tax cuts. For that reason, C. Eugene Steuerle concludes that virtually all tax cuts, no matter how they are distributed, will ultimately be regressive because they will likely lead to cuts in government spending.

CONCLUSION

The tax and transfer system in the United States offers resources to politicians in their policymaking fights, and politicians from both parties have sought to use policies to advance their political agendas. In this, Republicans have been advantaged by features of the American tax system that are visible and resented—the much-disliked income and property taxes that gave rise to the antitax drive of the late 1970s. This enabled conservative politicians and strategists to turn a set of elite, antigovernment ideas into an electoral platform with wide support. Since then, the Republican antitax stance has yielded political gains, giving politicians a clear message that resonates with many people, even those who otherwise favor government social programs. Democrats have had difficulties responding to the antitax movement, given the truncated and often hidden nature of the American welfare state that seems to do little for the non-elderly, non-poor population. They have successfully defended existing, popular programs like Social Security, but have had difficulties developing new social programs for which they could claim credit. Both budget constraints and the antitax environment have stymied such initiatives. Thus, while left parties in many West European countries continue to reap political power resources from universalistic welfare states, Democrats in the United States have struggled to develop a positive, pro-government message in an antigovernment environment.

This case study of the antitax, antigovernment movement in the United States offers some confirmation for those who argue that the form of taxation is consequential for the ability of governments to build up expansive welfare states. Income and property taxes have consistently been the most resented forms of taxation in the United States and Social Security and sales taxes have been more acceptable. The latter forms of taxation may therefore enable greater growth of government, as appears to be the case in many West European countries.[16] Crucial, however, has been the behavior of political elites who choose to politicize these taxes, drawing on latent discontent with features of the tax system to create a larger movement against government. One can imagine a similar campaign in a country with a national sales tax, and there have been tax revolts against the VAT in some countries over the past few decades (Martin and Gabay 2007).[17] In general, however, these revolts have been sporadic and limited, and they have not restructured the political space around a pro-tax, antitax cleavage. Only future research on this topic will tell whether this is because of the opaqueness of the VAT burden or the calculations of political elites not to emphasize it.

In the United States, the 2001-to-2006 tax cuts could have tremendous feedback effects on the politics of social policy in the years ahead. Most of these tax reductions are scheduled to expire in 2010, but many commentators believe it will be difficult for legislators to allow what may by that time seem to the public like a tax increase. The problem of the alternative minimum tax will also require attention, potentially with a very high price tag. If "Reagan's revenge" was to stymie the Clinton administration's social spending agenda, one legacy of the Bush II administration could be the decreased fiscal capacity of government at a time of rising needs. The retirement of the baby boom generation and continued problem of medical inflation will continue to fuel entitlement spending, and the United States is poorly positioned to cope with these costs after six years of tax cuts. The fiscal squeeze and continuing fights over taxation will also make it harder for Democrats to push new social programs, and will likely shape social policy strategies on the left and the right for many years to come.

This chapter has benefited from the very helpful comments of Christopher Jencks, James Sparrow, and the editors of this volume.

NOTES

1. There also is a large public choice literature on "fiscal illusion"—the idea that because many public finance issues are opaque or misunderstood by the public, policymakers can exploit this and push the growth of government beyond that which would be publicly acceptable (see, for example, Becker and Mulligan 1998).
2. Complicating this is the fact that payroll taxes can be structured in a more progressive manner. In much of northern Europe, for example, payroll taxes are integrated with the income tax, using a similar base and thresholds as the income tax. This makes them more like an income tax that is earmarked for social insurance programs (Messere, Kam, and Heady 2003, 242).
3. All of the liberal welfare regimes except for the United States have adopted a VAT, although the rates are lower than those in most other European countries (Kato 2003).
4. For example, in response to the question "What kind of taxes are most in need of being lowered?" 68 percent of respondents cited the federal income tax in 1945 and 1953. The second tax most often mentioned, the local property tax, garnered 29 percent (1945) and 17 percent (1953) of responses (Campbell and Morgan 2005b).
5. In 1945, personal and corporate taxes made up over 76 percent of all federal revenues; this figure dropped to 64 percent by 1970 as payroll taxes expanded in significance (Office of Management and Budget 2007, *Budget of the U.S. Government*).
6. The Congressional Budget Act of 1974 defines tax expenditures as the "revenue losses attributable to provisions of the Federal tax laws which allow a special exclusion, exemption, or deduction from gross income or which provide a special credit, a preferential rate of tax, or a deferral of tax liability" (U.S. Congress 1974).
7. Monica Prasad (2006) also emphasizes the importance of government regulation in mobilizing the business community and cementing their support for free-market policies.
8. The question was whether people get excellent value for the dollar, or good value, or only fair value for the dollar, or poor value for the dollar of federal income taxes. In 1980, only 15 percent of recipients said they got excellent or good value from these taxes, whereas 39 percent said they received fair value, and 39 cited said they got poor value (Roper Organization 1980). Another survey at the time, a 1977 Harris Survey, found that 74 percent of respondents rated negatively the value they got from their tax dollars paid to the federal government (Roper Organization 1977).
9. The mismatch between the highly visible and resented tax system and less visible welfare state helped generate a feeling that people's hard-earned money was financing a wasteful and useless government apparatus—one that not only failed to provide them with benefits or services but that also had lost the public's trust (Ladd et al. 1979).
10. On the tax revolt as symbolic politics, see David Lowery and Lee Sigelman (1981).
11. C. Eugene Steuerle (2004) points out that the Reagan administration did not propose or endorse the indexing of tax brackets, as many feared the lasting fiscal consequences. The proposal was pushed by conservatives in Congress.
12. In the final vote on the conference report for the Omnibus Budget Reconciliation Act of 1990, 47 House Republicans voted for it, and 126 voted against. The vote was more bipartisan in the Senate, where 19 Republicans voted for the conference report and 25 voted against it.
13. The alternative minimum tax is a parallel tax system that is intended to make wealthy taxpayers pay a minimum amount of federal taxes by eliminating most of the deductions and exemptions that normally reduce their tax liability. More middle-class taxpayers will face this tax in future years because its brackets and exemptions are not indexed for inflation, and because the 2001-to-2006 tax cuts reduced many people's tax liability.
14. For example, in a 2001 survey carried out by NPR, Kaiser, and the Kennedy School of Government, the question was posed "Do you feel the government will help you if you fall on bad times, or do you think you'll have only yourself to rely on?" Only 29 percent said the government would help, whereas 65 percent said they would have to rely on themselves ("Poverty in America," accessed at http://www.npr.org/programs/specials/poll/poverty/summary.html).

15. At the end of 2002, Congress enacted and the President signed a law that essentially suspended the PAYGO requirements for Fiscal Years 2003 to 2006.
16. Steffen Ganghof (2006) points out that the key may lie in the ability of certain forms of taxation to appease powerful groups in society, such as business or the rich. Heavy reliance on VAT and Social Security taxes may achieve this by enabling lower taxes on capital, but this goal could also be accomplished by maintaining an extensive income tax and taxing capital income at a lower rate. This is the Danish model of taxation, which relies heavily on income taxation, as well as a VAT, but levies lower taxes on capital.
17. For example, France has experienced revolts against the VAT in the past.

REFERENCES

Adema, Willem. 2001. *Net Social Expenditure.* 2nd edition. Labor Market and Social Policy Occasional Papers no. 52. Paris: Organization for Economic Cooperation and Development.

Advisory Commission on Intergovernmental Relations. 1975. *Trends in Fiscal Federalism 1954–1974.* Washington: ACIR.

Alesina, Alberto, and Edward L. Glaeser. 2004. *Fighting Poverty in the U.S. and Europe: A World of Difference.* Oxford: Oxford University Press.

Babilot, George, and Joan Anderson. 1967. "Empirical Evidence of the Changing Patterns of Personal Income Taxes Paid by Income Classes, 1951–1962." *Southern Economic Journal* 33(April): 518–25.

Baron, Jonathan, and Edward J. McCaffery. 2006. "Masking Redistribution (or Its Absence)." In *Behavioral Public Finance,* edited by Edward J. McCaffery and Joel Slemrod. New York: Russell Sage Foundation.

Bartels, Larry. 2003. "Homer Gets a Tax Cut: Inequality and Public Policy in the American Mind." *Perspectives on Politics* 3(March): 15–31.

Bartlett, Bruce. 2004. "Explaining the Bush Tax Cuts." *Commentary* 117(6): 23–27.

Becker, Gary S., and Casey B. Mulligan. 1998. "Deadweight Costs and the Size of Government." NBER Working Paper 6789. Cambridge, Mass.: National Bureau of Economic Research.

Becker, Gary S., Edward P. Lazear, and Kevin M. Murphy. 2003. "The Double Benefit of Tax Cuts." *Wall Street Journal,* October 7: A20.

Blendon, Robert J., Mollyann Brodie, and John Benson. 1995. "What Happened to Americans' Support for the Clinton Health Plan?" *Health Affairs* 14(2): 7–23.

Blomqvist, Paula, and Christoffer Green-Pedersen. 2004. "Defeat at Home? Issue-Ownership and Social Democratic Support in Scandinavia." *Government and Opposition* 39(4): 587–613.

Boeri, Tito, Axel Boersch-Supan, and Guide Tabellini. 2002. "Pension Reforms and the Opinions of European Citizens." *American Economic Review* 92(2): 396–401.

Brownlee, W. Elliot. 2004. *Federal Taxation in America: A Short History.* 2nd edition. Cambridge: Cambridge University Press.

Brownlee, W. Elliot, and C. Eugene Steuerle. 2003. "Taxation." In *The Reagan Presidency: Pragmatic Conservatism and Its Legacies,* edited by W. Elliot Brownlee and Hugh Davis Graham. Lawrence, Kan.: University Press of Kansas.

Burns, John W., and Andrew J. Taylor. 2000. "The Mythical Causes of the Republican Supply-Side Economics Revolution." *Party Politics* 6(4): 419–40.

Campbell, Andrea Louise, and Kimberly J. Morgan. 2005a. "Federalism and the Politics of Old-Age Care in Germany and the United States." *Comparative Political Studies* 38(8): 887–914.

———. 2005b. "Financing the Welfare State: Elite Politics and the Decline of the Social Insurance Model in America." *Studies in American Political Development* 19(Fall): 173–95.

———. 2006. "The Medicare Modernization Act and the New Politics of Medicare." Paper presented at the annual meeting of the American Political Science Association. Philadelphia, Penn., August 31 to September 3, 2006.

Clayton, Richard, and Jonas Pontusson. 1998. "Welfare-State Retrenchment Revisited: Entitle-

ment Cuts, Public Sector Restructuring, and Inegalitarian Trends in Advanced Capitalist Societies." *World Politics* 51(October): 67–98.
Congressional Budget Office. 2007. *The Budget and Economic Outlook: Fiscal Years 2008 to 2017.* Washington: Congressional Budget Office.
Danziger, Sheldon, and Sandra K. Danziger. 2005. "The U.S. Social Safety Net and Poverty: Lessons Learned and Promising Approaches." Unpublished manuscript. Gerald R. Ford School of Public Policy, University of Michigan.
DeMuth, Christopher. 2006. "Unlimited Government." *American Enterprise* 17(1): 18–23.
Edsall, Thomas Byrne. 1984. *The New Politics of Inequality.* New York: Norton.
Engelhardt, Gary, and Jonathan Gruber. 2004. "Social Security and the Evolution of Elderly Poverty." NBER Working Paper 10466. Cambridge, Mass.: National Bureau of Economic Research.
Esping-Andersen, Gøsta. 1985. *Politics Against Markets.* Princeton, N.J.: Princeton University Press.
———. 1990. *The Three Worlds of Welfare Capitalism.* Princeton, N.J.: Princeton University Press.
Friedman, Milton. 2003. "What Every American Wants." *Wall Street Journal,* January 15: A10.
Ganghof, Steffen. 2006. "Tax Mixes and the Size of the Welfare State: Causal Mechanisms and Policy Implications." *Journal of European Social Policy* 16(4): 360–73.
Gilens, Martin. 1999. *Why Americans Hate Welfare: Race, Media, and the Politics of Anti-Poverty Policy.* Chicago, Ill.: University of Chicago Press.
Graetz, Michael J. 1997. *The Decline (and Fall?) of the Income Tax.* New York: Norton.
Grogan, Colleen, and Eric Patashnik. 2003. "Between Welfare Medicine and Mainstream Entitlement: Medicaid at the Political Crossroads." *Journal of Health Politics, Policy and Law* 28(5): 821–58.
Hacker, Jacob S. 2002. *The Divided Welfare State: The Battle over Public and Private Social Benefits in the United States.* Cambridge: Cambridge University Press.
———. 2004. "Privatizing Risk Without Privatizing the Welfare State: The Hidden Politics of Social Policy Retrenchment in the United States." *American Political Science Review* 98(2): 243-60.
Hibbs, Douglas A., Jr., and Henrik Jess Madsen. 1981. "Public Reactions to the Growth of Taxation and Government Expenditures." *World Politics* 33(3): 413–35.
Himelfarb, Richard. 1995. *Catastrophic Politics: The Rise and Fall of the Medicare Catastrophic Coverage Act of 1988.* University Park, Penn.: Pennsylvania State University Press.
Howard, Christopher. 1995. "Protean Lure for the Working Poor: Party Competition and the Earned Income Tax Credit." *Studies in American Political Development* 9(Fall): 404–36.
———. 1997. *The Hidden Welfare State: Tax Expenditures and Social Policy in the United States.* Princeton, N.J.: Princeton University. Press.
Kato, Junko. 2003. *Regressive Taxation and the Welfare State.* Cambridge: Cambridge University Press.
Kincaid, John. 2003. "The Crisis in Fiscal Federalism." *Spectrum: The Journal of State Government* 76(Summer): 5–10.
Kinder, Donald R., Nancy Burns, and Dale B. Vieregge. 2005. "Liberalism, Race, and Exceptionalism: Understanding the American Appetite for Tax Reduction." Paper presented at the annual meeting of the American Political Science Association. Washington. August 31-September 4, 2005.
Klein, Jennifer. 2003. *For All These Rights: Business, Labor, and the Shaping of America's Public-Private Welfare State.* Princeton, N.J.: Princeton University Press.
Ladd, Everett Carll, Jr., Marilyn Potter, Linda Basilick, Sally Daniels, and Dana Suszkin. 1979. "The Polls: Taxing and Spending." *Public Opinion Quarterly* 43(Spring): 126–35.
Leiserson, Greg, and Jeffrey Rohaly. 2006. "The Distribution of the 2001-2006 Tax Cuts: Updated Projections, November 2006." The Tax Policy Center. Accessed June 20, 2007 at http://www.urban.org/UploadedPDF/411378_tax_cuts.pdf.
LeLoup, Lance T. 2005. *Parties, Rules, and the Evolution of Congressional Budgeting.* Columbus, Oh.: Ohio State University Press.
Lindert, Peter H. 2004. *Growing Public: Social Spending and Economic Growth Since the Eighteenth Century.* Cambridge: Cambridge University Press.

Lowery, David, and Lee Sigelman. 1981. "Understanding the Tax Revolt: Eight Explanations." *American Political Science Review* 75(December): 963–74.

Mahler, Vincent, and David Jesuit. 2004. "State Redistribution in Comparative Perspective: A Cross-National Analysis of the Developed World." Luxembourg Income Study, Working Paper No. 392. Luxembourg: LIS.

Martin, Cathie Jo. 1994. "Business and the New Economic Activism: The Growth of Corporate Lobbies in the Sixties." *Polity* 27(Fall): 49–76.

Martin, Isaac. 2007. *The Politics of the Tax Revolt.* Unpublished manuscript. University of California, San Diego.

Martin, Isaac, and Nadav Gabay. 2007. "Do Visible Taxes Cause Protest? Tax Institutions and Tax Protest in Thirteen OECD Democracies." Unpublished paper. University of California, San Diego.

Messere, Ken, Flip de Kam, and Christopher Heady. 2003. *Tax Policy: Theory and Practice in OECD Countries.* Oxford: Oxford University Press.

Mettler, Suzanne, and Andrew Milstein. 2007. "American Political Development from Citizens' Perspective: Tracking Federal Government's Presence in Individual Lives over Time." *Studies in American Political Development* 21(1): 110–30.

Niskanen, William A., and Peter Van Doren. 2004. "Some Intriguing Findings About Federal Spending." Paper presented at the Public Choice Society. Baltimore, Md. March 11 to 14, 2004.

OECD (Organization for Economic Cooperation and Development). 2001. Social Expenditures Database. Paris: OECD.

———. 2002. Social Expenditures Database. Paris: OECD.

———. 2004. *Revenue Statistics.* Paris: OECD.

———. 2006. *Revenue Statistics.* Paris: OECD.

Office of Management and Budget. 2007. *Budget of the U.S. Government.* Washington: Government Printing Office.

Ornstein, Norman, and John Fortier. 2002. "Relations with Congress." *PS: Political Science and Politics* 35(1): 47-50.

Page, Benjamin I., and Robert Y. Shapiro. 1992. *The Rational Public: Fifty Years of Trends in Americans' Policy Preferences.* Chicago, Ill.: University of Chicago Press.

Patashnik, Eric. 2005. "Budgets and Fiscal Policy." In *The Legislative Branch*, edited by Paul J. Quirk and Sarah A. Binder. Oxford: Oxford University Press.

Pechman, Joseph A. 1985. *Who Paid the Taxes, 1966–1985?* Washington: Brookings Institution Press.

Peters, B. Guy. 1991. *The Politics of Taxation: A Comparative Perspective.* Cambridge, Mass.: Basil Blackwell.

Peterson, Mark A. 1998. "The Politics of Health Care Policy: Overreaching in an Age of Polarization." In *The Social Divide: Political Parties and the Future of Activist Government*, edited by Margaret Weir. Washington: Brookings Institution Press.

Petrocik, John R. 1996. "Issue Ownership in Presidential Elections, with a 1986 Case Study." *American Journal of Political Science* 40(3): 825-50.

Pierson, Paul. 1993. "When Effect Becomes Cause: Policy Feedback and Political Change." *World Politics* 45(4): 595–628.

———. 1994. *Dismantling the Welfare State? Reagan, Thatcher, and the Politics of Retrenchment.* Cambridge: Cambridge University Press.

———. 1998. "The Deficit and the Politics of Domestic Reform." In *The Social Divide Political Parties and the Future of Activist Government*, edited by Margaret M. Weir. Washington: Brookings Institution Press.

Ponnuru, Ramesh. 2005. "Spendaholics." *National Review* 57(19): 32-34.

Posner, Paul L. 1998. *The Politics of Unfunded Mandates: Whither Federalism?* Washington: Georgetown University Press.

Prasad, Monica. 2006. *The Politics of Free Markets: The Rise of Neoliberal Economic Policies in Britain, France, Germany, and the United States.* Chicago, Ill.: University of Chicago Press.

Rae, Nicol C. 1989. *The Decline and Fall of Liberal Republicans.* Oxford: Oxford University Press.

Rauch, Jonathan. 2006. "Stoking the Beast." *Atlantic Monthly* 297(5): 27–28.

Rivlin, Alice M. 1989. "The Continuing Search for a Popular Tax." *American Economic Review* 79(2): 113–7.

Rohde, David. 2005. "Committees and Policy Formulation." In *The Legislative Branch*, edited by Paul J. Quirk and Sarah A. Binder. Oxford: Oxford University Press.

Roper Organization. 1977. Survey by Louis Harris and Associates, August 13-August 20, 1977. The Roper Center for Public Opinion Research, University of Connecticut. Accesed June 21, 2007 from the iPOLL Databank, http://www.ropercenter.uconn.edu/ipoll.html.

———. 1980. Survey by the Roper Organization, April 26-May 3, 1980. The Roper Center for Public Opinion Research, University of Connecticut. Accesed June 21, 2007 from the iPOLL Databank, http://www.ropercenter.uconn.edu/ipoll.html.

Sausgruber, Rupert, and Jean-Robert Tyran. 2004. "Testing the Mill Hypothesis of Fiscal Illusion." Department of Economics Working Paper No. 04-18. Copenhagen: University of Copenhagen.

Schickler, Eric. 2001. *Disjointed Pluralism: Institutional Innovation and the Development of the U.S. Congress*. Princeton, N.J.: Princeton University Press.

Schulman, Bruce J. 2001. *The Seventies: The Great Shift in American Culture, Society, and Politics*. New York: Free Press.

Sears, David O., and Jack Citrin. 1982. *Tax Revolt: Something for Nothing in California*. Cambridge, Mass.: Harvard University Press.

Skocpol, Theda. 1991. "Targeting Within Universalism: Politically Viable Policies to Combat Poverty in the United States." In *The Urban Underclass*, edited by Christopher Jencks and Paul E. Peterson. Washington: Brookings Institution Press.

———. 1997. *Boomerang: Health Care Reform and the Turn against Government*. New York: Norton.

———. 2000. *The Missing Middle: Working Families and the Future of American Social Policy*. New York: Norton.

Smeeding, Timothy. 2004. "Public Policy, Economic Inequality, and Poverty: The United States in Comparative Perspective." Unpublished manuscript. Maxwell School, Syracuse University.

Smeeding, Timothy, Lee Rainwater, and Gary Burtless. 2001. "U.S. Poverty in a Cross-National Context." In *Understanding Poverty*, edited by Sheldon H. Danziger and Robert H. Haveman. New York: Russell Sage Foundation.

Steinmo, Sven. 1993. *Taxation and Democracy: Swedish, British, and American Approaches to Financing the Modern State*. New Haven, Conn.: Yale University Press.

Steuerle, C. Eugene. 1992. *The Tax Decade: How Taxes Came to Dominate the Public Agenda*. Washington: Urban Institute Press.

———. 2003. "Can the Progressivity of Tax Changes Be Measured in Isolation?" *Tax Notes*, September 1: 1187–8.

———. 2004. *Contemporary U.S. Tax Policy*. Washington: Urban Institute Press.

Stevens, Beth. 1988. "Blurring the Boundaries: How the Federal Government Has Influenced Welfare Benefits in the Private Sector." In *The Politics of Social Policy in the United States*, edited by Margaret Weir, Ann Shola Orloff, and Theda Skocpol. Princeton, N.J.: Princeton University Press.

Stonecash, Jeffrey M. 2000. *Class and Party in American Politics*. Boulder, Colo.: Westview Press.

Stonecash, Jeffrey M., and Andrew E. Milstein. 2000. "Parties and Taxes: The Emergence of Distributive Divisions, 1950–2000." Paper presented at the Midwest Political Science Association Conference. Chicago (April 27 to 30).

Strudler, Michael, Tom Petska, and Ryan Petska. 2004. "Further Analysis of the Distribution of Income and Taxes, 1979–2002." Paper presented at the Joint Statistical Meetings of the American Statistical Association. Toronto, Ontario. August 8, 2004.

Sundquist, James L. 1983. *Dynamics of the Party System. Alignment and Realignment of Political Parties in the United States*. Revised edition. Washington: Brookings Institution Press.

Taylor, Andrew J. 2002. "The Ideological Roots of Deficit Reduction Policy." *Review of Policy Research* 19(Winter): 12–29.

Tempelman, Jerry H. 2006. "Does 'Starve the Beast' Work?" *Cato Journal* 26(3): 559–72.

U.S. Congress. 1974. Congressional Budget and Impoundment Control Act of 1974. Pub.L. 93-344, 88 Stat. 297.

Vogel, David. 1989. *Fluctuating Fortunes: The Political Power of Business in America.* New York: Basic Books.

Wilensky, Harold L. 2002. *Rich Democracies: Political Economy, Public Policy, and Performance.* Berkeley, Calif.: University of California Press.

Zelizer, Julian E. 1998. *Taxing America: Wilbur D. Mills, Congress, and the State, 1945–75.* Cambridge: Cambridge University Press.

Chapter 3

Entrepreneurial Litigation: Advocacy Coalitions and
Strategies in the Fragmented American Welfare State

When the Republican-dominated 104th Congress restructured welfare policies in 1996, it also launched a major assault on welfare litigation. The law that replaced Aid to Families with Dependent Children (AFDC) with the new Temporary Assistance for Needy Families (TANF) virtually shouted "NO INDIVIDUAL ENTITLEMENTS." This part shall not be interpreted to entitle any individual or family to assistance under any state program funded by this part." Just to be sure that federal judges got the message, the statute announced that federal eligibility standards "shall not be interpreted to require States to provide assistance to *any* individual for *any* period of time under the State program under this part" (PL 104-725, sections 401(b) and 408(a)(2)(D), emphasis added). The 1996 law attempted to circumvent a 1969 Supreme Court decision that had prevented states from denying welfare benefits to those living in the state for less than a year (*Shapiro v. Thompson*). It also tried to override a 1990 Supreme Court decision that had expanded the number of disabled children eligible for Supplemental Security Income (SSI) (*Zebley v. Sullivan*). The 104th Congress not only slashed funding for the federal Legal Services Corporation but also prohibited Legal Services from initiating class-action suits, receiving attorneys' fees, representing illegal immigrants, or becoming involved in "any effort to reform a Federal or State welfare system" (PL 104-134, sections 501 to 509). House Republicans would have eliminated the federal Legal Services Corporation altogether had they not been thwarted by the Senate. Conservatives recognized that for three decades the federal judiciary had played a major role in developing the programs they were now determined to reconfigure, and they feared that subsequent litigation would dilute their new welfare prescriptions. In short, conservative welfare reform was coupled with an effort to "defund the left" and to defang the federal judiciary.

Congress succeeded in curtailing federal court involvement in TANF eligibility determinations, but not in ending Legal Service's role as an advocate for its diverse clientele. In 2001 the Supreme Court struck down the congressional restriction on welfare reform litigation, arguing that it violated the First Amendment rights of lawyers and unduly interfered with the judicial process (*Legal Services Corporation v. Valasquez*). Long accustomed to political attacks and statutory restrictions on their activities, Legal Services attorneys found innovative ways to hand off many of these restricted activities to allied organizations. Some of the legal advocacy and research centers affiliated with Legal Services were able to replace federal funding with foundation grants in order to escape the new restrictions. State bar associations helped by providing financial assistance and identifying lawyers willing to do pro bono work. Legal Services has continued to receive political and financial support from the American Bar Association (ABA), which for over thirty years has played a key role in guaranteeing the organization's independence. In the words of two experienced Legal Services strategists, "Despite these restrictions, most of the work that needs to be done to address the individual and systemic problems that poor people face can still be done" (Houseman and Perle 2002, 245; see Smith and Silverstein 2004; Houseman 1998).

A quick glance at Legal Service's major publication, *Clearinghouse Review*, shows how important litigation remains in many public assistance programs, as well as the central role Legal Services and its "national support centers" play within an extended advocacy network. Each bimonthly issue of *Clearinghouse Review* lists fifty to seventy significant recent state and federal decisions, and notes that many additional decisions can be found on its website. These cases are arrayed by "practice areas" that illustrate both the diversity and the specialization of Legal Service's efforts: Social Security and Supplemental Security Income, veterans, food projects, migrants, mental health, housing, employment, health, disability, education, consumer protection, immigrants, and family law.

Legal Services attorneys throughout the country rely heavily on the twenty-seven "national support centers" listed in table 3.1. These centers not only offer legal research, policy analysis, and strategic advice to attorneys, but coordinate the activities of an array of state, local, and professional organizations within their area of expertise. For example, the National Employment Law Project describes itself as an advocate for low-wage workers, the poor, and the unemployed. Its work includes "supporting worker organizing and alliance-building among key constituent groups working with low-wage workers," and providing advice to "legal services attorneys and other advocates working directly with low-wage workers and the unemployed, including community-based organizations, service providers, [and] labor unions." Its strategies include "litigation; policy advocacy; research, analysis, and technical assistance in support of organizing; and publications, training sessions, and other educational activities" (see website at http://www.help.org/about/index.cfn). The National Law Center on Homelessness and Poverty notes that it was established "two years after Congress passed the McKinney-Vento Homeless Assistance Act," serves "as the legal arm of the nationwide movement to end homelessness," and "pursues three main strategies: impact litigation, policy advocacy, and public education" (see National Law Center on Homelessness and Poverty website, http://www.nlchp.org/about). Support centers receive funding and other forms of assistance from foundations, universities, government, private law firms, and individual donations. Hugh Heclo (1978, 99) has famously described "issue networks" as "specialized subcultures composed of highly knowledgeable policy watchers." Anyone interested in mapping the issue network surrounding public assistance programs would do well to start with the web of organizations affiliated with Legal Services and its National Support Centers.

This advocacy network is relatively new, and it is largely the result of government action. Most of its elements arose in the wake of the Great Society, and are organized around the numerous programs that were either created or federalized in the decade and a half after 1964. Legal Services was created in 1965 by Sargent Shriver within the Office of Economic Opportunity. Many of the national support centers began as Legal Services "backup centers" funded by government grants and foundations. Crucial to the success of the fledgling Legal Services was a shift in legal doctrine initiated by the Supreme Court in the second half of the 1960s. Without the federal courts' innovative rulings on matters such as jurisdiction, standing, due process, and remedies, many of the activities of Legal

TABLE 3.1   National Support Centers

AARP/Legal Counsel for the Elderly
ABA Commission on Legal Problems of the Elderly
ABA Center on Children and the Law
Center for Adolescent Health and the Law
Center for Law and Education
Center for Law and Social Policy
Center for Social Gerontology
Child Care Law Center
Farmers' Legal Action Group
Food Resources and Action Center
Bazelon Center for Mental Health Law
Indian Child Welfare Law Center
Health Care for All
Center for Medicare Advocacy
Migrant Legal Action Program
National Center for Youth Law
National Center on Poverty Law
National Consumer Law Center
National Economic Development and Law Center
National Employment Law Project
National Health Law Program
National Housing Law Project
National Immigration Law Center
National Law Center on Homelessness and Poverty
National Senior Citizens Law Center
National Veterans Legal Service Project
Welfare Law Center

Source: Author's compilation.

Services and its allies would have been impossible. Moreover, as Jeffrey Berry (1999, chapters 4, 5) has pointed out, liberal advocacy groups benefited enormously from changes in Congress in the late 1960s and early 1970s that increased their access to subcommittee hearings and deliberations. Each of these changes reinforced the others. Advocates for a variety of disadvantaged groups learned how to take advantage of these institutional shifts, using victories in court to force further action in Congress, and victories in Congress as leverage within the judicial and administrative process (Melnick 1995).

The central theme of this volume is E. E. Schattschneider's (1935, 288) famous dictum that "new policies create a new politics." As Jacob Hacker, Suzanne Mettler, and Joe Soss explain in the opening chapter, the contributors all try to explore "how policies, once established, become part of the political process and transform it by their presence" and how "policies shape the resources and capacities of citizens or affect the content and articulation of public concerns." Several chapters in this volume explore the ways in which program design shapes the perceptions and political activities of beneficiaries (for example, families receiving TANF or workers eligible for Unemployment Compensation). But new programs and new institutional rules (such as those governing access to the courts) can also create and affect the behavior of three other types of organizations that help shape public policy.

First and most obvious are those government agencies responsible for running the new programs. As Martha Derthick's (1979) classic analysis of the Social Security Administration (SSA) demonstrates, the driving force behind the expansion of Social Security and the creation of national disability insurance and health-care programs was the cadre of long-term Social Security officials she calls the "program administrators." Similarly, state officials who had developed welfare-to-work programs in Wisconsin and elsewhere became leading proponents of the 1996 welfare reform act (Mead 2004; Weaver 2000, chapters 8, 10, 12). A key feature of the American welfare state is its decentralized and categorical structure. Not only are there scores of programs targeting particular populations, but within each program authority is divided among state, federal, and sometimes local agencies. As a consequence, there are always many expert agencies pushing a variety of policy innovations. It also means that many government officials are seeking creative ways to shift costs (and blame) to other levels of government.

Second, many government programs require a large number of service providers. Another peculiar characteristic of the American welfare state is that means-tested programs frequently provide benefits in the form of goods and services rather than cash. Rarely are these providers of goods and services employed directly by the federal government. Sometimes they are hired by state and local governments: teachers are the most obvious and important example. Sometimes they are simply reimbursed by the government (for example, doctors for Medicaid and landlords for Section 8 housing), and sometimes the government contracts out to nonprofits to provide social services. These providers will all develop a keen interest in the operation of the program. Frequently they will be more politically engaged and more efficacious than those who ultimately receive the goods and services provided.

Third, many welfare state programs engage the interest of professional groups, which inevitably insist upon the application of professional norms within those programs. In the 1980s, as we will see, mental health professionals insisted that the Social Security Administration incorporate new methods for measuring disabilities in its disability benefits programs. Local schools hire an array of specialists to determine what constitutes an "appropriate education" for children with disabilities. The American Bar Association has a long track record of working to protect the professional autonomy of Legal Service attorneys. Four decades ago Daniel Patrick Moynihan (1969, 23) wrote, "Increasingly efforts to change the American social system for the better arise from initiatives undertaken by persons whose profession was to do just that." What he termed "the professionalization of reform" has grown more pronounced as the variety, the prestige, and the ranks of the "learned professions" have increased.

If an army of highly professional service providers worked for a single national agency, then we could be confident that such a program would command significant clout, regardless of the political influence of the recipients of these services. But in the United States, matters are seldom so simple. Government authority is dispersed; services are contracted out; and professional groups are often at odds with one another. Commenting on the exceptional nature of American bureaucratic politics, Joel Aberbach, Robert Putnam, and Bert Rockman (1981, 95–96) have written, "American bureaucrats, to a degree unmatched elsewhere, are responsible for shoring up their own bases of political support. American bureaucrats must find allies where they can." As a result American bureaucrats "are clearly more political in their role focus than their European counterparts" and demonstrate "an entrepreneurial style of behavior." Much the same can be said of those program advocates (some inside government, some outside, many in the vast gray area in between) who seek to protect and expand public programs on behalf of politically weak clients. They, too, need to find allies where they can, exploit opportunities as they unpredictably appear, and build coalitions on an ad hoc basis. In American society it is frequently lawyers who play this entrepreneurial role, negotiating agreements and alliances, moving from the courtroom to the committee room to the press gallery, translating the jargon of specialists into a language understandable to generalist judges, juries, and the public. Thus it is not surprising that lawyers with policy specialties play a central role within the diffuse "issue networks" that have grown up around various elements of our fragmented welfare state.

This chapter examines the entrepreneurial role legal advocates have played in three quite different programs: Aid to Families with Dependent Children (AFDC) in the late 1960s and early 1970s; disability benefits in the 1980s; and state programs for the homeless in the 1990s. The sections of the chapter devoted to each of these three programs emphasize the ways in which their idiosyncratic structure created opportunities and obstacles for reformers. The subsequent section takes a broader look at how legal advocates have adapted their strategies to the fragmented and categorical nature of the American welfare state.

NATIONALIZING AFDC ELIGIBILITY STANDARDS

When Legal Services was created in 1965, most of its litigation focused on AFDC, which at the time was not only the largest program serving poor families but also the gateway to many other benefits. The most famous part of this effort was the campaign to constitutionalize a right to welfare. Led by a small group of experienced lawyers and welfare experts associated with the Columbia Center for Law and Social Policy, this carefully coordinated campaign achieved several notable successes—including *Goldberg v. Kelly* (establishing a right to a pre-termination hearing in welfare cases) and *Shapiro v. Thompson* (invalidating state durational residency requirements)—before losing pivotal cases in the early Burger Court. For years reformers and academics have debated the reasons for the failure of this high-risk, high-visibility strategy (Krislov 1973; Davis 1993; Lawrence 1990; Sunstein 2004; Rosenberg 1991).

From the point of view of the structure of the AFDC program itself, though, the Supreme Court's most important decisions were three seemingly more prosaic statutory rulings issued between 1968 and 1972. In the so-called "King-Townsend-Remillard trilogy" (referring to three landmark cases, *King v. Smith*, *Townsend v. Swank*, and *Carleson v. Remillard*) the Court in effect reversed the presumption about AFDC eligibility that had guided policymaking for the preceding thirty years. Prior to 1968 states could impose any rule not explicitly prohibited by federal statute. But by 1972 states needed explicit authorization from the federal government to limit eligibility or to attribute income to a recipient family. As Justice Brennan explained in a unanimous 1971 opinion (*Townsend v. Swank*, 286),

> In the absence of congressional authorization for the exclusion clearly evidenced from the Social Security Act or its legislative history, a state eligibility standard that excludes persons eligible for assistance under federal AFDC standards violates the Social Security Act and is therefore invalid under the Supremacy Clause.

Given the fact that federal administrators and liberals in Congress had for decades failed in their effort to curtail state control over AFDC, this was a remarkable shift in the operation of the program. As the conservative Senate Finance Committee complained,

> These decisions have used the very broadness of the Federal statute (intended to allow States more latitude) against the States by saying sometimes that anything the Congress did not expressly prohibit it must have intended to require—and sometimes that what Congress did not expressly permit it must have intended not to permit (U.S. Congress, Senate Finance Committee 1972, 16).

Once the Supreme Court had established this surprising new policy, Legal Services attorneys flooded the courts with cases contesting nearly every facet of state programs.

Although the Supreme Court later expressed some misgivings about this novel reading of the statute, the lower courts were quick to apply and extend the logic of the "trilogy." Federal circuit and district courts struck down state rules requiring AFDC mothers to identify the father of their children, requiring the recipient to accept various types of work, disqualifying those previously found guilty of fraud, and requiring stepparents to disclose their income. The lower courts also prohibited states from automatically reducing benefits to families receiving Social Security benefits, child support payments, tax refunds, or income from a stepparent (Melnick 1993, 97–102). The high point of judicial expansion came when five circuit courts ordered states to treat a fetus as a "dependent child" under the act, thus making pregnant women eligible for benefits. The First Circuit explained (*Carver v. Hooker*, 1247):

> A finding of eligibility for the unborn is consistent with the purposes and policies of the Social Security Act. The Supreme Court has declared that the "paramount goal" of the AFDC program to be protection of needy children. Payments to the unborn are an appropriate, if not essential measure to that end.

Although the Supreme Court reprimanded these circuit courts for their "departure from ordinary principles of statutory interpretation" (*Burns v. Alcala*, 580), it periodically reverted to its previous habit of establishing a virtually unrebuttable presumption of eligibility (*Miller v. Youakim*).

Serendipity played an important role in this story, as it does in almost all such litigation. The pivotal case *King v. Smith* was virtually made to order for exposing the hazards of the existing AFDC arrangement. It arose from a 1964 Alabama eligibility rule that had thrown 16,000 children—90 percent of them African American—off the welfare rolls. The rule announced that any man who either "lives in the house" of an AFDC family or even "visits frequently for the purpose of cohabiting" automatically becomes a "substitute father." Since Alabama provided benefits only to one-parent families, AFDC families with such a "substitute father" lost all benefits, whether or not the man in question provided any support to the family. To challenge this rule, welfare reform litigators filed suit on behalf of a hard-working widowed black woman who was raising four children. Mrs. Smith lost her meager benefits when an anonymous informant told her case worker that she had had occasional relations with a neighbor who was supporting nine children of his own. The fact that the rule had been issued by Governor George Wallace and that the case came from Selma made the racial element unmistakable.

Just as important as the extreme nature of the case was the decision by the plaintiffs' attorneys to rely on statutory interpretation rather than constitutional law when the case got to the Supreme Court. The lower court had found the Alabama rule so arbitrary as to violate the equal protection clause of the Fourteenth Amendment. Governor Wallace, spoiling for a fight as usual, imprudently appealed. Shortly after the Supreme Court agreed to hear the case, Mrs. Smith's attorneys decided that a statutory ruling would have broader ramifications than a constitutional one. If the Court based its decision on the equal protection clause, then in future cases poverty lawyers would bear the burden of proving that the challenged rule was discriminatory either in its intent or in its effect. A statutory ruling, in contrast, would prohibit the states from imposing certain restrictions on eligibility without any finding of discrimination. "If the decision goes off as the lower court's did," Martin Garbus (1971, 194–95) told the Court in oral argument, "then very little will have been accomplished. Even if we win in Alabama, HEW [Department of Health, Education, and Welfare] will not stop similar practices in other states." A statutory argument, though, "would give us all we wanted" and provide "a way in which the narrowest of rulings would have the broadest of implication."

This is precisely what Chief Justice Warren's opinion for a unanimous Court did. Although Alabama's statutory arguments "would have been quite relevant at one time," the times they were a-changin': "[F]ederal welfare policy now rests on a basis considerably more sophisticated and enlightened than the 'worthy-person' concept of earlier times." To uphold Alabama's rule "would require us to assume that Congress, at the same time that it intended to provide programs for the economic security of *all* children, also intended arbitrarily to leave one class of destitute children without meaningful protection. . . . Such an interpretation of congressional intent would be most reasonable, and we decline to adopt it" (*King v. Smith*, 330). Warren suggested that any eligibility requirement other than economic need was arbitrary and thus legally suspect. This, of course, was an assumption at war with the categorical nature of the American welfare system.

In 1968 the Supreme Court was willing to play fast and loose with the language, structure, and political history of title IV of the Social Security Act in order to invalidate an egregious, racially motivated state regulation. Given the fact that four Nixon appointees joined the Court between the time King was decided in 1968 and *Carlson v. Remillard* was decided in 1972, one might have expected the Court to back away from the most adventuresome dicta of King. But it did the opposite. In relatively mundane cases coming from northern and western states, it strengthened the presumption in favor of eligibility and repeatedly rebuked states' efforts to broaden the definition of income that is "available" to welfare families. Adopting such a liberal interpretation of the Social Security Act, Justice Brennan explained in *Townsend v. Swank* (291), allowed the Court to "avoid the necessity of passing upon the equal protection issue." One of the peculiar features of the Burger Court was that it frequently adopted innovative and counterintuitive interpretation of statutes in order to avoid contentious constitutional issues. The justices could allay their concerns about excessive judicial activism by arguing that if Congress disagreed, it could always change the law.

The efforts of antipoverty lawyers to increase state benefit levels proved far less successful (Rabin 1970; Melnick 1993, 94–97; *Rosado v. Wyman*). Not only did they lack a case as compelling as *King v. Smith*, but the aggregate costs and potentially redistributive nature of court-ordered benefit increases were readily apparent to most judges. Losing on benefits litigation forced Legal Services attorneys to rely more heavily on the limits on attribution of income suggested in the "trilogy" in order to offset the effects of inflation on benefit levels. The emphasis judges place on precedent makes litigation particularly path-dependent: early victories and losses establish patterns that persist for years.

Alexander Bickel (1970) once wrote of the Warren Court, "What informed the enterprise was the idea of progress. . . . Man-made progress was the new faith, and the supremacy of judges as its carriers and executioners was not denied" (13, 17). In the late 1960s and early 1970s the Court's "sophisticated and enlightened" understanding of welfare policy was in its ascendance. But it also had persistent foes. Two of the most determined were the governor of California and the chair of the Senate Finance Committee. Governor Ronald Reagan was on the losing end of many federal court decisions on welfare. Senator Russell Long (D-Louisiana), not only helped to scuttle Nixon's Family Assistance Plan but also led one effort after another to reverse the courts' rulings and to defund Legal Services ("Only an idiot," Long never tired of saying, "would hire someone to sue himself"). The features of American politics that make it difficult to pass legislation on controversial topics protected the courts' holdings from legislative reversal for years. In 1981 and 1982 Reagan and Long were able to use the budget reconciliation process and the president's popularity to reverse a few court rulings (Melnick 1993, 120–30). Not until 1996—nearly thirty years after the first legal assault on AFDC practices—did Congress hand control of eligibility standards back to the states.

RECONCEPTUALIZING DISABILITY

Just as litigation on AFDC was running out of steam in the federal courts and facing reversals in Congress, new court battles were brewing over disability benefits. During the 1970s the disability rights movement had won impressive victories in three areas: the reform of large state facilities for the mentally ill and developmentally disabled; requiring local school systems to provide a "free appropriate education" for all children, regardless of the nature and severity of their disability; and making public transportation more accessible to those with physical disabilities. In each instance advocates for the disabled artfully combined litigation with lobbying before Congress, state legislatures, and a variety of administrative agencies, using victories in one arena to increase their leverage in others (Katzmann 1986; Melnick 1995; Burke 1997). Until the early 1980s these advocacy groups paid little attention to the two major income-maintenance programs for the disabled, Social Security Disability Insurance (SSDI) and the disability component of Supplemental Security Income (SSI). Many leaders of the disability rights movement were hostile to programs that had the effect of removing those with disabilities from the workforce rather than eliminating those physical and social barriers that prevented them from working. The Supreme Court's due process rulings suggested that it would more readily defer to administrative expertise in these programs than it did in AFDC (*Mathews v. Eldridge*). Lower courts heard a steady trickle of SSDI cases, but their holdings were usually limited to the particular facts of each case. Nine times out of ten the courts upheld the SSA. Legal Services and its backup centers never developed special expertise in the field.

This changed suddenly in 1981 when the Reagan administration undertook an unprecedented review of the eligibility of hundreds of thousands of SSDI and SSI recipients. Legislation enacted in 1980 had mandated a review of existing cases. The Reagan administration proceeded with great speed and zeal in order to achieve major budget savings. As Derthick (1990, 36) put it, "What was set in motion in 1981 was more like a purge." During the first three years of the review the SSA reexamined over a million cases and terminated more than half of those examined. State officials conducting the reviews for the SSA found that the best way to keep up with the crushing workload was to terminate benefits after cursory review.

Many of the initial administrative rulings were overturned on appeal. Administrative law judges blocked termination in 40 percent of these cases—over 90 percent of the time in cases involving those with mental impairments. Reversal rates in the federal courts jumped from 10 to 15 percent before 1980 to almost 50 percent after the reviews began. By late 1983 the SSA faced almost 35,000 disability lawsuits, including 95 class-action suits that affected tens of thousands of recipients (Erkulwater 2006, 124; Derthick 1990, 42–46). Federal judges regularly excoriated the SSA for conducting reviews with "no medical, vocational, or other empirical basis whatever" (*Mental Health Association of Minnesota v. Schweiker*, 162). In an especially important class-action case, Judge Jack Weinstein described the SSA review process as a "paper charade" in which "[p]hysicians were pressured to reach 'conclusions' contrary to their own professed beliefs" (*City of New York v. Heckler*, 1124).

The SSA fueled the controversy by adopting a policy of "non-acquiescence." This meant it would follow court orders on the specific individuals named in the court proceedings, but would not alter its general policies until the Supreme Court had ruled on the issue in question. But whenever the government lost a case in the circuit courts, it would not ask for Supreme Court review—which meant that the Supreme Court would never hear any of these issues. Federal judges responded by issuing hundreds of contempt citations. According to Derthick (1990, 140), "Judges all over the country were berating the SSA from the bench." A judge on the Ninth Circuit likened non-acquiescence to the "pre–Civil War doctrine of nullification." United States Attorney Rudolph Giuliani "virtually apologized for the SSA's policy in a letter to the judge in his district" (Derthick 1990, 140, 144). Fearing that those dropped from SSDI and SSI would end up in state-financed public assistance programs, state and local government joined the chorus of criticism of the SSA.

The immediate crisis ended in 1984 and 1985 when Congress passed legislation clarifying the standards governing disability reviews, and the Reagan administration abandoned its efforts to trim the rolls substantially. The judicial response to the Reagan disability reviews thus provides a graphic example of the role courts can play in blocking executive-led retrenchment efforts. But that was only the beginning of the story. The disability review confrontation led to a long-term transformation of the way the SSA defines disability for children and for adults with mental illness.

Two issues lay at the heart of the decade-long struggle between the SSA and the courts. One was the legal standard for terminating benefits: the SSA claimed that beneficiaries must prove that they remain disabled; the courts maintained that the burden lay on SSA to demonstrate "medical improvement." Congress resolved this dispute in 1984 by writing the courts' "medical improvement" standard into law. The second, more subtle and less easily resolved, issue was the role of professional judgment in disability determinations. The federal courts routinely criticized the SSA for failing to place sufficient weight on the individualized assessments of treating physicians and mental health professionals. This issue, never directly confronted by Congress, lay at the heart of the SSA's rewriting of rules on mental disabilities after the crisis of the mid-1980s, the Supreme Court's 1990 *Zebley* decision, and the regulations SSA wrote in response to *Zebley*.

Jennifer Erkulwater's (2006) detailed and subtle analysis of disability determinations by the SSA shows that the crisis of the early Reagan years led to a far-reaching conceptual shift within SSA. In response to the barrage of litigation, the SSA changed its regulations and informal practices to emphasize an individual's capacity to function rather than to rely entirely on the severity of isolated but observable "clinical signs and symptoms." The new approach required the examiner to make a more holistic—but inevitably more subjective—determination about the claimant's capacity to find, perform, and retain a job in the real world. Erkulwater (121) notes that

> the shift from an approach that looked at objective clinical measures to one that emphasizes functional deficits was so subtle that it might be tempting to regard it as a distinction without a difference. But the implications for disability certifications were enormous. In a system as large as Social Security with a significant number of borderline cases, small shifts of emphasis could translate into considerable changes in the aggregate size and cost of the program.

The result is readily apparent in the number of program beneficiaries. From 1985 to 1995 the number of SSDI recipients nearly doubled, rising from about 2.5 million to almost 4.5 million (U.S. Congress, House Ways and Means Committee 2000, 79). The increase was even steeper for SSI. Just under 2.5 million disabled individuals received SSI benefits in 1984. This rose to almost 3 million in 1988, over 4 million in 1992, and more than 5 million in 1996 (U.S. Congress, House Ways and Means Committee 2004, 3-5).

Litigation contributed to this transformation in at least three ways. First, the legal challenges to the Reagan administration's disability reviews forged an alliance between mental health professionals and attorneys affiliated with the Judge David L. Bazelon Center for Mental Health Law, a Washington-based support center that describes itself as "the nation's leading civil rights organization representing people with mental illnesses or mental retardation." This alliance proved particularly important in the long rule-making process within the SSA. It also had the effect of insulating that rule-making from congressional attack. As Erkulwater (2006, 225–36) explains, "By arguing that disability standards should conform to the prevailing medical diagnostic standards, advocates appealed to the congressional penchant for dodging the contentious distributive decisions by delegating the truly difficult decisions to experts."

Second, the long series of high-visibility losses in court left both long-term SSA officials and newly appointed political executives deeply chagrined and eager to "get it right this time." Years after the disability review fiasco the former associate commissioner of the Office of Supplemental Security Income confessed (Davis 1996),

> [W]e began the slaughter of the innocents. . . . By the time [we] realized we had to slow it down,. . . it was too late in the sense of having the outside world have faith that our intentions were credible, and that we are an honorable group of people who want to do the right thing because every action that we took was to the contrary. . . . We created the nightmare in the courts.

Throughout the organization there was broad agreement that wholesale change was in order and that the agency had to reestablish its deeply strained relations with physicians and mental health professionals.

Third, the federal courts emerged from the confrontation with the SSA far less willing to defer to the expertise of the SSA. According to Erkulwater (2006, 141–2), by the early 1990s

> federal courts had issued rulings that touched every aspect of the disability programs. They reworked the criteria the SSA used to evaluate cardiovascular disease, AIDS and HIV, pain, diabetes, and hypertension. They even contested routine administrative details, including the methods for calculating the amounts of SSI payments, counting veterans' benefits, determining whether the claimant's impairment has lasted for twelve months or longer as required by law, and deciding whether a claimant's impairment was "severe" enough to warrant benefit payments. In 1992, the SSA confronted forty-six threatened or pending class action lawsuits and thousands of individual lawsuits dealing with issues pertaining to its disability program.

The Supreme Court's major contribution came in *Zebley v. Sullivan*, a class-action suit brought on behalf of over three hundred thousand children. The controversial regulations the SSA promulgated in response to *Zebley* produced a huge increase in SSI beneficiaries. Indeed the Legal Services attorney who argued the case before the Court concluded that the litigation had been "more successful than could possibly [have] been imagined." Paradoxically, the federal courts were increasing their scrutiny of the SSA just as the Supreme Court was ordering the lower courts to show more deference to administrative agencies (*Chevron v. Natural Resources Defense Council*).

The federal judiciary remained distrustful not only of the SSA but of any efforts to substitute hard and fast administrative rules for individualized professional judgment in disability determinations. The Supreme Court's *Zebley* opinion exemplified this judicial insistence on an "individualized, functional analysis" of disability. According to Justice Harry Blackmun's majority opinion (*Zebley v. Sullivan*, 539),

> No decision process restricted to comparing claimants' medical evidence to a fixed, finite set of medical criteria can respond adequately to the infinite variety of medical conditions and combinations thereof, the varying impact of such conditions due to the claimants' individual characteristics, and the constant evolution of medical diagnostic techniques.

These cases provide a graphic illustration of what Jerry Mashaw (1983, 29) has called the "professional treatment model of justice," which places its faith "in having the appropriate professional judgment applied to one's particular situation in the context of a service relationship."

Court action thus contributed to a major turnabout on disability policy. In the early 1980s disability policies were facing unprecedented cuts and political attacks. The courts not only blocked the Reagan administration's retrenchment effort, but served as a catalyst for a decade of rapid expansion. This expansion in turn attracted congressional attention. In 1996 Congress tried to reverse the expansion of spending on the SSI children's disability program. The resulting rules reduced the number of families receiving SSI benefits by about a hundred thousand, a significant number, but only a fraction of the increase that had followed Zebley (U.S. Congress, House Ways and Means Committee 2000, 251–52).

FINDING A HOOK FOR HOUSING

Homelessness, another problem that received a good deal of attention in the Reagan years, was the subject of a much different type of litigational campaign. Although Congress passed legislation to address the issue in 1987 and 1990, most of the burden of providing emergency shelter and finding ways to reduce homelessness fell on state and local governments. This is where advocates for the homeless focused much of their attention. One early example was *Callahan v. Carey*, a case brought by the Coalition for the Homeless in 1979. The New York State Supreme Court issued a preliminary injunction ordering the City of New York to provide shelter to any homeless man who requested it. The City subsequently signed a consent decree with the Coalition that guided city policy on shelters for years to come (Main 1983). A decade later Legal Services attorneys used litigation to force five states—California, Illinois, New York, Massachusetts, and Washington—to take steps to reduce homelessness among families with children. Beth Harris's (2004) detailed description of this multistate effort provides us with a third view of welfare litigation in action.

In California the effort to respond to the problem of homeless families was spearheaded by the Western Center on Law and Poverty, one of the oldest and most experienced of the Legal Services backup centers. Stymied by their inability to convince state officials to raise AFDC grants to reflect rising housing costs, the center's lawyers "scrutinized the public assistance and child welfare statutes to find a legal hook to establish the state's responsibility to provide shelter to homeless families" (Harris 2004, 41). They found it in a California statute passed to bring the state into compliance with the federal Adoption Assistance and Child Welfare Act (AACWA) of 1980. The law announced that a primary goal of the California child welfare agency was "preventing the unnecessary separation of children from their families by identifying family problems, assisting families in resolving their problems, and preventing breakup of the family where the prevention of child removal is desirable and possible" (Harris 2004, 59). The center's lawyers argued that because the state child welfare agency provided emergency shelter only to children who had been removed from the family—and not to children in intact homeless families—the agency was failing to prevent family breakup and thus was violating its statutory mandate.

The center's lawyers recognized that this was not the most convincing of legal arguments. Consequently they developed what Harris (2004, 60) describes as "an intensive factual record based on the compelling stories of those who were victimized, on social science studies, and on expert testimony concerning the seriousness of harms to destitute families caused by current agency practices." One experienced attorney explained,

> You're not just appealing to judges to enforce statutes, but you're appealing to them to be human beings. The briefs in these cases were trivial compared to the affidavits and declarations. They are powerful stories of people suffering outrageously, and any judge who has half a heart, who had any authority to do anything, would do something. So your job as a lawyer is then to give them the legal authority (Harris 2004, 61).

Shopping for the judicial audience most sympathetic to these compelling stories, the center's lawyers decided to file suit not in federal court (where it could argue that the state had violated the federal AACWA), but in state court.

They chose wisely, winning at both the trial and appellate levels. The California Court of Appeals found that the "preservation of the family unit is an objective which courses throughout the body of California's laws governing the AFDC program"; that the Department of Social Service's regulations were "subversive of those goals, in that their application has the actual potential of needlessly forcing homeless AFDC families into the clutches of child dependency proceedings, and thereby effecting the disintegration of families"; and that "a society that sacrifices the health and well-being of its young upon the false altar of economy endangers its own future, and, indeed, its own survival" (Harris 2004, 62–63).

The California Department of Social Services (DSS) did not object to the goal of providing housing assistance to at-risk families. But already overburdened with running the nation's largest foster-care system, DSS did object to the court's insistence that it somehow come up with the money necessary to pay for the judicial mandate. After the court announced its decision, lawyers for the plaintiff and for DSS entered into negotiations with state legislators. They reached this deal: if the plaintiffs would agree to terminate the litigation, the legislature would establish a new program providing $140 million for homeless families over the next two years. This agreement offered something for everyone. Most important, it created a program that aided ninety thousand families in its first year. DSS was able to avoid responsibility for running a program that lay well outside its area of expertise, and the state legislature was able to tap into federal emergency assistance funds to defray most of the cost. The disadvantage of the negotiated settlement was that it did not lock in this level of spending. When federal money dried up and California faced a huge budget deficit, spending on the program plummeted.

A few years later poverty lawyers in Illinois filed a similar suit. Attorneys in the Children's Rights Program of the Legal Assistance Foundation of Chicago decided to take their chances in federal court. Unlike their colleagues in Los Angeles, they had a higher opinion of federal judges in Illinois than of state court judges, whom they considered too reluctant to order the state to spend money. This, too, proved to be a shrewd choice. The federal district court accepted the argument that the AACWA required the state to take "reasonable efforts" to keep families together by helping them avoid homelessness. The federal magistrate who initially issued the injunction claimed that children who fall into a condition of homelessness are "likely to sustain deep psychological injury." The net cost to the government, she maintained, would be minimal because the agency would save money by reducing the number of children in foster care (Harris 2004, 67).

The new head of the Illinois Department of Children and Family Services agreed. In *Norman v. Johnson*, he signed a detailed consent decree that was in effect for the next six years. The two sides worked together relatively congenially over that period. The budget for the Illinois program was smaller than that of California, but (unlike California) gradually expanded over time. The so-called Norman program served 1,500 families per year in 1994 and 4,500 in 2002. Current costs are about $2 million annually.

New York presents yet another variation on this theme. Here the litigants relied on state law and the state constitution. The New York AFDC statute established a separate shelter grant for AFDC recipients and stated that public assistance allowances "shall be adequate to enable the father, mother, or other relation to bring up the child properly." The trial court in *Jiggetts v. Grinder* issued a preliminary injunction ordering the state to increase the shelter allowance for families facing eviction. It was upheld on review. Although the lower court never issued a final decision, it ordered the state to pay back rent and monthly rent for all the named plaintiffs. When additional families asked to join the suit, the judge simply added their names to the list. This process continued for many years. In 1991 the number of families receiving *Jiggetts* payments was 135. Six years later the number of *Jiggetts* households peaked at a little over 26,000, with an annual cost of a little over $70 million. Governors Cuomo and Pataki tried to convince the legislature to end the program, but both failed.

Harris (2004, 98–99) provides this evaluation of the New York litigation:

> Although the program for *Jiggetts* relief lacked any statutory foundation and the rule-making process was *ad hoc* for fifteen years, it has significant redistributive consequences for many families receiving public assistance benefits in New York City. The ad hoc bureaucracy created for implementation supported the employment of workers in community organizations as well as Legal Aid attorneys, and contributed to the incomes of landlords. A kind of temporary bureaucratic stability developed within the very unstable context of continuing litigation.

Ironically, one of the critics of the *Jiggetts* process was the attorney who initially brought the case. "Processing *Jiggetts* relief," he explained, "is very uninteresting, boring work. At Legal Aid, it has become a very difficult issue that people don't want to do these cases. It is debilitating for a Legal Services office to have lots and lots of extremely routine boring cases" (Harris 2004, 98). It is obviously more fun to be a critic of bureaucracy than to be a cog in one.

These "right to housing" cases illustrate how litigational strategies and outcomes can differ not just from policy area to policy area but from state to state within the same policy area. The consequences of these cases were not nearly as dramatic as the AFDC and disability litigation. Florence Roisman (2005, 759) notes that "although the cases were filed during years of hostility to programs for poor people (1986–1991), each produced substantial new financial and other benefits that have survived the federal welfare 'reform' of 1996, state budget deficits, and other negative forces." Such cases help us understand the myriad of small victories, defeats, and negotiated settlements that form the routine of legal advocates for the disadvantaged.

CATEGORICAL PROGRAMS, FRAGMENTED AUTHORITY, AND LITIGATIONAL STRATEGIES

Litigation expanding public assistance benefits was not merely a fleeting phenomenon cultivated by the Warren Court in the halcyon years of antipoverty programs. Why and when does this litigation succeed? These case studies suggest the difficulty of providing a systematic answer to this question. Their legal arguments are usually based on the idiosyncratic structure of the program at hand. Litigants move from one judicial forum to another. To succeed, their strategies must shift with the disposition of incumbent presidents, members of Congress, and judges. Litigation on behalf of potential recipients of public assistance programs is thus inherently entrepreneurial: litigators must search for creative ways to take advantage of unusual sets of circumstances. One thing all these litigational strategies have in common, though, is that their architects have discovered ways to take advantage of two central features of the American welfare state, its fragmentation and its categorical nature.

The lower tier of the American welfare state is a baffling collection of categorical programs. The House Ways and Means Committee's *2004 Green Book* (U.S. Congress,

House Ways and Means Committee 2004, K-10—K12) lists eighty-five separate means-tested programs funded in whole or in part by the federal government. They range from the behemoth Medicaid to the tiny Special Milk Program, from such well-known programs as Temporary Assistance for Needy Families, Food Stamps, and SSI to Head Start, Pell Grants, and adoption assistance to Indian housing improvement grants and weatherization assistance. Categorical programs single out particular categories of needy people—children, the elderly, widows, single parents, the disabled, veterans—and particular types of human needs—nutrition, health care, shelter, education—for special attention. Categorized programs at one and the same time impose *limits* (we will provide benefits to those who are unemployed because they are disabled, but not to those who are unemployed because employers have fled the area; food stamps can be used only to buy nutritious groceries and cannot be used to defray housing costs) and establish a *rationale* for public assistance (we cannot expect those with serious disabilities to work; in a nation that produces such a huge agricultural surplus no one should go hungry).

Successful welfare litigation usually requires plaintiffs' lawyers to convince the judge that some of the limitations imposed by federal or state laws and regulations or by informal administrative practices somehow conflict with the program's underlying rationale. The trick is to convince the court to adopt a broad reading of the program's rationale and then to explain why this rationale should trump the limitations imposed by legal authorities charged with the program's implementation. Thus, in the King-Townsend-Remillard trilogy the Supreme Court announced that the purpose of AFDC was to provide assistance "to *all* needy dependent children." State rules that conflicted with this federal mandate suddenly became invalid. In Food Stamp cases the lower federal court found that the purpose of federal legislation was to guarantee the right to a nutritionally adequate diet. Any federal regulation that threatened to leave some people without adequate nutrition became suspect (Melnick 1993, 207–16). State child welfare laws charge state agencies with helping keep families together. States that provided foster care to children removed from troubled homes but failed to provide emergency shelter or housing assistance to intact families threatened with homelessness seemed to violate that broad legislative mandate.

Several features of the adjudicatory process help litigators exploit the tension between categorical programs' rationales and their limitations. First, in most welfare reform litigation, the attorneys can select their lead plaintiffs to illustrate how destitute and blameless people can fall though holes in the existing social safety net. Experienced litigators stress the importance of finding plaintiffs who will engage the sympathies of the judge, educate the judge about the harsh realities of the welfare system, and expose incongruities in the maze of rules on eligibility and benefit levels. The lawyer who brought many of the early Food Stamp cases explained that his strategy was to find "plaintiffs whose situation would become so desperate if the court did not rule in their favor that a judge could not help but think that the regulation under question was arbitrary or irrational" (Pollack 1969, 38). Those who brought the first AFDC cases looked for "the worst examples of a practice or rule, the gross or excessive form, so to speak, in the most highly suspect social setting" (Albert 1968, 28). Powerful stories of destitute families becoming the "victim of an uncaring bureaucracy" make judges significantly less likely to defer to administrative expertise. Conversely, as a Legal Service manual warns (Smith and Silverstein 2004, 46),

> No matter how good your legal claim, if your clients are completely unsympathetic, are responsible in good measure for the bad outcome of which you are complaining, or are

perceived to be undeserving, the outcome will not be to your liking. The court may be forced to rule in your favor on the law, but will do so parsimoniously, and you will not achieve your broader objectives.

Good plaintiffs personify a problem that deserves public attention and that is at least vaguely related to a problem previously identified by legislators.

Because litigation allows advocates to focus on particularly compelling stories, it fits seamlessly into a broader strategy of publicity and exposure. The publicity generated by litigation has several purposes and audiences outside the courtroom: to embarrass or shame administrators; to alert and organize potential beneficiaries; to attract the attention of entrepreneurial politicians and electoral challengers; and, of course, to appeal directly to public opinion. One reason that many cases settle before a ruling by a judge is that politicians and administrators do not relish the type of attention such cases attract. They will be willing to make modest adjustment to make the problem and the attendant publicity go away as soon as possible.

Adjudication, as Donald Horowitz (1976, 37) has noted, is both focused and piecemeal. It manages to zero in on a small number of issues by defining closely related matters as irrelevant or out-of-bounds. In Horowitz's words, adjudication "isolates[s] artificially what in the real world is merged." A major factor that is often considered irrelevant in welfare reform litigation, of course, is cost. Agencies will frequently argue, in effect, "We would like to do this, but we don't have the money." Just as often judges will reply, "This is a legal mandate; it's not our job to worry about the cost." In practice, very large costs will make judges think twice—if only because they must worry about the possibility of noncompliance by the agency before them. But small sums—a few million here and there, as Everett Dirksen would say—usually seem manageable. Administrators recognize that losing a case can increase their leverage within the budgetary process. "The judge made me do it" is a powerful argument in negotiations with legislators and budget offices (Wood 1990, chapter 3).

A more subtle consequence of the narrow focus of adjudication is that judges can sidestep many of the dilemmas that so often preoccupy legislators and administrators—and endlessly tie them up in knots. As Kent Weaver (2000, 45) has shown, welfare reform invariably presents us with what he calls policy "traps:"

> [W]elfare reform initiatives have usually created hard choices for policymakers because they could not increase the prospects that they would get more of something they wanted without also increasing the risk that they would get more of something that they did not want in political or policy terms.

Most prominent is what Weaver (2000, 45) labels the "dual clientele trap:"

> [P]olicymakers usually cannot take the politically popular step of helping poor children without the politically unpopular step of helping their custodial parents; they cannot take politically popular step of increasing penalties for refusal to work or for out-of-wedlock childbearing that may hurt parents without also risking the politically unpopular result that poor children will be made worse off.

Moreover, "No policy intended to help poor families can entirely avoid creating incentives for recipients that policymakers and the public are likely to see as undesirable, and no plausible welfare reform initiative is likely to avoid creating some new perverse incentives or making some existing ones worse" (Weaver 2000, 48). This, as Henry Aaron (1973) has explained, is "why welfare is so hard to reform." The narrow focus of litigation affords judges the luxury of separating the immediate problem before them from the unintended and undesirable long-term consequences of the actions they mandate. Worrying about these secondary consequences is someone else's job. As Weaver shows, welfare politics usually involves strategies for emphasizing one side of each "trap" and keeping the other under wraps. Litigation not only allows plaintiffs' lawyers an opportunity to frame the issue in a way favorable to their cause, but allows judges the opportunity to sidestep the hardest choices.

Appealing to judges' sense of compassion and pointing out anomalies or irrationalities in government programs is a necessary ingredient of welfare reform litigation, but it is seldom sufficient. To prevail, litigators must find what they often call a "legal hook." A central feature of the American legal system is that it produces a wide variety of sources and types of legal authority (Atiyah and Summers 1991; Kagan 2001) (see table 3.2). Most means-tested programs are run jointly by the federal government, the states, and localities, which means that they involve the application of legal rules from all levels of government and many types of legal authority to which litigants can often appeal.

Table 3.2   Sources of Legal Authority

Federal constitutional provisions
Federal statutes
Federal legislative histories
   House and Senate reports and hearings
   Floor debate
   Presidential signing statements
Federal administrative regulations
Federal administrative guidelines and informal directive
Cross-cutting administrative rules (Title VI, Title IX, and the Americans with
   Disabilities Act)
Executive orders
Federal court decisions
   Supreme Court decisions
   Circuit court decisions
   District court decisions
Treaty provisions

State constitutional provisions
State statutes
State legislative histories
State regulations, guidelines, and informal guidance
State court decisions interpreting the above
State court common law rulings

Local ordinances
Tribal law

Source: Author's compilation.

The potent combination of federalism, separation of powers, decentralized legisla-tive bodies, and a weak senior civil service produces a cacophony of legal rules and ob-jectives that are all too frequently in conflict with one another. Some of these legal author-ities—especially federal grant-in-aid statutes, state constitutions, and cross-cutting regulatory commands—are likely to contain hortatory or aspirational language. Others—especially administrative rules at both the state and federal level—try to be much more specific. Lawyers routinely use the more abstract statements of purpose and principle to attack the more specific limitations on eligibility and benefit levels. A central feature of our legal system is that the so-called "canons" of statutory interpretation do very little to constrain judges' ordering of these many sources of legal authority. And a central feature of our political system is that it is very hard (but not impossible) for the other branches to reverse judicial decisions (Atiyah 1988).

An important corollary of this fragmentation of legal authority is the potential it cre-ates for forum shopping. Most obviously, plaintiffs can often chose between federal and state courts. In the 1960s and 1970s Legal Services attorneys preferred to challenge state policies in federal court, arguing that they conflicted with federal law. In the 1980s and 1990s they found that they were often more successful when they went to state court and relied on state statutes and state constitutional provisions. The California and New York housing cases are good examples of this. School finance reform litigation failed in the fed-eral courts in the early 1970s, but has been extremely successful in many state courts in recent years. Plaintiffs can also choose among federal district and circuit courts. Given the infrequency of Supreme Court review, lower court decisions will often drive agency policy.

Going hand in hand with this fragmentation of legal authority is the opportunity for cost shifting. Politicians and administrators at one level of the federal system can use lit-igation as a way to shift cost to another level. A good deal of welfare litigation in federal court involves defining and enforcing unfunded or partially funded mandates. Congress is fond of taking credit for providing new benefits which it expects subnational govern-ments to fund. Many of these mandates are enforced through private rights of action in federal court (Melnick 2005b). Conversely, state and local officials will often initiate or join with private litigants to force the federal government to fund what they see as its com-mitments. In the disability controversy described previously, state and local government joined with disability rights groups because they feared that they would be left with the cases that were dropped by the feds.

Many administrators have learned that losing a court suit can be a good way to pry more money out of a stingy state legislature. Nonetheless, most administrators do not relish losing court cases. Not only is this professionally and politically embarrass-ing, but it can also produce troublesome limitations on administrative discretion. Much better to sign a consent agreement with the plaintiffs. This allows administrators to gain leverage within the appropriations process and to lock in policies for many years. In the meantime, convenient adjustments can be made though informal negoti-ations with the original parties. Frequently the real adversaries in this form of litiga-tion—state legislators, future governors, other agencies competing for resources—are excluded from the initial litigation and subsequent negotiations (Sandler and Schoen-brod 2003).

An unusual feature of American politics since the late 1960s is that we have added a large number of tasks to the public sector at a time when trust in government has plum-meted (Melnick 2005b). Litigators have often managed to tap into this widespread hos-tility to "big government," bureaucracy, and administrative discretion by framing issues in terms of individual rights—the right to decent housing, a nutritious diet, adequate medical care—that are to be defined by professional norms and protected against administrative trimming. The clearest instance of this came in the disability cases and the subsequent rule-making within the SSA. Judges repeatedly berated the SSA for failing to accept the recommendations of medical and mental health professionals. Courts frequently read statutes to mandate individual determinations of appropriate treatment by members of the helping professions. This comports not only with their understanding of due process but also with their inclination to believe that highly educated, high-status professionals (like themselves) are more trustworthy and thoughtful than mere politicians and bureaucrats.

An important consequence of this judicial preference for professional judgment is that litigants are often able to gain informal help from professionals within the agency being sued. As one advocate for the disabled explained (Abeson 1976, 240),

> Changes sought through litigation may be very similar to directions the party named as "defendant" has tried to achieve. . . . Litigation (or the threat of litigation) may be used as a lever to bring about the action desired by both the potential defendant and the plaintiff. . . . [In some cases] named defendants have spent days preparing defenses for the suit, and nights assisting the plaintiffs to prepare their arguments.

To the extent that litigation boosts the standing of professionals within government, it shifts influence from those who tend to be highly cost-conscious (especially political executives) to those who are not.

CONCLUSION

The conventional wisdom in political science holds that contributory programs such as Social Security, Medicare, and veterans' pensions command a powerful political constituency, but means-tested programs such as TANF, Medicaid, and SSI serve a constituency that is politically weak, even despised. Several chapters in this volume provide evidence suggesting that the political influence of the constituents of the latter group of programs has significantly declined in recent decades. Thus it would seem that those at the bottom of the economic ladder are caught in a vicious cycle: lack of political influence increases their vulnerability to unfavorable market forces, further reducing their political and social standing.

Given the Republican Party's success in national politics between 1980 and 2006, the huge deficits that began in the Reagan years, and the high level of public antipathy toward "welfare" in the 1980s and 1990s, the growth rates of means-tested programs in recent decades are rather remarkable. The House Ways and Means Committee's *2004 Green Book* reports that measured in constant 2002 dollars, total federal, state, and local spending on means-tested programs rose from less than $90 billion in the late 1960s to almost $240 billion in 1980, about $300 billion in 1990, $450 billion in 2000, and almost $525 billion in 2002. The share of the federal budget devoted to means-tested programs—a fairly good indication of how these programs have fared in comparison with the competing programs—rose from less than 6.5 percent in the late 1960s to well over 17 percent in 2000.

Lawrence Brown and Michael Sparer (2003, 3) of the Columbia School of Public Health have pointed out that spending on Medicaid has outstripped spending on the allegedly more popular Medicare. Since the early Reagan years, the number of Medicaid recipients has doubled. Medicaid, they write, "has contrived to stabilize its benefits and expand its number of beneficiaries with success that is surprising in a poor people's program." Other scholars have noted this apparent anomaly as well (Wildavsky 1988; Nathan 2005; Greve and Smith 2003). According to Brown and Sparer (2003),

> The evolution of the two programs over nearly four decades shows that the conventional wisdom about the political inferiority of poor people's programs—at least in the health policy area—misses much. Medicare has indeed been stable and politically successful, but the program has seen very little expansion, whereas Medicaid has enjoyed more stability and growth than "theory" predicts.

Regardless of where one stands on the question of the adequacy of Medicaid and other public programs, their incremental growth in an era of conservatism and fiscal austerity in Washington presents a puzzle. This chapter has suggested that two factors help us understand the unexpected resilience of means-tested programs. The first and most obvious is that these programs have an array of organized supporters in addition to their principal beneficiaries. This includes many well-educated, affluent, and politically engaged professionals whose influence has increased in recent decades. The second is that advocates for these programs have found multiple ways to take advantage of the fragmented, categorical nature of the lower tier of the American welfare state in order to expand eligibility and benefits levels. The ordinary politics of these programs is complex, technical, and (let's face it) often boring. It generates far fewer books and articles than the passage of legislation such as the Social Security Act of 1935, Medicare and Medicaid in 1965, or the Welfare Reform Act of 1996. But it is no less important. In the words of Congressman Henry Waxman, who has done as much as anyone to extend Medicaid benefits, "Incrementalism may not get much press, but it does work" (Brown and Sparer 2003). Not always, of course, but frequently enough to command our attention.

At the same time, recognizing the political influence of professionals, providers, and the intergovernmental lobby raises in stark form the perennial question of how well these organizations speak for the disadvantaged and for the intended beneficiaries of government programs. Many elements of the disabilities rights movement claim that professionals arbitrarily categorize, stigmatize, and even infantilize those with disabilities. Raising reimbursement rates for Medicaid might be good for physicians, but might also force states to reduce the number of covered services. In some cities, African American parents support voucher programs, which are adamantly opposed by teachers' unions. New policies create new politics both by establishing new sets of actors and by structuring the opportunities for cooperation and conflict among them. Such is the complexity of politics in the mature welfare state.

REFERENCES

Aaron, Henry J. 1973. *Why Is Welfare So Hard to Reform?* Washington: Brookings Institution Press.

Aberbach, Joel D., Robert Putnam, and Bert A. Rockman. 1981. *Bureaucrats and Politicians in Western Democracies.* Cambridge, Mass.: Harvard University Press.

Abeson, Alan. 1976. "Litigation." In *Public Policy and the Education of Exceptional Children,* edited by Fred J. Weintraub et al. Washington: Council for Exceptional Children.

Albert, Lee. 1968. "Choosing the Test Case in Welfare Litigation: A Plea for Planning." *Clearinghouse Review* 1(November): 4–28.

Atiyah, Patrick. 1988. "Judicial-Legislative Relations in England." In *Judges and Legislators: Toward Institutional Comity*, edited by Robert Katzmann. Washington: Brookings Institution Press.

Atiyah, Patrick, and Robert Summers. 1991. *Form and Substance in Anglo-American Law: A Comparative Study of Legal Reasoning, Legal Theory, and Legal Institutions*. New York: Oxford University Press.

Berry, Jeffrey M. 1999. *The New Liberalism: The Rising Power of Citizen Groups*. Washington: Brookings Institution Press.

Bickel, Alexander M. 1970. *The Supreme Court and the Idea of Progress*. New York: Harper & Row.

Brown, Lawrence D., and Michael S. Sparer. 2003. "Poor Program's Progress: The Unanticipated Politics of Medicaid Policy." *Health Affairs* 22(1): 31-49.

Burke, Thomas F. 1997. "On the Rights Track: The Americans with Disabilities Act." In *Comparative Disadvantages? Social Regulations and the Global Economy*, edited by Pietro Nivola. Washington: Brookings Institution Press.

Burns v. Alcala, 420 U.S. 575 (1975)

Callahan v. Carey, #49-42582 (Sup. Ct. N.Y. County; Cot. 18, 1979)

Carleson v. Remillard, 406 U.S. 598 (1972)

Carver v. Hooker, 501 F. 2d 1244 (1st Cir., 1974)

Chevron v. Natural Resources Defense Council, 467 837 (1984)

City of New York v. Heckler, 578 F.Supp.1109 (EDNY, 1984)

Dandridge v. Williams, 397 U.S. 471 (1970)

Davis, Martha F. 1993. *Brutal Need: Lawyers and the Welfare Rights Movement*. New Haven, Conn.: Yale University Press.

Davis, Rhoda. 1996. Interview, February 5, 1996. Transcript. Oral History Collection, Office of the Historian, Social Security Administration, Baltimore, Md.

Derthick, Martha. 1979. *Policymaking for Social Security*. Washington: Brookings Institution Press.

———. 1990. *Agency Under Stress: The Social Security Administration in American Politics*. Washington: Brookings Institution Press.

Erkulwater, Jennifer. 2006. *Disability Rights and the American Safety Net*. Ithaca, N.Y.: Cornell University Press.

Garbus, Martin. 1971. *Ready for the Defense*. New York: Farrar Straus and Giroux.

Goldberg v. Kelly, 397 U.S. 254 (1970)

Greve, Michael, and Jinney Smith. 2003. "What Goes Up May Not Go Down: State Medicaid Decisions in Times of Plenty." AEI Working Paper. Washington: American Enterprise Institute August 5, 2003. Accessed at http://www.aei.org/ publications/pubID.17115/pub_detail.asp.

Harris, Beth. 2004. *Defending the Right to a Home: The Power of Anti-Poverty Lawyers*. Burlington, Vt.: Ashgate.

Heclo, Hugh. 1978. "Issue Networks and the Executive Establishment." In *The New American Political System*, edited by Anthony King. Washington: AEI Press.

Horowitz, Donald L. 1976. *The Courts and Social Policy*. Washington: Brookings Institution Press.

Houseman, Alan W. 1998. "Civil Legal Assistance for the 21st Century: Achieving Equal Justice for All." *Yale Law and Policy Review* 17(1): 369-433.

Houseman, Alan W., and Linda E. Perle. 2002. "What You May and May Not Do Under the Legal Services Corporation Restrictions." In *Poverty Law Manual for the New Lawyer*. Chicago: National Center on Poverty Law. Accessed at http://www.povertylaw.org/poverty-law-library/research-guides/poverty-law-manual/houseman-perle.pdf.

Jiggetts v. Grinder, 75 NY 2nd 411 (1990)

Kagan, Robert A. 2001. *Adversarial Legalism: The American Way of Law*. Cambridge, Mass.: Harvard University Press.

Katzmann, Robert A. 1986. *Institutional Disability: The Saga of Transportation Policy for the Disabled.* Washington: Brookings Institution Press.

King v. Smith, 392 U.S. 309 (1968)

Krislov, Samuel. 1973. "The OEO Lawyers Fail to Constitutionalize a Right to Welfare: A Study in the Uses and Limits of the Judicial Process." *Minnesota Law Review* 58(2): 211-45.

Lawrence, Susan. 1990. *The Poor in Court: The Legal Services Program and Supreme Court Decisionmaking.* Princeton, N.J.: Princeton University Press.

Legal Services Corporation v. Velazquez, 531 U.S. 532 (2001)

Main, Thomas. 1983. "The Homeless of New York." *The Public Interest* 72(Summer): 3-28.

Mathews v. Eldridge, 425 U.S. 319 (1976)

Mashaw, Jerry L. 1983. *Bureaucratic Justice: Managing Social Security Disability Claims.* New Haven, Conn.: Yale University Press.

Mead, Lawrence. 2004. *Government Matters: Welfare Reform in Wisconsin.* Princeton, N.J.: Princeton University Press.

Mental Health Association of Minnesota v. Schweiker, 554 F.Supp. 157 (D.Minn., 1982)

Melnick, R. Shep. 1993. *Between the Lines: Interpreting Welfare Rights.* Washington: Brookings Institution Press.

———. 1995. "Separation of Powers and the Strategy of Rights." In *The New Politics of Public Policy*, edited by Marc Landy and Martin Levin. Baltimore, Md.: Johns Hopkins University Press

———. 2005a. "Deregulating the States: The Political Jurisprudence of the Rehnquist Court." In *Institutions and Public Law: Comparative Approaches*, edited by Tom Ginsburg and Robert Kagan. New York: Peter Lang.

———. 2005b. "From Tax and Spend to Mandate and Sue: Liberalism After the Great Society." In *The Great Society and the High Tide of Liberalism*, edited by Sidney Milkis and Jerome Mileur. Amherst, Mass.: University of Massachusetts Press.

Miller v. Youakim, 440 U.S. 125 (1979)

Moynihan, Daniel Patrick. 1969. *Maximum Feasible Misunderstanding: Community Action in the War on Poverty.* New York: Free Press.

Nathan, Richard. 2005. "Federalism and Health Policy." *Health Affairs* 24(6): 1458-66.

Norman v. Johnson, 739 F.Supp. 1182 (ND Ill., 1990)

Pollack, Ronald. 1969. "Legal Services and the Fight against Hunger." *Clearinghouse Review* 3: 38.

Rabin, Robert. 1970. "Implementation of the Cost of Living Adjustment for AFDC Recipients: A Case in Welfare Administration." *University of Pennsylvania Law Review* 118: 1143.

Roisman, Florence Wagman. 2005. "How Litigation Can Lead to Substantial Relief for Clients and Significant Social Change." *Clearinghouse Review* March–April: 759–67.

Rosado v. Wyman, 397 U.S. 397 (1970)

Rosenberg, Gerald. 1991. *The Hollow Hope: Can Courts Bring About Social Change?* Chicago, Ill.: University of Chicago Press.

Sandler, Ross and David Schoenbrod. 2003. *Democracy by Decree: What Happens When Courts Run Government.* New Haven, Conn.: Yale University Press.

Schattschneider, E. E. 1935. *Politics, Pressure, and the Tariff.* New York: Prentice-Hall.

Shapiro v. Thompson, 394 U.S. 618 (1969)

Smith, Gary F., and Susan Ann Silverstein. 2004. "Preparing For Litigation." *Clearinghouse Review* (May–June): 27-48.

Sunstein, Cass R. 2004. *The Second Bill of Rights: FDR's Unfinished Revolution and Why We Need It More than Ever.* New York: Basic Books.

Townsend v. Swank, 404 U.S. 282 (1971)

U.S. Congress, House Ways and Means Committee. 2000. *2000 Green Book.* Washington: Government Printing Office.

———. 2004. *2004 Green Book.* Washington: Government Printing Office. Accessed at http://waysandmeans.house.gov/ Documents.asp?section=813.

U.S. Congress, Senate Finance Committee. 1972. *Social Security Amendments of 1972.* Senate Report 92-1230, 92nd Cong., 2nd sess. Washington: Government Printing Office.

Weaver, R. Kent. 2000. *Ending Welfare As We Know It.* Washington: Brookings Institution Press.
Wildavsky, Aaron. 1988. *New Politics of the Budgetary Process.* Glenview, Ill.: Scott, Foresman.
Wood, Robert. 1990. *Remedial Law: When Courts Become Administrators.* Amherst, Mass.: University of Massachusetts Press.
Zebley v. Sullivan, 493 U.S. 521 (1990)

Part III

Elite Efforts to Reshape the
Political Landscape

Lawrence R. Jacobs

Chapter 4

The Implementation and Evolution of Medicare: The Distributional Effects of "Positive" Policy Feedbacks

In the early 1950s, a small group of stalwart reformers concluded that the failure to establish universal access to health insurance under Franklin Roosevelt and Harry Truman required a change in strategy. Passing universal health insurance in one fell swoop was unlikely to succeed, they reasoned, because of the public's general philosophical uneasiness with "big government" and the mismatch in organized pressure in Congress—the constitutional process created numerous opportunities for delay and obstruction by well-organized narrow interests such as the American Medical Association (AMA) that intensely opposed health reform while reform advocates lacked encompassing organizations to represent and garner the support of the diffuse public that would benefit from national health insurance (Poen 1979; Jacobs 1993).

Instead of achieving universal access in a single legislative moment, reformers opted in the early 1950s for an incremental strategy that would take a series of gradual steps over time to extend health insurance to all Americans—a form of "salami slicing" (as one reformer put it)—and to build public and elite confidence in national government administrative capacity to operate the program.[1] The starting point would be establishing hospital insurance for Social Security beneficiaries—what later became known as "Medicare." This approach—"Medicare incrementalism"—identified a popular and narrow set of recipients (seniors) and health services (hospital care), built on an existing government program that Americans strongly supported and was not tarnished as "big government" (Social Security), and rallied a relatively well-organized group of advocates that intensely supported government health insurance (Social Security beneficiaries).

Following Medicare's passage, reformers stuck to their strategy of incrementally expanding the pool of those eligible for the program. From 1965 through 1968, officials in the Johnson White House and in the Department of Health, Education, and Welfare (DHEW) formulated and advocated an expansion of Medicare to include new segments of the population, children, and additional health services to meet the new demand. By 2004, however, national health reform advocates no longer concentrated on using Medicare as a platform for reaching universal coverage: major reform efforts focused on expanding benefits to existing population groups and avoided Medicare as the foundation for expanding access.

The incremental strategy that gave rise to Medicare has had decidedly mixed results. On the one hand, Medicare is a programmatic success for its beneficiaries. The rights and treatment of its beneficiaries are universal (trumping the selectivity that characterizes much of the American welfare state), its coverage of medical care has steadily expanded (most recently with the passage of a new drug benefit in 2003), and its basic operating structure has been largely stable. Attempts to restructure Medicare continue, but its durability as a cornerstone of the American welfare state and as a mechanism for redistributing money and government authority to its target population is significant.

On the other hand, the prospective strategy of using Medicare to ignite a steady march to achieving national health insurance for all Americans has failed in big and small ways. The proposals during the Johnson administration to expand the program's beneficiaries to include children failed. Instead, health insurance for children was distanced from Medicare when it was introduced three decades later: it was established as a voluntary program run by states as part of its public assistance system rather than run by Medicare as part of a national social insurance system. In addition, proposals to incrementally expand Medicare (the principal objective of reformers in the 1950s) failed to receive sustained attention from authoritative government officials during America's episodic efforts at comprehensive health reform. During the 1993 and 1994 debate over comprehensive health-care reform, the Clinton administration and Congress rejected the proposal of several leaders in the House of Representatives to use Medicare as a foundation for reform. The failure of Medicare to serve as the launching pad for expanding access to health insurance in the early 1990s illustrates both the contemporary neglect (until quite recently) of Medicare's original strategy for incrementally expanding eligibility and the significance of strategic choices by reformers. Contrary to the expectations of its original designers, Medicare has become targeted at a discrete segment of the population, which receives ever more funding and services (epitomized by the new pharmaceutical benefit) even as the number of Americans who lack health insurance rises.[2]

This chapter has two purposes. The first is to explain a stillborn strategy for expanding access to health insurance—the initial steps to steadily expand Medicare's eligibility in the mid-1960s and its abandonment by authoritative government reformers in the early 1990s. The failure of access-expanding Medicare incrementalism has important implications for economic inequality and disparities in health in the United States. In other advanced industrialized countries, universal access to health insurance both removes a drain on the economic resources of families and provides medical care that is essential for treating serious illness and prolonging life. In the United States, 45.8 million people were uninsured in 2004 (an increase of 2 million from 2003); 74.7 million Americans under sixty-five were without health insurance for all or part of 2001 and 2002 (DeNavas-Walt, Proctor, and Mills 2004; Mills and Bhandari 2003). One impact of this extraordinary gap in health insurance is that Americans shoulder a financial burden unparalleled among advanced industrialized countries in personally paying the costs of premiums, uncovered medical services, and deductibles and co-payments (Anderson et al. 2005).

Gaps in insurance coverage also contribute to the comparatively wide disparity in longevity between higher and lower income groups and the frequency of acute illness in the United States. Essential medical services—from diagnostic procedures (prostate screenings, mammograms, and pap smears) to vaccinations, dentistry, and treatment for asthma and other medical conditions—that save lives and improve well-being are very unevenly available in the United States. Americans with good health insurance receive immediate treatment or hospital beds, but those without insurance are given care less frequently, receive treatment only in the later stages of illness, or are given temporary treatments in emergency rooms and then released. Untreated or delayed treatment of asthma, for instance, leads to premature death. A recent report by the Institute of Medicine blames gaps in insurance coverage for seventeen thousand preventable deaths a year (Smedley, Stith, and Nelson 2003; Morone and Jacobs 2005, introduction and chapter 1).

Given the profound implications for health and economic well-being, the failure to develop government policy to achieve universal—or even just wider—access to health insurance is a significant factor in generating inequality in the United States. This chapter explains a critical reason for this failure, focusing on the unfulfilled plans of Medicare's original reformers to incrementally build universal access to health insurance.

The second purpose of this chapter is to use the implementation and evolution of Medicare to extend research on policy feedbacks—ways in which policies affect politics—by introducing a methodological innovation and highlighting the importance of incorporating agency into structural accounts. Previous research tends to infer the evolutional paths of institutions from their observed development—namely, their continuation or discontinuation. The Medicare case and, specifically, the planning of its early reformers identify a wider set of possible directions of program evolution (i.e., variation on the dependent variable is increased). Studying the prospective feedback expectations of Medicare's original reformers illustrates a methodological opportunity for strengthening the explanatory power of policy feedback analysis. In addition, the Medicare case demonstrates the analytic importance of studying agency and, specifically, elite mobilization strategies in the context of the structural constraints of existing government institutions. In short, this paper contributes to explaining the distributional consequences of policy feedbacks by accounting for the stunted development of government health insurance and by contributing to new approaches to policy analysis.

The next section considers current research on policy feedbacks and the utility of incorporating agency and reformers' prospective expectations regarding institutional evolution. The second section examines the Johnson administration's implementation of Medicare in 1965 and 1966 and initial proposals during the second half of the 1960s to expand the program along the lines suggested by the original Medicare reformers. Although a large literature examines Medicare's legislative passage (see review in Marmor 2000) and evolution (Oberlander 2003), little attention has been devoted to the critical policy design decisions made during the second half of the 1960s to foster the expansion of Medicare's eligibility and to the implicit theory of policy feedbacks in the work of Medicare's reformers. The third section considers the strategic choices of President Clinton and his senior advisers in 1993 and 1994, which undermined the strategy of Medicare incrementalism that was proposed by several congressional leaders and that Clinton himself tried to return to in his second term.

PATHS OF INSTITUTIONAL DEVELOPMENT, AGENCY, AND POLICY FEEDBACKS

An important focus of research on policy feedbacks has been institutional survival—the evolution of institutions along a continuum from durability to termination. This analysis has tended to focus on "positive" policy effects ("self-reinforcing" cycles that reproduce and expand initial institutional developments due to the persistent support of beneficiaries and government officials) or "negative" policy effects (political opposition that scales back or terminates existing institutions) (Pierson 2000, but see Hacker 2004). Karen Orren and Stephen Skowronek (2002, 745), for instance, characterize policy feedbacks as either "reinforcing" or "threatening" established institutions. Theda Skocpol (1992) suggests that the corrupt administration of Civil War pensions undermined confidence in the government's competence and generated opposition to extending the benefits into a universal noncontributory pension program. Analysis of the impacts of Social Security and Aid to Families with Dependent Children on public opinion and political behavior helps to explain why the former endured whereas the latter did not (Soss 1999; Campbell 2003).

Discovering New Paths of Potential Institutional Evolution

Most analysis of policy feedbacks focus on a fairly narrow set of institutional paths, which are inferred from the continuation or discontinuation of actual government programs. Research on policy feedbacks can be strengthened, though, by broadening the analytic focus from a narrow set of currently observable paths to institutional developments that were expected by initial reformers but did not materialize.

Studying the expectations of institutional entrepreneurs offers an important methodological tool for identifying previously unrealized paths of potential institutional change that were conceivable and in fact anticipated by policy entrepreneurs but did not occur and therefore are not readily observable to contemporary analysts. This approach to expanding the set of institutional paths under investigation has the effect of increasing the variation of the dependent variable, which makes it possible to sharpen the explanatory power of policy feedback analysis by accounting for nondevelopments. In addition, widening policy feedback analysis to incorporate developmental paths that were initially conceivable but did not occur also reveals the contingent nature of institutional evolution and the impact of agency. This approach counters the tendency to "read back" into historical developments an interpretation that the fate of institutions to survive or die off is preordained by their beginnings and their initial structure.

In the case of Medicare, its institutional evolution developed in two distinct directions. The first trajectory was started in the early 1950s by Medicare's initiators, who expected that a program for the retired would generate political support over time for incrementally expanding coverage to new client groups until universal access was achieved. Officials in the Johnson administration continued to pursue this eligibility-expanding strategy after Medicare's passage by pursuing two approaches: first, establishing among elites and the general public who harbored unease about bureaucracy a perception of the government's competence to manage Medicare; second, empowering the recipients of Medicare by instilling a favorable identity of themselves as a group and by increasing their resources to participate in the program and its development. The Clinton White House pursued a different direction in 1993 and 1994, one that repudiated the original "Medicare strategy" as a "big government" approach in favor of a new hybrid of "managed competition" among private health plans (Hacker 1997). Although some Democratic leaders in the House of Representatives attempted to resuscitate the Medicare approach as Clinton's plan headed for defeat, they were unable to overcome the opposition of the White House and others and place it on the agenda for sustained attention.

Studying the real and anticipated paths of Medicare's development raises a series of questions for policy feedback analysis. How did the Johnson administration attempt to pursue access-expanding Medicare incrementalism? More to the point, why did the Clinton White House fail to pursue Medicare incrementalism in the early 1990s? Did the failure of Medicare to expand incrementally reflect a flawed calculation by Medicare's initial reformers that underestimated the structural constraints facing the program? Alternately, did the Clinton White House miscalculate?

Elite Mobilization Strategies and Policy Feedbacks

Paul Pierson (1993) persuasively argues for strengthening policy feedback research by replacing the general question "Do policies produce politics?" with "more precise questions about how policies matter and under what conditions" (627). Pierson's analysis cogently points to two effects of major policies. The first concerns resources and incentives: significant government programs both equip individuals and groups with material resources and access to the authority that promotes (or retards) politically meaningful actions and establishes strong incentives that induce individuals to make particular choices (Pierson 1993, 597–610).

The second policy effect Pierson identifies concerns the interpretations of elites and, especially, the mass public that guide their actual behavior. Calling for a "significant reevaluation of the psychological foundations of individual choice," Pierson (1993, 627–28) suggests that "some of . . . [the] most important effects [of policies] may be cognitive" and involve the "efforts of individuals to interpret the social world." In particular, he appears to propose a "memory-based" cognitive process: established policies transmit information and promote "learning," which in turn is stored by individuals as "knowledge" and accessed by them to "make sense of their environment" (Pierson 1993, 611–24). Suzanne Mettler and Joe Soss (2004, 61) link this policy-generated interpretative process to the definition of group membership: "Public policy defines the boundaries of political community, establishing who is included in the membership" and how they are perceived. For instance, eligibility rules that rely on means tests convey messages about the beneficiary group as deviant and "undeserving," whereas eligibility rules tied to payroll contributions signify "earned" rights, "deservedness," and "dignity."

Jacob Hacker's (2002) analytic framework suggests a structural account that rests on the resource and interpretative effects of "inherited legacies" of established policies. The early establishment of Social Security and employer-based health insurance generated, according to Hacker, systemic predispositions and political coalitions that tend to reproduce each of these core arrangements while channeling, halting, and limiting what government can do on health insurance and what the private sector is likely to achieve on old-age pensions. The implication for health insurance is that private social benefits have induced a structural dependence on and comfort with private-sector plans among employers and employees and an unease with (if not outright opposition to) the disruptions of government intervention. The 1965 Medicare legislation succeeded because its limited focus on seniors worked around (rather than trying to radically supplant) the social interpretation of employer-based private health insurance as desirable without provoking the defenders of this system to mobilize their formidable resources in its defense.

Policy feedback research by Pierson (1993, 2000), Hacker (2002), and others highlight the structural constraints on institutional development and corrects for the lopsided emphasis on material resources by incorporating the interpretative effects of policy. Extending this contribution requires further development of the concepts of information processing and institutionally nested agency. The next two sections expand these concepts.

Information Processing and Motivated Behavior   Research on policy effects can be strengthened by developing a more explicit model for how individual agents (both elites and ordinary citizens) process information and reach judgments. Research in a variety of fields of psychology demonstrates that most individuals neither store facts in memory nor draw on them when forming interpretations and evaluations. Instead, individuals rely on the cognitively less-taxing process of reaching judgments "on line." Individuals commonly engage in on-line reasoning by integrating new information into a "running tally" of current impressions of, for instance, a political party or a government program (Hastie and Park 1986; Lodge and McGraw 1995; Lodge, McGraw, and Stroh 1989, 1990; Lodge and Stroh 1993; McConnell, Sherman, and Hamilton 1994).

Cognitive processes interact with the intense motivations of authoritative government officials engaged in struggles for institutional position and political power (Fiske 1993; Greenstein 1969). Rather than passively observing this process, authoritative officials have strong incentives to shape on-line information processing by members of the mass public.

Motivated on-line information processing has two implications for analyses of policy feedback effects and the history of Medicare incrementalism. First, although reformers and far-sighted administrators may have long-term strategies, elected officials and their aides are likely to be guided by their intense electoral concerns and by their own on-line processing of information to focus on early-order rather than the delayed-feedback effects essential to institutional development. In particular, the strategic decisions of government officials about detailed program design and implementation put a high premium on the immediate costs of defying the intense demands of political opponents and prompt them to discount the delayed benefits tied to longer-term institutional developments that generate interpretations and resources for expansion.

The implication for Medicare was apparent in the program's formulation during the presidencies of John Kennedy and Lyndon Johnson, when antistatist criticisms primed them to focus on the immediate political costs of centralized budgetary control and to reject the administrative gains of "direct federal administration," which was recommended by officials in the Department of Health, Education, and Welfare (Jacobs 1993). Minimizing short-term political costs by rejecting centralized budgetary control led to rapid cost escalation within a decade, which undermined Medicare reformers' original long-term goal of establishing a publicly credible national administrative capacity for managing government health insurance.

Second, the struggle for political power and institutional position motivates political elites to augment the public's informational resources and to dominate the public's on-line thinking and its interpretation of new government programs. Rather than passively leaving this process to structural dynamics, political elites have strong incentives to develop and use governmental capacities to communicate with the public and to influence the volume and specific content of the information that reaches citizens. In the Medicare case, Johnson administration officials in the White House and in DHEW developed a federated communications capacity at the local, state, and national levels both to build a sense among potential beneficiaries that they were part of a cohesive and efficacious group (the "Medicare beneficiaries") and to mobilize them as a group to sustain and expand the program in the future.

Agency and Structure   Even as established policies and embedded structures constrain future policy options and generate structural predispositions, human agency and, specifically, the calculated strategies of political elites and interest groups can be significant. Agency can be a factor in accurately identifying the opportunities and constraints of existing structures, formulating policies that exploit these conditions, and giving rhetorical expression to policy proposals. For instance, presidents are institutionally and politically constrained but their unrivaled public stature gives them extraordinary personal latitude in setting policy agendas and in framing policy debates by how they express themselves and publicly present their policies (Greenstein 1969).

The Medicare case illustrates the role of both agency and structure. The established structure of the existing private, employer-based system created durable constraints against a direct, explicit, and immediate reorganization that substantially expanded government responsibility for the financing and delivery of medical care (Hacker 2002). Bill

Clinton and other reformers failed to appreciate the stubbornness of these constraints; instead, they publicly stressed the value of private-sector arrangements and minimized and denigrated the need for government intervention. The result was that he contributed to the efforts of reform opponents to prime the on-line processing of Americans to focus on the threat of government and to preclude the consideration of Medicare incrementalism—a direction favored by leaders in the House in 1994 and by Clinton himself during his second term.

We now examine several selected aspects of Medicare's complicated history to explore potential avenues for expanding access to health insurance as well as broader themes related to policy feedback analyses (for detailed discussions of Medicare's history, see Oberlander 2003; Jacobs 1993, 2007; Marmor 2000). We begin by considering aspects of Medicare's history during its original implementation in the second half of the 1960s and then turn to the debate over health reform during the early 1990s.

IMPLEMENTING MEDICARE: BUILDING ADMINISTRATIVE CAPACITY AND INITIATING EXPANSIVE POLICY FEEDBACKS

As Medicare moved toward law in 1965, the Johnson White House and, especially, officials in DHEW were convinced that a smooth implementation of the new program would yield political points for Johnson and other Democrats in future elections. One senior White House official predicted to Johnson that the "simple and efficient administrative system" that DHEW was developing "will redound to the credit of this administration."[3] To drive the point home to Americans, DHEW officials boasted of the labor savings gained by their advanced computer system and the President publicly proclaimed, "Never before, except in mobilizing for war, has any government made such extensive preparations for any undertaking as we have made in connection with Medicare."[4]

Civil servants in the Bureau of the Budget and DHEW made a strong and persistent recommendation to the Kennedy and Johnson White Houses: centralized budgetary control over Medicare offered the most effective long-term administrative structure for the program. Specifically, they recommended to Presidents Kennedy and Johnson that Medicare establish "direct federal administration" over the disbursement and use of Medicare's funds to control the quality of care and prevent waste and unreasonable costs (Jacobs 1993, chapters 5 and 7).

Although administration officials appreciated the political stakes in effective implementation, their primary attention was focused on defusing the intense opposition of medical providers to "big government" and the potential receptivity of Americans to their antistate charges. The intense protests of a concentrated and organized set of opponents led the Kennedy and Johnson White Houses and their allies in Congress to reject the advice of DHEW officials to pursue the beneficial but diffuse and delayed effects of centralized budgetary control. Instead, they used private intermediaries like Blue Cross, Blue Shield, and private insurance companies in order to deflect the immediate charges of "big government" interference in the "free choice" of patients and the decisions of doctors (Jacobs 1993, chapters 5 and 7).

The short-term orientation of administration officials had two implications—the significance of which would grow over time: it enormously complicated implementation in 1965 and 1966 and it hobbled the program's financial management in ways that would diminish elite and public confidence in the program's administration. During the year after Johnson signed Medicare into law in July 1965, the administration and DHEW launched an extraordinary campaign to implement Medicare—a challenge that was made significantly more difficult by the structural limitation imposed by the outsourcing of financial oversight.

Medicare's implementers did face a number of challenges that were typical for launches of major new programs (for example, recruiting, training, and organizing new personnel and certifying providers for quality). But DHEW's job of administering Medicare was complicated by its indirect, mediated relationships with health-care providers. Rather than directly administering the process of reimbursing health-care providers, officials in DHEW were forced to work one step removed, negotiating contracts with the intermediaries who were then expected to serve as frugal and responsible spenders of public funds. Relying on these go-betweens to handle the claims from providers required, DHEW officials acknowledged, "very extensive contacts and negotiations" to identify their role and obligations.[5] Working through an army of intermediaries to keep track of the bills and reimbursements of thousands of medical providers literally defied human capacity; it required state-of-the-art computer processing and optical scanning technology.

Despite the heroism of DHEW and the breakthroughs in information technology to implement Medicare, the initial decisions to reject centralized budgetary authority in response to the intense demands of reform opponents opened the door to rapid cost escalation. Critics of Medicare attributed the cost hikes to bureaucratic waste and inefficiency even though much of the problem resulted from third-party reimbursement. (Ironically, it was Ronald Reagan—a prominent opponent of the Medicare legislation in the 1960s—who resuscitated centralized budgetary authority in the 1980s.) The effect was to complicate and hinder the goal of Medicare's original reformers to use the program's "first step" to build public and elite confidence in the government's national administrative capacity to manage government health insurance.

Federated Communications and the Forming of Public Interpretations

Policy feedbacks—as current research suggests—generate structural predispositions, but political actors rarely (if ever) passively defer to structure. Government officials engaged in struggles for political power and institutional position have strong motivations to attempt to influence the public's on-line processing by shaping the information it receives about new programs (Jacobs and Shapiro 1994, 2000; Druckman, Jacobs, and Ostermeier 2004).

The Johnson administration's strategy in 1965 and 1966 for implementing Medicare rested in important respects on launching a public communications barrage that was expected to give Johnson immediate political credit for Medicare's passage and to build future support by signing up nearly every eligible American. Johnson instructed the secretary of DHEW that he would "not be satisfied so long as anyone who is qualified for this program fails to enroll because he did not learn in time."[6] The administration did succeed in pushing enrollment, which rose to over 90 percent by its first day of operation, an accomplishment that the White House publicly heralded as a vivid demonstration of support for Medicare and the president.[7]

To improve the administration's public communications, Johnson's aides instructed DHEW officials to strengthen their capacity to fulfill their "obligation to inform the public . . . of its great new programs" and to give Johnson "nourishment to sustain his capacity to build support for these programs."[8] The department responded with an "extensive reorganization of . . . [its] public information activities" and the department secretary declared "the job of informing people" and shaping press coverage (especially television's) to be "one of our most important jobs."[9]

The White House and DHEW developed a federated communications capacity at the local, state, and national levels to use the mass media and to make personal direct contact and recontact with individuals who were eligible for Medicare.[10] At the national level, they staged events for Johnson that would saturate national news coverage and prepared broadcast and print advertising blitzes. They also identified hundreds of thousands of people by using income tax returns from the IRS, the rolls of the Welfare Administration, and televised public service announcements by well-known personalities.[11]

In an important innovation to "pu[t] Medicare into effect," officials linked these national efforts with state and local campaigns to shape the perceptions of the new Medicare program. Part of DHEW's "tooling up" involved adding one hundred new Social Security district offices in order to "reach local communities" and (Johnson was informed) to "significantly . . . make it easier for people to get information about the new program."[12]

Administration officials concentrated their institutional capacity to "make an imprint upon the public mind" on dominating the acquisition and processing of information by two groups of Americans—the broad diffuse public and a narrower segment of harder-to-reach citizens.[13] To reach diffuse national, state, and local audiences, the administration launched "extensive public information activities in Washington and more than six hundred Social Security district offices using briefings, news releases, [and] television spots."[14]

In addition, administration officials organized national, state, and even local collaborations to reach populations whose income level or language singled them out as unlikely to receive or understand government information. For instance, DHEW funded nearly five hundred community action programs associated with the Office of Economic Opportunity to organize community meetings and to make direct face-to-face contact with eligible citizens. The purpose of these efforts was to "reach uneducated, foreign-language groups, and minority group members" and to put information about Medicare into their hands.[15] DHEW also recruited the Agriculture Department to use its state and local employees to organize community meetings that explained Medicare, to arrange for private transportation of the elderly to these meetings, and to provide information to seniors not able to attend meetings.[16] In effect, the administration used its federated communications apparatus to subsidize the cost of learning about the program's "most important facts."

Motivated politicians and civil servants developed and used a federated communications capacity to dominate on-line processing by Americans and Medicare's potential beneficiaries in order to achieve two interpretative aims: to isolate the program's most vociferous opponents and to instill a positive identity for the program and mobilize energetic support for it.

The Making of "Medicare Beneficiaries"   According to the initial logic of Medicare's founders, the most effective route to universal access was to create intense backing for a seniors-oriented program among its beneficiaries and the general public and then to rely on the positive feedback effects of the program to expand its eligibility to new population groups. The Johnson White House and DHEW officials treated the implementation of

Medicare as an opportunity to initiate this process. In particular, they used the government's federated communications system to craft and widely distribute information to Americans that would define Medicare's beneficiaries as a positively constructed group and jump-start what they expected to be an ongoing process of routinely cultivating values and participatory behaviors that rallied disparate individuals in support of Medicare's expansion.

The administration's federated communication apparatus was used to distribute information that primed the public to focus on the problems of seniors as genuine and to view them as "deserving" of assistance. The secretary of DHEW explained that public communications was directed at "inform[ing] the public about the problems of the elderly and to show that they are shared by all age groups."[17] He calculated that the problems of seniors would be highlighted and brought to the forefront of the public's mind by urging Americans to "look over community programs for the aged, to support them where they exist, and to help start them where they are needed."[18]

Medicare's public information crusade was also designed to initiate a particular interpretation of Medicare as establishing "rights and responsibilities." Administration officials distributed information that highlighted the "rights" of the program's clients and their group identity. Their public messages were fashioned, according to archival records, to "effectively inform all persons over sixty-five of their *rights* under Medicare" (emphasis added).[19]

The very term "Medicare" was calibrated to project a particular interpretation of the program. The Social Security Administration (SSA) initially resisted the term "Medicare" out of concern that it inaccurately described a broader range of medical services than was included. In the face of pressure from other officials, SSA relented and conceded that "most people were familiar with this term from media coverage and might not understand the more "correct" title in the law."[20] "Medicare" became a socially useful concept for instilling group identity and a positive interpretation of the program.

The Unmaking of the AMA and Segregationists   The administration's use of its federated communications apparatus to shape the public's interpretations was directed not only at cultivating positive perceptions of Medicare beneficiaries but also at undermining the opponents of Medicare's implementation—the threat of the American Medical Association to lead a strike of doctors and the opposition of southern segregationists to racially integrating medical facilities, which were required by title VI of the 1964 Civil Rights Act.

To defuse the opposition to Medicare's implementation, the administration relied on its federated communications capacity to launch a two-prong attack. On the one hand, it publicly projected great confidence that Medicare's start on July 1, 1966, was assured, private reservations notwithstanding. The administration used its hundreds of federated offices to "make the broadest possible presentation to the American public of our state of readiness to carry out [Medicare]."[21] At the national level, Johnson's statements and a series of DHEW press releases highlighted the "steps taken to put the Medicare program into effect on July 1st" in order to encourage the perception of inevitability.[22] Johnson urged "local groups [to] abandon any opposition they have had to Medicare," predicting that "within a very short time Medicare will be as accepted . . . as the Social Security program." To drive home the expectation that Medicare's start was certain, Johnson asked his cabinet members to "spea[k] out publicly in explanation of the fine job of organization that [D]HEW has done."[23] As July 1 approached, Johnson matter-of-factly informed the leaders of the medical profession and hospitals that the largest domestic health reform in the nation's history was starting "15 days from now."[24] Meanwhile, DHEW's state and local offices issued regular press releases on the number of organizations and medical personnel who had agreed to work for Medicare to provide care, serve as contractors, and assume other responsibilities.[25]

On the other hand, Johnson and his aides also developed distinctive strategies to undermine the AMA and segregationists. Their strategy for quelling the AMA's opposition publicly played on the medical profession's cherished reputation among its patients. In the year between Johnson's signing ceremony and the program's start on July 1, 1966, the White House staged a series of highly visible "on the record" meetings between Johnson and the AMA to firmly establish the public expectation (as the president put it) that "the hospitals and medical profession will cooperate fully in making Medicare a success."[26] These public meetings were calculated by White House officials to "take the initiative in making clear to them that . . . it is time to work together to make the new act work" and to let "the public . . . know that you are making this effort."[27] Although the administration was confident that "opposition among doctors will be dispelled,"[28] it kept open the nuclear weapon of public pressure—"a direct television appeal [by the President] to the Doctors . . . [that] appeal[ed] to their wise restraint to insure its success."[29] The message to doctors was clear: failure by the medical profession to cooperate would be punished by their public vilification as violating the public's trust to serve a vulnerable population and to "begin the greatest contribution to the older citizens."[30]

The administration's highly public campaign against doctors contrasts with its more private approach on race to isolate segregationists without antagonizing racial tensions (see Quadagno 2000). With senior White House and departmental officials holding regular confidential meetings to monitor compliance, Johnson encouraged low-visibility envoys of administration officials (including three hundred DHEW staff), a southern governor and southern members of Congress, the American Hospital Association, and Blue Cross to "wor[k] extensively" to urge individual hospitals to desegregate their facilities.[31] He instructed Vice President Hubert Humphrey to "get in touch with the mayors in communities [where hospitals were not in compliance and] to take a strong line with the mayors, pointing out the dire consequences of failing to be ready for Medicare by July 1st." Humphrey reported back to the White House that the "mayors have been uniformly appreciative of his efforts and are ready to cooperate."[32] As the July 1 launch approached, Johnson met behind closed doors with the administration's most senior officials to plan for the use of medical facilities run by the Defense Department, the Veterans Administration, and other agencies to compensate for significant refusal to desegregate—a possibility that was averted.[33]

In short, implementing Medicare offered an opportunity—one that the Johnson administration seized—to inculcate an interpretation of Medicare as establishing a new set of rights, the right to health insurance, and as forming a new group that was deserving and worthy of the program's benefits. The administration's implementation of Medicare also rested on managing public perceptions to marginalize and deter the program's most determined opponents.

WHAT HAPPENED TO MEDICARE FOR ALL?

In the months after Medicare's passage, the original reform strategy of using the program as a departure point for incrementally moving toward universal health insurance appeared to work. By the time of Bill Clinton's reform effort in the early 1990s, however, it was no longer receiving serious and sustained attention among authoritative government officials, including the president.

The development of the private health insurance system and the operation of Medicare created structural pressures that diminished the probability of successfully introducing in one stroke significant new government control over both the financing and delivery of health care (Hacker 2002). Structural predispositions affect the probabilities of power but do not mechanically dictate how authoritative government officials respond to the circumstances facing them (Greenstein 1969). The essence of strategic choice is navigating the rocky shoals of the firm structural coastline to find inlets of opportunity. Decisions by authoritative government officials to set policymaking agendas and to frame policy options can exploit or bypass the opportunities created by inherited policy and political legacies. Medicare's history in the mid-1960s and early 1990s illustrate the interaction of structure and agency.

The "Second Great Society:" Johnson's Plans to Expand Medicare

Following Medicare's passage in 1965, political ambition and the structural dynamics of the program's operations combined to keep the incremental expansion of Medicare eligibility and health-care services on the agenda during the second half of the 1960s. By widening the access of seniors and the indigent, the establishment Medicare immediately contributed (as DHEW explained) to a "shift from a concern with discrete and independent issues with health affairs to the entire continuum of the health enterprise," including what became seen as the growing problem of inadequate supplies of medical professionals and facilities.[34] The White House and a task force it established on health care reported that Medicare had "added to the present demands for services" and created the "problem [of] . . . insur[ing] adequate hospital services in a nation already feeling the pinch of inadequate facilities."[35]

Medicare's launch also created a beachhead for proposing expansions in eligibility, which Johnson and his allies seized on to appeal to the program's supporters and to hold together an increasingly fractured coalition from the New Deal (Matusow 1984). Shortly after Johnson signed Medicare into law in 1965, officials in the White House and DHEW started to "plan our next steps toward the Great Society" and the "second stage of the War on Poverty," which could be promoted during the 1968 presidential campaign and enacted during the second term of a Johnson presidency. After 1965, when Vietnam increasingly frayed Democratic loyalties to Johnson, White House allies viewed continued domestic reform as necessary to fend off the "feeling of a diminishing of the Great Society goals because of Vietnam" and the widespread "stories that the Great Society is being drastically cut back to accommodate the war budget."[36] The head of the Council of Economic Advisers, Walter Heller, recommended to Johnson that even with the rising costs of Vietnam he should continue to invest in sustaining the Great Society because it "spell[ed] the difference . . . between political affection and disaffection of key groups."[37]

The broad political pressures on the Johnson White House created incentives to single out Medicare as an opportunity to dramatically "emphasize . . . the more hopeful dimensions of America's face today" and offset the "danger of [Johnson] presenting a one-dimensional appearance to the public [as] . . . the wartime leader in a war which frustrates and disturbs people."[38]

The confident expectation of senior officials in the Johnson administration was that Medicare's launch created "new opportunities to effectively make quality medical care available to all Americans."[39] To continue along the path of gradually expanding eligibility, Johnson administration officials proposed incremental steps to "[b]roade[n] Medicare to include additional beneficiaries—disabled workers, children of the disabled or deceased workers, mothers of sick children." The objective was to "extend medical insurance under Social Security" in order to "enable every child to have the medical care he needs to develop his capabilities" and to ensure that "no child is handicapped by the lack of proper medical care in reaching the fullest development of his talents." Unlike Medicaid and the State Child Health Insurance Program, which was developed two or three decades later, the Johnson administration designed a "Medicare program for the children" to rely on the "standards [of] . . . health rather than welfare considerations."

After Johnson withdrew from the 1968 campaign and Vice President Humphrey stepped in, White House aides prepared proposals to expand Medicare to equip the Democratic nominee to "heighten the contrast between Nixon's vague promises and your concrete proposals for dealing with America's most urgent problems."[40] If Humphrey had won the closely fought 1968 presidential election, he would have come into office with a proposal sitting on his desk to launch "Kiddicare"—the first major expansion of Medicare's eligibility.[41]

The Demise of the Medicare Incrementalism

In 1968, political motivations and the structural dynamics of Medicare's operations fueled a process of planning for the incremental expansion of Medicare eligibility that the program's original reformers anticipated. By the early 1990s, however, the expansion of Medicare's eligibility remained an option, but Bill Clinton as a candidate and president avoided and, indeed, initially opposed it. The private health insurance system and the development of Medicare created a structurally ambivalent situation for politicians who considered using Medicare as a platform for comprehensive health reform. On the one hand, there was strong and intense opposition to Medicare's expansion that resulted from enduring philosophical conservativism, alarm about the program's current and projected budgetary costs, and the protests of the program's well-organized stakeholders. On the other hand, Americans' pragmatic view of Medicare as providing concrete assistance to a deserving and needy group fueled strong support for the program and for incrementally expanding it. President Clinton's decisions in 1994 to rigidly insist on immediately achieving universal coverage and on hewing to his idiosyncratic approach to reform missed an opportunity to widen Medicare's eligibility to new population groups—a misstep that the president would implicitly acknowledge when he returned to it later in his presidency after Democrats had lost control of Congress. Even if Medicare expansion could not have been passed in 1994, Clinton's decisions squandered the unrivaled power of the president to set the policymaking agenda and frame policy choices into the future.

Clinton's "Third Way" and the Medicare "Second Way"   As a candidate and then president, Bill Clinton partially rested his claim to be a "New Democrat" on his efforts to combine government and markets to produce an innovative "third way" to reform the health-care system. The plan he outlined during the campaign and then formulated during his first year in office proposed to establish "managed competition within a budget" by relying on conservative means (private markets) to achieve liberal ends (universal health insurance coverage). Clinton and his aides believed that this approach made sense both substantively (it would produce enough savings to finance universal coverage and avoid stifling bureaucracy) and politically (its embrace of private markets would shield it from damaging charges of "big government" that had repeatedly torpedoed past efforts to achieve national health insurance). Given his New Democrat commitments, Clinton and his aides entered the White House with deep suspicions of Congress, established health policy experts, and what they saw as the "old" government approach embodied in Medicare and Medicaid. Expanding Medicare was anathema to Clinton's initial "third way" approach; the President and his aides concluded that it was run by "the regulators" and was a hopelessly inflexible government approach when a dynamic, cross-sectoral framework promised wider coverage for less (Hacker 1997; Jacobs and Shapiro 2000, chapters 3 and 4).

After Clinton introduced his reform plan to Congress and the country in September 1993, it dominated debate for the next nine months. By the summer of 1994, however, it was clear that the Clinton plan lacked support to pass in Congress (even though Democrats held majorities in the House and Senate) and congressional leaders attempted to forge new proposals that could pass. One of the main initiatives came from the leadership in the House, which proposed to use Medicare as the platform for health reform.[42] The chairman of the health subcommittee of the House Ways and Means Committee, Fortney (Pete) Stark (D-CA), resurrected Medicare incrementalism for just the reasons that the program's original reformers envisioned—"people understand the Medicare program, know it has worked well and trust it" and "Medicare is simple: no new rules, no new bureaucracy" (Rich 1994a, 1994b; Pear 1994). Stark's approach—which was approved by the full Ways and Means Committee by July 1994 and which formed the backbone of the proposal offered by the majority House leader, Richard Gephardt, at the end of the month—pursued the same goals identified by Clinton: achieving health insurance for all Americans and controlling medical spending.[43]

The Stark approach proposed to achieve universal access through a patchwork of public and private programs. Employers would continue to be the primary source of health insurance and would be required (as under the Clinton plan) to pay 80 percent of the cost of private insurance for full-time employees. What was distinctive about Stark's approach was that it proposed to create Medicare, part C, a new component that would be separate from the continuing (and unaffected) program for seniors and funded through a combination of premiums charged to individuals and small firms as well as increased taxes on cigarettes and large corporations to pay for the poor and subsidize the charges to low-income Americans. It could be used by small businesses with less than a hundred workers to satisfy the new employer mandate as well as by part-time workers, the uninsured, and vulnerable populations on Medicaid, which would be terminated. Recipients of Medicare Part C could—as in the Medicare program for seniors—choose their own private doctors and hospitals, which would be paid on a fee-for-service basis. The new expanded Medicare was projected to encompass about half of the population of the United States, with the other half covered by private health plans (Rich 1994b).

Much as Medicare's original reformers anticipated, Stark emphasized that Medicare Part C would effectively control health- care costs by relying on the program's relatively recent prospective payment systems for paying doctors and hospitals. He insisted, "No payer has done a better job of holding down costs and fighting fraud" (Rich 1994a). (Medicare's budgetary controls on provider reimbursement have produced lower rates of growth and per-enrollee costs than private health insurers since the 1980s.) In addition to extending Medicare's existing prospective payment system to providers of services to Part C beneficiaries, Stark's plan would have established federal cost controls on fees charged by doctors, hospitals, and insurers in the private sector.

Although Sparks, Gephardt, and other House leaders were initially confident about passing the Medicare Part C proposal, it was soon overtaken by the same chorus of complaints that washed over President Clinton's proposal: the reforms introduced massive new government regulations, costs, and taxes that interfered with and disrupted private-sector arrangements. As with the well-known attacks on the Clinton plan (Johnson and Broder 1996; Jacobs and Shapiro 2000), Stark's Medicare approach was criticized (as two congressional Republicans, Bill Thomas and Jim McCrery, put it) for "extend[ing] government control over millions of Americans" and establishing a "new government entitlement program" (Rich 1994a; Pear 1994). Stakeholders opposed it as a direct threat to their livelihoods: one representative of insurers blurted out, "We hate it, we hate it, we hate it!" because "it could put us out of business." The American Medical Association, American Hospital Association, and other providers opposed a "vast expansion of Medicare" that restricted their reimbursement until "every hospital would be bankrupt," and the United States Chamber of Commerce expressed the "crazy" opposition of businesses to picking up the burden of higher health insurance costs (Rich 1994b).

The opposition to Medicare Part C tapped into public unease during the 1990s toward an explicit and rapid change to folding all Americans and health-care providers into one plan. An expansion of Medicare that was encompassing (rather than targeted to discrete population groups) lacked public support. Public opinion polls consistently found that using Medicare to cover all the uninsured drew the least support among five alternatives that included an employer mandate, state government programs, tax deductions, and a single-payer approach.[44] In addition, the public harbored suspicions that government intervention would lower the quality of medical care and fail to control costs (Jacobs and Shapiro 2000, chapter 7). Criticisms of the Stark approach for launching a Medicare takeover of the existing private system resonated with public reservations about an overbearing national government.

The irony is that the doubts and opposition to the Medicare approach were fueled in the early 1990s by Bill Clinton and his administration. The Clinton Administration's managed-competition proposal and its public framing of it as embracing private markets and shunning government squandered two opportunities.

The Medicare Expansion Act of 1994   The fact that the Johnson administration was in the advanced stages of planning incremental expansions of Medicare and that some Medicare expansion proposals were floated in 1993 does not, of course, demonstrate that Clinton faced a simple choice between his approach that ultimately failed and success in widening Medicare. Efforts at incremental expansion of Medicare in the early 1990s did face intense opposition and the possibility of failure was real. Nonetheless, the history behind Medicare's original design and the Johnson administration plans open up another possible institutional trajectory. A proposal that rested on the incremental extension of Medicare and a familiar and proven program may well have been better positioned than Clinton's managed competition plan to reassure and win over conservative Democrats and some Republicans.

Medicare incrementalism might have improved the probability of widening access to health insurance during the early 1990s by avoiding three strategic errors by the Clinton White House. First, Clinton's search for an alternative to Medicare and government led him to falsely frame his managed-competition approach as relying on private markets, which delegitimized government and set the expectation that reform should avoid it. Clinton contributed (as one op-ed put it) to "wailing against government bureaucracy and the specter of Armageddon [created by] . . . nationalized (socialized) medical system" and invited moderate Republicans, Democrats, and even members of the administration to harp on the dangers of government and the virtues of private health-care markets (Trafford 1994). Once launched as a way to promote his own proposal, Clinton's public presentations were exploited by Democrats and some Republicans not only to question the

President's own proposal but also to assail Stark's Medicare approach (Pear 1994). The National Governors Association launched a bipartisan barrage against Medicare Part C as "highly bureaucratic." Governor Howard Dean led the antistatist charge, railing against its "huge federal bureaucracy" and the notion that the "federal government is capable" of running it (Broder 1994; Rich 1994b). In the context of Clinton's offensive against government, the *New York Times* editorial page (a friend of widening access and, in the early 1990s, sympathetic to Clinton's third-way approach) found the "Stark plan . . . dismayingly backward-looking" in relying on government in contrast to the "better way" of "control[ing] costs by forcing large health plans to compete against one another" (*New York Times*, March 10, 1994).

Second, the public supported incremental changes in Medicare during the 1990s that expanded coverage to discrete population groups, as the program's original designers anticipated. A number of polls showed that majorities supported lowering Medicare's eligibility from sixty-five years of age to sixty-two (62 percent support) or fifty-five (56 percent support) in exchange for a monthly premium that covered its cost ($300 and $400, respectively).[45] Polls that identified these reforms as having been proposed by Bill Clinton found less support for them, though majorities still supported them.

Public support for incremental expansion of Medicare to the "near retirees" is most apparent in "balanced-frame" questions that ask respondents to choose between competing positions—one that favored the reform and one that opposed it. When presented with contrasting arguments for lowering Medicare's eligibility to sixty-two in exchange for a higher premium, 60 percent favored it to "give uninsured early retirees access to health insurance" and only 37 percent opposed it because it would "add costs" and was "unlikely to help many people."[46] When asked about proposals that lowered the age of eligibility to fifty-five and attributed the arguments to Bill Clinton and Republicans, the magnitude of support for widening access declined but was still supported by a 48 to 39 percent plurality.[47]

These data suggest that Stark's "Medicare for All" strategy may well also have been too expansive for most Americans. Indeed, Dan Rostenkowski signaled before he was forced to resign as chairman of the powerful House Ways and Means Committee that he would abandon the goal of comprehensive reform in favor of taking "a step in the right direction" by adopting a "much more conservative" version of Stark's Medicare proposal—one that focused on discrete population groups, dropped broad-based taxes, and narrowed its impact on the private medical system (Priest and Rich 1994). Without this kind of moderating leadership that pushed for an incremental approach based on Medicare, moderate and conservative Democrats were left to bemoan (as one did) the fact that the leaders failed to "addres[s] our concerns about the very strong employer mandate and backup price controls" (Broder and Priest 1994).

Third, the operation of the Medicare program (much as structuralists and the program's original designers expected) generated resource and interpretative effects that prompted organized groups to support incremental expansion. Groups representing consumers, organized labor, physicians, and seniors supported Medicare Part C in 1994. John Rother from the AARP (American Association of Retired Persons) explained that seniors and the disabled liked the addition of Part C because "Medicare is a known quantity," neatly summarizing a finding from research on positive feedback effects (Rich 1994b). The incremental expansion of Medicare was also supported by the experts from medicine, nursing, business, and other related fields who served on the Physician Payment Review Commission (Trafford 1994).

Drawing Battle Lines for Future Debates   Even though there are grounds for suspecting that an incremental approach to Medicare expansion may have picked up more congressional swing votes, it is certainly plausible that this approach may well have met the same leg- islative fate as Clinton's plan and other scaled-back plans offered by several congressional groups.[48] Clinton's dogged insistence on his managed-competition proposal missed a sec- ond opportunity—to orient future policymaking agendas and to orient policy options to- ward incremental expansions of access to Medicare. By August 1994, as the prospects for enacting health reform faded, the *Washington Post* (1994) joined others in recommending a "fallback position" of "retain[ing] the notion of a Medicare Part C" in order to make incremental improvements for discrete groups (Trafford 1994). Indeed, in his second term, Clinton himself turned to Medicare incrementalism as a more promising path for- ward instead of a maximalist approach and the attempt to open Medicare to all Ameri- cans in one fell swoop. By then, Democrats were a minority party in Congress and Clin- ton's change of heart came too late.

The first decade of the twenty-first century has seen a resurgence of interest among Democratic policymakers and allies in building health reform on the foundation of Medi- care because it offers favorable institutional and political vantage points. One set of con- gressional liberals led by Senator Ted Kennedy and Congressmen Stark and Dingell (and others) have returned to the "Medicare for All" approach to extending health insurance to all Americans. Many of these reformers explicitly argue that Clinton went wrong in not embracing Medicare as a reform approach because of the resource and interpretative advantages it lends reformers.

There are also renewed calls to focus health reform efforts on incrementally expand- ing Medicare to discrete population groups (near retirees). The rationale mirrors the ar- guments of Medicare's original designers and the Johnson administration, that cutting off one more "salami slice" (rather than reaching for universal coverage) would narrow the scope of those feeling its concentrated costs while identifying a clear winner that was in- creasingly organized by an encompassing organization. (The AARP has widened its membership to near retirees and has become a strong advocate for them.) This approach scales back legislative ambition in clear recognition that many Americans will remain un- covered out of respect for America's Madisonian system of multiple veto points and a confidence that future reformers will work to further widen access to Medicare.

THE DISTRIBUTIONAL POLITICS OF POLICY FEEDBACKS

Studying the origins, implementation, and evolution of Medicare opens a window onto institutional development, agency within structured contexts, and the enduring failure of the United States to establish universal or, more modestly, wider access to health insur- ance—a critical contributor to economic inequality and health disparities. The Medicare case reveals how the cognitive mechanism of on-line processing primes elites to privilege short-term considerations over longer-term institutional consequences and motivates au- thoritative government officials to establish a federated communications capacity to influ- ence the public's interpretations and augment its resources for making sense of new gov- ernment programs. It also demonstrates the significance of agency. Structure creates durable pressures that are conducive to some policies while erecting barriers to others; but authoritative government officials like presidents exercise critical leeway in interpreting these opportunities and constraints.

The interactions of structure and agency shape in important respects the distributional consequences of policy feedbacks. In the case of Medicare, they created the opportunity for ambitious politicians to establish health insurance for tens of millions of Americans;

they also generated possibilities for further expansions of access that were not exploited—witness Kennedy's and Johnson's rejection of fiscally sound budgetary control and Clinton's initial decision to reject Medicare as a platform for reform. Structure not only creates opportunities; it also imposes substantial constraints on political actors, as illustrated by its delimiting of Clinton's (and Stark's) efforts to supplant the private medical system grounded in employer-based health insurance.

America's enduring private medical system and the strategic miscalculations of its leaders have produced a troubling dynamic in its health policy. On the one hand, a narrow segment of the population enjoys a national health insurance system that continues to offer substantial and growing benefits. On the other hand, a large and growing number of Americans lack health insurance to cover the costs of even essential medical care. American political leadership and enduring institutional patterns sustain policies that defer to private market distributions when it comes to most Americans while establishing generous social rights for the relatively few.

Although the first four decades of Medicare's history have largely failed to follow the projections of its original designers, the program's access-expanding opportunities remain. Recent proposals to build off of Medicare reflect a sober reappraisal of the Clinton White House's initial rejection of the program as a reform platform. Moreover, the dynamic of discrete, small steps that add up over time has been amply demonstrated by Medicaid and Social Security, establishing a potent model of incremental institutional development (Derthick 1979; Grogan and Patashnik 2005). The intensifying stress in America's private medical system combined with a heightened strategic awareness by reform leaders may create in the future an opportunity for widening eligibility to Medicare's health insurance to new population groups.

I would like to acknowledge the helpful feedback of the editors, colleagues at the conference on "Make the Politics of Poverty and Inequality," April 21–22, 2005, University of Wisconsin at Madison, as well as the feedback of two anonymous reviewers.

NOTES

1. Wilbur Cohen, author interview, Austin, Texas, April 1, 1987.
2. Although Medicare did not expand as its founders initially expected, it did come to include the disabled and Americans suffering from end-stage renal disease.
3. Douglas Cater, memo to Lyndon B. Johnson, May 27, 1966, attached to memo from James Jones to Robert Kinter, May 31, 1966, Ex IS1, Box 1, Lyndon Baines Johnson Library and Museum, University of Texas, Austin, Texas. All archival materials cited are housed at the LBJ Library.
4. Administrative History of the Department of HEW and the Social Security Administration During the Johnson Presidency (henceforth: Admin. History, HEW and SSA), pp. 148–54; President's Remarks, June 15, 1966, Ex IS1.MC, Box 3; Bill Moyers and Hayes Redman, HEW reports to the Johnson White House, Ex FG/RS/PR18.
5. Admin. History, HEW and SSA, p. 147.
6. LBJ, letter to John Gardner, April 7, 1966.
7. Admin. History, HEW and SSA, volume 1, part XVII, pp. 183–87; Ex FG165: Horace Busby, memo to LBJ, July 16, 1965, Ex FG165, Box 239; LBJ, memo to A. Celebrezze, July 16, 1965,

Ex FG165, Box 239; Anthony Celebrezze, memo to LBJ, July 1, 1965, Ex FG165, Box 239; John Gardner (secretary, HEW), memo to LBJ, May 23, 1966, Ex LE/ISI, Box 75.

8. Douglas Cater, memo to LBJ, September 3, 1965, Ex FG165, Box 239.
9. Harold Levy, memo to Bill Moyers, March 7, 1966, Ex FG165, Box 239; Admin. History, HEW and SSA, Volume 1, Part XVII, pp. 183–88.
10. Admin. History, HEW and SSA, Volume 1, Part XVII, p. 34.
11. Harold Levy, memo to Hayes Redman, November 19, 1965, Ex FG165, Box 239; Robert Ball, "Report on the Implementation of the Medicare Provisions" EX FG165, Box 739; Robert Ball, memo to John Gardner, March 1, 1966, Ex IS1, Box 1.
12. Celebrezze, memo to LBJ, July 1, 1965; DHEW, "Putting Medicare into Effect," report, June 1966, Ex IS Box 1; Admin. History, HEW and SSA, Volume 1, Part XVII, pp. 183–87.
13. Horace Busby, memo to Wilbur Cohen, 19TK, Ex LE IS1, Box 75; Jack Valenti, memo to LBJ, July 19, 1965, Ex LE IS1, Box 75; Horace Busby, memo to Jack Valenti, Doug Cater, and Bill Moyers, W, Marvin Watson, July 22, 1965, Ex LE IS1, Box 75.
14. Harold Levy, memo to Bill Moyers, July 30, 1965, Ex FG1/RS/PR18, Box 5.
15. R. Ball, "A Report on the Implementation of the Medicare Provisions of the 1965 Amendments to the SSA as of May 23, 1966 from R Ball," Ex IS1, Box 1; Howard Levy, memo to Hayes Redman, December 3, 1965, FG165, Box 239.
16. Howard Levy, memo to Hayes Redman, December 17. 1965, Ex FG/RS/PR18, Box 7.
17. Anthony Celebrezze, memo to LBJ, July 1, 1965.
18. Ibid.
19. Howard Levy, memo to Hayes Redman, November 19, 1965, Ex FG165, Box 239; Admin. History, HEW and SSA, Volume 1, Part XVII, p. 10; "Your New Health Insurance," EX WE6, Box 15, August 1965.
20. Admin. History, HEW and SSA, Volume 1, Part XVII, pp. 183–87.
21. Assistant SSA Commissioner, memo to All Regional Assistant Commissioners, June 16, 1966. Ex WE6, Box 5.
22. Press release, "Progress Report to President on Launching of Medicare," Ex IS, Box 1.
23. LBJ, comments to cabinet, June 6, 1966, CF FG100/MC, Box 22.
24. LBJ, remarks to meeting of medical professionals, June 15, 1966, Ex IS1.MC, Box 3.
25. See, for instance, "Press Release: HEW, SSA," February 10, 1966, Ex IS, Box 1.
26. LBJ, letter to John Gardner, June 3, 1966, Ex FG165, Box 239; Wilbur Cohen, memo to Doug Cater, June 8, 1966, Ex IS, Box 1; CF FG100/MC, Box 22.
27. Doug Cater, memos to LBJ, July 26 and 28, 1965, Cater Box 13.
28. John Gardner, memo to LBJ, December 13, 1965.
29. Doug Cater, memo to LJB, May 27, 1966, Ex IS Box 1.
30. Ex IS1.MC, Box 3.
31. Doug Cater, memo to LBJ, June 18, 1966, Cater Box 15; John Gardner, memo to LBJ, June 10, 1966.
32. Doug Cater, Memo to Hubert Humphrey, June 10, 1966; Cater, memo to LBJ, June 18, 1966, Cater Box 15.
33. Ex IS1, Box 1; Robert Kinter, memo to LBJ, June 16, 1966, CF HE5, Box 54; Cater, memo to LBJ, May 25, 1966, Cater Box 14; Farris Bryant (director, Office of Emergency Planning), memo to LBJ, May 23, 1966, Ex FG165, Box 239.
34. Admin. History, HEW and SSA, Volume 1, Part 1, pp. 9, 42.
35. Ibid.; Gardner, memo to LBJ, May 23, 1966, Ex LE/ISI, Box 75; Cater, memo to LBJ, May 27, 1966, Ex IS1, Box 1; Cater, memo to LBJ, October 1, 1965, Ex HE, Box 1; Cater, memo to LBJ, December 27, 1965, Ex HE5, Box 17.
36. Robert Kinter, memo to LBJ, April 25, 1966, CF FG1, Box 16; Joseph Califano, memo to LBJ, December 21, 1965, regarding conversation with Ray Scherer. CFFGI, Box 16.
37. Joseph Califano, memo to Gardner, August 27, 1965, CF FG165, Box 130; Wilbur Cohen, memo to Joseph, December 21, 1965. CFFG165, Box 130.
38. Erwin Duggan, memo to Cater, May 31, 1966, Cater Box 12.
39. Joseph Califano, Memo to Wilbur Cohen, August 5, 1965, Confidential File, FG600, Box 36;

Califano, memo to LBJ from Califano, August 11, 1965, Ex LE, Box 4; "Health Care Task Force," September 10, 1965; "Administratively Confidential," CF FG600, TF on Health, Box 36; Wilbur Cohen, memo to Califano, September 13, 1965, "HC TF Proposals for FY 1966 Legisl Progr," CF FG600, Box 36; Cater, memo to LBJ, October 1, 1965, Ex HE, Box 1; Wilbur Cohen, memo to LBJ, March 15, 1966, Ex WE6, Box 15.

40. Califano, memo to Hubert Humphrey, September 25, 1968, McPherson Box 30.

41. Wilbur Cohen, author interview, Austin, Texas, April 1, 1987; Joseph Califano, memo to Hubert Humphrey, September 25, 1968, McPherson Box 30.

42. The other principal effort to formulate health reform developed in the Senate and focused on the majority leader's effort to compromise on several key components of Clinton's plan (including universalism) while still relying on its basic framework

43. Stark's approach was developed in the Ways and Means subcommittee on health and was largely adopted by the full Ways and Means Committee, which was chaired by Sam Gibbons after Dan Rostenkowski's indictment on corruption charges.

44. Lawrence R. Jacobs and Robert Y. Shapiro (2000, chapter 7) review the findings of surveys sponsored by the Henry J. Kaiser Family Foundation and Harvard School of Public Health, from December 3 to 13, 1999, using a national adult sample of 1,515 respondents.

45. ABC News and Washington Post Poll, January 15 to 19, 1998, using a national sample of 1,206 adults.

46. Henry J. Kaiser Family Foundation and Harvard School of Public Health, August 14 to September 20, 1998, national sample of 1,909 adults (Princeton Survey Research Associates).

47. The question was worded as follows: "President Clinton has proposed allowing people age sixty-two to sixty-four to participate in Medicare if they pay a monthly premium, and giving people as young as age fifty-five the right to buy Medicare coverage if they have lost their job. He says this step is necessary to help people who have trouble getting private insurance. Republicans say Medicare is already in financial trouble and that it's too costly to add new people to a system that can't handle them. Who do you agree with more on this issue —President Clinton or the Republicans?" The survey was carried out by Hart and Teeter Research Co., for NBC News and the Wall Street Journal, January 17 to 19, 1998, on a national sample of 1,005 adults.

48. Among the proposals that were circulated in August 1994 in an effort by Democrats and moderate Republicans to find compromise legislation were those prepared by Senate Majority Leader George Mitchell and a bipartisan coalition in the House and Senate of moderate Republicans and Democrats, which dropped the politically controversial aspects of previous proposals—the employer mandate and tax increases (Broder and Dewar 1994).

REFERENCES

Anderson, Gerald, Peter Hussey, Blanca Frogner, and Hugh Waters. 2005. "Health Spending in the United States and the Rest of the Industrialized World." *Health Affairs* 24(July–August): 903–14.

Broder, David S. 1994. "House Leaders Cancel All Leaves Until Health Bill Comes to a Vote." *Washington Post*, August 4, 1994.

Broder, David S., and Helen Dewar. 1994. "Senate Republicans Impede Health Legislation." *Washington Post*, August 13, 1994.

Broder, David S., and Dana Priest. 1994. "Gephardt Announces Health Plan; Democratic Leaders Back Universal Coverage, Employer Mandate." *Washington Post*, July 30, 1994.

Campbell, Andrea Louise. 2003. *How Policies Make Citizens: Senior Political Activism and the American Welfare State*. Princeton, N.J.: Princeton University Press.

DeNavas-Walt, Carmen, Bernadette D. Proctor, and Robert J. Mills. 2004. "Income, Poverty, and Health Insurance Coverage in the United States: 2004." Current Population Reports No. P60-226. Prepared for the U.S. Census Bureau. Washington: Government Printing Office. Accessed at http://www.census.gov/prod/2004pubs/p60-226.pdf.

Derthick, Martha. 1979. *Policy Making for Social Security*. Washington: Brookings Institution Press.

Druckman, James N., Lawrence R. Jacobs, and Eric Ostermeier. 2004. "Candidate Strategies to Prime Issues and Image." *Journal of Politics* 66(November): 1205–27.

Fiske, Susan. 1993. "Cognitive Theory and the Presidency." In *Researching the Presidency*, edited by George Edwards III, John Kessel, and Bert Rockman. Pittsburgh, Pa.: University of Pittsburgh Press.

Greenstein, Fred. 1969. *Personality and Politics: Problems of Evidence, Inference, and Conceptualization.* Chicago, Ill.: Markham.

Grogan, Colleen, and Eric Patashnik. 2005. "Medicaid at the Crossroads." In *Healthy, Wealthy, and Fair*, edited by James Morone and Lawrence Jacobs. New York: Oxford University Press.

Hacker, Jacob. 1997. *The Road to Nowhere: The Genesis of President Clinton's Plan for Health Security.* Princeton, N.J.: Princeton University Press.

———. 2002. *The Divided Welfare State: The Battle over Public and Private Social Benefits in the United States.* New York: Cambridge University Press.

———. 2004. "Privatizing Risk Without Privatizing the Welfare State: The Hidden Politics of Social Policy Retrenchment in the United States." *American Political Science Review* 98(May): 243–60.

Hastie, Reid, and Bernadette Park. 1986. "The Relationship Between Memory and Judgment Depends on Whether the Judgment Task Is Memory-Based or On-Line." *Psychological Review* 93(3): 258–68.

Jacobs, Lawrence. 1993. *The Health of Nations: Public Opinion and the Making of American and British Health Policy.* Ithaca, N.Y.: Cornell University Press.

———. 2007. "The Medicare Approach: Political Choice and American Institutions." *Journal of Health Politics, Policy and Law.* 32(2): 159-86.

Jacobs, Lawrence R., and Robert Y. Shapiro. 1994. "Issues, Candidate Image and Priming: The Use of Private Polls in Kennedy's 1960 Presidential Campaign." *American Political Science Review* 88(September): 527–40.

———. 2000. *Politicians Don't Pander: Political Manipulation and the Loss of Democratic Responsiveness.* Chicago, Ill.: University of Chicago Press.

Johnson, Haynes, and David Broder. 1996. *The System: The American Way of Politics at the Breaking Point.* Boston, Mass.: Little, Brown.

Lodge, Milton, and Kathleen McGraw, editors. 1995. *Political Judgment: Structure and Process.* Ann Arbor, Mich.: University of Michigan Press.

Lodge, Milton, and Patrick Stroh. 1993. "Inside the Mental Voting Booth: An Impression-Driven Process Model of Candidate Evaluation." In *Explorations in Political Psychology*, edited by Shanto Iyengar and William McGuire. Durham, N.C.: Duke University Press.

Lodge, Milton, Kathleen McGraw, and Patrick Stroh. 1989. "An Impression-Driven Model of Candidate Evaluation." *American Political Science Review* 83(2): 399–419.

———. 1990. "On-Line Processing in Candidate Evaluation: The Effects of Issue Order, Issue Importance, and Sophistication." *Political Behavior* 12(1): 41–58.

Marmor, Theodore. 2000. *The Politics of Medicare.* 2nd edition. New York: Aldine de Gruyter.

Matusow, Allen. 1984. *The Unraveling of America: A History of Liberalism in the 1960s.* New York: Harper & Row.

McConnell, Allen, Steven Sherman, and David Hamilton. 1994. "On-Line and Memory-Based Aspects of Individual and Group Target Judgments." *Journal of Personality and Social Psychology* 67(2): 173–85.

Mettler, Suzanne, and Joe Soss. 2004. "The Consequences of Public Policy for Democratic Citizenship: Bridging Policy Studies and Mass Politics." *Perspectives on Politics* 2(March): 55–73.

Mills, Robert J., and Shailesh Bhandari. 2003. "Health Insurance Coverage in the United States: 2002." Current Population Report No. P60-223, prepared for the U.S. Census Bureau. Washington: Government Printing Office. Accessed at http://www.census.gov/prod/2003pubs/p60-223 .pdf.

Morone, James, and Lawrence Jacobs, editors. 2005. *Healthy, Wealthy, and Fair.* New York: Oxford University Press.

Oberlander, Jonathan. 2003. *The Political Life of Medicare.* Chicago, Ill.: University of Chicago Press.

Orren, Karen, and Stephen Skowronek. 2002. "The Study of American Political Development." In *Political Science: The State of the Discipline,* edited by Ira Katznelson and Helen Milner. New York: Norton.

Pear, Robert. 1994. "The Health Care Debate: The Legislation." *New York Times,* July 1, 1994.

Pierson, Paul. 1993. "When Effect Becomes Cause: Policy Feedback and Political Change." *World Politics* 45(4): 595–628.

———. 2000. "Increasing Returns, Path Dependence, and the Study of Politics." *American Political Science Review* 94(June): 251–67.

Poen, Monte. 1979. *Harry S. Truman Versus the Medical Lobby.* Columbia, Mo.: University of Missouri Press.

Priest, Dana, and Spencer Rich. 1994. "Rostenkowski Sees Limited Health Reform." *Washington Post,* March 24, 1994.

Quadagno, Jill. 2000. "Promoting Civil Rights through the Welfare State: How Medicare Integrated Southern Hospitals." Social Problems 47(February): 68–89.

Rich, Spencer. 1994a. "Medicare C: A Massive New Program." *Washington Post,* July 1, 1994.

———. 1994b. "Plan to Expand Medicare Pains the Health Industry." *Washington Post,* August 5, 1994.

Skocpol, Theda. 1992. *Protecting Soldiers and Mothers.* Cambridge, Mass.: Harvard University Press.

Smedley, Brian, Adrienne Stith, and Alan Nelson. 2003. *Unequal Treatment: Confronting Racial and Ethnic Disparities in Health Care.* Report prepared for the Institute of Medicine. Washington: National Academy Press.

Soss, Joe. 1999. "Lessons of Welfare: Policy Design, Political Learning, and Political Action." *American Political Science Review* 93(2): 363–80.

Trafford, Abigail. 1994. "A Significant, If Small, Step for Down-to-Earth Reform." *Washington Post,* April 5, 1994.

Washington Post. 1994. "Senator Mitchell's Rescue Effort." August 3.

Chapter 5

A Public Transformed?
Welfare Reform as Policy Feedback

An old saw in political science, often attributed to E. E. Schattschneider (1935), holds that "new policies create a new politics." It is an insight lost on few successful politicians. Like good chess players, lawmakers must often "think two moves ahead" when designing policy. As they gauge how a new policy will affect relevant social problems, they also consider its potential to mobilize or mollify the opposition, create pressures for further action, appease or outrage the party faithful, redistribute political resources, change the terms of debate, and so on. To strategic politicians, policies are not only efforts to achieve social and economic goals, but also ways of achieving long-term political goals.

In this chapter, we analyze welfare reform as a means of achieving a specific political goal that was clearly on the minds of liberal advocates of reform from the mid-1980s onward—the softening of public attitudes toward the poor and the popular rehabilitation of the Democratic Party. It was thought that "ending welfare as we knew it" would make the public more willing to help the poor and support the Democratic Party. By bringing welfare policy more into line with public values, liberal advocates of reform reasoned, welfare reform not only would change the economic condition of the poor but also would transform the politics of public assistance, insulating Democrats from the charge that they coddled the idle and irresponsible, undermining the "racialization" of antipoverty programs, and ultimately paving the way for ambitious new efforts to fight poverty.

Although liberal advocates of welfare reform may not have known it, the argument that they were advancing—that policies transform politics—is one with which political scientists have increasingly grappled, under the banner of "policy feedback" (Skocpol 1992; Pierson 1993). Policy feedback research has considered how policies, once enacted, reshape political institutions, interests, and dynamics. In most of this literature, the political effects under examination have been largely unintended. Most of this research, moreover, has focused on the effects of policies on either elites and organized interests (Hacker 2002) or the proximate targets of public policies, such as welfare recipients (Soss 2000; Campbell 2003; Mettler 2005). In this chapter, we move beyond existing scholarship to address the use of policy design as a conscious political strategy that is used to alter the preferences, beliefs, and behaviors of broad mass publics, not simply organized elites or program beneficiaries.

Our analysis reveals that welfare reform in the 1990s produced few changes in mass opinion, a result directly contrary to that expected by advocates of the liberal argument for reform. Indeed, public opinion was remarkably unaffected by the dramatic restructuring of welfare that occurred in the mid-1990s. This leads to a further question: How and when should we expect governing elites to be capable of using policy actions to reshape beliefs and preferences in the citizenry? To answer this question, we propose a general framework for the analysis of mass feedback effects that shows when policy is more or less likely to affect mass public opinion—and why the argument that welfare reform would jump-start American antipoverty efforts missed some of the most enduring elements of this thorny policy area.

THE PROMISE OF MASS FEEDBACK EFFECTS

For political liberals in the United States, the 1980s were hard times. The Republican Party controlled the White House and was winning key votes from traditional Democratic Party constituencies in the white working class and the South (Teixeira and Rogers 2000). Efforts to cut back social supports were gaining steam, and antiwelfare rhetoric seemed to resonate with the public (Block et al. 1987). Among liberals, these developments gave rise to intense self-reflection and, eventually, a reformist perspective that Harold Meyerson (1996) dubbed "progressive revisionism."

Progressive revisionists argued that "Democratic doctrine went off track during the Johnson years [of the 1960s]," turning toward divisive policies that favored the very poor and racial minorities over the white working-class mainstream (Meyerson 1996). The new policies transformed the political landscape, generating a public backlash against taxes and programs for the disadvantaged and creating a set of wedge issues related to crime, welfare, and race that Republicans were using to win over decisive votes (Edsall with Edsall 1991).

A variety of prominent policy scholars made arguments that resonated with the progressive revisionist thesis. Well-known liberal social scientists argued that targeted social policies had "veered off course" (Skocpol 2000), become mired in "helping conundrums" (Ellwood 1988), and could never build "a bridge over the racial divide" (Wilson 1999). Conservative policy scholars argued that permissive welfare had undermined "progressive politics," based on questions of distributive justice, and given rise to "dependency politics," based on questions of social behavior (Mead 1992). Some said that by rewarding irresponsibility, the Aid to Families with Dependent Children (AFDC) program had fueled racial stereotypes, bred pathology among the poor, undercut public support for antipoverty efforts, and put liberals at an ongoing political disadvantage (Mead 1992).

The clock could not be turned back, but progressive revisionists suggested that these political legacies might be reversed if Democrats used policy proposals to signal renewed commitments to personal responsibility and the white working class. In a widely discussed 1986 article and 1992 book, Mickey Kaus (1992, 177–78) succinctly expressed a view that was gathering momentum among moderate "New Democrats," who sought to move the Democratic Party toward the political center:

> If voters are faced with a Democrat who wants to spend money to end welfare, they will open up their wallets—both for ending welfare and for other government projects. . . . To regain the taxpayers' confidence . . . Democrats must be ruthless in drawing the work/nonwork distinction. . . . Declaring that government benefit programs . . . will only help working families or those who can't work . . . neatly solves the political dilemma [Thomas] Edsall and others say the Democrats face: how to help the poor without seeming to underwrite the underclass.

Variants of this thesis gained influence rapidly in the early 1990s, and by the time of the 1992 presidential campaign, the Democratic candidate, Bill Clinton, "was well on his way to mastering the progressive revisionist two-step" (Meyerson 1996). As R. Kent Weaver (2000) recounts, Clinton's pledge to "end welfare as we know it" did not reflect a detailed set of policy plans in 1992. Promoted by Bruce Reed and other advocates of a centrist strategy at the Democratic Leadership Council (DLC), the pledge was deployed more as a move in "the grand strategic game of realigning the image of the Democratic Party on welfare issues" (Weaver 2002, 116).

As the push for reform heated up, the idea that welfare reform could move the public in a progressive direction gathered momentum, suggesting a reason why moderate Democrats should abandon the standoff among political elites over AFDC and join a centrist coalition for reform (Teles 1996). Lawrence Mead (1992, 204) counseled that if AFDC could be reformed to raise work levels, "politics probably would revert to progressive themes and shift to the left." "If liberals genuinely accepted [behavioral expectations], they could parry the strongest weapon conservatives hold in the current dependency politics" (Mead 1992, 253). Moreover, they could deracialize poverty politics. "Opposition to welfare exacerbates racism. . . . To reform welfare and enforce work . . . would serve [blacks] by reducing black reliance on welfare, raising black work levels, and thus undercutting racism" (Mead 2001, 207–8).

With poverty politics widely viewed as a frustrating and politically costly quagmire, liberal versions of these arguments found an audience among Democrats looking for a way to change the political terrain—and especially in the new Clinton White House. Many in the Clinton administration hoped to strike a legislative bargain along the lines suggested by David Ellwood (1988), in which liberals signed onto time limits and work requirements in exchange for conservatives' signing onto substantial social investment.

After Republicans took Congress in 1994, however, hopes for such a bargain gave way to discussions of a sequential political strategy. In the months leading up to the Personal Responsibility and Work Opportunity Reconciliation Act (PRWORA), presidential advisors argued that "the welfare restrictions—time limits and work requirements—would do more than revamp one discredited program. [They] would help create a political climate more favorable to the needy. Once taxpayers started viewing the poor as workers, not welfare cheats, a more generous era would ensue. Harmful stereotypes would fade. New benefits would flow. Members of minorities, being disproportionately poor, would disproportionately benefit" (DeParle and Holmes 2000).

Although Clinton considered some aspects of the Republican proposals too punitive (DeParle 1999; Weaver 2000), he came to see welfare reform "as an effort to quiet racial disputes about social supports for the vulnerable" (Theda Skocpol, quoted in DeParle and Holmes 2000, 12). His trusted pollster, Dick Morris, played a key role in promoting this view. "By ending welfare," Morris advised, "Clinton wasn't rejecting liberalism; he was clearing the way for its rejuvenated influence over one of its central concerns, ghetto poverty" (quoted in DeParle 1999, 12).

Progressive revisionists made similar arguments in public venues. Writing in *The New Republic,* Theda Skocpol (1996) urged liberals to "bury the corpse [of AFDC] and move on [to] work and family policies applicable to everyone, yet structured to give extra help to the least privileged working parents." Writing in the *New York Times* as the welfare reform bill awaited Clinton's signature, Mickey Kaus (1996) promised both electoral and policy payoffs: "AFDC has poisoned the public against all government spending. Republicans have skillfully used the program's unpopularity to taint all Democratic antipoverty efforts, indeed all government. . . . But, with government cleansed of AFDC's taint . . . Democrats [will be] liberated to meet the public's legitimate, unfilled expectations of government. I suspect we will see the results clearly, if not in this election then the next."

In the ensuing years, as Temporary Assistance for Needy Families (TANF) became viewed as a policy success and public spending shifted from cash aid to work supports, these sorts of predictions morphed into claims of actual effects on public opinion, sometimes cited to justify further New Democratic strategies. "The results so far have borne out the central New Democrat insight that inspired Clinton's promise to end welfare: The way to make American social policy both more effective and more generous is to make it more morally demanding. . . . [Welfare reform is] visibly restoring public confidence in government's ability to help the poor lift themselves up" (Marshall 2002).

Far from being held only by New Democrats, the idea that welfare reform changed mass opinion has begun to take on the status of conventional wisdom in scholarly circles. Thus, Hugh Heclo (2001, 197) concludes that "the more [welfare] offices become employment-focused centers, not centers administering welfare checks, the firmer the political base for doing more to help those in the nation's inner cities for whom 'work' may be only a small part of the problem." Christopher Jencks (2005, 86) states that "welfare reform has at least reduced popular opposition to [government efforts to help poor single mothers]. Most Americans seem to share Clinton's view that 'those who work shouldn't be poor,' and they are now more likely to see single mothers as working mothers." Mead (2004, 274) contends that "the more the welfare rolls have declined . . . the more social politics has shifted to the left"; "Democrats were freed from the need to defend traditional welfare. Rather than speaking for the dependent, they could now defend the working poor or working families, which was what many welfare cases had become. This was immensely more popular" (Mead 2005, 185). Kaus (2002) states simply that one of "welfare reform's achievement was to enable a new consensus in favor of helping poor Americans who work."

STUDYING MASS FEEDBACK EFFECTS

What is important about the progressive revisionist thesis, for our purposes, is that prominent policy scholars, political scientists, and successful political actors advanced a common thesis: that welfare reform would reshape mass opinion. What is more, they offered coherent reasons for their expectations, reasons that were compatible with the evidence available at the time. Finally, and no less important, their logic was consistent with existing theories of policy feedback. The revisionists' political diagnosis hinged on the feedback effects of 1960s welfare policies; their prescription hinged on the idea that welfare reform could set new opinion dynamics in motion.

The concept of policy feedback disrupts the linear causal flow emphasized in most conventional political studies. Rather than treating policies as the culminating "outputs" of a political process (Easton 1953), scholars analyze policies as political forces in their own right (Pierson 1993). Policies can set political agendas and shape identities and interests. They can influence beliefs about what is possible, desirable, and normal. They can alter conceptions of citizenship and status. They can channel or constrain agency, define incentives, and redistribute resources. They can convey cues that define, arouse, or pacify constituencies.

By highlighting such possibilities, feedback theorists argue for a more balanced analytic stance in which scholars investigate how political processes and public policies shape each other over time. The key early works in this tradition focused on how policy designs influence the mobilization of organized interests and their interactions with elected officials (Lowi 1964; Wilson 1973). Recent works have maintained this emphasis: most of what we know continues to focus on state actors and organized interests (see Pierson 1994; Hacker 2002). Relative to mass publics, state actors and organized interests tend to have more clearly defined goals and interests; they pay closer attention to policy incentives and cues; and they are often embedded in institutions that shift visibly as a result of policy change. Thus, it is not clear how much one should generalize from these findings to predictions of mass feedback effects.

When researchers have considered effects on mass publics, they have usually done so by examining how policies affect the political attitudes and behaviors of policy "target populations." Some policies, for example, directly restrict a target group's standing to participate in politics, as in the case of felony disenfranchisement laws (Uggen and Manza 2002). Others distribute important resources for political engagement, such as education or wealth (Hochschild and Scovronick 2004; Katznelson 2005). Program benefits may generate new bases for self-interest and political participation, as in the case of seniors who vigorously defend Social Security and Medicare (Campbell 2003). And personal experiences with public programs may have educative effects that influence political beliefs and participation (Soss 2000; Mettler 2005). These sorts of effects contribute to general patterns of mass behavior, but they tell us little about what policies communicate to people who are *not* target-group members. We know less and confront greater analytic difficulties when we ask how policies affect broader mass publics.

To be sure, there has been no shortage of claims asserting the existence of mass feedback effects. Scholars have argued that the symbolic cues conveyed by government policies are powerful determinants of mass arousal and quiescence (Edelman 1971) that also shape mass perceptions of target groups (Schneider and Ingram 1997). Likewise, the structures of "major welfare-state institutions" have been singled out as potent influences on "the formation of values, attitudes, and interest among citizens" (Korpi 2003, 598). As Lawrence R. Jacobs and Theda Skocpol (2005, 226) note, "Research on the mass political effects of social policies" has emerged as "a growing new area in which exciting challenges loom." For all its progress, however, the study of mass feedback has produced few systematic analyses of survey data capable of testing predictions of policy-driven opinion change. Equally important, the field continues to lack explicit analytic frameworks capable of specifying the conditions under which mass feedback effects will occur.

Given this context, we see the case of welfare reform as a promising basis for advancing the field. The public opinion record on welfare is extensive, and there are a variety of reasons to see welfare reform as a "likely case" for mass feedback. Many observers have identified welfare as a potent symbol for Americans—a salient object of intense policy preferences for nonparticipating publics. Under AFDC, conflict over welfare largely followed party lines, which should have made it easier for publics to connect policy changes to broader political orientations. Participating political actors and observers considered mass feedback a likely outcome in this case. And finally, when policy reform occurred, it received extensive media coverage, and the resulting policy changes had large and widely reported effects.

In short, welfare reform offers a case in which predictions of mass feedback seem both plausible and amenable to testing. There is little in the existing literature on policy feedback that would cast doubt on such predictions. Thus, where positive evidence would affirm the theory in the context of a new and important case, the largely negative results reported in this article offer a stronger contrast to theoretical expectations and, hence, hold greater analytic value. Employing the limited effects of welfare reform as grist for theorizing, we attempt to specify the conditions under which mass feedbacks should occur.

SPECIFYING PREDICTIONS AND AN ANALYTIC APPROACH

To pursue a statistical analysis of the revisionist thesis, one must translate its narrative into a model with discrete, testable linkages. Figure 5.1 presents a path diagram, beginning with the initiating policy event: welfare reform. It distinguishes between two variants of the thesis based on the mechanism underlying expected effects. In the first, revisionists hoped to transform welfare into a program that would affirm majority values and present Americans with an antipoverty program they could support (path A). In this scenario, New Democrats would move mass opinion by associating the poor with work, refusing to abet those who failed to "play by the rules," and publicly claiming credit for it. A second variant of the thesis implied that reform would move mass opinion by removing welfare, with all its pejorative meanings and heavy political baggage, as a controversial issue in public discourse (path B). The assumption underlying this mechanism was that welfare discourse had distorted public sentiment. "Welfare" distracted Americans from their real desires to reduce poverty and artificially suppressed support for the Democratic Party. By taking "welfare" off the table, reform would allow these underlying preferences to emerge. Thus, rather than focusing public attention on the positive qualities of a reformed program, this strategy sought the opposite: to move opinion by removing "welfare" as a source of concern in the public consciousness.

For each variant, we can also distinguish a direct and indirect channel for effects. The direct channels are implied by the variant descriptions. Under the logic of transformation, the public would become more willing to invest because public aid would now be conditioned on responsible behavior and beneficiaries would be associated with work. The public would move back toward the Democratic Party because of the party's decisive rejection of permissive welfare in favor of a positive alternative (path C). Alternatively, under the logic of negation, where welfare would be erased from public discourse, support for public aid and the Democratic Party would rise simply because these inclinations would no longer be suppressed by the specter of welfare (path D). Each variant also suggests an indirect channel for effects: welfare reform would deracialize poverty politics, which would then redound to the advantage of both the poor and the Democratic Party. In the transformative variant, the image of a "handout to lazy blacks" would be neutralized by a design that clearly required work and responsible behavior (path E). Under the logic of negation, removal of the racialized welfare issue would yield a similar outcome (path F). Deracialization, in turn, would yield a more generous public and an electorate more favorable to the Democratic Party (path G).

It is tempting to test these predictions by simply comparing opinion in the final years of AFDC to opinion after 1996. Pursuing this approach, scholars have found that negative welfare attitudes in the mid-1990s softened after 1996, a pattern that seems consistent with the progressive revisionist thesis (Shaw and Shapiro 2002; Dyck, Hussey, and Williams 2005; Hetling, McDermott, and Mapps 2006). For example, based on changes in spending preferences from the period 1994 to 1996 to that of 2000 to 2001, Robert Shapiro concludes that "the [positive] shift in public opinion on welfare spending seems due to the adoption of stricter eligibility guidelines and work requirements for welfare recipients" (quoted in Devitt 2002). The problem is that such comparisons invite spurious conclusions by ignoring the heated reform campaign from 1992 to 1996—a period that

FIGURE 5.1 Path Diagram of the Progressive Revisionist Thesis

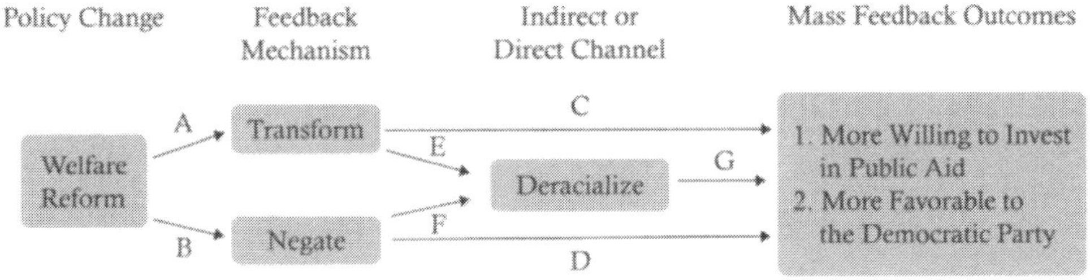

| Policy Change | Feedback Mechanism | Indirect or Direct Channel | Mass Feedback Outcomes |

Source: Authors' compilation.

saw a dramatic spike in media coverage of welfare (Schneider and Jacoby 2005) as well as in the mobilization and racialization of public anxieties over welfare policy (Soss and LeClair 2004).

Thus, analyses that use the period from 1992 to 1996 as a baseline risk conflating the effects of policy designs (AFDC versus TANF) with the effects of communication streams (a major reform campaign versus a more normal period). As policy analysts often note, it is easy to be misled by a time series if one compares an artificially high baseline to a later post-measure (for example, because of regression to the mean or cyclical trends; Cook and Campbell 1979). To obtain a more valid assessment of welfare reform's feedback effects, one must compare opinion at its steady state under AFDC (pre-1992) to opinion at its steady state under TANF (post-1997). Here, we treat the public opinion record as a simple interrupted time series (Cook and Campbell 1979, 209–14). Because there is no reasonably comparable control series, we pursue standard alternatives to enhancing validity: we examine pre-post differences that discount the 1992-to-1996 period; we rely on a variety of outcome measures rather than basing conclusions on a single measure; and we examine key relationships both with and without control variables.

EMPIRICAL ANALYSIS

Did welfare reform transform public aid in a way that improved public views of aid to recipients, the poor, and welfare policy itself (path A)? This prediction receives little support from the survey data. Here, it is important to return to the distinction between public satisfaction with a policy and feedback effects that yield changes in underlying political attitudes. In 2001, about 61 percent of those who knew about welfare reform said it was working well and, of these, 64 percent said the most important reason was that "the law requires people to go work" (NPR/Kaiser/Harvard). (Unless otherwise noted, results can be obtained from the cited polling organization and Bowman 2003.) Beyond this satisfaction, however, we find considerable stability in perceptions of welfare, welfare recipients, and the poor.

Mechanism

A policy promoting work does not seem to have allayed public anxieties about welfare dependency. In 1989, 64 percent of the public thought "welfare benefits make poor people dependent and encourage them to stay poor" (Gallup). We have no identical question for the TANF period, but available data do not suggest that reform banished negative beliefs about welfare dependency. In 2003, 71 percent of Americans agreed that "poor people have become too dependent on government assistance" (Pew). In 2001, 2002, and 2003, a steady 40 percent of women and 50 percent of men agreed with the hostile statement that "most welfare recipients are lazy cheats" (DDB Needham Worldwide). In 2002, 53 percent of Americans stated that "the current welfare system" makes things worse "by making able-bodied people too dependent on government aid" (Pew). Perhaps most remarkable in light of work-conditioned aid, 49 percent endorsed the statement that "poor people today do not have an incentive to work because they can get government benefits without doing anything in return" (Greenberg, Quinlan, and Rosner).

Wording differences make it impossible to know how strongly these results indicate stability. But responses to questions with consistent wording offer corroborating evidence. For example, "In your opinion do you think most people who receive money from welfare could get along without it if they tried, or do you think most of them really need this help?" The "could get along without it" view was endorsed by 40 percent in 1986 (CBS/NYT), 44 percent in 1992 (NBC/WSJ), and 44 percent in 2001 (NPR/Kaiser/Harvard). Similarly, work requirements have not diminished the belief that lack of effort explains why poor people are poor. "In your opinion, which is more often to blame if a person is poor—lack of effort on his part, or circumstances beyond his control?" From 1988 to 1990, 35 to 40 percent of Americans endorsed "lack of effort," and 37 to 45 percent endorsed "circumstances" (Gallup). Between 1998 and 2001, 40 to 48 percent chose "lack of effort," while 38 to 45 percent chose "circumstances" (Gallup; CBS; NPR/Kaiser/Harvard). The National Election Studies (NES) "feeling thermometer" scores also allow us to assess changes in Americans' feelings toward welfare recipients and the poor. For welfare recipients, the average score "warmed" from 50.7 (1980 to 1990) to 53.6 (1998 to 2004). By contrast, the score for the poor "cooled" from 72.5 (1980 to 1990) to 70 (1998 to 2004). These changes are statistically significant. But they are cross-cutting and, with standard deviations running in the fifteen-to-twenty point range, they are not substantively large.

Did policy reform negate welfare as an object of public concern (path B)? The NES time series survey contains two relevant measures. The first indicates the percentage of respondents each year who volunteered the answer "welfare" when asked, "What do you think are the most important problems facing this country?" From 1976 to 1986, welfare was named by 8 to 12 percent of NES respondents (mean = 9.2). In the political lull between the Family Support Act of 1988 and Clinton's pledge to end welfare, this number fell to 4.7 in both 1988 and 1990. The reform campaign produced a large spike, starting at 7 percent in 1992, rising to 16.8 percent in 1994, and then 26.6 percent in 1996. After reform, salience declined to 8 percent in 1998 and then to 4.8 percent in 2000. The NES series for this item ends here. Thus, we are left to conclude only that welfare's salience in 2000 (95 percent C.I. = 3.4 to 6.2) was discernibly lower than in the 1976-to-1986 period and was equivalent to the 1988-to-1990 period.

Fortunately, the NES series also allows us to follow the number of respondents each year who volunteered the answer "welfare" in response to any variant of the question "Is there anything in particular that you [like/dislike] about the [Democratic/Republican] party?" The observations here are slightly higher but follow a similar pattern. From 1976 to 1986, "welfare" was named as a basis of party evaluation by 7.3 to 17.7 percent of respondents (mean = 12.3). After remaining high at 17.1 percent in 1988, we see a dip in 1990 (11.9) and 1992 (11.4), followed by a spike in 1994 (23.2) and 1996 (19.6). In 2000, the percentage (10.4 percent; 95 percent C.I. = 8.5 to 11.6) falls below the AFDC-period norm and, in 2004, it falls to 4 percent (95 percent C.I. = 2.8 to 5.3), a level well below the low point under AFDC (7.3 in 1978).

Causal inference here is complicated by the possibility that welfare was pushed off the agenda after 2000 by other issues—most notably, national security and the Iraq War—rather than by the abolition of AFDC. Indeed, other domestic spending issues with little relation to welfare reform also declined in salience between 2000 and 2004. For example, although Social Security was a major domestic policy issue during this period, its salience dropped between 2000 and 2004 at a rate (7.8 to 2) almost identical to that of welfare (10.4 to 4). Thus, it seems plausible that agenda crowd-out accounted for some of welfare's declining visibility. Nevertheless, a variety of competing issues came and went in the pre-reform era, and none neutralized welfare's salience to this extent. Although outstanding causal questions remain, we consider these results consistent with the negation variant of the progressive revisionist thesis. In sum, then, we find evidence of issue negation (path B) but no transformation of views on welfare policy, welfare recipients, and the poor (path A and, hence, paths C and E). After 1996, welfare faded from the public agenda, but underlying images of welfare and policy-relevant groups shifted little.

The Indirect Channel: Deracialization

The General Social Survey (GSS) includes a number of measures that can be used to assess the prediction that welfare reform would deracialize poverty and welfare politics. Although this diversity precludes the satisfaction of a single definitive test, it allows us to avoid an overly tidy conclusion that hinges on the validity of a single measure.

We can begin by examining changes over time in the extent to which white preferences for spending on African Americans are related to white preferences for spending on welfare and the poor. To control for demographic differences over time, we estimate the relationships with controls for age, sex, education, marital status, and family income. (For full models underlying all results reported in this paper, as well as supplemental analyses, please see http://www.polisci.wisc.edu/~soss/public_transformed.pdf.) In the period from 1984 to 1991, whites who opposed efforts to "raise the living standards of blacks" were significantly more likely to oppose efforts to "raise the living standards of the poor" ($b = .270$, $p = .00$). This relationship grew stronger in the 1998-to-2004 period ($b = .334$, $p = .00$; test of difference $t = 3.4$, $p = .00$). The relationship between preferences for "spending to assist blacks" and "spending to assist the poor" held steady across the 1984-to-1991 period ($b = .278$, $p = .00$) and the 1998-to-2004 period ($b = .260$, $p = .00$; test of difference $t = -.84$, $p = .40$). And finally, whites who opposed efforts to raise black living standards were significantly more likely to oppose welfare spending in both the 1984-to-1991 period ($b = .168$, $p = .00$) and the 1998-to-2004 period ($b = .149$, $p = .00$; test of difference $t = -1.01$, $p = .34$). Thus, white Americans' tendency to equate welfare and aid to the poor with forms of aid targeted to blacks seems not to have been affected by welfare reform.

In addition to policy associations, the GSS time series includes two measures that allow us to assess change in the relationship between stereotypes of black work effort and white preferences for spending on public aid. The first, available in every GSS from 1985 to 2004, asks respondents to agree or disagree that economic disparities between blacks and whites exist because "most blacks just don't have the motivation or will power to pull themselves up out of poverty." The second, available in the GSS only between 1990 and 2004, asks all respondents to place "most blacks" on a seven-point scale running from hardworking to lazy. We find that neither measure exhibits a significant change in trend related to the passage of welfare reform.

To test for changes in stereotype influence, we constructed multivariate models predicting white opposition to spending on welfare and aid to the poor. The models consist of (1) respondents' sex, age, education, family income, marital status, party identification, liberal-conservative identification, and support for individualism; (2) dummy indicators for the reform and post-reform periods, with the pre-1992 era serving as the baseline; (3) one of the two stereotype measures; and (4) interactions between the period dummies and all included variables. In models that employ the laziness measure, our tests depend on an AFDC baseline that consists of only one pre-1992 year, 1990. The motivation measure, available for six years in the 1985-to-1991 period, offers a more substantial baseline for tests of pre-post differences.

Examining the sources of white welfare opposition, we find little evidence that stereotype effects weakened after welfare reform. Whites who believed that "blacks lack motivation" were significantly more likely to oppose welfare spending from 1985 to 1991 (b = .64, p = .00). The TANF period interaction term indicates no change (b = −.02, p = .87), leaving the relationship intact in the 1998-to-2004 period (b = .61, p = .00). Our second specification also fails to produce evidence of deracialization. The effect of the "black laziness stereotype" is actually insignificant in 1990 (b = .11, p = .25) and increases slightly over time (b = .18, p = .11) to yield a statistically significant relationship in the post-reform period (b = .29, p = .00).

Relative to "welfare," "assistance to the poor" has historically drawn stronger public support and has been less central to racialized poverty discourses (Gilens 1999; Schram 1995). Even so, we find a significant relationship in the 1985-to-1991 period between white preferences for aid to the poor and the belief that "blacks lack motivation" (b = .51, p = .00). The TANF period interaction is insignificant (b = −.07, p = .71), leaving this relationship substantially the same in the 1998-to-2004 period (b = .44, p = .00). By contrast, results using the "black laziness stereotype" suggest a pattern of change. In 1990, the only baseline year where we can observe it, this stereotype is a significant predictor of white opposition to assistance for the poor (b = .22, p = .03). This effect then weakens over time—not enough to make the relationship in the 1998-to-2004 period statistically distinct from the relationship in 1990 (b = −.14, p = .23), but enough to render the laziness stereotype statistically insignificant in the 1998-to-2004 period (b = .08, p = .19).

Because they pool years into periods, these pre-post tests benefit from larger samples in each time unit. Separate-year analyses force us to rely on samples that are smaller and more variable, but they also allow us to examine whether racialization has become less stable under the TANF program. Using this approach, we find little evidence that white welfare preferences have become less racialized. Counting results for both our GSS measures, we find that stereotypes of black effort are significant predictors in five of six separate-year analyses in the 1985-to-1991 period and seven of eight analyses in the 1998-to-2004 period.

For white opposition to spending on the poor, however, we find a more intriguing pattern. The black motivation stereotype is significant in three of five models in the 1985-to-1991 period and two of four models in the 1998-to-2004 period. Notably, the insignificant results in the post-reform period appear as the final two observations, 2002 and 2004. The samples available in 2002 (n = 182) and 2004 (n = 175) are small relative to earlier years, and the 2004 coefficient is comparable in size to the coefficient that is significant with a larger sample in 2000. But this weak indication of change is strengthened by results for the black laziness stereotype. Significant in 1990 as a predictor of white opposition to spending on the poor, this measure yields significant results in only one of four years in the 1998-to-2004 period, 2000. Thus, it seems plausible that these stereotypes exerted less influence on preferences for aid to the poor after welfare reform. With similar samples, the GSS shows no similar disruption of stereotype effects for "welfare."

In sum, we find mixed results for the deracialization hypothesis. The public remains as likely as earlier to equate welfare and generic aid to the poor with targeted efforts to assist blacks. Likewise, we find no reduction in the influence that black-effort stereotypes exert on white welfare preferences. By contrast, for aid to the poor, we find a mixed pattern: no discernible change in analyses that pool years into periods but evidence of weakening effects in separate-year analyses.

End Goals: Public Generosity and Partisan Advantage

Ultimately, the progressive revisionist thesis promised greater public support for efforts to help the disadvantaged and for the Democratic Party. One way reform might generate the first of these effects would be to strip the taint of "welfare" away from antipoverty efforts. As we have seen, welfare retained negative connotations for large segments of the public in the post-reform era: it remained associated with dependence, laziness, and aid to blacks. One critical question, then, is whether the quieting of welfare disputes weakened the relationship between disdain for welfare and resistance to helping the poor.

In the subsample of the GSS that contains the welfare preference question, two items measure willingness to help the poor: a five-point scale indicating opposition to the idea that government "should do everything possible to improve the standard of living of all poor Americans" and a seven-point scale indicating opposition to the idea that government should "reduce the income differences between the rich and the poor, perhaps by raising the taxes of wealthy families or by giving income assistance to the poor." To test whether these policy preferences have become less tied to welfare attitudes, we use a regression analysis that includes controls for respondents' sex, age, education, family income, marital status, party identification, liberal-conservative identification, and support for individualism. For the first measure, we find a significant relationship to welfare opposition in the 1984-to-1991 period ($b = .307$, $p = .00$) that if anything increases slightly in the 1998-to-2004 period ($b = .345$, $p = 00$; test of difference: $t = .71$, $p = .48$). We find the same pattern using the second measure (1984 to 1991: $b = .316$, $p = .00$; 1998 to 2004: $b = .388$, $p = .00$; test of difference: $t = .82$, $p = .41$). Both results prove robust in analyses of subsamples restricted to white respondents and whites making below the median income.

Despite its lingering association with welfare, the public's willingness to invest in the poor could have risen as welfare became a less salient issue. Comparing means across periods, we find no evidence of such a shift. Opposition to improving "the standard of living of all poor Americans" actually increased significantly in the years after welfare reform (mean$_{1984-1991}$ = 2.81, mean$_{1998-2004}$ = 2.98; $t = 8.57$, $p = .00$), as did opposition to reducing "income differences between the rich and the poor" (mean$_{1984-91}$ = 3.57, mean$_{1998-2004}$ = 3.83; $t = 7.86$, $p = .00$). For the key spending preferences, we find continuity. There was a negligible increase in opposition to spending on aid to the poor (mean$_{1984-1991}$ = 1.42, mean$_{1998-2004}$ = 1.44; $t = 1.68$, $p = .09$). We observe no significant changes in preferences regarding aid to blacks (mean$_{1984-1991}$ = 1.93, mean$_{1998-2004}$ = 1.93; $t = .41$, $p = .68$) and welfare (mean$_{1984-1991}$ = 2.29, mean$_{1998-2004}$ = 2.21; $t = -1.04$, $p = .30$). All five results are robust in analyses of subsamples restricted to whites and to whites below the median income, and yearly observations corroborate the analyses based on periods.

Thus, in the post-reform era, the tendency to attribute poverty to lack of effort has held steady, feelings toward the poor have grown slightly cooler, efforts to aid the poor have remained associated with "welfare," and willingness to aid the poor has stayed the same or diminished. Finding little change in the public climate for policymaking, we turn to partisan and electoral dynamics. In the years leading up to welfare reform, revisionists argued that Democrats labored under unacceptable disadvantages as a result of their association with "permissive" welfare. By signing a tough reform bill, President Clinton would clear the way for Democrats to gain support among Americans who opposed permissive public assistance.

Figure 5.2 offers support for some aspects of this argument. The "balance" trend line for each party indicates the proportion of NES respondents in each year that cited welfare as a reason to like a specific party minus the proportion citing it as a reason to dislike that party. The bars represent welfare's salience to the public, as indicated by the NES "important problem" question. In most years from 1976 to 2004, the Republican Party shows a net positive evaluation on this issue; the Democratic Party shows a net negative. The changing distance between the lines clearly supports those who argued that Democrats suffered a substantial disadvantage on welfare in the late 1970s and early 1980s. At its widest in 1982, there was a 20.2-point gap favoring the Republicans. At the end of the 1980s, however, we see parallel shifts in partisan advantage and issue salience. In the wake of the Family Support Act of 1988, amid the much-discussed "new consensus" in welfare policy, public attention to welfare wanes *and* the Republican advantage on this issue evaporates. This state of affairs proved ephemeral, however. After Clinton reopened the issue with his 1992 campaign pledge, and Republicans responded, welfare reemerged on the public agenda and the Republican Party promptly reestablished its advantage. Indeed, the Republican issue advantage follows the trend in issue salience very closely. It reappears with Clinton's pledge in 1992; it expands markedly in 1994; it peaks in 1996; and then falls away in the years after reform.

Several points merit our attention here. First, in periods of higher salience, the welfare issue redounded to the Republican Party's advantage, regardless of whether leading Democrats were defending welfare (pre-1988) or demanding its reform (1992 to 1996). Thus, contrary to the transformative variant of the revisionist thesis, if any party was in a position to claim credit for ending permissive welfare, it was the Republicans. Second, the periods that follow major legislative actions (1988 to 1990 and 2000 to 2004) are characterized by dissipation: public attention drops and the party balance measures drift toward each other at the neutral point on the scale. Third, public concern and Republican issue advantage were not constants under AFDC; they were variables tied to elite interaction. Fourth, while bipartisan legislative action neutralized the welfare issue briefly after 1988, it did not prevent the issue's resurgence or the reestablishment of partisan advantage. When elite conflict returned, so did the earlier patterns. Thus, just as the welfare issue can be taken off the table, it can be put back on. A key question, then, is whether welfare reform changed underlying political dynamics (or constrained political discourse) in a more fundamental and durable way.

The welfare issue became less salient after 1996, but did this change produce dividends for the Democrats? One way to interpret the progressive-revisionist strategy is to say that it aimed to make partisan competition less "about" the most divisive targets of social spending: blacks and welfare recipients. Success in this strategy would be indicated by an electorate in which preferences for welfare spending and assistance to blacks became less predictive of partisanship. Because opponents of such spending would feel

FIGURE 5.2   Percentage of People Naming Welfare as a Reason to Like or Dislike the Democratic and Republican Parties; Comparison of Party Balances and Issue Salience over Time

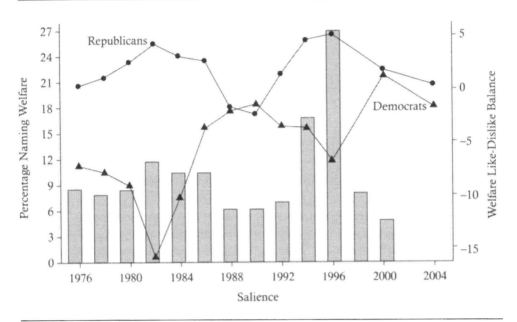

Source: Authors' calculations.

more comfortable identifying as Democrats, the correlation between attitudes toward these "stigmatized" policies and party identification would diminish.

The GSS time series suggests no such pattern of change. Outside the South, the bivariate correlation between party identification and welfare preferences was r = .21 between 1980 and 1991, and it remained r = .21 in the 1998-to-2004 period. In the South, where conservatives were moving toward the Republican Party during this time, the correlation rises across the two periods from r = .18 to r = .24. A stronger version of the same patterns emerges for the relationship between party identification and preferences for spending on aid to blacks. Outside the South, the average bivariate correlation between these measures was r = .21 between 1980 and 1991; it rises to r = .26 in the period from 1998 to 2004. In the South, the correlation rises from r = .19 to r = .32. None of these patterns suggests that welfare reform helped the Democrats win over opponents of stigmatized public assistance.

Indeed, welfare opponents who lived outside the South identified with the Democratic Party at a rate that was 84 percent of the general electorate between 1980 and 1991 but only 77 percent of the electorate between 1998 and 2004. Democratic identification among welfare opponents in the South fell from 89 percent of the general electorate (1980 to 1991) to 73 percent of the general electorate (1998 to 2004). Outside the South, people who opposed aid to blacks identified as Democrats at a rate that was 79 percent of the general electorate in the AFDC era (1980 to 1991) but only 73 percent of the general electorate in the TANF era (1998 to 2004). Within the South, the rate of Democratic identification among those who opposed aid to blacks fell from 86 percent of the general electorate (1980 to 1991) to 63 percent (1998 to 2004). Thus, opponents of these two forms of spending remained just as numerous in the post-reform era as they were before; survey data suggest that "welfare" symbolized the same things it had in the past to these opponents; and even if one isolates Americans outside the South, public aid opponents were at least as hesitant to identify with the Democratic Party after welfare reform as they had been before.

If we shift our attention from party identification to electoral choice, a similar story emerges. Because issues related to national security and the Iraq War dominated the election of 2004, diminishing the influence of domestic social policy issues in general, 2004 offers an uncertain basis for assessing relevant changes. Instead, we focus on the two presidential elections immediately prior to Clinton's welfare pledge (1984 and 1988) and the election four years after reform (2000). The 1984 election took place under AFDC, in a year when the welfare issue was salient and favored the Republican Party over Democrats. The 1988 election was also contested under AFDC, but in this year welfare was much less salient and the Democrats enjoyed parity on the party balance measures. The 2000 election was contested after welfare reform, in a period when welfare was once again low on the public agenda and the party balance measures were in parity. How did the Republican advantage among welfare-opposing voters shift across these elections? If we take the Republican candidate's share of the two-party vote among welfare opponents and divide it by this candidate's share of the two-party vote among all voters, we obtain a ratio indicating how much better the Republicans performed among welfare opponents than among the electorate as a whole. Outside the South, this ratio was 1.15 in 1984, 1.20 in 1988, and 1.19 in 2000. In the South, this ratio was 1.32 in 1984, 1.16 in 1988, and 1.21 in 2000. These patterns of stability hold even if we restrict our samples to white voters or to white voters below the median income.

In sum, we find that reform made welfare less salient as a basis for party evaluation, but decreased salience does not seem to have yielded broader political gains for the Democratic Party. Welfare opponents remained just as numerous after 1996 as in the AFDC era, and these individuals became no more likely to identify with the Democratic Party or vote for Democratic candidates.

WHY WELFARE REFORM DIDN'T TRANSFORM PUBLIC ATTITUDES

Progressive revisionists were right about many things. In the wake of political and policy changes in the 1960s, a racialized view of welfare emerged as a major contributor to negative views of the Democratic Party. Pre-1996 majorities did indeed want to reform welfare, and post-1996 majorities took a positive view of work-oriented welfare reform. Nonetheless, few of the opinion effects that revisionists predicted actually materialized. Social welfare policies have, in the past, been catalysts for major changes in mass opinion. New Deal policies, for example, encouraged new public beliefs about government's responsibility for citizens' economic well-being and new categories for perceiving and evaluating public policy—a "big bang" of opinion change (Piven and Cloward 1982; Skocpol 1995). In the 1960s and 1970s, civil rights policies set in motion major changes in racial attitudes and political values. In light of those changes, the weak opinion effects associated with contemporary welfare reform pose a genuine puzzle for students of American politics and poverty policy. These weak effects invite an effort to explain the conditions under which policy changes should have stronger or weaker effects on public opinion. Is it possible to provide a general explanation for why the progressive revisionist thesis went wrong?

The primary problem, we argue, is that progressive revisionists focused on the visibility of welfare for Americans without attending to the fact that this policy had little proximity to the lives of most Americans. Public policies vary not only in their visibility, but also their proximity (see figure 5.3). Regardless of their visibility in public discourse, policies may be distant from citizens' everyday lives as a result of geography (as with some foreign policies), the patterning of social relations (as with an income-targeted policy in a class-segregated city), or time (as with policy effects that will be felt personally but only at some remote date). When highly visible policies have proximate, tangible effects on people's lives, mass publics will experience them more directly and, hence, will gain greater ability to evaluate them through "individual observation rather than mass response to others' cues"(Edelman 1971). By contrast, when highly visible policies exist primarily as distant objects of perception for mass publics, they may elicit rapt attention and powerful emotion, but they will lack concrete presence in most people's lives. In such instances, claims and beliefs about policies cannot easily be tested against experience. As a result, public perceptions will depend more heavily on elite rhetoric, media frames, and widely held cultural beliefs.

Welfare reform, in our view, offers a paradigmatic example of the politics that surround distant-visible policies of this sort. (It falls into the upper-left quadrant of figure 5.3.) As Jacob Hacker (2004) points out, AFDC was "a fiscally tiny program with . . . a clientele that never exceeded 6 percent of the population," yet it became "liberalism's symbolic beachhead and conservatives' poster child for everything wrong with American social policy." Details of the AFDC policy design mattered greatly for recipients but very little in most Americans' lives. "Welfare," on the other hand, symbolized to large numbers of Americans a deeply felt sense that government was giving special favors to a group of undeserving others. It evoked an image of easy living on government largesse, in contrast to the experiences of "normal, hard-working Americans."

Based on this "distant-visible" status, we outline four general propositions that explain why welfare reform had limited effects on public opinion.

1. When a policy exists as a potent but distant symbol for mass publics, the details of its material design will seldom anchor public understandings of the policy. Unaffected publics will rarely pay close attention to changing policy realities, and new facts on the ground will rarely force the abandonment of old myths. Before 1996, researchers repeatedly found that public perceptions of welfare had only the loosest relation to the AFDC program's actual features. A 1994 poll, for example, found that most Americans thought that AFDC—which, at its peak, cost less than 5 percent of Social Security—was one of the two largest items in the federal budget (Hacker 2004). In the TANF era, evidence suggests that 40 to 50 percent of Americans have never had a clear understanding of exactly how welfare provision changed. For example, when asked in 2001 whether welfare had been reformed in any significant way over the past five years, 50 percent of respondents answered either "No" or "Don't know" (Weaver 2000, 338). Thus, one part of our explanation is that, no matter how visible a policy may be in symbolic terms, changes to its material design will tend to go unnoticed if the policy affects few citizens' lives directly.

2. When policies are highly visible but have few concrete effects on most citizens' lives, they will often be valued less for what they achieve, in fewer people's lives, than for what they affirm, about society as a whole (Gusfield 1963). Policy actions, in such cases, are valued primarily for what they say about who we are, what we stand for, and what we

FIGURE 5.3   A General Framework for the Analysis of Mass Feedback
Processes: Policy Visibility and Proximity

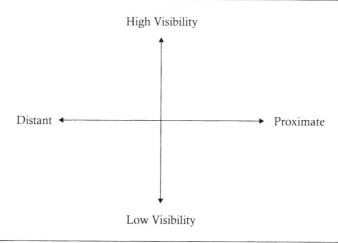

Source: Authors' compilation.

expect of one another. The fact that such actions express majority opinion does not mean that they will change majority opinion. In particular, when a policy action affirms dominant, widely held values by rewarding individuals who live up to them or by punishing individuals who do not comply with them, we should expect the policy to reinforce rather than disrupt existing patterns of mass opinion.

Here, we encounter a major problem in the progressive revisionist argument that "work attachment" would make welfare recipients appear more deserving. The language of "work attachment" elided a crucial distinction between policies that reward work and policies that compel work as a condition of aid. In the politics that led to welfare reform, "work" was not identified as a prior status indicating the deservingness of recipients; it was cast as a behavioral standard that had been violated. For most Americans, welfare reform was about holding violators of the work ethic accountable. This observation helps to explain how revisionists could be right about the popularity of welfare reform but wrong to predict that reform would improve the image of aid recipients. Majorities may like it when legislators pass tough sentencing laws that hold criminals accountable, for example, but such policies rarely lead publics to view criminals in a positive light. Work requirements followed an analogous logic. "Legislation requiring welfare recipients to work engenders the belief that laziness is at the heart of the welfare problem and that jobs are plentiful" (Edelman 1977).

3. When a policy is not directly experienced by many in the public, it exists primarily as a symbol. So it is essential to recognize that symbols only evoke underlying beliefs; they do not account for their existence. The power of a symbol lies not in itself but rather in what it stands for. (Thus, a shrug of the shoulders may symbolize and convey the idea "I don't know," but the absence of a shrug does not prevent this idea from being conveyed in other ways.) As long as there is a shared public understanding that two objects signify the same thing, they will suffice as substitutes (Edelman 1964, 1988). Drawing on this in-

sight, we can see that the withdrawal of a distant-visible policy will only yield changes in mass perception if no alternative symbol is deployed as a substitute. Progressive revisionists were wrong to assume that beliefs about welfare could be banished simply by "ending welfare as we know it." Images of the poor as idle and immoral flourished long before the AFDC program, as did the idea that public aid perversely encourages dysfunctional behavior (Gordon 1994; Katz 1989). Negative images of the poor can be, and at times have been, successfully contested with alternative images and discourses. But they cannot be negated simply by removing any single symbol—even one as potent as "welfare."

4. The material features of distant-visible policies do have consequences for mass opinion, even if these effects are mediated by the ways policies are portrayed in elite rhetoric, mass media, social conversation, and so on. The crucial point is that mass perceptions of public policies depend upon both a policy's internal characteristics and its positioning within the larger structure of a policy regime. When policies are directly experienced, people will tend to judge them according to both their internal design characteristics (which they experience) and the contrast between this policy and others (which they observe).

As the distance between policy and public grows, however, internal design characteristics fade from view, leaving perception more dependent on the contrast of one policy with another. In this regard, state institutions and the structures of policy regimes may be quite important. The establishment of "separate departments of government to deal with . . . supposedly distinct problems" presents the public with an organizing schema that helps to fix the meanings of particular social problems, social groups, and government activities (Edelman 1977). The bifurcated structure of the American welfare state, for example, provides an institutional contrast—"Social Security versus welfare"—that is frequently cited as a basis for public distinctions between the deserving and the undeserving. Public perceptions depend heavily on the symbolic oppositions conveyed by this contrast: contract versus charity, independence versus dependence, white versus black, masculine versus feminine, universal versus particular (Gordon 1994; Schram 1995; Schneider and Ingram 1997).

Thus, it is significant that welfare reform changed the conditions of public aid for the poor but did not displace or reconfigure this basic contrast in American social politics. As a result, welfare reform did not alter the way Americans distinguish the deserving from the undeserving or think about policies for the disadvantaged. Changes to welfare were far less salient to most Americans than the enduring distinction between this type of program and the policies that "deserving" Americans receive benefits from. Today, the positive image of Social Security is held in place not just by its own policy design, but also by the idea that it is "not welfare." Conversely, although the TANF program has restricted the pool of recipients of aid to those who "play by the rules," its meaning remains tied to its contrast with programs that offer "earned, contributory" benefits.

Thus, the case of welfare reform, we believe, does not cast doubt on the idea that policy changes can move public opinion. Rather, it helps to clarify the circumstances under which such changes are likely to occur. It underscores that the categories of a policy regime can structure public understanding in powerful ways, and that stable institutional contrasts can matter more than changes in the design of even a highly visible policy. When a policy change directly touches only a few citizens' lives, when it is valued primarily as a symbolic affirmation, when it eliminates one symbolic distraction only to replace it with others, when it leaves salient categories of the regime intact, and when its introduction is framed in ways that reinforce prevailing discourse, we should not be surprised if it fails to shift entrenched public opinion.

REFERENCES

Block, Fred, Richard A. Cloward, Barbara Ehrenreich, and Frances Fox Piven. 1987. *The Mean Season.* New York: Pantheon Books.

Bowman, Kathryn. 2003. "Attitudes About Welfare Reform." AEI Studies in Public Opinion. Washington: American Enterprise Institute.

Campbell, Andrea Louise. 2003. *How Policies Make Citizens: Senior Political Activism and the American Welfare State.* Princeton, N.J.: Princeton University Press.

Cook, Thomas, and Donald Campbell. 1979. *Quasi-Experimentation: Design and Analysis Issues in Field Settings.* Boston, Mass.: Houghton Mifflin.

DeParle, Jason. 1999. "The Silence of the Liberals: Liberals Need to be More Active in Welfare Reform." *Washington Monthly* 51(April): 12. Accessed at http://www.washingtonmonthly.com/features/1999/9904.deparle.silence.html.

DeParle, Jason, and Steven A. Holmes. 2000. "A War on Poverty Subtly Linked to Race." *New York Times*, December 26, 2000, A1.

Devitt, James. 2002. "Six Years After Welfare Reform, Public Opposition to Welfare Spending Declines." *Columbia News*, April 1, 2002. Accessed at http://www.columbia.edu/cu/news/02/04/welfare_spending.html.

Dyck, Joshua J., Laura Hussey, and Linda Williams. 2005. "The End of Welfare As We Know It?" Paper presented at the American Politics Workshop, University of Maryland, Department of Government and Politics. College Park, Md. March 4, 2005. Accessed at http://www.bsos.umd.edu/gvpt/apworkshop/DHW.pdf.

Easton, David. 1953. *The Political System: An Inquiry into the State of Political Science.* New York: Knopf.

Edelman, Murray. 1964. *The Symbolic Uses of Politics.* Urbana, Ill.: University of Illinois Press.
———. 1971. *Politics as Symbolic Action.* Chicago, Ill.: Markham.
———. 1977. *Political Language: Words That Succeed and Policies That Fail.* New York: Academic Press.
———. 1988. *Constructing the Political Spectacle.* Chicago, Ill.: University of Chicago Press.

Edsall, Thomas Byrne, with Mary D. Edsall. 1991. *Chain Reaction: The Impact of Race, Rights, and Taxes on American Politics.* New York: Knopf.

Ellwood, David. 1988. *Poor Support: Poverty in the American Family.* New York: Basic Books.

Gilens, Martin. 1999. *Why Americans Hate Welfare: Race, Media, and the Politics of Antipoverty Policy.* Chicago, Ill.: University of Chicago Press.

Gordon, Linda. 1994. *Pitied but Not Entitled: Single Mothers and the History of Welfare.* New York: Free Press.

Gusfield, Joseph. 1963. *Symbolic Crusade.* Urbana, Ill.: University of Illinois Press.

Hacker, Jacob S. 2002. *The Divided Welfare State: The Battle of Public and Private Social Benefits in the United States.* New York: Cambridge University Press.
———. 2004. "After Welfare." *The New Republic.* October 11, 2004.

Heclo, Hugh. 2001. "The Politics of Welfare Reform." In *The New World of Welfare*, edited by Rebecca Blank and Ron Haskins. Washington: Brookings Institution Press.

Hetling, Andrea, Monika L. McDermott, and Mingus Mapps. 2006. "Does Policy Affect Public Opinion: The Case of 1996 U.S. Welfare Reforms." Unpublished manuscript. Political Science Department, University of Connecticut.

Hochschild, Jennifer, and Nathan Scovronick. 2004. *The American Dream and the Public Schools.* New York: Oxford University Press.

Jacobs, Lawrence R., and Theda Skocpol, editors. 2005. *Inequality and American Democracy: What We Know and What We Need to Learn.* New York: Russell Sage Foundation.

Jencks, Christopher. 2005. "What Happened to Welfare?" *The New York Review of Books*, December 15, 2005, 76-86.

Katz, Michael. 1989. *The Undeserving Poor.* New York: Pantheon.

Katznelson, Ira. 2005. *When Affirmative Action Was White: An Untold History of Racial Inequality in Twentieth-Century America.* New York: Norton.

Kaus, Mickey. 1992. *The End of Equality.* New York: Basic Books.

———. 1996. "The Revival of Liberalism." *New York Times*, August 9, 1996, A27.

———. 2002. "Making the Case: Has Welfare Reform Worked? Yes, Smashingly." *Blueprint* (Democratic Leadership Council) 14(January–February). Accessed at http://www.ndol.org/ndol_ci.cfm?contentid=250083&kaid=114&subid=143.

Korpi, Walter. 2003. "Welfare-State Regress in Western Europe: Politics, Institutions, Globalization, and Europeanization." *Annual Review of Sociology* 29: 589–609.

Lowi, Theodore. 1964. "American Business, Public Policy, Case-Studies, and Political Theory." *World Politics* 16 (July): 677–715.

Marshall, Will. 2002. "After Dependence." *Blueprint* (Democratic Leadership Council) 14(January–February). Available at http://www.dlc.org/ndol_ka.cfm?pagenum=2&kaid=132.

Mead, Lawrence M. 1992. *The New Politics of Poverty: The Nonworking Poor in America*. New York: Basic Books.

———. 2001. "The Politics of Conservative Welfare Reform." In *The New World of Welfare*, edited by Rebecca Blank and Ron Haskins. Washington: Brookings Institution Press.

———. 2004. *Government Matters: Welfare Reform in Wisconsin*. Princeton, N.J.: Princeton University Press.

———. 2005. "Welfare Reform and Citizenship." In *Welfare Reform and Political Theory*, edited by Lawrence M. Mead and C. Beem. New York: Russell Sage Foundation.

Mettler, Suzanne. 2005. *Soldiers to Citizens: The G.I. Bill and the Making of the Greatest Generation*. New York: Oxford University Press.

Meyerson, Harold. 1996. "Wither the Democrats." *The American Prospect Online*, 7, 25(March): 79.

Pierson, Paul. 1993. "When Effect Becomes Cause: Policy Feedback and Political Change." *World Politics* 45(July): 595–628.

———. 1994. *Dismantling the Welfare State? Reagan, Thatcher, and the Politics of Retrenchment*. New York: Cambridge University Press.

Piven, Frances Fox, and Richard A. Cloward. 1982. "The American Road to Democratic Socialism." *Democracy* 3(3): 58–69.

Schattschneider, E. E. 1935. *Politics, Pressure, and the Tariff*. New York: Prentice-Hall.

Schneider, Anne, and Helen Ingram. 1997. *Policy Design for Democracy*. Lawrence, Kan.: University Press of Kansas.

Schneider, Saundra K., and William G. Jacoby. 2005. "Elite Discourse and American Public Opinion: The Case of Welfare Spending." *Political Research Quarterly* 58(3): 367–79.

Schram, Sanford F. 1995. *Words of Welfare: The Poverty of Social Science and the Social Science of Poverty*. Minneapolis, Minn.: University of Minnesota Press.

Shaw, Greg M., and Robert Y. Shapiro. 2002. "The Polls—Trends: Poverty and Public Assistance." *Public Opinion Quarterly* 66(Winter): 105–28.

Skocpol, Theda. 1992. *Protecting Soldiers and Mothers: The Political Origins of Social Policy in the United States*. Cambridge, Mass.: Harvard University Press/Belknap Press.

———. 1995. *Social Policy in the United States: Future Possibilities in Historical Perspective*. Princeton, N.J.: Princeton University Press.

———. 1996. "Bury It: Welfare: Where Do We Go From Here? *The New Republic* 215(7): 20–21.

———. 2000. *The Missing Middle*. New York: Norton.

Soss, Joe. 2000. *Unwanted Claims: The Politics of Participation in the U.S. Welfare System*. Ann Arbor, Mich.: University of Michigan Press.

Soss, Joe, and Danielle LeClair. 2004. "Race, Sex, and the Implicit Politics of Welfare Reform." Paper presented at the Annual Conference of the Midwest Political Science Association. Political Science Department, University of Wisconsin, Madison.

Teixeira, Ruy, and Joel Rogers. 2000. *America's Forgotten Majority: Why the White Working Class Still Matters*. New York: Basic Books.

Teles, Stephen M. 1996. *Whose Welfare? AFDC and Elite Policies*. Lawrence, Kan.: University Press of Kansas.

Uggen, Christopher, and Jeff Manza. 2002. "Democratic Contraction: Political Consequences of Felon Disenfranchisement in the United States." *American Sociological Review* 67(6): 777–803.

Weaver, R. Kent. 2000. *Ending Welfare as We Know It*. Washington: Brookings Institution Press.

———. 2002. "Polls, Priming, and the Politics of Welfare Reform." In *Navigating Public Opinion*, edited by Jeffrey Manza, Fay L. Cook, and Benjamin I. Page. New York: Oxford University Press.

Wilson, James Q. 1973. *Political Organizations*. New York: Basic Books.

Wilson, William Julius. 1999. *Bridge over the Racial Divide: Rising Inequality and Coalition Politics*. Berkeley, Calif.: University of California Press.

Part IV

Policies and Participation:
The Interplay of Structure
and Agency

Andrea Louise Campbell

Chapter 6

Universalism, Targeting, and Participation

Political inequality is one of the defining characteristics of our time. Some groups—the wealthy, the educated, and the organized—participate in politics at much higher rates than others. As a result, they tend to get more of what they want from the government (Campbell 2003a; Hill and Leighley 1992; Martin 2003). This wouldn't matter if their preferences across issue areas were the same as everyone else's—but they are not: the highly participatory also tend to have different policy preferences (Verba, Brady, and Schlozman 2004; Verba, Schlozman, and Brady 1995). The result of political inequality is that the vocal and organized get their preferences fulfilled while the quiescent do not. Thus we care about inequalities in political participation because they influence what kind of policies come out of government.

The factors that determine the likelihood that different individuals and groups will participate in politics arise from a variety of sources—formal education, childhood socialization, and social environments such as work, church, and nonpolitical organizations (Verba, Schlozman, and Brady 1995). The most prominent explanations of political participation today are what Suzanne Mettler and Joe Soss (2004) term "sociological": how individuals fare in the political arena is determined by their social backgrounds and affiliations.

However, these models tend to overlook a crucial source of political participation and inequality: public policy itself. As Jacob Hacker, Suzanne Mettler, and Joe Soss note in the introduction to this volume, we often think of public policies as being the outcomes of democratic processes. However, such policies are also profoundly influential inputs in the democratic process. The designs of policies—what they do, to whom they are targeted, and how generous they are—are not just the result of the struggle of contending groups as they make their way through the institutional processes of American government. The designs of public policies are also a key factor in determining who enters that struggle and how they fare. Government policies shape the ability of members of the mass public to participate in politics. In turn that participation influences subsequent policy outcomes. This chapter explores a variety of social policy areas, showing how government policies are key determinants of economic and in turn political equality. The particular characteristics of public policies that enhance or diminish recipient political participation will be examined. In the United States, constellations of these factors tend to come together, so that universal programs typically enhance participation while targeted programs undermine it. These program effects feed back into the political system, affecting subsequent policy initiatives and reforms.

PARTICIPATORY DIFFERENCES: WHERE
DO THEY COME FROM?

The chief method by which members of the mass public can be heard in the political arena is through political participation. When citizens vote, make campaign contributions, write letters to elected officials, work on campaigns, sign petitions, and attend rallies and protests, they send messages to the government about their political preferences. These participatory acts vary in how difficult they are, how much information they convey to policymakers, and how egalitarian they are (Verba and Nie 1972). But in each case, whether individuals become involved in these activities is a function of the participatory factors of resources, engagement, and mobilization (Verba, Schlozman, and Brady 1995). These factors determine whether individuals can participate in political action, whether they want to, and whether they are asked to do so. These participatory factors share two important characteristics: they tend to build on each other, and they are each influenced by public policy.

Resources help determine whether individuals are able to participate in politics.[1] Politically relevant resources include formal education, income, civic skills, and free time. Those with more education find the bureaucratic hurdles associated with political participation—registering to vote in advance of election day, locating mailing addresses for members of Congress—less daunting than do the less educated. Political knowledge and interest tend to increase with education, as does location in social groupings where participation is the norm. Income, too, aids participation, particularly in activities such as making campaign donations, where it is a necessary ingredient. As with the educated, more affluent individuals tend to be surrounded by social and work environments in which politics is discussed and participation expected. And income typically increases engagement with politics, as stakes in government policies increase with higher incomes (think of tax policy, where the more one earns, the more one has at stake). Possessing politically relevant skills such as letter writing and speech making also increases the likelihood of participation. These skills are often developed in nonpolitical settings such as workplaces and churches and can be transferred to the political arena. Finally, participation in some activities, particularly time-intensive ones such as working on campaigns, tends to increase with free time. This relationship has been more difficult for political scientists to determine, largely because of difficulties in measuring how much free time people have (Verba, Schlozman, and Brady 1995, 440–44). However, we do know that retired people are far more likely to participate in a variety of political activities, in part because of their great stakes in public affairs, but also because of the enormous boost in free time that comes with the cessation of formal paid work.

Political engagement refers to a variety of characteristics that capture whether individuals want to participate. Political interest is chief among these: having an interest in public affairs, either general or issue-specific, is a major predictor of participation. Political knowledge helps facilitate participation; knowing about politics generally or specifically both increases the rewards of participation and reduces the costs associated with political action, such as information gathering (Hutchings 2003). Finally, political efficacy figures prominently in participation. Feeling that the government pays attention to people like oneself and that there is some payoff to participation makes individuals much more likely to engage in political activity.

The third major participatory factor is mobilization: whether individuals are asked to participate. Mobilization can come from a variety of sources—a personal request from someone at work or in a group one is involved with; a letter from an interest group; a phone call from a political party. Being asked is often the trigger that gets those with the potential to participate to actually join in.

These participatory factors tend to cluster together. If one is educated, one is more likely not only to know about politics and feel prepared to participate but also to be situated in social environments where participation is the social norm and where information about public affairs is readily available. A well-educated individual is more likely to get a high-paying job, providing income that can be used for campaign donations, but also providing opportunities to exercise high-level and politically relevant skills such as speechmaking.

The other key characteristic of these participatory factors is that they can arise from public policies. As Paul Pierson (1993) first suggested, public policies are important sources of politically relevant resources. Some public policies, such as Social Security and welfare, literally confer cash income on recipients, while others provide in-kind benefits such as health care and housing.

Perhaps even more important are policies' "interpretive effects" (Pierson 1993)—how policies shape both individuals' stakes in politics and public affairs and their sense of standing as members of the political community. These interpretive effects are similar to the political engagement effects just discussed. Public policies can tie individuals' interests to public action in tangible and significant ways that spark political participation. Moreover, public policies can have a powerful "political learning" effect: how policies are designed—who receives benefits, how generous they are, and how they are administered—sends messages to clients about their worth as citizens, which in turn affects their orientation toward government and their likelihood of political participation (Ingram and Schneider 1993). Program recipients learn what actions are appropriate for their group and how legitimate and successful such actions are likely to be. "Advantaged" groups such as Social Security recipients hear messages that they are "good, intelligent" people with legitimate claims on the government (Ingram and Schneider 1993, 89–90). Less-advantaged groups hear the opposite lesson, that they are not worthy of the full rights and benefits of democratic citizenship, which undermines their political interest and efficacy and therefore their participation.

Finally, public policies define groups and create targets for mobilization. Public policies can take otherwise disparate groups of people—persons aged sixty-five and over, for example—and turn them into a politically relevant group—Social Security recipients—by virtue of their receipt of a public program. Such a group can then be mobilized to political activity by political parties, interest groups, and political entrepreneurs on the basis of this policy-forged identity.

PUBLIC POLICIES AS SOURCES OF PARTICIPATORY DIFFERENCES

The effect of public policies on participation through the resource, engagement, and mobilization mechanisms can be either positive or negative. The effects of universal programs such as Social Security, Medicare, and the G.I. Bill tend to be positive, fostering participation among client groups, whereas the effects of targeted programs tend to be negative (although not necessarily so). This section will compare what is perhaps the prototypical universal program, Social Security, with a targeted one, welfare, to show the effects of program design on resources, engagement, and mobilization, and therefore on client participation.[2] Findings on a third program, Head Start, show that means-tested programs are not necessarily harmful to clients' civic engagement and capacity, and can be designed to have positive effects.

These program effects are profoundly consequential because they can feed back through the political process. Over time a "participation-policy cycle" can emerge, whereby programs influence the level and nature of client political participation, and that participation in turn influences policy outcomes. These cycles can be positive or negative, with policies enhancing recipient participation levels and policy outcomes (as with Social Security) or undermining participation and leading to less favorable subsequent policies (welfare). Thus the design of public policies can put programs and their client groups on upward or downward trajectories that change the face of political inequality and policy outcomes in the United States.

Social Security

Senior citizens today are one of the most prominent groups in American politics.[3] Decades ago, however, seniors were quite marginalized, both economically and politically. The development of Social Security helped lead to this remarkable transformation, in part creating this now politically active constituency, which is able to shape policy outcomes by vigorously protesting policies seen as inimical to its interests. Over time, an iterative participation-policy cycle developed in which the program enhanced senior participation, lawmakers had an incentive to further increase their programs, and those increased programs further enhanced senior participation. Social Security thus put seniors on an upward political and policy trajectory.

Back in the early 1950s, before Social Security was widespread or very generous, senior citizens voted, made campaign contributions, and worked on campaigns at lower rates than younger citizens. As the program grew, senior voting and contributing grew absolutely, and their campaign work rates grew relative to those of younger people, so that by the 1980s, seniors constituted the most politically active age group. The result of Social Security's development over time, as coverage became universal and as benefits nearly tripled in real value, was increased senior participation. Social Security contributed to this increase in senior participation by enhancing the group's participatory resources, interest in politics, and mobilization opportunities.

Over time Social Security conferred the politically relevant resources of money and free time. Scholars believe that during the Depression, the senior poverty rate was at least 50 percent (Achenbaum 1986, 53). As of the late 1950s, more than one-third of seniors still lived in poverty (Campbell 2003a, 91). Today, the senior poverty rate is 10 percent, two-thirds that of children (Federal Interagency Forum on Aging Related Statistics 2000, 63). In part because of increased Social Security payments, senior incomes grew at the highest rate of any age group during the 1970s and 1980s (U.S. Census Bureau 1991). The program's cash benefit hardly makes recipients rich, but it does lift most seniors out of poverty and provides them a steady, inflation-adjusted income, freeing them to pursue luxuries such as politics.[4] Furthermore, the program makes retirement a reality for many, providing a large increase in free time. During the 1950s, half of senior men worked, whereas now that figure is one in six; furthermore, continuing to work is now more likely to be a matter of choice than of necessity (U.S. House Ways and Means Committee 1998, 1032). Studies show that seniors have twelve to fourteen hours of free time per day, two to three times that of working people (Campbell 2003a, 42). Over the past five-plus decades, the reduction in senior poverty and increases in income and retirement rates have significantly enhanced senior capacity to participate in politics.

Social Security also increased seniors' engagement with public affairs because their financial well-being became linked in a significant and obvious way to government activity. National Election Study data show that over time, seniors' interest in politics increased dramatically, as Social Security made up an increasingly greater share of their income as a result of legislated increases in coverage and benefit levels. Social Security now accounts for nearly half of senior incomes on average, up from one-fifth in the late 1950s (Cutler 1996, 127; Federal Interagency Forum on Aging Related Statistics 2000). Seniors also feel more efficacious toward government than younger people, and the gap between the age groups has increased over time as lawmakers and political parties have grown increasingly responsive to seniors and their concerns (Campbell 2003a, chapter 4).

In addition, the program creates a political identity for what is otherwise merely a demographic category. There is nothing particularly significant about being sixty-two or sixty-five except that a major government benefit is conferred on the basis of age. Interest-group and political-party mobilization takes place on the basis of this government-created identity, further enhancing senior participation. The rate at which seniors are mobilized by the political parties has increased over time, both absolutely and relative to younger citizens—seniors are now the age group most likely to be contacted by the political parties during campaign seasons. Furthermore, the existence of Social Security and Medicare is the raison d'être for many interest groups. Contemporary senior interest groups such as the AARP (formerly the American Association of Retired Persons), the National Committee to Preserve Social Security and Medicare, and the Alliance for Retired Americans did not exist or were not yet politicized when Social Security was adopted in 1935 and Medicare in 1965. Indeed, rather than the groups being the impetus behind the programs, the programs provided the rationale for founding and maintaining the groups. Program limitations provided service niches for interest groups to fill—like the AARP's large supplemental "medigap" insurance business. The interest groups in turn educate and mobilize seniors around relevant policy issues.

Thus the development of Social Security greatly increased the ability, desire, and opportunities for seniors to engage in political activity. Over time they overtook younger citizens in the rates at which they vote and make campaign contributions, ultimately constituting a greater proportion of both the electorate and of all campaign contributors than of the general adult population. The result of growing senior participation is that elected lawmakers have had an increasing incentive to address the needs and preferences of this constituency. Congress started to devote a greater number of congressional hearings to senior concerns, and mentions of seniors and their programs in political party platforms grew as well (Campbell 2003a, chapter 4). Lawmakers are keenly aware that although seniors are a diverse group and certainly do not always vote as a bloc, they are of similar mind on Social Security—surveys show that 98 percent want federal spending on Social Security kept at the same level or increased (Campbell 2003a, 98). Furthermore, seniors are vigilant about their programs. The culmination of decades of the participation-policy cycle is that when Social Security and Medicare were threatened during the 1980s, seniors responded with surges of letter writing to Congress (Campbell 2003a, 2003b). Frightened lawmakers withdrew the offending proposals: the pattern of senior participation shaped policy outcomes. In fact, the more seniors there are in congressmen's and senators' districts or states, the likelier these legislators are to vote in a pro-senior direction, regardless of their own ideological positions.[5]

The development of Social Security increased senior participation in politics, both absolutely and relative to that of younger people. Although the effect was strongest for activities with a federal focus, such as writing letters to congressmen and senators, senior participation in all activities increased as their politically relevant resources grew. Social Security helped increase political inequality between age groups, raising senior participation above what it was previously and above that of younger people.

Indeed, Social Security's effects on senior political participation suggest that what might be good for the democratic participation of one group might not be in the interests of others. Social Security's development raised seniors' participatory capacity and political interest. In addition, seniors absorbed positive citizenship lessons from the bureaucratically efficient manner in which Social Security benefits are conferred and from lawmakers' increasing responsiveness to seniors' concerns. They learned that they are a respected, important, and electorally crucial group that has the right to fight for its programs. Because seniors are disproportionately active in politics, lawmakers have an incentive to fulfill their preferences over those of younger people, not only on senior programs, but in other areas as well, resulting in policy crowd-out. Thus, in this instance policy feedbacks undermine democratic governance, which is predicated on the equal distance of all citizens to government.

However, Social Security is not entirely detrimental to participatory democracy. Although the program increases political inequality between age groups, it reduces inequality within the senior population: its participatory effects are greater on low-income seniors, who are more dependent on the program (Campbell 2002, 2003a). Seniors in the bottom two income quintiles get over 80 percent of their income from Social Security; the middle quintile, 64 percent; the fourth quintile, 45 percent; and the highest quintile, just 18 percent (Federal Interagency Forum on Aging Related Statistics 2000, 66). Because low-income seniors have such a large stake in the program, they are more likely to participate specifically with regard to the program—they are more likely to vote, contact elected officials, and make campaign contributions with Social Security in mind than their high-income counterparts for whom the program is less crucial. This reduces the overall income-participation gradient among seniors. One of the most long-standing regularities of participation research is that participation increases with income, and this is true for seniors as well, for political activity concerning issues other than Social Security. But for the portion of all senior activity animated by Social Security, the income-participation gradient is negative, not positive, so that overall senior participation is less unequal than that of other age groups.[6] This effect is apparent not only cross-sectionally (across seniors at a given time) but also over time. As Social Security developed, the participation of low-income seniors increased more than that of high-income seniors, especially for political activities concerning Social Security. Thus Social Security works against political inequality among senior citizens. Mettler (2002, 2005) found a similar effect for another universal program, the G.I. Bill: the program's education benefits had the greatest effect on the likelihood of civic group membership and political participation among veterans from low-to-medium and medium socioeconomic backgrounds.

Thus Social Security illustrates both aspects of the policy-participation cycle: it has enhanced senior political participation, and with their high rates of participation, and particularly with their vigilance over age-related issues, seniors have been able to beat back threats to their programs, shaping subsequent policy outcomes. By forging from a politically marginal and quiescent population the most vocal and active constituency in contemporary politics, Social Security has fundamentally transformed the terrain of mass politics in the United States.

Welfare

In contrast to Social Security, welfare has negative feedback effects on its clients. Where Social Security benefits are large enough to lift most seniors out of poverty, welfare benefits leave most clients poor—they are intentionally kept low so that they do not provide a disincentive to work (Gilens 1999). Welfare recipients' level of interest in public affairs is lower than that of senior citizens as well (Campbell 2003a, 128). Furthermore, unlike seniors, welfare recipients do not have mass membership groups that educate and mobilize them to political activity. Although half of all seniors are members of the AARP, only 2 percent of public assistance recipients belong to organizations concerned with their program (Campbell 2003a, 129). The National Welfare Rights Organization (NWRO) briefly flourished in the late 1960s and early 1970s, and welfare take-up rates peaked at 90 percent in 1971 (Weaver 2000, 55), but the era of politicized welfare claiming is long over.

Thus welfare recipients do not have the same levels of participatory resources or political interest as senior citizens, and are far less mobilized to participate in politics. Furthermore, Joe Soss (1999, 2000) shows that the way in which welfare benefits are conferred, through a demeaning process of proving eligibility to caseworkers who appear to have great discretion over benefits, actually undermines recipients' feelings of external political efficacy. They are more likely than other citizens to assert that they have little say about what the government does and that public officials don't care what they think (Campbell 2003a, 157). Their participation levels are even lower than would be predicted from their socioeconomic characteristics, whereas seniors' participation is higher.[7]

With few resources and little mobilization, welfare recipients suffer from having a muted political voice. As a consequence, during the 1980s, when their programs were threatened, they did not respond with surges in participation as did seniors (Campbell 2003a). The data on participatory reactions to policy threats do not extend to the 1996 legislation that replaced Aid to Families with Dependent Children (AFDC) with Temporary Assistance for Needy Families (TANF)—which ended the entitlement to aid and introduced time limits and work requirements—but I have not found any mention of significant participatory actions by recipients in journalistic accounts of the period. Lack of participatory capacity is exacerbated by the stigma of means-tested benefits, which imposes a moral bar that dampens recipients' defense of their programs.[8]

Unlike Social Security recipients, welfare clients experience a negative participation-policy cycle. Welfare's trajectory is downward: recipients' resources are low to begin with, their efficacy is actually undermined by their program, and neither mass membership groups nor political parties view them as worthwhile targets of mobilization, exacerbating their political marginalization. This low political participation has made welfare a relatively easy political target: benefits were never indexed to inflation at the national level and have been flat or decreasing over time, and the program was fundamentally altered in 1996—one of the few examples of significant welfare state retrenchment.

Head Start

The evidence from Head Start shows that means-tested programs do not necessarily undermine client participation. Indeed, Soss's (1999) study shows that although Head Start serves very much the same population as AFDC, the participatory nature of the program, in which parents are included in policy decisions and work together on the form and substance of their children's education, actually increases client political efficacy. This participatory design engenders positive citizenship learning and empowerment.[9] The program provides an exercise in participatory democracy that potentially has spillover effects into other arenas. Although there are no national participation surveys with Head Start identifiers to corroborate Soss's interview-based findings, he is able to show that even within his small sample, Head Start participants had higher external political efficacy than AFDC-only participants, despite the higher average education level of the AFDC clients in his study.

These studies begin to illuminate the ways in which public policies shape the attitudes and behaviors of their mass clienteles. The designs of social programs such as Social Security, welfare, the G.I. Bill, and Head Start influence the interest, ability, and opportunities for political participation. Whether these effects are positive or negative, and therefore whether clients' participation is enhanced or diminished, shapes the ongoing politics of program expansion or retrenchment.

POLICY CHARACTERISTICS

Existing case studies such as those just described allow us to make some generalizations about the specific characteristics of policies that create these positive and negative feedback effects. How a program fares politically depends both on the attitudes and participatory behaviors of client groups and on broader public support. Client groups are influenced by all three program design effects—resources, engagement, and mobilization effects. Public opinion about programs is affected primarily by "interpretive effects"—program designs communicate not only to the client groups themselves but also to the general public images and judgments about the apparent "worth" of program clienteles, a process Anne Schneider and Helen Ingram (1993) term the "social construction of target populations." The combination of client political participation and broader public attitudes shapes the politics surrounding programs.

Benefit Size

For public policies to have a resource effect—to affect meaningfully the ability of client groups to participate in politics—they must confer a significant level of benefits. One reason that Social Security has had such a profound effect on senior citizens is that the benefits it confers are pretty large, both absolutely and as a percentage of senior incomes. The average monthly Social Security benefit for a retired male worker was $1,129 in 2005; for those who had earned the most over their lifetimes, it was $1,874 (Social Security Administration 2005). Medicare has a number of shortcomings as a form of health insurance but nonetheless pays for half of seniors' health care and most of the big-ticket items (Moon 2001). Welfare payments, by contrast, are extremely low. The average monthly TANF benefit was $166 per recipient, or $397 per family in 2004 (Social Security Administration 2005), and fell in real value between the 1970s and 1990s (Mettler and Milstein 2003). Welfare benefits do not bring most recipients above the poverty line: the benefit paid by the median state comes out to just 34 percent of the United States poverty line (see U.S. House Ways and Means Committee 1998, 418). Such low benefits do not confer the resources that might facilitate recipients' greater political participation. Welfare recipients enjoy neither the direct effect of resources (they lack disposable income for campaign contributions, for example) nor the more indirect effects (they also lack resources to hire a baby-sitter to free up time for political work). Trying to keep body and soul together does not facilitate participation in a "luxury" such as political activity (Rosenstone and Hansen 1993, 13).

Level of Government

In the United States, the size of benefits tends to be related to the level of government that carries program responsibility. The national programs such as Social Security and Medicare have uniform benefits nationwide, and these tend to be relatively generous. Programs run at the state level, or in a joint federal-state partnership, tend to be targeted, means-tested programs with less generous benefits—welfare and Food Stamps, for example.[10] Moreover, benefit levels vary tremendously by state: in 2004, the average monthly TANF payment per recipient in New York was more than four times Tennessee's average payment (Social Security Administration 2005). Some scholars argue that states should not be in the business of running means-tested programs because they have an incentive to provide the lowest possible benefits to avoid becoming magnets for welfare recipients (Peterson 1995). Although evidence about such a "race to the bottom" is not conclusive (see Peterson and Rom 1990 and Schram, Nitz, and Krueger 1998 for opposing views), state officials believe such an effect exists, and that colors their policymaking (Rom 2004).

Distribution of Benefits

The distribution of benefits across income levels within programs is a crucial factor in determining both the participatory effects of programs and the political support they enjoy among clients and the greater public. The universal programs of Social Security, Medicare, and the G.I. Bill redistribute benefits toward the poor. Low-income Social Security recipients receive higher benefits, as a proportion of their pre-retirement incomes, than do higher-wage workers. Low-income Medicare beneficiaries over a lifetime receive more benefits because on average they are sicker and are less likely to have supplemental insurance than their more affluent counterparts (Campbell 2005). And the G.I. Bill made a far greater difference to World War II veterans from modest backgrounds in providing educational opportunities than it made to better-off veterans (Mettler 2002, 2005). In each case, the participatory effects of these programs are greatest on low-income clients because of the magnitude of the resource to those who have very little, raising their participation levels relative to the affluent, and democratizing participation within client groups.

We cannot forget, however, the sizable benefits these universal programs confer on middle-class and affluent beneficiaries, too, populations that form a crucial component of the programs' overall political support. Particularly in Social Security, high-income retirees get large benefits, reflecting their higher payroll tax contributions. Moreover, the contributory finance mechanism creates a sense of earned entitlement. Because they have paid into the program, affluent beneficiaries feel a moral claim to get these benefits "back," even if they are not particularly dependent on them to make ends meet. Even with Medicare, where the affluent are more likely to have employer-provided or privately purchased supplemental coverage (Pourat et al. 2000), the program covers major hospitalizations. Universal programs, by conferring large benefits on the affluent—even as they redistribute to the poor in a hidden, nonstigmatizing way—win the support of the most active and politically crucial portion of the population. Unlike their low-income counterparts, affluent beneficiaries would be able to participate politically without the participation-enhancing effects of the programs. But the designs of the programs give them an incentive to participate. Thus, when Social Security was threatened with cuts in benefits for early retirees (two-thirds of individuals take their benefits before age sixty-five) and a delay in the annual cost-of-living adjustment in the early 1980s, affluent seniors' surge of letter writing to Congress in protest was the greatest among all senior groups, helping bury those proposals (Campbell 2003b). The distribution of benefits within universal programs produces political protection by giving both high- and low-income recipients the means and motive to participate concerning the programs.[11]

Thus, universal programs have two important effects: their design secures political support by including the middle class as beneficiaries (Skocpol 1991), and also enhances political equality by incorporating low-income beneficiaries into full democratic citizenship.

Financing and Budgetary Status

Financing is a characteristic of public policies that influences both the resource and "interpretive effects" that policies have on client groups and on public opinion more broadly. One reason that Social Security and Medicare benefits are relatively generous is that those programs have dedicated funding sources: payroll tax contributions to the Social Security and Medicare Hospital Insurance trust funds. The next most secure programs are those that are funded by general revenues (regular tax dollars) but are also entitlements, meaning that all individuals categorically eligible for a program will be covered, without a separate appropriations process and without regard to total cost. Medicare Part B is such an example—seniors' physician visits and outpatient hospital services are financed by a combination of monthly premiums paid by beneficiaries (which now account for about 25 percent of Part B spending) and general revenues (which account for 75 percent).[12] Worst off are programs that are subject to appropriations or that require some action to prevent the erosion of their value, like Pell Grants and unemployment insurance. Over time the real value of benefit levels have eroded (Mettler and Milstein 2003) and this has reduced their likelihood of having a positive resource effect on recipient groups.

The method of financing is also crucial to the interpretive effects programs convey. As mentioned, contributory finance creates an earned entitlement and sense of legitimate claim to benefits. But benefits can be "earned" in other ways, as veterans benefits are earned in a most profound way through service to the nation. Moreover, certain kinds of benefits that are not earned per se but that promote desirable behavior, such as the Earned Income Tax Credit (EITC) and the home mortgage interest deduction, also create a sense of deservingness on the part of recipients even if not earned through a payroll tax. The EITC, which subsidizes the working poor by refunding part or all of their federal income taxes, and the home mortgage interest deduction, which subsidizes home ownership, are funded by general revenues (in the form of forgone taxes), yet that form of financing is not stigmatizing, apparently because of the nature of the behavior rewarded.[13]

Deservingness and Stigma

As alluded to previously, two characteristics of public policies that have profound interpretive effects on both clients and the broader public are deservingness and stigma. Whether clients feel that it is their place to participate politically concerning their benefits—and how the rest of the public feels about those benefits—has much to do with perceptions of deservingness and the presence of stigma. Clients' groups that are considered deserving are those who have earned the benefit, either by paying into a social insurance system (Social Security and Medicare Hospital Insurance) or serving the nation (veterans' benefits), or those whose neediness is beyond their control (the disabled and poor children). Those who are viewed as least deserving are those whose difficulties are perceived to be their own fault, such as welfare recipients. Perceptions of fault and deservingness profoundly influence public opinion around social welfare policies. Most highly supported are the "earned" programs such as Social Security and Medicare. Means-tested programs are held in lower regard—welfare scores the lowest—but there is some variation. Medicaid, the health insurance program for the poor, is viewed more benignly than welfare, presumably because needing health care is perceived as less one's fault than needing a cash payment from the government because one is a single mother (Cook and Barrett 1992).

These perceptions of deservingness and stigma affect clients' beliefs and behaviors as well. The stigma associated with means-tested programs is one reason that take-up rates—the percentage of those eligible who actually enroll—are lower than those for the earned programs. Virtually all persons eligible for Social Security and Medicare participate in the programs. Even though Medicare Part B, insurance for doctor's visits and outpatient services, is voluntary, 98 percent of those eligible take part. By contrast, only about half of the poor elderly who are eligible for Medicare and Medicaid take up the latter—in part because of ignorance (Medicaid is not nearly as well known among the target group as is Medicare) and in part because of stigma (Kaiser Commission on Medicaid and the Uninsured 2002).

Stigma affects not only program take-up rates but also the likelihood that recipients will press their claims on government (Soss 2000) or band together to fight for their rights (Little 1999). Stigma undermines both individual efficacy and participation and the possibilities for collective action. Thus stigma is an interpretive effect of program design that deeply affects both public opinion and client political participation.

Duration

Some programs are of long duration, in some cases for the rest of one's life, such as Social Security or Medicare. Others are of shorter duration or are more episodic—welfare, unemployment insurance, and college loans, for example. If one is likely to drift in and out of eligibility for a program, or only hopes to need it for a short period of time, one is less likely to participate politically around it compared to a long duration program, where one is more likely to enjoy the fruits of one's labor.

Risk Assessment

A further factor is that opinions about public programs are shaped by one's assessment of whether one will ever need the program. Everyone hopes to retire and enjoy a long life, and so everyone perceives a stake in Social Security and Medicare. Part of the political advantage such "universal" programs enjoy is that everyone thinks they will benefit from them, in part because they cover everyone and in part because they protect against a "risk"—old age—that everyone believes they will face. For other programs, perceptions of risk are much lower, and this diminishes public support. In some cases risk perceptions are erroneously low, leaving programs with less public support than they "ought" to enjoy. For example, one reason that long-term care for disabled older persons continues to be relegated to a means-tested, inadequate provision within Medicaid is that people vastly underestimate their risks of needing such care. They confuse the cross-sectional likelihood that someone aged sixty-five and over is in a nursing home—5 percent—with the longitudinal likelihood that one will need long-term care at some point in one's life—72 percent for home care, 49 percent for nursing-home care (Friedland 2002). Contrast the perceived risk of needing long-term care, 5 percent, with the fact that over 80 percent of today's seniors take a prescription medication (*NewsHour with Jim Lehrer* et al. 2000). Little wonder that seniors and their interest groups like the AARP agitated for a prescription drug benefit in Medicare rather than an improvement in long-term-care provision, which nearly as many will need in the future. And this despite the fact that the expected lifetime uncovered cost of long-term care is four times that of uncovered prescription drugs (Knickman and Snell 2002). Similarly, calculations by the sociologists Mark Rank and Thomas Hirschl (2002) show that two-thirds of persons will make use of a means-tested program for at least a year before they reach the age of sixty-five, but very few people probably think they will be poor, and that undermines public support for such programs as compared to other programs where the perceived risks and the likelihood of receiving benefits are higher. Thus risk assessment is partly a function of the particular risk—old age versus poverty or unemployment—and partly a function of program design. Universality makes all individuals think of themselves as potential beneficiaries, whereas targeted programs make many think of themselves only as taxpayers.

Because we lack data sets that allow us to measure the effects of each aspect of program design on resources, engagement, and mobilization, we cannot know with precision the relative contribution of each to recipient political attitudes and participation. I strongly suspect that program effects are cumulative rather than competing—large benefit sizes mean larger resource effects *and* greater political engagement—although perhaps the presence of multiple participation-enhancing elements reduces the marginal effect of each. Empirical assessment of the magnitude of effects is something we must leave for future research.[14]

CHANGING POLICY DESIGNS

The argument that policy designs influence the mass public's feelings and actions suggests that changes in the designs of policies will change such feelings and actions. The designs of Social Security and Medicare, for example, have three important effects: they democratize participation within their target groups because their resource effects are tilted toward the poor; they enjoy the support of middle-class and affluent individuals because of large benefits to these groups; and they encourage in all these income groups political activity, because the programs are so clearly government programs for which political participation is an expected and productive form of activity.

But what happens if the designs of these programs are changed? Proposals to introduce more market-oriented elements, to privatize Social Security and Medicare, have been on the political agenda since the early 1980s. And some efforts, like the Medicare Modernization Act of 2003 (MMA), have actually been enacted. By examining the political effects of design changes that have previously taken place, and by thinking through the implications of current and proposed design changes for the factors discussed in the previous section, we can speculate about the likely effect of such reforms on client political activity and public opinion around these programs more broadly.

The idea of privatizing aspects of these large entitlement programs gained ground during the Reagan administration, when conservatives, long wary of the welfare state, began attempts to wean Americans from public provision by increasing the availability and attractiveness of private alternatives (see Butler 1983). The creation of individual retirement accounts (IRAs) and 401(k) programs are early examples of this, and the more recent push to introduce private accounts in Social Security is a more overt challenge to the traditional program. Most proposals for Social Security privatization would create a hybrid program where some portion of payroll taxes would continue to be invested by the government in the traditional plan while the other portion would be invested by individuals, who under the typical proposal would choose from a list of investment options. To date such a reform has not been achieved, in part because of the "double payment" problem: today's payroll taxes finance today's benefits, and therefore the setting aside of funds to invest in individual accounts would require higher taxes or lower benefits, neither of which is politically attractive. However, the idea of Social Security privatization remains on the agenda.

Greater change has been achieved in the Medicare program. The 2003 MMA, which provided a new drug benefit as of January 2006, changed the design of Medicare by introducing private elements in three ways. The new drug coverage is administered through private firms rather than through traditional Medicare. The law increases subsidies to private plans such as health maintenance organizations (HMOs) to make those companies view elderly enrollees as more attractive customers. And it stipulates demonstration projects in which traditional Medicare must compete with private plans in six cities in 2010. Compared to Social Security privatization, changing the design of Medicare is fiscally and politically easier, in part because many aspects of Medicare have always been "private"—the care itself is delivered by private hospitals and physicians, and administration is handled through the private Blue Cross and Blue Shield system. It is true that the privatization aspects of the MMA as enacted are considerably watered down compared to Republican hopes at the outset—proponents had wanted the prescription drug program to be available only for those enrolled in private plans, not traditional Medicare, and they wanted price competition between private plans and the traditional program, not merely demonstration projects in the future. However, the MMA's proponents were successful in encouraging seniors to consider private alternatives to Medicare both for drug coverage and for their overall health care. Enrollment in both has been strong, with just over half of all seniors enrolling in private drug plans and 17 percent in private health plans such as HMOs by late 2006 (Kaiser Family Foundation 2006a, 2006b).

What might be the effects of these changes in program design, of the privatization of these previously government-run programs? The characteristics of programs most likely to be altered by these proposed and enacted reforms are the level and distribution of benefits, perceptions of deservingness and stigma, and processes of risk assessment.

Privatizing Social Security or Medicare could undermine the programs' resource effects on lower-income individuals, whose guaranteed benefits are reduced under the new designs. For poorer seniors, Social Security benefits could decrease under privatization because the defined benefit (traditional) portion would be smaller, and the new defined contribution (private account) portion may not make up the difference if the individual makes poor investment choices, the equity market sours, or administrative fees eat into returns. Medicare benefits may also decrease under privatization, because of adverse selection: healthier seniors may opt into private plans, leaving traditional Medicare with a sicker, poorer, and more expensive population, which may force either an increase in premiums or a decrease in benefits, impacting precisely the population that can least afford negative financial outcomes.

Reduced benefits from these programs, and possibly higher premiums for Medicare, could undermine poorer seniors' political participation. Their disposable incomes would be lower, setting off a series of effects. More would have to work during their senior years, reducing their free time for political activity. Poorer seniors would worry more about their finances—indeed, some would drop below the poverty line—which would diminish their ability to engage in leisure activities such as political participation. Economic inequality would increase among the senior population, exacerbating differences in political activity between high- and low-income seniors, undermining the programs' earlier democratizing effects.

In addition to the effects on low-income seniors of reducing their resources, the changed levels and distribution of benefits could undermine the interest of high-income seniors in Social Security and Medicare and thus reduce the likelihood of their political participation concerning these government programs. With Social Security, for instance, it is already the case that affluent seniors get a smaller share of their total incomes from the program. With private, self-directed accounts, their stake in the traditional government-controlled defined-benefit program would be even smaller and the visibility of government in their retirement security even less. They could become less motivated to support the program with political activities because it would have less relevance to their financial well-being.

We already know from previous changes to Social Security what happens when the stake of the affluent in Social Security is reduced. Throughout Social Security's history, the affluent have been somewhat less supportive of the program than poorer citizens. In the 1930s, the affluent were about 10 percent less likely to support old-age pensions or to support extending them to new groups (Schiltz 1970, 38, 65). Later, the gap between rich and poor in their attitudes toward Social Security grew as a result of a series of design changes as well as alterations in private retirement savings and in the larger political environment (Campbell and Morgan 2005). Rescue legislation in 1977 and 1983, intended to address crises in the Social Security trust fund, disproportionately affected high-wage earners. These changes raised their payroll taxes, increased their payback times (the number of years it would take to earn back their contributions in benefits), and taxed their benefits. In all, these changes made the program a worse deal for the affluent by reducing their net lifetime Social Security benefits. At the same time, options for private retirement savings proliferated, with the introduction of 401(k) programs in 1980 and clarification and liberalization of IRAs in 1981. Moreover, new critiques from the political right of Social Security's "low rate of return" compared to the stock market made the comparison between the public pension program and private savings vehicles look even starker. As a result, the gap in support for Social Security across income groups, about ten percentage points in the thirties, increased to twenty- or thirty-point differences after the 1980s (Campbell and Morgan 2005).

This experience shows the potential for changes in program design to diminish the politically crucial support of the affluent and to create a rift in the heretofore cross-class coalition behind Social Security. With privatization, affluent seniors who can afford the risks of equity investing will have less of a stake in the traditional, defined benefit portion of Social Security and may not defend it, to the detriment of divorced and single older women, the disabled, the poor, and others who are disproportionately dependent on it.

Encouraging seniors to leave traditional Medicare for HMOs and other private health plans could have similar effects in reducing the interest and participation of privately enrolled seniors in the government-run programs. It is already the case that many seniors in Medicare managed-care plans believe that they are no longer in a government program (Bernstein and Stevens 1999). If they feel that their health care is provided by a private plan and not by the government, they may fail to be a political force in the defense of Medicare. Similarly, compared to clients of traditional Medicare, seniors in Medicare HMOs exhibit lower levels of group consciousness, are less likely to support strategies of collective action, and are more likely to see health care as an individual rather than a societal responsibility (Schlesinger and Hutchings 2003). These feelings may undermine their political activity concerning the program. With seniors split among different plans—

some in traditional Medicare, others in various private plans—we may see a senior constituency divided and weakened politically, unable to fend off future threats to their welfare state benefits. In these ways, design changes that alter the level and distribution of benefits fundamentally change patterns of resources, interests, and hence participation concerning these programs.

Beyond their effects on the level and distribution of benefits, privatizing Social Security and Medicare could alter perceptions of deservingness and stigma. Privatization signals a profound transformation, from uniform programs serving all clients in a similar manner to a new situation in which some clients benefit mostly from the remaining government-run portion while others mostly from the new private portion. The constituency not only becomes divided, but divided largely along income lines, so that the remaining government portion of these formerly universal programs begins to resemble a means-tested program. Stigma could become associated with the government portion when most of the affluent have sorted themselves into the more privatized options. As with existing means-tested programs, stigma could reduce the likelihood of political participation among clients as well as undermine broader public support.

Finally, privatization could change individuals' risk assessment processes. In the transformation of universal programs to public-private hybrids segregated by income, the risk calculation is no longer about being older and retired—which everyone hopes to be and therefore wants universal Social Security and Medicare to be there for them. Rather, the calculation is about the risk of being old *and poor*—which no one thinks they will be. Then public support for, client activity concerning, and the political trajectory of the remaining government-run portions of Social Security and Medicare will no longer resemble their robust selves from the universal era, but instead will look more like the politics of Medicaid for old-age care: politically and fiscally marginalized.

Privatization is so significant to the politics of these programs because it unmakes politically crucial aspects of their heretofore universal designs. Privatization reduces the redistributive effects of these programs, diminishing their ability to democratize senior political participation. It also reduces the stake of the middle class and especially the affluent—those who are most attracted to private alternatives because they can afford to self-insure—reducing their crucial support for the public programs. Sorting by income across the private and public aspects raises the specter of stigma and political marginalization. Thus, changing the designs of universal programs through privatization threatens to fracture the political constituencies from both the top and bottom. Privatization would unravel the political and economic gains these programs have forged.

CONCLUSION

Social Security is the most effective antipoverty program in American history—its clients are among the least likely of all citizens to be poor. Medicare renders seniors the age group most likely to have health insurance. In contrast, AFDC and TANF have left most of their recipients in poverty, and benefits have declined over time. Somewhat better off are low-income workers, who are assisted by the EITC and in some cases Medicaid. For the most part, however, the participants in universal programs have fared far better economically than those in targeted programs. These programs have played a crucial role in defining the topography of poverty in the United States.

But just as important, these universal programs also shape the American political terrain. Through effects on clients' politically relevant resources, on the interpretation of their place in the polity, and on their political opportunities, these programs play a key and largely overlooked role in determining who participates in politics and what they say. Public policies have the power to elevate some groups, such as senior citizens, both economically and politically, while relegating others, such as the poor, to even more marginalized status.

In assessing who participates and why, researchers then must consider not just how an individual was schooled, or where she works, or what voluntary groups she belongs to, but also what government programs she participates in. These profoundly affect her ability to participate, her interest in doing so, and her opportunities. Similarly, when designing policies, lawmakers, policy analysts, and academics must consider not just whether a policy is efficient or effective in its narrow goals, but also what effects those policies will have on recipients and on public opinion about those recipients. These policy effects cycle through in an iterative manner, altering the place of client groups in the polity and therefore the possibilities for future policymaking.

More broadly, public policies affect not only the political participation of target groups, but also the regard of citizens for government. Those who have benefited from the government in significant ways—for example, the current generation of the elderly who benefited from the G.I. Bill early in life and Social Security and Medicare later on—are more likely to trust government and to feel that it is a positive force in citizens' lives. The much-noted decline in trust in government since the early 1970s has taken place hand in hand with the receding of government from the lives of many Americans, especially the working non-elderly. After peaking in the 1970s, the role of government in health security, job security, wage security, and access to education has diminished, with decreases in the minimum wage, unemployment insurance, Pell Grants, and government support of the labor movement (Mettler and Milstein 2003). One reason people don't trust the government is that it does not do much for them—or what it does do, such as providing tax deductions for home mortgage interest, is not seen as a government benefit. The inescapable conclusion is that the designs of government policies help shape the very nature of American democracy.

NOTES

1. This section on participatory factors draws on the work of Sidney Verba, Kay L. Schlozman, and Henry E. Brady (1995). Also see Verba and Norman H. Nie (1972); Steven J. Rosenstone and John Mark Hansen (1993); and Raymond E. Wolfinger and Rosenstone (1980) on the factors behind political participation.
2. I use the popular term "welfare" to refer to Aid to Families with Dependent Children (AFDC) and the program that replaced it in 1996, Temporary Assistance for Needy Families (TANF).
3. This section is adapted from Campbell 2003a.
4. On average senior incomes are modest compared to those of non-seniors. But they are also more predictable, and surveys show that seniors are less worried about their finances than any other age group. They are also far less likely to have been forced to make lifestyle changes like cutting back on food or entertainment, putting off medical or dental care, or delaying rent or mortgage payments than younger people in order to make ends meet (Campbell 2003a, 20).
5. In particular this is true for Republicans. Democrats, who are more ideologically inclined to vote pro-senior, do so at the same rate no matter what the age composition of their constituencies (Campbell 2003a, chapter 6).
6. There is a similar effect with Medicare: because low-income seniors are more dependent on the program (they are typically sicker, use more Medicare benefits over a lifetime, and are less likely to have supplemental heath insurance), they are more likely to vote, contact, and make campaign contributions concerning Medicare than are high-income seniors (Campbell 2005).
7. Perhaps welfare recipients' depressed political participation is due to stress in their lives rather

than to their claiming experience. However, Soss (1999) shows that Social Security Disability (SSDI) recipients, who presumably also suffer from stress but whose program is run in a bureaucratic-rational manner by the Social Security Administration rather than by local welfare offices, do not experience lowered political efficacy and participation levels, thus eliminating this alternative hypothesis.

8. The stigma associated with welfare is evident even among program clients, who speak disparagingly of other recipients as "the *real* dependents" who keep having "'all' these babies" (Little 1999, 175–76; emphasis in the original).

9. The difference in political efficacy between Head Start and AFDC participants is not due solely to selection effects—that is, to systematic differences in the two groups' preexisting characteristics. Soss (2000, 140) finds that among his subjects who participated in both programs, those who "shared their fellow recipients' fears and doubts about speaking up in AFDC . . . felt quite opposite sentiments about client involvement in Head Start." This suggests that policy design has an effect; otherwise "one would expect [the same] clients to hold a single orientation toward involvement across different program contexts."

10. For arguments attributing these differences historically to the role of race and gender in American politics, see Robert C. Lieberman (1998), Suzanne Mettler (1998), and Jill Quadagno (1994).

11. Suzanne Mettler finds that veterans from moderate to higher-income backgrounds who took advantage of the G.I. Bill reported that they probably would have gone to college even if the program had not existed, but were grateful nonetheless because the program allowed them to attend under better circumstances—to attend better or more expensive institutions, to go full-rather than part-time, or to attend longer. Some managed to graduate with savings accounts because of the bill (2005; personal communication). Length of time on the G.I. Bill positively affects later political participation (2005, 187); in this way the bill's effects fed back into the political system. Given the nature of the program—supporting higher education—the feedback effects do not appear to be issue-specific, as is the case with Social Security and Medicare, where the lifetime duration of the program also affects participatory incentives. See the "Duration" section of this chapter.

12. What form of financing is the most stable and potentially most expansionary is the subject of some debate among scholars of the welfare state. In the United States, payroll tax contributions paid into trust funds were adopted as the mechanism for Social Security and later for Medicare because liberals felt that an earmarked source of funding was crucial to the programs' stability and would allow for program expansion. Fiscal conservatives viewed the same mechanism as constraining growth in benefits because they would be linked with payroll tax increases (Derthick 1979; Zelizer 1998). Ironically, the trust fund mechanism has become a trigger for program crises and reform, as trust funds can go "bankrupt" in ways that general-revenue-funded programs never can (Patashnik 2000; Oberlander 2003).

13. On these tax expenditure programs, see Christopher Howard (1997).

14. With senior citizens we can measure the relative contribution of resources, engagement, and mobilization to their increased political participation over time, even if we cannot parse those effects out across specific Social Security and Medicare design elements precisely. Following the example of Steven Rosenstone and John Mark Hansen (1993, 213), using National Election Study data I "transformed" the senior citizens of 1960 (the earliest year in which all the variables are available) into seniors of 1996 and calculated how much of the increase in senior voting and contributing was due to resource effects (income, marital status, age, and work status), to engagement effects (political efficacy and interest), and to mobilization effects (party contacting). This calculation shows that 43 percent of the increase of senior voting is due to enhanced resources, 25 percent to increased engagement, and 32 percent to greater party mobilization. The effect of resources on contributing is greater, as we might expect, given the importance of income in particular to contributing rates (Verba, Schlozman, and Brady 1995): 74 percent of the increase in senior contributing is due to greater resources, 5 percent to greater engagement, and 21 percent to higher rates of party mobilization. Thus the resource effects appear most important, followed by mobilization effects and then by

engagement effects. We have to take these estimates with a grain of salt, however, because we cannot attribute all of seniors' increased resources to their social welfare programs (senior incomes increased because of increases in private pensions and savings as well, while medical advances, and not just the increased access to health care provided by Medicare, contributed to their longevity and greater likelihood of being married rather than widowed in old age, which preserves social ties and incomes, and hence rates of political participation). Engagement and mobilization effects are more directly attributable to program design.

REFERENCES

Achenbaum, W. Andrew. 1986. *Social Security: Visions and Revisions.* Cambridge: Cambridge University Press.

Bernstein, Jill, and Rosemary A. Stevens. 1999. "Public Opinion, Knowledge, and Medicare Reform." *Health Affairs* 18(1): 180–93.

Butler, Stuart. 1983. "Privatization: A Strategy for Cutting Federal Spending." Heritage Foundation Report No. 310. Washington: Heritage Foundation, December 7, 1983.

Campbell, Andrea Louise. 2002. "Self-Interest, Social Security, and the Distinctive Participation Patterns of Senior Citizens." *American Political Science Review* 96(3): 565–74.

———. 2003a. *How Policies Make Citizens: Senior Citizen Activism and the American Welfare State.* Princeton, N.J.: Princeton University Press.

———. 2003b. "Participatory Reactions to Policy Threats: Senior Citizens and the Defense of Social Security and Medicare." *Political Behavior* 25(1): 29–49.

———. 2005. "The Political Consequences of Program Design: The Case of Medicare." Unpublished manuscript. Department of Political Science, MIT.

Campbell, Andrea Louise, and Kimberly Morgan. 2005. "Financing the Welfare State: Elite Politics and the Decline of the Social Insurance Model in America." *Studies in American Political Development* 19(2): 173–95.

Cook, Fay Lomax, and Edith J. Barrett. 1992. *Support for the American Welfare State: The Views of Congress and the Public.* New York: Columbia University Press.

Cutler, David M. 1996. "Reexamining the Three-Legged Stool." In *Social Security: What Role for the Future,* edited by Peter A. Diamond, David C. Lindeman, and Howard Young. Washington: National Academy of Social Insurance.

Derthick, Martha. 1979. *Policymaking for Social Security.* Washington: Brookings Institution Press.

Federal Interagency Forum on Aging Related Statistics. 2000. *Older Americans 2000: Key Indicators of Well-Being.* Washington: U.S. Government Printing Office.

Friedland, Robert B. 2002. "The Coverage Puzzle: How the Pieces Fit Together." Paper presented at the annual conference of the National Academy of Social Insurance. Washington, D.C., January 24-25, 2002.

Gilens, Martin. 1999. *Why Americans Hate Welfare.* Chicago, Ill.: University of Chicago Press.

Hill, Kim Quaile, and Jan E. Leighley. 1992. "The Policy Consequences of Class Bias in State Electorates." *American Journal of Political Science* 36(2): 351–65.

Howard, Christopher. 1997. *The Hidden Welfare State: Tax Expenditures and Social Policy in the United States.* Princeton, N.J.: Princeton University Press.

Hutchings, Vincent L. 2003. *Public Opinion and Democratic Accountability: How Citizens Learn About Politics.* Princeton, N.J.: Princeton University Press.

Ingram, Helen, and Anne Schneider. 1993. "Constructing Citizenship: The Subtle Messages of Policy Design." In *Public Policy for Democracy,* edited by Helen Ingram and Steven Rathgeb Smith. Washington: Brookings Institution Press.

Kaiser Commission on Medicaid and the Uninsured. 2002. "Barriers to Medicaid Enrollment for Low-Income Seniors: Focus Group Findings." Washington: Kaiser Family Foundation, January 2002.

Kaiser Family Foundation. 2006a. "Prescription Drug Coverage Among Medicare Beneficiaries." Accessed at www.kff.org/medicare/upload/7453.pdf.

————. 2006b. "Tracking Medicare Health and Prescription Drug Plans." Accessed at www.kff .org/medicare/upload/ medicaretracking1106.pdf.

Knickman, James R., and Snell, Emily K. 2002. "The 2030 Problem: Caring for Aging Baby Boomers." *Health Services Research* 37(4): 849–84.

Lieberman, Robert C. 1998. *Shifting the Color Line: Race and the American Welfare State.* Cambridge, Mass.: Harvard University Press.

Little, Deborah L. 1999. "Independent Workers, Dependable Mothers: Discourse, Resistance, and AFDC Workfare Programs." *Social Politics* 6(2): 161–202.

Martin, Paul S. 2003. "Voting's Rewards: Voter Turnout, Attentive Publics, and Congressional Allocation of Federal Money." *American Journal of Political Science* 47(1): 110–27.

Mettler, Suzanne. 1998. *Dividing Citizens: Gender and Federalism in New Deal Public Policy.* Ithaca, N.Y.: Cornell University Press.

————. 2002. "Bring the State Back In to Civic Engagement: Policy Feedback Effects of the G.I. Bill for World War II Veterans." *American Political Science Review* 96(2): 351–65.

————. 2005. *Soldiers to Citizens: The G.I. Bill and the Making of the Greatest Generation.* New York: Oxford University Press.

Mettler, Suzanne, and Andrew Milstein. 2003. "'A Sense of State': Tracking the Role of the American Federal Government in Citizens' Lives over Time." Paper presented at the annual meeting of the Midwest Political Science Association. Chicago, Ill., April 3-6, 2003.

Mettler, Suzanne, and Joe Soss. 2004. "The Consequences of Public Policy for Democratic Citizenship: Bridging Policy Studies and Mass Politics." *Perspectives on Politics* 2(1): 55–73.

Moon, Marilyn. 2001. "Medicare." *New England Journal of Medicine* 344(12): 928–31.

NewsHour with Jim Lehrer/Kaiser Family Foundation/Harvard School of Public Health. 2000. National Survey on Prescription Drugs. July 26 to September 5, 2000. Accessed at http://www .kff.org/rxdrugs/3065-index.cfm.

Oberlander, Jonathan. 2003. *The Political Life of Medicare.* Chicago, Ill.: University of Chicago Press.

Patashnik, Eric M. 2000. *Putting Trust in the US Budget: Federal Trust Funds and the Politics of Commitment.* Cambridge: Cambridge University Press.

Peterson, Paul E. 1995. *The Price of Federalism.* Washington: Brookings Institution Press.

Peterson, Paul E., and Mark C. Rom. 1990. *Welfare Magnets: A New Case for a National Welfare Standard.* Washington: Brookings Institution Press.

Pierson, Paul. 1993. "When Effect Becomes Cause: Policy Feedback and Political Change." *World Politics* 45(4): 595–628.

Pourat, Nadereh, Thomas Rice, Gerald Kominski, and Rani E. Snyder. 2000. "Socioeconomic Differences in Medicare Supplemental Coverage." *Health Affairs* 19(5): 186–96.

Quadagno, Jill. 1994. *The Color of Welfare: How Racism Undermined the War on Poverty.* New York: Oxford University Press.

Rank, Mark R., and Thomas A. Hirschl. 2002. "Welfare Use as a Life Course Event: Toward a New Understanding of the U.S. Safety Net." *Social Work* 47(3): 237–48.

Rom, Mark Carl. 2004. "Transforming State Health and Welfare Programs." In *Politics in the American States: A Comparative Analysis*, edited by Virginia Gray and Russell L. Hanson. 8th edition. Washington: CQ Press.

Rosenstone, Steven J., and John Mark Hansen. 1993. *Mobilization, Participation, and Democracy in America.* New York: Macmillan.

Schiltz, Michael E. 1970. *Public Attitudes Toward Social Security: 1935–1965.* Washington: Government Printing Office.

Schlesinger, Mark, and Vincent L. Hutchings. 2003. "Affiliation, Collective Identification and Public Policy: Medicare Privatization and Elders' Attitudes Toward Federal Involvement in Medical Care." Unpublished paper. Yale University.

Schneider, Anne, and Helen Ingram. 1993. "Social Construction of Target Populations: Implications for Politics and Policy." *American Political Science Review* 87(2): 334–47.

Schram, Sanford, Lawrence Nitz, and Gary Krueger. 1998. "Without Cause or Effect: Reconsidering Welfare Migration as a Policy Problem." *American Journal of Political Science* 42(1): 210–30.

Skocpol, Theda. 1991. "Targeting Within Universalism: Politically Viable Policies to Combat Poverty in the United States." In *The Urban Underclass,* edited by Christopher Jencks and Paul E. Peterson. Washington: Brookings Institution Press.

Social Security Administration. 2005. *Social Security Bulletin: Annual Statistical Supplement.* Accessed at www.ssa.gov/ policy/docs/statcomps/supplement/2005/index.html#toc.

Soss, Joe. 1999. "Lessons of Welfare: Policy Design, Political Learning, and Political Action." *American Political Science Review* 93(2): 363–80.

———. 2000. *Unwanted Claims: The Politics of Participation in the U.S. Welfare System.* Ann Arbor, Mich.: University of Michigan Press.

U.S. Census Bureau. 1991. *Money Income of Households, Families, and Persons in the U.S.* Washington: Government Printing Office.

U.S. House Ways and Means Committee. 1998. *1998 Green Book.* Washington: Government Printing Office.

Verba, Sidney, Henry E. Brady, and Kay L. Schlozman. 2004. "Why No Confiscation in America? Political Participation, Political Parties, and the Median Voter Theorem." Paper presented at the Annual Meeting of the American Political Science Association. Chicago, Ill., September 2-5, 2004.

Verba, Sidney, and Norman H. Nie. 1972. *Participation in America: Political Democracy and Social Equality.* New York: Harper & Row.

Verba, Sidney, Kay Lehman Schlozman, and Henry E. Brady. 1995. *Voice and Equality: Civic Voluntarism in American Politics.* Cambridge, Mass.: Harvard University Press.

Weaver, R. Kent. 2000. *Ending Welfare As We Know It.* Washington: Brookings Institution Press.

Wolfinger, Raymond E., and Steven J. Rosenstone. 1980. *Who Votes?* New Haven, Conn.: Yale University Press.

Zelizer, Julian E. 1998. *Taxing America: Wilbur D. Mills, Congress, and the State, 1945-1975.* Cambridge: Cambridge University Press.

Chapter 7

Institutions and Agents in the
Politics of Welfare Cutbacks

The idea that welfare-state programs are not only the consequence of politics but that, once created, they are powerful influences on the politics that subsequently shapes the programs is by now familiar. On the one side, social democratic analysts have argued persuasively not only that labor parties and their union allies support welfare-state programs, but also that these programs, when they are structured to build class solidarity, in turn strengthen the working-class formations on which the programs depend. On the other side, American programs, and to a lesser extent the programs of other Anglo countries, are often criticized because they enfeeble rather than strengthen their beneficiaries in politics. Programs are fragmented, and fragmented programs divide constituency groups, with consequences that weaken the program. Thus means-tested programs for selected constituencies provide meager benefits and are punitively administered, and these features in turn generate wider public opposition rather than support. The incidence of taxes that provide the revenues for the programs can also generate divisions among groups that might otherwise be political allies. The moral is that "categorical" programs—those that are targeted toward specific groups—isolate and enfeeble program beneficiaries politically, whereas more universal programs nourish broad political support.

In this paper I argue that although there is some truth in an institutionalist view that focuses on welfare-state policies, this view is both misstated and overstated. It is misstated because its proponents tend to treat welfare-state institutions as virtually a bounded world, ignoring the multiple ways that the politics generated by other and larger institutions in the society shape the politics of the welfare state and its beneficiaries. It is overstated because, although institutions do influence politics, they are not singularly determining. Institutions matter largely in the construction of political actors, in forming their identities and interests, and in making possible the strategies they employ. But political actors also innovate and interact in ways that not only reflect but also escape the structured and continuous influence of institutions. Indeed, if that were not so, there would be little need to scrutinize the realm of political action, of interest groups, social movements, and political parties, for with a sufficiently complex analytical model, all of that political activity could presumably be deduced from the institutions that shape it.[1]

First, let me highlight what we all do indeed know, at least most of the time: that welfare-state institutions are neither bounded and isolated nor necessarily primary in the development of the politics of the welfare state. Rather, the policies that govern the welfare state are formulated in the context of the larger institutions of the economy, the polity, the church, the family, and so on. Decisions about social policy are of great moment to many groups. They involve the expenditure of billions of dollars with large implications for taxation and government borrowing, and for capital and labor markets. These decisions also affect the well-being of large strata of the population, including the recipients of services and income supports, and the growing numbers of service providers, as well as the local communities that depend on government programs for infrastructure support. Moreover, social-policy politics has become a kind of political theater played to wide audiences and managed by politicians trying to sway voting publics.[2]

In fact, a fair amount of attention has been given to the role of political institutions in the formation of social policies. The school known as "historical institutionalism" is preoccupied with the impact of formal features of the American political system, such as federalism, or the design of our electoral-representative arrangements, on the evolution of our social policies. These arrangements of course matter, but the impact of politics on social policy is not circumscribed by the formal features of political institutions. The historical-institutionalism school tends to give short shrift to political agents, especially when the emergence of these agents does not seem to flow naturally from institutionalized features of the American polity. In particular, this school of thinking is at some pains to underplay the role of economic interest groups and social movements.

It should not need saying, but economic institutions also matter mightily in the politics of social policy. The preoccupation of welfare-state policymakers with the effects of relief, or unemployment insurance, or disability programs, or pension programs, on labor markets provides suggestive evidence of the bearing of economic institutions on social policy. The age-old concern of employer interests with social policy has always reflected the fear that programs that provide income that is politically conditioned instead of work-conditioned will relax labor-market discipline (Piven and Cloward 1971, 1993). The more recent celebration of expanded income-support programs as "decommodifying" makes the same point in reverse (Esping-Andersen 1985, 1999). And the contemporary drive for "labor-market flexibility" across the developed welfare states is in part a drive to reassert the primacy of labor markets in structuring welfare-state policy.

Economic actors also have large stakes in welfare-state programs because the programs require government expenditures and therefore taxation. A generous welfare state means higher taxes; a tight-fisted welfare state means lower taxes. Obviously, economic actors will be interested not only in the level of taxation associated with social policies but with their incidence. This also can be complicated, for it involves not only the straightforward question of who bears the cost, but which level of government extracts the taxes, because subnational governments concerned to keep investors and affluent residents within their jurisdictional boundaries will tend toward more regressive patterns of taxation. Finally, there are the stakes of market actors in the opportunities for profit that can result from the privatization of welfare-state programs, a development that appears to be of growing importance.

The institution of the family also matters, as a glance at the history of poor relief in the United States makes evident. During the long period that the primacy of the maternal role of at least middle-class mothers was taken for granted, our social policies reflected that institutional arrangement, first in the design of "mothers' pensions," and then in the design of the Aid to Families with Dependent Children (AFDC) program. Once family roles began to change and more and more women moved into the labor force, that development was registered in the design of poor relief, as the "Work first" slogan of Temporary Assistance for Needy Families (TANF) program created in 1996 makes evident (for a comparative discussion of this development, see Esping-Andersen 1999).

And then there is the church, which before the rise of commercial capitalism in the

West was the main source of poor relief, and is again becoming more important. As government benefits shrink, hard-pressed Americans turn to the churches, and especially to the fundamentalist Protestant churches that have become part of the administration's "faith-based" social service network. Individual churches receive government funds to expand their services and their membership, and the churches in turn urge their parishioners to vote against candidates who favor abortion and gay rights, which in practice means voting against Democrats. This is an attempt by a Republican regime to revive the clientelist uses of relief, especially in the African American and Hispanic communities that have hitherto been the bulwark of Democratic Party support. Here indeed is an attempt to use policy to shape politics.

But the considerable influence of these institutions is still only part of the explanation of the politics of social policy. Institutional arrangements help constitute the identities, interests, and strategies of political actors, and they also stand as constraints on political action. Nevertheless, identities and strategies change in ways not predicted by specific institutions, and institutional constraints can be overcome. Sometimes these unexpected developments can be illuminated by attention to developments in institutional spheres outside the purview of the analyst. After all, political actors are not bounded by the analytical lines we draw around particular institutions, and given human capacities for reflection and innovation, the ideas, identities, even resources generated in one institutional sphere can migrate to influence political action in other institutional spheres (on this point, see Sewell 1992).

The point I am making is thus two-sided. On the one hand, institutions, even broadly considered, do not entirely shape the politics of social policy. And on the other hand, even the most striking expressions of agency are nevertheless also shaped by and limited by institutional structures. In other words, structure and agency each inform the other. Or in the words of Anthony Giddens (1984, 174), structural constraints "serve to open up certain possibilities of action at the same time they restrict or deny others."

I begin to elaborate these observations by focusing on welfare, by which I mean mainly means-tested cash and in-kind assistance programs for the poor. From their origins in poor relief, these programs have always been designed to control, or regulate, the work behavior of the poor and the near-poor. Whether poor relief, or mothers' pensions, or Aid to Dependent Children (ADC), or Aid to Families of Dependent Children, or Temporary Assistance for Needy Families, the programs have included elaborate safeguards to restrict aid to the people once called "unemployables," on the one hand, and to ensure that those who do get aid get less, usually much less, than the lowest wage earner. Even that little aid has always been given on harsh and degrading terms. So there are institutional continuities in American relief policy.

But there are also periods of dynamic and radical change in these traditional practices that cannot be predicted from the structure-induced stability that an institutional analysis posits. In fact, American social-policy development is widely agreed to have developed in periods of explosive change. Almost all of the social-welfare legislation of consequence in the industrial era was enacted in just two six-year periods: 1933 to 1938 and 1963 to 1968 (with the exception of the Supplemental Security Income program of 1972, a delayed federal reaction to the state and local fiscal burdens resulting from the great expansion of the relief rolls in the 1960s).[3] None of this can easily be explained as a simple evolutionary outgrowth of earlier policies.

Thus, during the first big bang, national income support programs were initiated,[4] at first in the form of emergency relief, which reached millions of people, and supported them at levels that amazed and often outraged local elites (Piven and Cloward 1993, chapter 3). The Civil Works Administration work relief program created during the bad winter of 1933 to 1934 went so far as to eliminate the means test and pay wages far more generous than the average relief benefit. Together, relief and work relief programs reached 28 million people, or 22.2 percent of the population, and social spending increased rapidly, from 1.34 percent of Gross National Product (GNP) in fiscal 1932 to 5 percent by 1934 (Patterson 1981, 57). In 1935, the Social Security Act established the framework for almost all of our income support programs, beginning with old age pensions, unemployment benefits, and "categorical" programs for the otherwise uncovered aged, the blind, and orphans. These were the programs that came to be known as welfare. Subsidized housing programs were also introduced. By 1938, social spending in the United States was proportionally higher than that of any European power at the time (Amenta 1998, 7, 77).[5]

The 1960s saw the major expansion of the entitlements inaugurated in the 1930s, including the liberalization of old age pensions and unemployment insurance through extension of coverage and higher benefits, a quadrupling of the numbers of women and children on the Aid to Dependent Children program, the creation of Medicare for the elderly and Medicaid for the poor, new nutritional and housing programs, of which the Food Stamps program was most important, since it expanded from only 49 thousand monthly participants in 1961 to over 11 million by 1972 (Finegold 1988, 223). Overall, federal expenditures in support of individual and family income increased from $37 billion to $140 billion in the decade after 1965. By the mid-1970s, official poverty levels had dropped to an all-time low, from 20 percent in 1965 to 11 percent (O'Connor 2001, 240). Federal spending on the programs was projected to reach $373 billion in fiscal year 1982. Together with matching funds contributed by states and localities for AFDC and Medicaid, projected to reach $25 billion, these sums were equal to 12 percent of the estimated GNP (Piven and Cloward 1985, 14–19).

The historical institutionalists who review this history try to answer two questions. Why was the United States a laggard in welfare-state development when it was not a laggard either in industrial or political development?[6] And why, when the European experience seems to suggest the gradualist development of policy, was the pattern of American policy development so explosive, with most welfare-state policy initiatives concentrated either in the mid-1930s or the mid-1960s (Weir, Orloff, and Skocpol 1988, 9)?

To explain the late development of the American welfare state, the historical institutionalists point to unique institutional constraints on policy and politics that limited the growth of social-policy initiatives. Thus, much attention is devoted to the inhibiting effects on new initiatives of the federal system in the United States. The constraining influence of subnational authorities on federal policy formation presumably explains why, for example, the implementation of unemployment benefits in the 1930s was ceded to the states. Similarly, they argue that a distinctive American "policy heritage" and the more limited capacities of our national government explain why, for example, World War II led to broad national social welfare reforms in Great Britain, but only to fragmented programs in the United States (Amenta and Skocpol 1988).[7]

Other limits on new social-policy initiatives were generated by distinctive American electoral arrangements, including a party system that relied on patronage, thus making elites fearful of the potential abuses of social policy. More recently, Edwin Amenta (1998) has borrowed from the "legal-institutional" explanation of low voter participation in the United States, invoking the argument that legal and procedural restrictions on the franchise kept voting low among the less-well-off, who had large stakes in social-policy reform.[8] Then, also, constitutional and congressional arrangements privileged a southern congressional delegation determined to prevent federal policies that would interfere with the southern system and especially with its low-wage and chattel labor supply. These more specific elaborations aside, the overall point of view is clear. As Margaret Weir (1992) says, "One of the most powerful factors determining how groups define their policy interests and which alliance they enter is the organization of political institutions."

There is ample evidence of institutional constraints, and surely they are part of the answer to the question of why the United States was a social-policy laggard. However, and perhaps inevitably, a theoretical tool kit dominated by inherited institutional limits fares far less well in explaining periods of rapid change.[9] If features of American political institutions inhibited policy development, those features were nevertheless at least partly overridden during the big bangs of social-policy creation. And once initiated, new policies obviously change institutional arrangements. The big bangs led to an enormous growth in national government capacity as a result of the enlargement of its policy and spending authority.

For example, much is made by the historical institutionalists of the impediments to national initiatives posed by preexisting state and local policy authority. At first glance, the federal emergency relief program of 1933 seems to provide evidence of the influence of this state-centered constraint. Relief had always been a state and county responsibility and the new national emergency relief program was designed, in principle, to conform with that precedent. Responsibility for operating the programs was delegated to the states and counties, and they were required to contribute three dollars for every one dollar from Washington. So institutional precedents mattered, somewhat. But many states wouldn't or couldn't allocate the funds. The Roosevelt administration ignored this, and fielded a mass relief program anyway, and did so rapidly.

Why? Amenta (1998), who relies on the full battery of state-centered explanations to explain why the United States was a welfare laggard, nevertheless surreptitiously reverts to an electoral argument to explain the rapid expansion of welfare policy in the 1930s. He argues that during the Depression, there were more "pro-spenders" in the congress. True. But why did congressional representatives become pro-spenders in the 1930s? What happened that led voters and politicians to break with the fiscal conservatism of American politics?

Electoral shifts themselves have to be explained. And electoral change in the 1930s was at least in part propelled by the protest movements of the era, which raised new and urgent issues and threatened to wreak havoc with a still unstable majority Democratic electoral coalition. Insurgency by the unemployed, in the form of rallies and riots, rent strikes and looting, and takeovers of local and private relief offices, was mounting, and strapped and besieged local officials were clamoring for help. So the federal money poured out, whether or not state governments paid their share. Indeed, national officials simply federalized the administration of relief in six resistant states (Patterson 1981, 58).

When the tumultuous politics of the 1930s subsided, the emergency programs were terminated. What was left for the very poor were the state-administered categorical assistance programs legislated in the Social Security Act, including AFDC. Few women and children actually received AFDC benefits, however, and those who did had virtually no rights. They were subject both to bureaucratic runarounds, if they were permitted to apply at all, and to the often arbitrary decisions of agency staff. Benefit levels were miserably low. And the procedures for getting on the rolls, and staying on the rolls, were laden with shaming rituals of interrogation and investigation. There was a theatrical aspect to the shaming as well, as politicians periodically called for investigations to clean up "welfare fraud," by requiring more home investigations, more midnight raids to search for men, and so on. That the program was decentralized, was largely run by states and counties, and also relied in part on state and county funding gave extra bite to the politics of welfare scandal.

One might speculate that the poor-relief policy precedents of the pre–New Deal period somehow reasserted themselves after the interregnum of the Great Depression. But surely it is unsatisfactory to arbitrarily invoke one set of policy precedents and put aside another. More likely the explanation is that the mass insurgency that drove welfare expansion in the 1930s had subsided, at the same time as business interests shaped by markets reasserted themselves after the temporary hiatus of the Depression. Jacob Hacker and Paul Pierson (2002) offer an exceptionally illuminating analysis of the reasons for the decline of business influence during the 1930s. Their analysis is institutional, but their work is unusual because they examine the interplay of economic and political institutions. Their main conclusion is that although business occupies a privileged structural position in the decentralized American system, the "Great Depression and its political aftershocks shifted the locus of policy making to the federal level, stripping business of a significant source of its structural influence" (Hacker and Pierson 2002, 279). Once the Depression and its "political aftershocks" subsided, business influence again increased. In particular, business influence, and especially the influence of agricultural interests that depended on low-wage labor, loomed large in the design and implementation of the largely state-administered means-tested programs.

Welfare policy again changed dramatically during the course of the 1960s. Benefit levels were raised, application procedures were simplified, more of those who applied were accepted, intrusive investigations were less likely, there were fewer terminations for unspecified reasons, and the federal courts handed down decisions that created something like a "right" to welfare. It is not reasonable to think that these changes were a response to the constituency politics created by the AFDC program which had worked for a long time to strip people of rights, to isolate them, and to stigmatize them. In New York City, which was soon to receive notoriety for its welfare liberalism, the department regularly turned away new applicants, giving them bus tickets to return to the southern counties from which they had migrated instead.

To be sure, institutions mattered in shaping the tumultuous politics that interrupted these patterns. The institution that mattered most in generating the political upheavals that were eventually registered in welfare liberalization was not welfare itself, but the Democratic Party, and especially the presidential wing of the Democratic Party. Beginning in 1948, the party, which rested on a peculiar and fragile electoral coalition between the white South and the urban North, was buffeted by the complex interaction of massive demographic change and civil rights agitation. Rural African Americans, displaced from the plantations, flooded into northern cities, and therefore into the industrial states with large blocs of votes in the Electoral College. Meanwhile, urban whites who were traditionally Democratic were leaving the cities for the suburbs. Those who remained found themselves locked in conflict with the swelling ghettos that were encroaching on white neighborhoods, schools, and parks, setting off fierce racial conflicts in the cities.

These disturbances in the Democratic northern base were compounded by troubles in the "solid South." Blacks were also moving into the cities of the South, where their concentrated numbers, and their relative independence after generations of plantation servitude, helped to fuel the civil rights movement. Protests in the South were only encouraged by the ambiguous messages on civil rights communicated by Democratic presidential contenders seeking to hold the allegiance of newly volatile black voters in cities of the North without worsening southern white defections. The center could not hold, however. Together, the civil rights movement and Democratic presidential aspirants were driving white voters in the South to support insurgents such as Strom Thurmond and George Wallace in presidential elections.

The 1960 election cast these problems in sharp relief. Kennedy owed his victory to the heavy Democratic vote in key northern cities, especially the black vote. Reluctant at first to respond directly to civil rights demands, he instead inaugurated the first of the programs that came later to be known as the Great Society, a unique initiative that established a direct relationship between the federal government and ghetto neighborhoods. New federally-funded programs—ostensibly to deal with juvenile delinquency, or mental health, or poverty, or blighted neighborhoods—offered an array of services to ghetto residents, and also promulgated the message that the people in the neighborhoods had political rights.

A good deal of what these programs actually did, on the ground, was to help people get on the welfare rolls. Part of the reason was simply that many people were desperately poor, and needed cash, fast. Another part of the reason was that the old-line municipal agencies, with their entrenched constituencies of existing white residents in the civil services and in city politics, resisted making any service or employment concessions to the black newcomers, and the institutionalized apparatus of civil service regulations helped them to maintain this resistance.

By contrast, welfare had become, at least temporarily, a more accessible and softer institutional target. In the big cities, welfare offices were often located in the neighborhoods. New York City had thirty-seven such outposts, for example. And with riots spreading in the cities, the federal Department of Health, Education and Welfare, the predecessor to the current Department of Health and Human Services, issued new regulations requiring local welfare offices to accept oral applications. Meanwhile, the new poverty program also funded the lawyers who took the cases that led to the new court rulings establishing a modicum of "welfare rights." Under these conditions, welfare waiting rooms actually became organizing sites for the welfare protest movement.

And finally, the Great Society programs provided the rhetorical justification, and resources in the form of store-front offices, mimeograph machines, and Vista volunteers, that encouraged the emergence of a national "welfare rights" movement. But this was not a case of public policy, or political institutions, or markets, determining the emergence of a defiant movement, if there ever could be such a case. There was a large element of agency, of innovation and inspiration, in this development. Welfare recipients, blacks, Hispanics, and poor whites, the most benighted people in American society, banded together to claim their rights to welfare. By 1966, as urban protests over housing, schools, jobs, and so on escalated, along with federal promises to wage a "War on Poverty," demonstrations and sit-ins were spreading. Poor women across the country, especially African American and Hispanic women, were demanding welfare assistance.[10]

Many observers at the time, even observers sympathetic to the poor, were sharply critical of the welfare rights movement and its in-your-face demand for "more money now!" This was not the right demand, they scolded, and indeed, these were not the right people for a movement against poverty. The demand should not have been for welfare, but for jobs and job training. For example, when my collaborator Richard Cloward and I approached the noted civil rights leader Bayard Rustin for support for welfare rights organizing, Rustin replied disdainfully "I would rather get one black woman a job as an airline stewardess than get thousands of black women welfare." In today's political climate, one can see his point. But even back then, the women who massed together to demand welfare also saw his point.[11] Their problem was that there was little training available and few jobs for which they were suited, and they needed money to feed their children, now.

Along the same lines, other liberal critics complained about the failure of the welfare rights movement to form an alliance with unionized workers. Partly this reflected the long-standing conviction on the Left that the working class and only the working class was the motor for progressive change. Partly it reflected the reasonable fear that welfare rights demands would provoke the anger and enmity of those very workers. As a matter of historical fact, the movement's activists made repeated overtures to both workers and their unions, as the movement of the unemployed in the 1930s had done before them. To no avail, of course. Even an innovative movement could not overcome the label of pauperism perpetuated by the AFDC program. Nor could it bridge the social distance bred by a complex of institutional arrangements that fostered deeply imprinted attitudes about race and gender.

Or consider the curious influence of the family as an institution on the welfare rights protesters. Many of these women were divorced or separated, and others had never married. Yet they unfailingly addressed each other as "Mrs.," and their protests were justified in their eyes because they were mothers. Their fiercest protests were often for things such as clothing for school. In a way, the victories they won allowed them, to a small degree, to occupy the maternal role and to claim some respect for that role, even as developments in the American labor market were stripping an exclusively maternal role of legitimacy. So the welfare rights movement, even as it expressed the extraordinary defiance of the poorest and most benighted people in America, also reflected powerful institutional constraints on that defiance.

Nevertheless, these developments did indeed create a new politics of welfare, and its impact was large. The welfare rolls rose exponentially after 1964, and so did the Food Stamps and Medicaid rolls. Poverty rates fell sharply, from 15.6 percent in 1965 to 11.4 percent in 1978. The minority poverty rate fell from 42 percent in 1965 to 31 percent in 1978. And poverty in female-headed families dropped from 70 percent in 1966 to 48.6 percent in 1978 (Ylvisaker 1986; Williams 2001, 179). Writing in 1984, John Schwarz and John Volgy sum up the consequences:

> Programs such as food stamps virtually eliminated serious malnutrition among low-income children and adults in America. Medicaid and Medicare greatly increased the access of low income Americans to health care. In turn, the enlargement of both the nutritional and medical programs led to a decline in the infant mortality rates among minority Americans of 40 percent between 1965 and 1975, a drop that was eight times larger than the decline that had taken place in the ten years prior to 1965. The expansion of government housing programs helped to reduce the proportion of Americans living in overcrowded housing from 12 percent in 1960 to 5 percent in 1980. Those living in substandard housing declined from 20 percent to 8 percent.

These were political accomplishments. But they were not made possible by the institutional politics generated by the AFDC program. Obviously, that program had always worked to inhibit the political mobilization of its constituents. Instead, it was a chain of larger economic and demographic changes that destabilized the big political institutions of the nation, in combination with the ineluctable and unpredictable defiance of human agents that led to a measure of welfare reform.

Of course, more recent changes in welfare policy reversed these reforms. Features of American means-tested programs played a role in these reversals. The reforms of the

1960s did not overcome program fragmentation, and fragmented programs continued to be reflected in fragmented constituencies. Moreover, other features of the programs, including their revenue sources and their persisting stigmatizing rituals, also divided them from a larger working-class population.[12] Decentralization, in the case of AFDC and Medicaid, meant that the programs relied in significant measure on state and, in New York City, then the welfare capital of the nation, even on local taxation. And since the greater power of business on the state and local level, where investment exit threats are potent, leads to regressive tax policies, working-class animosities over welfare were easy to fan.

Ironically, some proponents of a more liberal or generous social policy did not regret the assault on AFDC.[13] Rather, they reasoned, once this much-derided program, the target of so much popular resentment, was done away with, new political possibilities for a more rational and inclusive set of policies would emerge. And besides, welfare, that old man of the sea, would finally be off the back of the Democratic Party. Needless to say, it did not turn out that way. And that was because the attack on welfare did not well up from the politics of the program. To be sure, popular resentments over taxation and program practices that degraded beneficiaries facilitated the campaign against welfare. But they did not create the campaign or give it the force and endurance that it had. Once again, larger institutions were at work, patterning—although not determining—the political campaign that emerged. The institution that mattered in activating political actors and shaping their interests was an increasingly competitive capitalist economy.

The liberalization of the means-tested programs in response to the tumult of the 1960s aroused opposition almost from the start. Generous income supports would make it possible for some people to withdraw from the labor market, and thus had the same effect as lower unemployment rates, effectively increasing the bargaining power of the low-wage workers who remained in the labor market. Even in-kind programs that provide subsidized health care or housing would have partial effects in relaxing the discipline of the market.

Nevertheless, for a time, opposition was muted. On November 8, 1954, Dwight Eisenhower had written to his brother Milton:

> Should any political party attempt to abolish social security, unemployment insurance, and eliminate labor laws and farm programs, you would not hear of that party again in our political history. Among them are H. L. Hunt (you possibly know his background), a few other Texas oil millionaires, and an occasional politician or business man from other areas. Their number is negligible and they are stupid.

In other words, American elites were cautious. Memories of the tumult of the 1930s, when business leaders had lost standing and legitimacy in politics, probably played a role in this,[14] and so did the extraordinary prosperity that American business enjoyed in the aftermath of World War II. After all, the United States was the only major industrial power to emerge from the war relatively unscathed. But this golden age of unchallenged American economic domination lasted a mere twenty-five years.

As Europe and Japan recovered, American corporations faced the unfamiliar prospect of tight competition with goods manufactured elsewhere, and this at a time when they were carrying the costs of the higher wages, more generous social programs, and workplace and environmental regulation that the turbulent 1960s had produced. By the early 1970s, as profit margins narrowed, the sorts of business leaders that Eisenhower had disparaged as marginal and stupid were leading a conservative counterassault that, as it gained momentum, threatened to wipe out the reforms of both the New Deal and the Great Society.

The business-led campaign to roll back the New Deal and Great Society reforms gained momentum as the protest movements of the sixties ebbed. The agenda of the campaign is by now familiar, and readily predictable as the agenda of market actors driven to increase their profit margins. The campaign worked to shift the brunt of taxation from business and the affluent to working people, and from capital to wages; to dismantle the environmental and workplace regulations that so irritated business and also cost them money; to reduce worker power by weakening unions, eviscerating regulatory protections of workers, largely through nonenforcement; and to roll back income-support programs so as to drive more people into the labor force and the scramble for work, and also to keep them anxious and insecure. Over time, as the campaign gained momentum, the agenda became more ambitious. Not only were the social programs to be slashed, but what remained of them would be targeted as another arena for profitability through publicly subsidized privatization.

If the agenda was predictable, the strategy of the campaigners was not. Rather, the strategy was constructed by imaginative and aggressive human agents who worked to create a powerful political apparatus. They launched new peak lobbying organizations, revived sleepy older organizations such as the Chamber of Commerce and industry trade groups, and built a political war machine on K Street. The campaign undertook to fold in the growing populist right rooted in the fundamentalist churches, and to cement their loyalty by rhetorically taking up their causes, especially opposition to abortion or gay marriage or gun control, no matter that the practical politics of the campaign was in fact mainly committed to the business agenda.

Liberals sometimes mourned that the right had launched a war of ideas. The ideas were obviously not new but a blend of market fundamentalism, or old-fashioned laissez-faire—a doctrine in which the individual stands unprotected before market forces and market "law"—and Christian fundamentalism, in which the individual is stripped of communal and political supports and stands unprotected before God's law. The core message, in the words of Linda Kintz (2005, 56), "spiritualized the market economy" (on this point, also see Gecan 2005).

What was new, rather, was the deliberate and strategic creation of an apparatus to promulgate these ideas. Rob Stein, formerly a Democratic political operative, calls it the "message machine" (Lapham 2004). Beginning in the early 1970s, with a handful of small right-wing foundations in the lead, a propaganda apparatus took shape. New think tanks were funded and a handful of older conservative think tanks were enlarged, including the Heritage Foundation, the American Enterprise Institute, the Cato Institute, and the Hoover Institution.

The think tanks elaborated the rollback agenda, hired the intellectuals who made the arguments, and spread those arguments widely, on talk shows, in op-ed columns, and so on. Grants from less politically aggressive corporations followed quickly, and the think tanks grew. The lead foundations also launched new periodicals and academic societies, and funded right-wing outposts in the universities, particularly in law and economics. They sponsored books by right-wing intellectuals and paid generously to publicize them, including *Freedom to Choose*, by Milton Friedman; *Losing Ground*, by Charles Murray; and *The Tragedy of Compassion*, by Marvin Olasky.

Market law and God's law are abstractions, and the campaign did not rely on abstractions. The organized right had a better symbol at hand. The propaganda of the message machine emphasized welfare, welfare recipients, and the Great Society, all codes to evoke and mobilize popular anxieties, and to turn the populist right against the programs and the political culture of the New Deal and Great Society eras.

There were good reasons for this strategy. The people on welfare were already marginalized, and vulnerable. Paupers have always been a despised caste in Western societies. Add to this long-standing distaste the fact that, in the wake of the mass migration of African Americans from the rural south to the urban north and the protests that ensued in the 1960s, welfare had become a disproportionately black (and Hispanic) program. The presidential campaigns of Barry Goldwater and George Wallace registered this fact and made evident the political uses to which it could be put. "Welfare" became a code word to evoke and mobilize rising white racial hatreds. In this limited sense, institutional precedents did matter.

At the same time, changing sexual and family mores were stirring a backlash of popular anxieties, anxieties that were fueled even more by the rise of the feminist movement. Since most recipients were single mothers, and black or brown, they were easily made into the symbol that captured all of this agitated hate politics. Ronald Reagan made the image of the "welfare queen" a staple of American popular culture. This was the politics of spectacle, a spectacle designed to evoke and intensify popular antipathies against Democrats, against blacks, against liberals, against licentious women, and against government, or at least those parts of government that provided support to poor and working people. In the background and out of the spotlight was the longer-term campaign of the organized right to defeat and dismantle the New Deal and Great Society policies.

Together, the alliance of business and the populist right took over the Republican Party, pouring new money into the electoral campaigns of hard-right candidates and pushing older-style conservatives to the margins. Business and business money was important in this process. Note, for example, that in 1980 big business broke with its usual practice of contributing to both major parties. The funds flowed to the Reagan campaign, and Reagan won. Then again in the midterm election of 1994, business money again tilted overwhelmingly to the Republican congressional races, and the Republicans swept the Congress, winning the House for the first time in many years, elevating Newt Gingrich to the speakership, and making the Contract with America and its distinguishing slogan of personal responsibility a template for its legislative initiatives.

But the real measure of the political success of the campaign was its influence on the Democratic Party, which had, for all its internal conflicts, and however reluctantly, championed the policies of the New Deal–Great Society period. Franklin Delano Roosevelt had talked of "strong central government as a haven of refuge to the individual."[15] By the 1990s, this tenet of the New Deal and Great Society was jettisoned by the Democrats. And welfare politics played a key role. The decades-long argument bubbling in the think tanks and regularly raised by Republican candidates had turned welfare into a metaphor for African Americans, sexual license, and liberalism. It had done its political work. In 1992, Bill Clinton made his bid for the presidency on the slogan of "ending welfare as we know it." As the 1996 election approached, the Republicans held his feet to the fire with their proposal for rolling back welfare called the Personal Responsibility and Work Opportunity Reconciliation Act (PRWORA). He turned for advice to his pollsters and consultants. Dick Morris told him to "fast-forward the Gingrich agenda." Clinton's pollster Stanley B. Greenberg (2005) argued that "progressives needed to transcend welfare politics."[16] Clinton signed the Personal Responsibility and Work Opportunity Reconciliation Act. The Democratic strategy, in a nutshell, was to beat the Republicans by adopting their positions.[17]

The PRWORA reproduced the features of the AFDC program as it existed before the reforms of the 1960s. Many of the legal and regulatory protections won under AFDC were wiped out simply because the AFDC program was eliminated. Under the "Work first" banner, which defined the new welfare program, state agencies, and in some places county agencies, or private agencies with whom state and local governments contracted to administer all or parts of the program, were now free to multiply the old-style administrative obstructions to distributing assistance. There was no longer a right to apply for welfare, and waiting rooms were heavily policed to prevent the kind of mobilization that had occurred in the 1960s. There were no statistics on how many people were turned away, or simply drifted away in discouragement. For those who succeeded in surmounting barriers to application, the conditions of continuing to receive aid multiplied, and compliance with these conditions was "individualized," leaving many decisions regarding benefits to the discretion of case managers. Work requirements in particular were stiffened, and sanctions—the reduction or termination of benefits—were freely used for noncomplying, or purportedly noncomplying, recipients (Fording, Schram, and Soss 2005).

These developments certainly reveal some feedback effects of the means-tested programs. Not only were the programs relatively undefended, but they bore the taint of their disproportionately African American and Hispanic and female clientele, and of the poor-relief practices that still characterized AFDC. But the main actors in the campaign did not emerge from the means-tested programs, but from business and politics. They included, importantly, the think tanks and lobbying organizations funded by business, and the politician-allies that business recruited. Their motives, and the political resources they deployed in their campaign, were formed in the context of the big institutions of the capitalist market and the electoral-representative system. But the campaign they mounted did not simply register market influences. Rather it was a bold and coordinated political initiative that used welfare as a foil for a larger redistributive agenda.

Thus, though the precarious political standing of the means-tested programs made them a tempting target and the focus of a good deal of political theater, the campaign was by no means mainly about welfare. With the political spotlight on the means-tested programs, and especially AFDC, a series of other programs were being chipped away. During the Reagan administration, big cuts were made in disability assistance; housing subsidies were scaled back massively; long-term unemployment insurance became harder to get, and much harder to get under George W. Bush; and new conditions were introduced into the Social Security program to encourage seniors to stay in the labor market. The president's budget proposals for 2006 continue the pattern, with big cuts proposed in Medicaid, supports for low-income housing, and a host of smaller social programs.

I turn now to the prospects for reversing the cutbacks in programs for the poor, whether to restore the damaged programs or to improve them. It is an important question, because the answer bears not only on the future of social policy but also on our confidence in democratic politics. After all, the cuts in the programs have increased hardship through a broad swath of American society, and the erosion of the safety net in turn is linked to stagnating wages, and even to the eroding strength of unions. For a long time, observers of American electoral politics were confident that such initiatives would lead to the defeat of political regimes. Voters might not be enlightenment thinkers, but at least they practiced a kind of pocketbook democratic politics, voting out incumbents—or defeating aspirants—on the basis of their assessment of how government policies were affecting their economic well-being. And, it was thought, politicians acted accordingly, striving to use government policy to affect the timing of downturns and upturns in the economy so that unemployment fell and personal income rose as election campaigns approached, and also arranging the timing of increases in transfer payments to coincide with electoral campaigns.[18] This was the heritage of the New Deal and the Great Society, and however limited, it was a kind of democracy, American style.

The campaign against welfare was an effort to discredit the political culture created during the New Deal and Great Society periods. The campaign was an effort not only to restrict the programs but also to change the understandings that influenced popular support. This was not done by making entirely new arguments, but by reviving and highlighting long-standing themes in American culture that had been partially displaced by the ideas formed during the New Deal and Great Society. To appreciate this cultural dimension, we have to return to the campaign to restrict welfare, because it cast a large shadow on American welfare-state politics.

Welfare reform was the beachhead, but other aspects of the right-wing cultural campaign, advanced under other slogans, meshed with the arguments about work and personal responsibility, and also made these ideas more seductive. Even before talk about the "ownership society" was being bruited about as part of the campaign to privatize Social Security, employment-based pension programs were being transformed by the contraction of guaranteed benefit plans and the expansion of guaranteed contribution plans that were often invested in company stocks, including 401(k)s, individual retirement accounts (IRAs), and direct-contribution pensions. (The Bush administration is also proposing tax-free lifetime savings accounts and retirement savings accounts.) Employment-based benefits have long been understood by some analysts as a way of tying employees to their employers. The expansion of the numbers of workers who hold these stock accounts bind them not only to their companies, however. It binds them to the market. More and more workers now own stock, and no matter that most workers have pitifully small holdings, even small holdings give some substance to the old idea "Every Man a Speculator."[19] Hoodwinked workers whose pensions are invested in the stock market tie their hopes to the Dow Jones average and watch the roulette wheel whirl, while the age-old struggle of workers for better wages, working conditions, and public programs sinks in hopelessness.

CONCLUSION

All of which is to say that political resistance to the campaign to transform the American welfare state will require some very heavy lifting. It is not likely to be accomplished by politics as usual. True, this round of Social Security proposals may be deadlocked, or end in compromise. But the compromise will continue the process of undermining public pensions.

We can get some perspective on the political prospects for authentic welfare-policy reform, by which I mean of course liberalization, in the face of determined and powerful business and political opposition by reflecting on the conditions that led to the policies now under attack. The initiation of the American welfare state in the 1930s, and its expansion and elaboration in the 1960s, occurred at moments of convulsive instability in American politics that gravely weakened business as a political force and brought new but insecure political leaders to power.

These conditions gave claimants for government support some leverage. Movements arose during the 1930s demanding government responses to economic hardship, first among the unemployed and then among the aged. These movements were nourished, however, by widespread popular discontent and even panic in the United States as the economy collapsed. Business leaders were stripped of standing, and new leaders came to power. Massive discontent also led Franklin Delano Roosevelt, even before he actually won the presidency, to give voice and legitimacy to the claims of the poor and the old.

And the instabilities that nourished these movements also made them more threatening. Indeed, in the early 1930s, even business leaders in the big American cities were calling for emergency-relief programs.

The conditions generating political instability in the 1960s were different, compounded as they were of massive demographic upheaval and racial conflict. What was similar, however, was that political instability nourished the emergence of protest movements, and not only over civil rights or education or housing or jobs; instability and the message of potential power it conveyed also sparked a wave of labor militancy, especially in the public sector. LBJ declared a war on poverty not in response to welfare-state claimants but in response to these broader disturbances. Only then did it become possible for welfare mothers, the poorest of the poor, to mobilize to assert their rights as well.

I do not expect either of these scenarios to be repeated exactly, of course. The moral, rather, is that the marginalized constituencies of the American welfare state cannot rise up alone. But then, if American leaders proceed on their current course, they may not be alone for very long.

NOTES

1. Steven Lukes (1974) makes this point.
2. David Bobrow makes a similar argument when he asserts that policy analysis is really about rationalization as much as reform. However, Bobrow seems to think that all sorts of advocates generate policy analysis, and ignores the reality of differential political power and its effects on the market for policy analysis.
3. On the concentration of progressive reform in these periods, see Alexander Hicks (2003, 271–88).
4. I exclude from consideration the veterans pensions, which were first inaugurated after the American Revolution.
5. Peter A. Swenson (2004) takes issue with Amenta, however, claiming that Sweden actually surpassed the United States modestly in social spending, 8.5 percent of GDP compared to 6.3 percent for the United States, when spending by all levels of government is considered.
6. The comparison deserves to be made with more caution than we exercise here. The United States did remain well behind some European powers—England and Belgium, for example—in the extent of industrialization. But it was ahead of other nations, such as Sweden and Norway, that initiated welfare programs early. The cross-national comparison of the development of democratic rights is also complicated, since the early-nineteenth-century expansion of the male voting franchise in the United States was followed half a century later by the introduction of drastic legal and procedural limits on the right to vote (see Piven and Cloward 1988).
7. Similarly, Margaret Weir (1992, 167) argues with regard to employment policy that "sequences of policy and institutional creation bounded later policymaking."
8. Limits on the franchise and their impact on party politics and policy are examined at length in Frances Fox Piven and Richard A. Cloward 1988.
9. Hacker and Pierson (2002, 277–325) also offer a broadly institutionalist argument in explaining the social policy initiatives of the 1930s. However, they focus not on political and policy institutions, but on economic institutions, and argue that the consequence of economic collapse was to weaken both the structural and instrumental power of business, allowing popular political claimants to exert more influence. For the argument that the institutionalists fasten on the wrong institutions in accounting for policy change, see Piven 2006.
10. For a more extended discussion of these political developments, see Piven and Cloward (2005 and 1993, chapters 8–10).
11. A meeting of the New York Citywide Coordinating Committee of welfare rights groups in 1967 was announced as a "training" meeting. The organizers intended training in the tactics

of demonstrating. The women who flocked to the meeting had understood they were coming for job training.

12. Heather Bouley (2004) emphasizes, as did Clinton administration officials, the injustice of allowing poor women to stay at home to care for their children while many working-class women not much better off were forced to work to make ends meet. Of course, there were other and better solutions to this injustice than the ones that were ultimately legislated.

13. See the assessment of this anticipated policy feedback effect in Joe Soss and Sanford F. Schram, "A Public Transformed? Welfare Reform as Policy Feedback" (chapter 5, this volume).

14. Hacker and Pierson (2002, 277–325) argue that what is important about the Great Depression is "the marked variation in business influence before, during, and after the New Deal. Prior to the Great Depression, business occupied a privileged position in American politics, thanks to the structural power conferred upon it by the decentralized character of American federalism." But business lost some of this structural power when the locus of decisionmaking shifted to the federal government. Moreover, business also lost instrumental power as a result of the widespread popular political mobilization.

15. The quotation is from a speech to the Commonwealth Club in 1932. See Aaron Singer, editor, *Campaign Speeches of American Presidential Candidates* (New York: Unger, 1976), cited in Ronald Schurin, "A Party Form of Government," Ph.D. dissertation completed at the Graduate School of the City University of New York, 1996. Schurin argues that this definition of the role of government was a strong and consistent theme in Roosevelt's public addresses.

16. Greenberg's analysis was considered a key guide for the 1992 Clinton presidential campaign.

17. See Jonathan Schell's (1999) review of two Morris books, *The New Prince: Machiavelli Updated for the Twenty-first Century,* and *Behind the Oval Office: Getting Reelected Against All Odds.*

18. Edward R. Tufte (1978, 39) made the original argument in 1978, and since then the propositions he advanced have become a standby in election predictions. "Unemployment levels twelve to eighteen months before presidential elections have exceeded unemployment at election time in six of the eight presidential elections between 1946 and 1976." Similarly, "In four of the last seven election years, government transfer payments have reached their yearly peak in October or November."

19. This is the title of a book by Steve Fraser, published in 2005: *Every Man a Speculator: A History of Wall Street in American Life.* New York: HarperCollins.

REFERENCES

Amenta, Edwin. 1998. *Bold Relief: Institutional Politics and the Origins of American Social Policy.* Princeton, N.J.: Princeton University Press.

Amenta, Edwin, and Theda Skocpol. 1988. "Redefining the New Deal: World War II and the Development of Social Provision in the United States." In *The Politics of Social Policy in the United States,* edited by Margaret Weir, Ann Shola Orloff, and Theda Skocpol. Princeton, N.J.: Princeton University Press.

Bobrow, Davis. B. 2006. "Social and Cultural Factors: Constraining and Enabling." In *The Oxford Handbook of Public Policy,* edited by Michael Moran, Martin Rein, and Robert E. Goodin. Oxford: Oxford University Press.

Bouley, Heather. 2004. "A House Divided: How Welfare Reform Pit Families Against the Non-Working Poor." *New Labor Forum* 13(3): 27–35.

Esping-Andersen, Goste. 1985. *Politics Against Markets: The Social Democratic Road to Power.* Princeton, N.J.: Princeton University Press.

———. 1999. *Social Foundations of Postindustrial Economies.* Oxford: Oxford University Press.

Finegold, Kenneth. 1988. "Agriculture and the Politics of U.S. Social Provision: Social Insurance and Food Stamps." In *The Politics of Social Policy in the United States,* edited by Margaret Weir, Ann Shola Orloff, and Theda Skocpol. Princeton, N.J.: Princeton University Press.

Fording, Richard, Sanford F. Schram, and Joe Soss. 2005. "Sanctioning Outcomes in the Florida TANF Program: Devolution, Privatization, and Performance Management." Paper presented to the Annual Meeting of the Midwest Political Science Association. Chicago, Ill. April 8, 2005.

Gecan, Mike. 2005. "Taking Faith Seriously." *Boston Review*, April–May: 17-20.

Giddens, Anthony. 1984. *The Constitution of Society: Outline of the Theory of Structuration.* Cambridge: Polity Press.

Greenberg, Stanley B. 2005. "How We Found—and Lost—a Majority." *The American Prospect* May 22, 2005: 27.

Hacker, Jacob, and Paul Pierson. 2002. "Business Power and Social Policy: Employers and the Formation of the American Welfare State." *Politics and Society* 30(2): 277–325.

Hicks, Alexander. 2003. "Back to the Future? A Review Essay on Income Concentration and Conservatism." *Socio-Economic Review* 1: 271–88.

Kintz, Linda. 2005. "God Goes Corporate." *New Labor Forum* 14(1): 56.

Lapham, Lewis. 2004. "Tentacles of Rage: The Republican Propaganda Mill, A Brief History." *Harper's Magazine*, September: 31-41.

Lukes, Steven. 1974. *Power: A Radical View.* New York: Macmillan.

O'Connor, Alice. 2001. *Poverty Knowledge: Social Science, Social Policy, and the Poor in Twentieth-Century U.S. History.* Princeton, N.J.: Princeton University Press.

Patterson, James T. 1981. *America's Struggle Against Poverty: 1900–1980.* Cambridge, Mass: Harvard University Press.

Piven, Frances Fox. 2006. "The Politics of Retrenchment: The U.S. Case." In *The Oxford Handbook of Public Policy*, edited by Michael Moran, Martin Rein, and Robert E. Goodin. Oxford: Oxford University Press.

Piven, Frances Fox, and Richard A. Cloward. 1971. *Regulating the Poor: The Functions of Public Welfare.* New York: Pantheon.

———. 1985. *The New Class War.* New York: Pantheon Books.

———. 1988. *Why Americans Don't Vote.* New York: Pantheon Books.

———. 1993. *Regulating the Poor: The Functions of Public Welfare.* Revised and expanded edition. New York: Vintage Books.

———. 2005. "The Politics of the Great Society." *In The Great Society and the High Tide of Liberalism*, edited by Sid Milkis and Jerome M. Mileur. Amherst, Mass.: University of Massachusetts Press.

Schell, Jonathan. 1999. "Master of All He Surveys." *The Nation*, June 21, 1999.

Schwarz, John, and John Volgy. 1984. "The War We Won: The Great Society's Fight Against Poverty." *New Republic*, June 18, 1984.

Sewell, William. 1992. "A Theory of Structure: Duality, Agency and Transformation." *American Journal of Sociology* 98(1): 1–29.

Swenson, Peter A. 2004. "Varieties of Capitalist Interests: Power, Institutions, and the Regulatory Welfare State in the United States and Sweden." *Studies in American Political Development* 18(3): 186–95.

Tufte, Edward R. 1978. *Political Control of the Economy.* Princeton, N.J.: Princeton University Press.

Weir, Margaret. 1992. *Politics and Jobs: The Boundaries of Employment Policy in the United States.* Princeton, N.J.: Princeton University Press.

Weir, Margaret, Ann Shola Orloff, and Theda Skocpol. 1988. "Introduction: Understanding American Social Politics." In *The Politics of Social Policy in the United States*, edited by Margaret Weir, Ann Shola Orloff, and Theda Skocpol. Princeton, N.J.: Princeton University Press.

Williams, Linda. 2001. *The Constraints of Race: Legacies of White Skin Privilege and the Politics of American Social Policy.* Albany, N.Y.: State University of New York Press.

Ylvisaker, Paul. 1986. "Poverty in the United States." In *The Great Society and Its Legacy: Twenty Years of U.S. Social Policy*, edited by Marshall Kaplan and Peggy L. Cuciti. Durham, N.C.: Duke University Press.

Part V

The People that Policies
Make: Roles, Identities,
and Democracies

Jennifer Hochschild and Vesla Weaver

Chapter 8

Policies of Racial Classification and the
Politics of Racial Inequality

In 1890, the United States Census Office reported that the nation contained 6,337,980 Negroes, 956,989 "mulattoes," 105,135 "quadroons," and 69,936 "octoroons."[1] In the early twentieth century it also reported the number of whites of "mixed parentage," the number of Indians with one-quarter, half, or three-quarters black or white "blood," and the "races" of Chinese, Japanese, and Hindoo. The boundaries between racial and ethnic groups, and even the definition of race and ethnicity, were blurred and contested. By 1930, however, this ambiguity largely disappeared from the census. Anyone with any "Negro blood" was counted as a Negro; whites no longer had mixed parentage; Indians were mainly identified by tribe rather than ancestry; and a consistent treatment of Asians was slowly developing. In other work we examine how and why these classifications rose and fell; here we examine the consequences for contemporary American politics and policy.

POLICY, POLITICS, INEQUALITY, AND RACE

Official governmental classification systems can create as well as reflect social, economic, and political inequality, just as policies of taxation, welfare, or social services can and do. Official classification defines groups, determines boundaries between them, and assigns individuals to groups; in "ranked ethnic systems" (Horowitz 2000), this process enshrines structurally the dominant group's belief about who belongs where, which groups deserve what, and ultimately who gets what. Official racial categories have determined whether a person may enter the United States, attain citizenship, own a laundry, marry a loved one, become a firefighter, enter a medical school, attend an elementary school near home, avoid an internment camp, vote, run for office, annul a marriage, receive appropriate medical treatment for syphilis, join a tribe, sell handicrafts, or open a casino. Unofficial racial categorizations have affected whether an employer offers a person a job, whether a criminal defendant gets lynched, whether a university admits an applicant, and whether a heart attack victim receives the proper treatment. In these and many more ways, racial classification helps to create and maintain poverty and political, social, and economic inequality. Thus systems of racial categorization are appropriate subjects for analysis through a policy-centered perspective because such systems are "strategies for achieving political goals, structures shaping political interchange, and symbolic objects conveying status and identity" (Hacker, Soss, and Mettler, chapter 1, this volume). Race is also, not coincidentally, the pivot around which political contests about equality have been waged for most of this country's history.

The same classification system that promotes inequality may also undermine it. Once categorization generates groups with sharply defined boundaries, the members of that group can draw on their shared identity within the boundary to mobilize against their subordinate position—what one set of authors calls strategic essentialism (Omi and Winant 1994). Thus classification laws are recursive, containing the elements for both generating and challenging group-based inequality. For this reason—and also because demographic patterns and other social relations on which classification rests can change—categorizations are unstable and impermanent.

We explore these abstract claims by examining the past century of racial classification in the United States. That period encompassed significant change in systems of classification and their attendant hierarchies; thus we can see how classification and inequality are related, and also trace the political dynamics that reinforce or challenge inequality-sustaining policies. From the Civil War era through the 1920s, the black population was partly deconstructed through official attention to mulattoes (and sometimes quadroons and octoroons), then reconstructed through court decisions and state-level "one-drop-of-blood" laws. As of 1930, a clear and simple racial hierarchy was inscribed in the American polity—with all the attendant horrors of full-scale Jim Crow segregation. However, the one-drop policy that reinforced racial inequality also undermined it. From the 1930s through the 1970s, that is, the black population solidified though a growing sense of racial consciousness and shared fate, and developed the political capacity to contest its poverty and unequal status.

Even this story is still too simple. While racial policies were deepening inequality and simultaneously creating the conditions to contest it, the remnants of the old classification scheme continued to have an impact. The category of mulatto disappeared, but the intragroup disparities that it implied did not. Inequalities among blacks, especially but not only in terms of skin color, have persisted into the twenty-first century with almost no public recognition. Thus classification systems can have a third impact, beyond reinforcing inequality and helping to create the conditions for fighting it; they can also mask disparities, which restricts citizens' capacity to derail them.

Currently, the black population is being partly deconstructed again, through official recognition of the new multiracial movement and through engagement with the growing Hispanic community and immigrants from Africa and the Caribbean. The United States is wrestling with an unstable set of conditions: mostly unrecognized but persistent skin-color differences among blacks, the growth of a class structure and political disparities among blacks, a new multiracial advocacy community, a continuing ideology of racial solidarity in the black community, and a principle of colorblind equality held by many whites. The possible implications of all of this for racial classification are multiple. Whether changing classification systems will reinscribe racial inequality, as some fear, or allow submerged inequalities and old hierarchies to be vigorously fought, as others hope, remains to be seen. Thus a central element of democratic citizenship—equality of respect and dignity—is at stake.

We aspire in this chapter to make both particular and general contributions to this volume. In particular, we show how the policy-centered perspective operates outside the more commonly studied social welfare system. In each era between the Civil War and the new millennium, contending political forces shaped official policy, the new policy helped to reshape political forces, and the new forces in time contributed to a new policy. That construction of the American racial order in the twentieth century is too simple and circular, of course, but we lack the space to develop all of its zig-zagging complexities here. What we can do is trace the stages of racial classification policy and their connections

with politics and inequality in order to show how a policy-centered perspective illumi-
nates American racial dynamics.

More generally, we hope to establish in this chapter a larger argument about democracy and public policy in an age of inequality. Just as American politics and scholarship
are impoverished by paying too little attention to class, so they are diminished by a lack
of attention to racial inequality. We mean five things by racial inequality:

First, a ranked social order created through a system of official classification is itself
a structure of inequality.

Second, racial inequality is not reducible to an observation that a disproportionate
share of a given group is poor or rich; being a member of a favored or disfavored race
can shape one's life chances independent of one's economic standing. For example,
middle-class blacks remain almost as residentially segregated as poor blacks, with
powerful consequences for quality of life, school achievement, wealth acquisition,
social relations, and political impact.

Third, the American structure of poverty and inequality is itself highly racially inflected. Fully 24.9 percent of blacks, compared with 8.3 percent of non-Hispanic
whites, lived below the poverty line in 2005 (see "People and Families in Poverty, by
Selected Characteristics," www.census.gov/hhes/www/poverty/poverty05/table4
.pdf). With regard to inequality, if blacks are not included in measures of income inequality in the United States, it declines. The Gini coefficient for all Americans in
2005 was 0.469; for whites alone, it was 0.461 (see "Table H-4. Gini Ratios for
Households, by Race and Hispanic Origin of Householder: 1967 to 2005," www.census
.gov/hhes/www/income/histinc/h04.html).

Fourth, the existence of socially consensual nominal racial groups (a.k.a. races)
partly explains socioeconomic and political inequality. A crucial answer to the old
saw of "Why no socialism in the United States?" is that racial hostility and mistrust
prevented the working class from consolidating into a powerful movement to contest
structures of economic and political inequality. Similarly, one reason why the many
poor in the purportedly democratic United States have not wrested political control
from the few rich is that the former are deeply divided by racial animosity and mistrust (often fostered by the well-off themselves) (Morgan 1975; Woodward 1971).

Finally, the nature of the racial order partly explains social policies; American policies ranging from housing subsidies to Social Security to school finance to criminal
justice probably would have developed very differently if the black-white binary had
not existed or if it had been more fluid and fragmented, as in most other nations
(Quadagno 1994; Lieberman 1998; Katznelson 2005; Weaver 2007).

We share the editors' goal for this volume of showing that policy change "has both
reflected and propelled a major shift in the character of inequality." We foster that goal by
demonstrating how the very categories so often used to analyze inequality—black, white,
Hispanic—are not a given, but have causal force in their own right; they contribute to
"shap[ing] coalitions, set[ting] agendas, creat[ing] symbols, alter[ing] interests,
influenc[ing] common-sense understandings, and so on" (Hacker, Soss, and Mettler,
chapter 1, this volume).

RACIAL CLASSIFICATION OF MULATTOES

Throughout the nineteenth and early twentieth centuries, individuals were commonly identified as Negro or mulatto, with the latter group often subdivided into quadroons and octoroons and sometimes even more finely split into griffes (the child of a black and a mulatto) or sang-meles ("mixed-blood"; one sixty-fourth black). In principle, these categories identified the precise nature of a person's lineage; in practice, the categories were typically determined by reputation or physical appearance, with light skin serving as a proxy for mixed ancestry. Thus, for example, in the 1910 Louisiana case of *State v. Treadaway* (see Finkelman 1993, 2111), the court declared:

> The person too black to be a mulatto and too pale in color to be a negro is a griff. The person too dark to be a white, and too bright to be a griff, is a mulatto. The quadroon is distinctly whiter than the mulatto. Between these different shades, we do not believe there is much, if any, difficulty in distinguishing.

The Census Bureau also delineated races by mixture, counting mulattoes as a separate group from 1850 through 1920 except in 1900, and including the categories of quadroon and octoroon at the behest of Congress in 1890 (Nobles 2000; Hochschild and Powell 2007). Similarly, in 1869 the United States Sanitary Commission published a volume summarizing data on most of the roughly 2,500,000 volunteers and recruits in the Union Army. For many tables in the volume, blacks were separated into "full blacks" and "mixed races" (while whites were separated into soldiers, sailors, and students; Gould 1869).

Analysts producing or using census or military data usually accepted the view that blacks and mulattoes were meaningfully distinct. The Sanitary Commission's report showed that mulattoes tended to weigh a bit more than blacks, although they were not taller, and to have more muscular strength than either blacks or whites. Census analysts ("a corps of Negro clerks working under the efficient direction of three men of their own race," as the director of the census carefully pointed out in 1918) meticulously documented differences in population growth rates, birth and death rates, school attendance and literacy, and migration patterns (U.S. Census Bureau 1918, "Letter of Transmittal"). The 1918 report showed, for example, that "the proportion attending school in the population of school age among mulattoes exceeds the proportion among blacks in each section of the country" (U.S. Census Bureau 1918, 215).

A few people saw mulattoes as a separate race altogether. The self-trained social analyst Alfred Holt Stone (1908, 398) argued in 1908:

> The mulatto is not a Negro, and neither written nor social law can make him one. By consent of all parties, including himself, he may be called a Negro. But we can no more make a Negro by such a process than we can alter the life traits and nationality of a Russian peasant by bestowing upon him an English name. The essential fallacy which underlies this classification will sooner or later make the latter impossible to maintain.

In his view, "there can no longer be a question as to the superior intelligence of the mulatto over the Negro" (Stone 1908, 401). Marcus Garvey saw an equally wide gap, but in the other direction—reportedly describing W. E. B. Du Bois as "a mulatto, . . . a monstrosity" (see "People and Events: W. E. B. DuBois, 1868-1963," http://www.pbs.org/wgbh/amex/garvey/peopleevents/p_dubois.html). Still others saw little meaningful difference between Negroes and mulattoes; the Census Bureau frequently denied the accuracy of its own distinctions, especially between mulattoes, quadroons, and octoroons.

State laws ranged across this array of assumptions. Elevated legal status for mulattoes was the rare exception.[2] Nevertheless, in at least twenty-five laws mulattoes were legally distinguished from blacks, for example by specifying that whites were forbidden from marrying "Negroes or Mulattoes." More generally, states' classifications diverged widely from each other, changed over time, and often contained no clear boundary between groups (authors' analysis from data in Murray 1950/1997). In three states, marriage to a white was prohibited if the person was one-fourth black; in seven others the formula was one-eighth, and in still others the law was simply unclear. States could employ one calculus for laws on marriage and another for purposes of segregation. For instance, in Tennessee, a marriage was interracial and therefore illegal if the person was "descended from a Negro to the 3rd generation inclusive" but in another Tennessee law Negroes were defined as including "mulattoes, mestizos and their descendants, having any blood of the African race in their blood."

These distinctions had deep symbolic and substantive impact; most saliently here, they created inequalities within as well as across groups. We need not detail the stratification between blacks and whites in the early days of Jim Crow, or remind readers of the depths of poverty to which designation as black consigned people. Less well known, for reasons that we discuss presently, is the significant stratification between blacks and mulattoes. The inequalities covered all arenas—social, economic, and political. Well before the Civil War, the Census Office noted the "preference they [mulattoes] have enjoyed in the liberation from slavery" (U.S. Census Office 1864). Free mulattoes in the lower South were "afforded a status superior to that of blacks," and they "tended to dominate the free black community in both numbers and influence. The lightest of the light-skinned lived almost as well as their white neighbors." Some owned slaves (Jones 2000, 1506–7).[3] Among Union soldiers in the Civil War, lighter-skinned blacks held more skilled occupations and higher military ranks than their darker counterparts; they were taller (a measure of nutrition) and less likely to die in the war (Hochschild and Weaver 2003). Mulattoes were more likely to be literate than blacks, and their children were more likely to attend school (U.S. Census Bureau 1918).

On average, mulattoes also enjoyed economic advantages over blacks. Before the Civil War, free mulattoes were more likely to own their own farms (Bodenhorn 2003), and their households had much greater wealth than black households (Bodenhorn and Ruebeck forthcoming). Those differences continued, and perhaps deepened, after emancipation. "Complexion homogamy"—the tendency for people to marry others of a similar color—prevailed, and couples in which both spouses were mulatto had at least 30 to 90 percent more wealth than partnerships with at least one black (Bodenhorn 2006; see also Reuter 1917; Gatewood 1990; Hill 2000).

Skin-color differences similarly structured political opportunities when those became available. Of the two black senators and twenty black members of Congress during Reconstruction, only three were *not* mulattoes. Perhaps a majority of the prominent racial leaders of the era were light-skinned or had white ancestors, including Booker T. Washington, W. E. B. Du Bois, and A. Philip Randolph. The status of mulattoes was hardly risk-free, but in most cases they were better off and had more resources for fighting or avoiding the worst features of the unequal racial order.

Bottom-up social relations often mirrored these top-down systems of categorization. Marcus Garvey (1925/1969, II, 55) observed in 1923 that "unfortunately, there is a disposition on the part of a certain element of our people in America, the West Indies and Africa, to hold themselves up as the 'better class' or 'privileged' group on the caste of color. . . . The evil of it is working great harm to our racial solidarity." Another observer surely exaggerated, but he too worried that "often their [mulattoes'] arrogance and intolerance toward the thick-lipped, kinky-haired Negro were more marked than that of the whites, and within two generations after emancipation, they had erected a 'color-caste' system within the race somewhat analogous to that prevailing in India" (Brisbane 1949). Black colleges and fraternities preferred light-skinned applicants; churches and organizations made distinctions in who could join or enter (Frazier 1957; Graham 2000). Charles Chesnutt (1898), a prominent African American educator, lawyer, and activist, describes in one of his short stories, "The Wife of His Youth," a group whose

> purpose was to establish and maintain correct social standards among a people whose social condition presented almost unlimited room for improvement. By accident, combined perhaps with some natural affinity, the society consisted of individuals who were, generally speaking, more white than black. Some envious outsider made the suggestion that no one was eligible for membership who was not white enough to show blue veins.

To the charge that they discriminated against darker-skinned people seeking membership, the members of the society (called the Blue Veins in the story) "declared that character and culture were the only things considered; and that if most of their members were light-colored, it was because such persons, as a rule, had had better opportunities to qualify themselves for membership" (Chesnutt 1898).

RACIAL CLASSIFICATION OF WHITE NATIONALITIES

On the other side of the racial divide, the meaning of whiteness around the turn of the twentieth century was also contested. Congressional committees held hearings to decide whether members of the "Hebrew race" were a distinct race, and how to categorize Mexicans (Perlmann 2001; Hattam forthcoming; Márquez 1993; Schor 2000).[4] Before 1870, the census tabulated the few Asians in the United States as white, although a footnote distinguished them; conversely, the 1908 Dillingham Immigration Commission's *Dictionary of Races or Peoples* described Slavs as "approach[ing] the Asiatic" (U.S. Congress 1911, 128; see also Hodes 2006 on the classification of Asians in 1890).

Courts almost despaired of drawing legal bright lines; as one put it,

> Then, what is white? What degree of colorization . . . constitutes a white person as against a colored person, and is the court to take the responsibility by ocular inspection of determining the shades of different colorization where the dividing line comes between white and colored. The statute . . . is most uncertain, ambiguous, and difficult both of construction and application. . . . There have been a number of decisions in which the question has been treated, and the conclusions arrived at in them are as unsatisfactory as they are varying.[5]

An array of legal cases, in state and federal courts and across many decades, groups, and issues, ensued before the judiciary was able to settle "what is white." Criteria included physical appearance (in at least one famous case the defendant was required to partially strip before the jury),[6] community recognition, ancestry, behavior, personal history, property considerations, timing of the case, and other factors (Haney López 1996; Gross 1998; Elliott 1999; Mack 1999). A Supreme Court decision in 1923 almost resolved the issue,[7] but for decades after that school boards and state regulatory agencies were adjudicating whiteness for children and would-be marital partners (Douglas 2003; Kennedy 2003; Ford 1994).

The entry of European nationalities into whiteness is much better known than that of mulattoes into blackness, and its implications for social, political, and economic inequality are clear. Hence we will not consider it further here (Sollors 1989; Gerstle 1993; Jacobson 1998; King 2000; Perlmann 2001; Hattam 2004; Roediger 2005). Suffice it say that we differ from the many legal scholars and historians who have depicted liminal individuals or nationalities as anomalies in a basically dichotomous black-or-white world. That viewpoint gives insufficient weight to the fact that many public agencies and private actors at the turn of the twentieth century classified an array of groups and people as neither black nor white, but as something in between and perhaps separate from both.

Thus politics and policy interacted between the Civil War and the Great Depression in a complex racial reorganization with an equally complex impact on structures of inequality. Politics created the policies of emancipation, immigration, and Mexican labor migration. Those broad policies called forth more specific policies from the Census Bureau, state legislatures, courts, and other institutions that sought to label, classify, order, and otherwise manage people of mixed or ambiguous or merely foreign descent. In the process, mulattoes were sometimes distinguished from Negroes and elevated above them; light-skinned people sometimes took advantage of their ambiguous status to escape the poverty and degradation that dogged almost all blacks. The same dynamics occurred, mutatis mutandis, among European immigrants, American Indians, and Mexican migrants. The policies remained confused, and so did the politics and the structure of race-based inequality, although the basic system of ranked ethnic orders was never threatened.

THE ONE-DROP RULE, JIM CROW, AND RACIAL POLITICS

From 1930 onward, racial classification changed. Uncertainty about racial classification and boundaries gave way to the clear, simple set of categories with which we are now familiar. Several strands of classification came together to permit that outcome. First, the concept of ethnicity became widely accepted, and enabled officials to locate various European nationalities in the white race. As European immigration declined and immigrants' children increasingly intermarried, the concept of whiteness was consolidated. Second, protest in response to the 1930 experiment of classifying Mexicans separately ensured that they, too, were considered white. Thus the politics of immigration restriction and foreign relations with Mexico, combined with the conceptual breakthrough of "ethnicity," shaped the policy definition of whiteness. That policy in turn enabled the majority of Americans to see themselves as white, and therefore part of the mainstream, and to live in reasonable comfort with the hardening segregation of Jim Crow.[8]

On the other side of the basic divide, the boundary around blackness was hardened, and the consequences of being labeled black deepened, at the same time that more and more people were being placed inside the category of black. This occurred in several political institutions more or less simultaneously. At the Census Bureau, the category of mulatto was dropped in 1930, with these instructions: "A person of mixed white and Negro blood should be returned as Negro, no matter how small the percentage of Negro blood. Both black and mulatto persons are to be returned as Negroes, without distinction." In state legislatures, "as the likelihood that more biracial people could be classified as white under existing laws increased, the laws became more restrictive, often progressing from one-fourth to one-eighth . . . , and finally culminating in the one-drop rule" by about 1930 (Wright and Hunt 1900, 524). Virginia provides the classic case. The criterion for membership in the black category grew from one-fourth before 1910 to one-sixteenth in 1910;

the 1924 Act to Preserve Racial Integrity defined whites as having "no trace whatsoever of any blood other than Caucasian" (Finkelman 1993; Gilanshah 1993).[9] By 1930, Virginia defined blacks as people with "any Negro blood." At the same time, the legal rights of mulattoes were largely dissolved into those of blacks.[10] State laws stopped using the phrase "Negroes and Mulattoes," substituting for both terms "Colored" (Higgenbotham and Kopytoff 1989). Only two of the twenty-five state laws that were concerned specifically with mulattoes were enacted after 1930.

In public discourse, also, discussion of mulattoes as a separate category largely faded away. The term "mulatto" and its variants appeared on average forty-two times a year in the *Washington Post* between 1890 and 1910 but only seventeen times a year from 1920 to 1940—and only eight times a year in the latter period if three outlier years are set aside (authors' analysis of keywords in the *Washington Post*, 1865 to 2005).

The new one-drop policy was associated with two immediate and related effects with regard to classification: the rejection of an explicit multiracial identity within the group, and the suppression of recognition of skin-color differences both within and outside the group. Neither blacks nor whites described mulattoes any longer as evidence of a link between them, even if usually forced and shameful, or as a distinct category meaningful on its own terms. Since 1990, "mulatto" and its variants have appeared anywhere from zero to three times a year in the *Washington Post*. This was not merely a change in vocabulary, as was the decline of "colored" or "Negro" to describe blacks; the whole concept of a group that was neither fully black nor white faded from social legitimacy.

As the law of hypodescent—the formal term for "one-drop" rules—was consolidated, so was Jim Crow segregation; the relationship is mutually causal. Americans found it difficult to have a system of strict and elaborate segregation until they had eliminated the categories that blurred the lines between segregators and segregated. Conversely, the more elaborate and wide-ranging the system of segregation became, the less feasible was occupation of any middle ground. These two policies together generated or sustained several forms of inequality. Most obviously, black poverty and racial economic inequality persisted and perhaps worsened.[11]

We lack systematic income or poverty statistics for the decades around the turn of the twentieth century; the best long-term data are for life expectancy, which was always, and remains, lower for blacks than for whites (in 2000, blacks could expect to live about 93 percent as long as whites). But blacks' life expectancy actually *declined* by up to six percentage points as a proportion of whites' life expectancy between 1910 and 1940, a pattern shown in table 8.1. Given those results, it is no surprise to find that about two and a half times as many black as white families were poor in every year from 1947 (the first year for which these data are available) to 1970 (see table 8.2).

The policies of the one-drop rule and legal segregation shaped racial politics as well as economic inequality. Most important, they denied the enlarged black population access to political power to change the laws that kept them poor, and legal redress for harms done under those laws. All blacks, even those with very light skin or many white ancestors, were accorded an unambiguously inferior legal and political standing. Of course inferior social and cultural status went along with subordinated economic and political status.

Over the long run, however, the policies of the one-drop rule and segregation, in conjunction with other factors such as a long tradition of racial nationalism and white liberal support, generated a counterreaction that led to a very different form of racial politics. A black sociologist predicted as much in 1926: "The American Negro will be forced by outside compulsion to maintain his social and physical identity, independent of any purpose

TABLE 8.1   Life Expectancy for Blacks as a Percentage of Life Expectancy for Whites, 1900 to 1940[a]

Year	Both Sexes	Men	Women
1900	84.2	83.4	85.3
1910	84.6	84.4	84.8
1920	82.5	83.7	80.2
1930	78.3	80.4	79.0
1940	82.7	83.2	82.6

Sources: Column 2: Haines (2006a); columns 3 and 4: Haines (2006b).
a. 1900 is the first year for which these data are available; they are not available for 1950 and 1960.

or policy on his part. The Negro will thus become one with himself long before he becomes one with the American people" (Miller 1926, 249). That is just about exactly what happened. By 1961, 89 percent of southern black adults agreed that they felt close to other blacks, and over three-quarters reported a "good deal" of interest in "how Negroes as a whole are getting along in this country" (authors' analysis of the Negro Political Participation Study cited in Matthews and Prothro 1975). This was a far cry from the "color-caste" of the early twentieth century.

The politics of racial solidarity directly challenged the politics of racial hierarchy, through bus boycotts, sit-ins, freedom marches, voter registration drives, and other acts. In Albert Hirschman's (1970) terms, once partial or complete exit from being black was no longer possible for those with light skin or known white ancestry, imposed connection to the group became, over several decades, genuine loyalty. Loyalty was followed by an increase in voice, now from a stance firmly within the black community. Put in other terms, by reinforcing the line between black and white, the one-drop rule and segregation primed black group consciousness and reduced the likelihood of intragroup division by color, at least in the public arena.[12]

The third effect of the post-1930 system of racial classification, however, reinforced rather than undermined inequality within the group. Although recognition of skin-color

TABLE 8.2   Annual Family Income of Poorest and Most Affluent Black and White Families, 1947 to 1970 (in 1967 Dollars)

	Blacks		Whites	
Year	Less than $3000	More than $10,000	Less than $3000	More than $10,000
1947	62.4%	2.2%	24.1%	9.5%
1957	46.7%	3.7%	17.6%	15.4%
1967	27.2%	16.7%	10.7%	36.4%
1970	25.0%	20.6%	9.7%	40.7%

Source: U.S. Census Bureau (1975), series G 16-30.

differences was officially eliminated and publicly muted, its strong association with economic, social, and political outcomes for blacks persisted. In the 1961 survey of southern
blacks, family income and years of education were both higher for those identified as
light-skinned, and declined proportionally with darker pigments (authors' analysis of
Matthews and Prothro 1975). The 1968 Kerner Commission survey of blacks in fifteen
major American cities yielded the same results (authors' analysis of Campbell and Schuman 1997). This pattern of light-skin advantage within the black population has persisted
to the present, and ranges across arenas as diverse as the likelihood of marrying, visual
representation in the media, length of prison sentences, chances of becoming a political
candidate and winning elective office, and selection to a judgeship (Hochschild and
Weaver 2007).

Light-skinned blacks seldom, however, combined their status advantages with withdrawal from other blacks in the 1960s as mulattoes had often done in earlier decades; in
both the Negro Political Participation Study and the Kerner Commission survey, light-
skinned blacks were just as likely as their darker counterparts to have a strong sense of
group consciousness. That pattern, too, has continued to the present. Intraracial inequality moved in tandem with attacks on interracial inequality.

By the second half of the twentieth century, then, most blacks had embraced the one-
drop policy imposed on them by 1930. Despite the undisputed fact of racially mixed ancestry, racial mixture disappeared as an officially or unofficially recognized category. The
internal politics of the black community mirrored the external legal standing of African
Americans, but with three very distinct consequences: segregation and hypodescent first
reinforced racial inequality and poverty, then fostered the conditions for group solidarity
and the generation of energy and resources for fighting racial inequality and poverty.
These two dynamics coexisted with a third—paler blacks continued to enjoy higher social, cultural, and economic status and more political power, although their status was not
accorded public recognition. Thus between 1930 and roughly 1990, the policies of American racial classification contributed to a complex, intertwined set of political dynamics—which together set the stage for a new round of policymaking.

MULTIRACIALISM REEMERGES

By the 1990s, while the old politics of racial hierarchy persisted, the United States was
once again moving into a new era of politics and policymaking with regard to racial mixture. The impact of this new era on poverty, inequality, democracy, and citizenship remains to be seen; all one can do at present is analyze the beginning of a set of dynamics
that will take decades to play out.

Racial mixture has reemerged as a political issue because of several policy and social
changes. First, as a largely unintended consequence of the 1965 immigration law, hundreds of thousands and then millions of residents of nations outside Europe began moving to the United States in the 1970s. Senator Edward Kennedy asserted in 1965 that "this
bill is not concerned with increasing immigration to this country," and President Lyndon
B. Johnson concurred that "this is not a revolutionary bill. It will not reshape the structure of our daily lives or add importantly to our wealth and power." Both were wrong, as
were virtually all other supporters of the Hart-Celler Immigration Act. Only its opponents accurately predicted its impact on the demography of the United States: namely,
that overall levels of immigration would rise dramatically, and that more and more immigrants would come from "nonwhite" nations (Tichenor 2002; Graham 2002; Hochschild
and Burch 2007).

By 2005, immigrants represented about 12 percent of the American population, and their children added another 12 percent or more. Through both immigration and high birth rates, the Latino population rose from 4 percent of Americans in 1970 to 13 percent in 2000, and the Asian population similarly increased from 1 to 4 percent. Like European immigrants around the turn of the twentieth century, contemporary immigrants and their descendants are marrying across group boundaries. About 30 percent of Asian-American marriages are to non-Asians (Fryer 2007) and that figure is projected to rise to 50 percent soon (Edmonston and Passel 1999). At least 14 percent of the much larger population of married Hispanics have a non-Hispanic spouse (Lee and Edmonston 2005, 25), and these figures too are rising rapidly.[13]

A second policy choice has also contributed to the rising salience of racial mixture in the American racial order. In 1967 the Supreme Court banned state antimiscegenation laws. Black-white unions, and their biracial offspring, remained rare for decades but are now increasingly rapidly. About 10 percent of African Americans were married outside their race as of 2000, and about a quarter of cohabiting blacks have a nonblack partner. Over 13 percent of children with at least one black parent have a nonblack parent as well (Fryer 2005). Given the trajectory of the past three decades, it is reasonable to assume that black outmarriage will continue to rise, as will the number of partly black children. And, according to Joel Perlmann (2002), once "a fifth to a quarter of children with a black grandparent . . . also have a non-black grandparent, . . . the history of outmarriage in other groups suggests it might well soar within a generation" (15–16). In short, mixed-race ancestry has returned to salience in the United States.

These changes have contributed to a new politics of multiracial assertion. Advocacy groups argue that multiracial individuals are being treated unequally because of their lack of official recognition, their distinctive medical needs (see, for example, Beal, Chou, and Palmer 2006), and their desire to retain multiple identities rather than follow the one-drop rule (DaCosta 2007). The mission statement of the Association of Multiethnic Americans (AMEA) reads, in its entirety, "To educate and advocate on behalf of multiethnic individuals and families by collaborating with others *to eradicate all forms of discrimination*" (see AMEA mission statement at http://www.ameasite.org; emphasis added). One advocate developed a "Bill of Rights for Racially Mixed People" with twelve elements, including "I have the right . . . not to keep the races separate within me, . . . to identify myself differently than strangers expect me to identify, . . . to have loyalties and identify with more than one group of people" (Maria Root, University of Washington website, www.washington.edu/alumni/columns/dec96/blurring5.html).

The politics of racial mixture have by now permeated public discourse. The term "multiracial" was almost never used in the *Washington Post* from the 1870s through the 1950s. It began to be seen in the 1960s and appeared an average of sixty times a year through the 1990s. Between 1990 and the present, commercial polling organizations, academic survey researchers, and media outlets have asked forty-six questions on national surveys that include the terms "multiracial," "mixed race," or "biracial." At least one major national poll has been conducted with respondents who are in biracial marriages.[14] College campuses have witnessed the growth of many student groups devoted to understanding and expressing multiracial identities. Amazon.com reports tens of thousands of books whose titles include the words "multiracial," "mixed race," or "biracial." Advertising firms and marketers are developing new plans based on the premise that "in this new, urban market, it is essential to get beyond ethnic segmentation and understand that it is the very *intermingling* of cultures and ethnicities that defines the urban sensibility" (Waterston 2004, emphasis in original). The phenomenal rise of Senator Barack Obama

(D-Ill.) in the national political arena guarantees that multiracialism will remain politically salient for some years at least.[15]

Policies changed; the political dynamics regarding racial mixture then changed; policymakers are now scrambling to catch up. At present, official systems of racial classification reflect a complex balancing act between competing norms and inconsistent applications. An unsystematic sample of twenty-five universities' equal opportunity forms illustrates the vagaries of racial classification. Some allow the respondent to choose more than one racial category while others require a single choice; some include Hispanic as a race while others designate it as "ethnicity"; still others include nontraditional categories such as Cape Verdean, Italian, and Pakistani. For example, Penn State University and the University of California, Berkeley—two prominent public universities—treat racial classification very differently, as figure 8.1 indicates.

More generally, for several decades individuals have been able to choose both a Hispanic ethnicity and a racial identity on the census and other official documents, thus resolving (at least for now) the dilemma of the statistical agencies in 1930 as to whether there is a Mexican "race." In addition, in 2000, for the first time in history, the census invited people to select multiple racial identities, thus recreating in a very different political atmosphere the mixed-race categories that featured prominently in official statistics, state laws, and court cases between the Civil War and the Great Depression. (Health-related federal agencies have collected data on racial mixture for some time.) The Office of Management and the Budget (OMB) is working to ensure that other federal agencies, such as the military and the Department of Education, follow suit. Prominent private institutions such as universities, hospitals, and corporations are moving in the same direction, and the media are full of stories and visual images reflecting ethnic ambiguity and multiracial diversity.

Nevertheless, for many policy purposes and legal cases the OMB permits or encourages the reaggregation of mixed-race individuals into a single race, that of the smallest minority or the one charging discrimination in a particular context. Not all people even recognize or accord legitimacy to the idea of a mixed-race identity, as the cartoon shown in figure 8.2 demonstrates.[16] Furthermore, most federal policies, such as redistricting under the Voting Rights Act, and many private sector policies, such as affirmative action in universities and corporations, still operate on the assumption that people belong to only one race. The situation with regard to whether Hispanicity should count as another race, like black or white, or whether it should remain as a separate ethnic category independent of race is a complete statistical, substantive, normative, political, and administrative hodgepodge.

There is a third position in this balancing act: an effort to avoid racial classification in any form. Some important actors, such as hospitals and schools, find it embarrassing to ask about racial identity and either make a decision about classification by visual inspection or do not record race at all. A few states are legally banned from practicing affirmative action in public agencies or institutions, and referenda to ban collection of racial data have appeared and may reappear. Thus we see policies that permit or encourage multiracialism, that permit or encourage monoracialism, and that permit or require race-blind practices. The implications of all of this for inequality and citizenship are, not surprisingly, unclear.

The multiracial movement itself is very small at present. Fewer than 3 percent of census respondents chose more than one race for themselves or their children, and only seven states permit people to choose more than one race on official forms (Williams 2006). However, it is plausible that the multiracial category will grow rapidly over the next few

FIGURE 8.1   Racial Classification Forms from Two Public Universities

University of California, Berkeley
Race/ethnicity *Please choose one category. If more than one choose the one with which you most closely identify.*

❏ White, not of Hispanic origin: *persons having origins in any of the original peoples of Europe, North Africa, or the Middle East*

❏ African American, not of Hispanic origin: *persons having origin in any of the Black racial groups of Africa*

❏ American Indian or Alaskan native: *persons having origins in any of the original American Indian peoples of North America, including Eskimos and Aleuts, or who maintain cultural identification through tribal affiliation or community recognition*

❏ Unknown

Hispanic (including Black individuals whose origins are Hispanic)

❏ Mexican/Mexican American/Chicano: *persons of Mexican culture or origin, regardless of race*

❏ Latin-American/Latino: *persons of Latin American (e.g., Central American, South American, Cuban, Puerto Rican) culture or origin, regardless of race*

❏ Other Spanish/Spanish American: *persons of Spanish culture or origin, not included in any of the Hispanic categories listed above*

Asian or Pacific Islander

❏ Chinese/Chinese American: *persons having origins in any of the original people of China*

❏ Japanese/Japanese American: *persons having origins in any of the original people of Japan*

❏ Filipino/Pilipino: *persons having origins in any of the original people of the Philippine islands*

❏ Pakistan/East Indian: *persons having origins in any of the original people of the Indian subcontinent (India and Pakistan)*

❏ Other Asian: *persons having origins in any of the original people of the Far East (including Korea), Southeast Asia, or Pacific islands (including Samoa), not included in any of the Asian categories listed above.*

The Pennsylvania State University
Affirmative Action Data Card

PLEASE CHECK THE APPLICABLE CATEGORIES
(Group definitions can be found on the back of this card.)

❏ American Indian or Alaska Native   ❏ Asian or Pacific Islander

❏ Black (non-Hispanic)   ❏ Hispanic

❏ White (non-Hispanic)

❏ Disabled   ❏ Disabled or Vietnam Era Veteran

❏ United States Citizen or Permanent Resident

FIGURE 8.2

Source: Universal Press Syndicate (1990).

decades if two conditions obtain. First, the policies and demographic forces that impelled its emergence will need to continue for some decades. And second, the politics of multiracialism will need to develop in a way that makes a mixed-race identity attractive to the many Americans who could claim it. While sharing some characteristics with the old interest in boundary-blurring represented by mulattoes and whites of mixed parentage, multiracialism will have to take on the connotations of multiculturalism and identity choice if it is to be widely accepted.[17]

PERSISTENT DISPARITIES IN TREATMENT BASED ON SKIN-COLOR

While the politics and policy concerns around racial mixture were reemerging in the United States during the 1990s, albeit in a very different form from a century earlier, disparities of status and general treatment on the basis of skin color persisted with almost no public recognition and little change. The two issues are related, but not in a simple way. In the aggregate, skin-color differences within a given race are obviously a consequence of racially mixed ancestry. But in particular cases, the connection can be weak; a light-skinned black can have two black parents and a racially mixed person with Hispanic and American Indian parents may be darker-skinned than many of those classified as black. Most important for our purposes, the political dynamics and policy issues are very different for skin-color inequality than for multiracial identity.

The topic of skin tone is even more fraught with personal and political sensitivities than is multiracialism, and is much less part of the public discourse. Nevertheless, differential treatment on the basis of skin color is arguably more implicated in racial inequality and racially inflected poverty than is multiracial heritage. People of mixed race on average have a socioeconomic status (SES) between the average SES's of their parents' racial groups. Multiracial identifiers on the 2000 census were somewhat younger, better educated, and more urban than black identifiers (Hochschild 2005). So multiracials are relatively well-off compared with the average black. But dark-skinned African Americans (and Latinos, although we do not consider them in this chapter) are *worse* off than the average black person.

Many scholars, using the eight national surveys with a skin-color measure as well as local or more opportunistic surveys, have reached the same conclusion: darker skin color within a given race or ethnicity is associated with lower SES. For example, the 2,107 respondents of the 1979–1980 National Survey of Black Americans (NSBA) averaged 10.9 years of schooling (Jackson and Gurin 1999), but a gap of almost two years separated the schooling of the darkest and lightest among them.[18] The pattern is the same for income: blacks' mean family income, according to the NSBA, was $12,417, with almost a $5,000 annual difference in family income between the lightest- and darkest-skinned respondents. Put another way, in a year in which all black families' mean income was 63 percent of white families', dark-skinned blacks' incomes were 70 percent of light-skinned blacks'.[19]

Other features of life are affected by skin color as well, ranging from length of prison sentences (Burch 2005) and likelihood of receiving a death sentence (Eberhardt et al. 2006) to attractiveness as a dating or marital partner (Hunter 2002) to likelihood of being negatively stereotyped (Maddox and Gray 2002) to chances of being nominated for or elected to political office (Weaver 2005; Hochschild and Weaver 2007). People of all races, in short, treat light-skinned blacks differently from dark-skinned blacks; even beyond its impact through the assignment of individuals into nominal racial categories, skin color remains a vital part of private classification by citizens and public officials alike. As such, it is deeply implicated in racial inequality and poverty, perhaps as much as it was around the turn of the twentieth century.

Despite the centrality of skin color as a social reality, the United States has not witnessed a politics of skin color analogous to the politics of multiracialism, never mind the politics of racial group identity. Variation in appearance is neither a source of political mobilization, nor the subject of policies to address the disparities associated with it. To the contrary: policies to promote racial equality, such as majority-minority districting or affirmative action, treat a given racial category as though all of its members are essentially the same for purposes of that policy. As the editors of this volume put it, policies can not only provide benefits (or harms) but can also "obscure which groups are benefiting or being harmed" (see Hacker, Mettler, and Soss, chapter 1, this volume).

Skin color is not a subject of discourse in the public arena because of one of the other strands of racial politics that we discussed earlier—group solidarity. As Marcus Garvey (1925/1969, II, 61) wrote in 1923, "We desire to have every shade of color, even those with one drop of African blood, in our fold. . . . Whether we are light, yellow, black or what not, there is but one thing for us to do, and that is to get together and build up a race." Racial solidarity continues to play a pivotal role in suppressing attention to skin-color discrimination. This logic of racial solidarity was deeply internalized and was effective, and it continues to hold sway in the African American population. By this logic, any internal difference that diverts attention or generates conflict—differences by gender, class, skin color, sexuality, and so on—should receive low priority until the fight for racial equality is closer to being won. As Cathy Cohen (1999, 15) puts it, blacks

> must weigh concern over the respectability and legitimization of black communities in the eyes of dominant groups against concern over the well-being of those most vulnerable in our communities, as they struggle against very public, stigmatizing issues. It is this tension that informs the indigenous political processes that determine which issues will be embraced by black elites and organizations. (See also Shelby 2005 on the need for racial solidarity.)

Several other features of the American racial order reinforce the role of racial solidarity in suppressing attention to skin-color discrimination. Its effects can be submerged in perceptions of persistent racial inequality; thus in some (though not all) surveys, lighter-skinned blacks perceive just as much discrimination against themselves and their group as do darker-skinned blacks.[20] In addition, those who suffer most from skin-color discrimination have, almost by definition, the fewest resources and lowest social standing with which to fight it. Because they are subject not only to racial but also skin-tone discrimination (Maddox and Gray 2002) by both blacks and whites—what Cohen (1999) calls "advanced" or "secondary" marginalization—even when they have wanted to, they have not been in a position to challenge their situation very effectively.

Finally, the whole history of "mulattoes" that we recounted earlier in this chapter affects Americans' ability in the present era to publicly discuss skin-color differentiation. The history of American racial classification and boundary blurring provides very little by way of a usable past. The discourse that refers to mulattoes, quadroons, and octoroons (never mind griffs, half-breeds, sang-meles, and metis) has been rejected for public use, along with the complicated and ambivalent social interactions, political maneuverings, and individual emotions that those terms and their history evoke. It is hard, if not impossible, to find in American history attractive models or tested strategies for negotiating or overcoming intra-group ancestral differences. Since racial mixture was typically "proved" by appearance, including skin tone, disavowal of the earlier politics around the designation "mulatto" slides easily into disavowal of any current politics around light or dark skin. Conversely, as we noted earlier, the history and practice of the one-drop rule has generated a norm of public assertion of social equality *within* racial groups. In short, the United States lacks both a politics and a policy agenda with regard to skin-color inequality.

THE POSSIBLE FUTURES OF MULTIRACIALISM

At this point, no one can confidently predict whether the policies of recognizing multiracialism will persist, whether political contestation around the concept will grow or diminish, or whether recognition of racial mixture or skin-color differentiation might make a material difference in reducing inequality and enhancing citizenship. There are simply too many variables, interacting in too many ways—and there is too much room for political entrepreneurship—for any prediction to be worth much.

Consider, for example, the array of responses to the idea of publicly recognizing racial mixture in the 2000 census (Williams 2006). All but one member of the Congressional Black Caucus opposed the proposal for a "multiracial" category. Some opponents feared a diminution of still-essential racial solidarity; as Arthur Fletcher (1993, 273), then chair of the United States Commission on Civil Rights, commented, "I can see a whole host of light-skinned Black Americans running for the door the minute they have another choice. . . . All of a sudden they have a way of saying—in this discriminatory culture of ours— . . . 'I am something other than black.'" Others cautioned against undermining policies designed to ameliorate racial inequality and poverty. Thus Harold McDougall (1997, 308) of the National Association for the Advancement of Colored People (NAACP) testified to a congressional committee: "The creation of a multiracial classification might disaggregate the apparent numbers of members of discrete minority groups, diluting benefits to which they are entitled as a protective class under civil rights laws and under the Constitution. In our quest for self-identification, we must take care not to recreate, reinforce, or even expand the caste system we are all trying so hard to overcome."

Conversely, some people supported official recognition of multiracialism as a first step toward replacing racial classification with color-blind policies and politics. Speaker of the House of Representatives Newt Gingrich (R-Ga.) (1997, 661–62), testified before a House subcommittee investigating the impact of race and ethnicity on the planned 2000 census: "[I]deally, I believe we should have one box on federal forms that simply reads, 'American.' But if that is not possible at this point, . . . allow[ing] them [Americans] the option of selecting the category 'multiracial' . . . will be an important step toward transcending racial division and reflecting the melting pot which is America."[21]

That is the conservative version of color-blindness; there is also a liberal version, held by people who argue against strong racial identities on the grounds that they inhibit class-based loyalties and political contestation around economic inequality (Gitlin 1995; Wilson 1999; Warren 2001).

Public opinion on the issue of multiracial classification is largely unformed. In 1995, more blacks (49 percent) than whites (36 percent) thought the census should add a multiracial category (*Newsweek* 1995). Overall, only 38 percent of respondents endorsed the addition. In 2001, however, perhaps as a result of the policy change in the census that invited respondents to "mark one or more" races, public opinion shifted. About two-thirds of a national sample then agreed that it is "good for the country . . . if more Americans think of themselves as multi-racial rather than as belonging to a single race" (Gallup/CNN/*USA Today* 2001). There was no significant difference between whites' and blacks' responses.[22] Both survey questions, like most others asking about multiracialism, showed high rates of "Don't know" responses. Looking across the full array of survey items since 1990, it seems clear that on balance Americans now favor recognition of multiracialism and that respondents identified as biracial are largely content with their situation (Fears and Deane 2001; Massey and Charles 2006).[23] None of these views are firmly grounded, however; political activity could surely push them in one or another direction.

We do not expect to see political activity developing around skin-color disparities. The subject is simply too emotionally laden, for blacks and whites equally—although for different reasons. (It might emerge in the Latino population as part of the debate over racial classification[s] of Hispanic Americans.) Nor do we expect much decline in African Americans' perceptions that regardless of internal tensions and inequality, their fates are linked and their commitment to racial solidarity must persist. In fact, unlike most ethnic groups in which those who are upwardly mobile become less committed to their ethnic identity, middle-class blacks are, if anything, *more* committed to their racial identity than are poorer or less-educated blacks (Hochschild 1995).

Reducing the argument to its simplest terms, policies of racial classification over the past century have generated four elements now yoked in unstable tension: differentiation by ancestry, differentiation by skin color, an ideology of color blindness, and deepening of the one-drop rule for African Americans. In official rules and public discourse, color blindness contests with black solidarity, solidarity that implicitly derives from the old one-drop rule; in practice, multiracialism and skin-color hierarchy complicate both of those simple principles. As a consequence of this history, efforts to "help blacks" risk disproportionately benefiting the best-off within the group, while efforts to help the worst-off blacks risk undermining group connectedness by drawing attention to intragroup inequities. It remains unclear whether fostering the new identity of multiracialism or giving attention to the old problem of discrimination against the dark-skinned would weaken or strengthen efforts to ameliorate racial inequality and black poverty. What is clear is that racial classification is a central form of policymaking that affects and is affected by inequality, norms of citizenship, and political formations—but not in any linear or simple way.

The project of which this paper is a part is jointly written with Traci Burch of Northwestern University. She has been fully involved in developing these arguments, but bears no responsibility for the exact content of this paper. We thank Gwen Clark, Ariel Huerta, Tiffany Jones, Frankie Petrosino, Brenna Powell, Robert Young, and Jasmine Zhang for heroic research assistance. We also thank Lisa Garcia Bedolla, Melissa Nobles, the editors of this volume, and the anonymous reviewers for insightful comments. Finally, we are grateful to the Guggenheim Foundation, the Radcliffe Institute for Advanced Studies, Harvard's Weatherhead Center for International Affairs, and Harvard's Center for American Political Studies for their financial and institutional support.

NOTES

1. After a first usage which is often in quotations, we continue by using the terminology common to the time period about which we are writing. We do not intend thereby to endorse these terms, which are often offensive to contemporary ears. But endless quotation marks or phrases such as "so-called" are tedious to read.
2. Before the Civil War, mulattoes were sometimes permitted to testify in court cases, although blacks were not, and in carefully specified circumstances, mulattoes were permitted to marry whites (Finkelman 1993).
3. Throughout the nineteenth century, "instead of grouping mulattoes into the undifferentiated category of black, the Lower South treated mulattoes as a third category, an intermediate class between blacks and whites. Pragmatic reasons drove southern whites to maintain this buffer class" (Jones 2000, 1508). South Carolina and Louisiana were especially slow and reluctant to adopt a one-drop rule, preferring often to give special status to mulattoes of good reputation.
4. The 1930 census enumerated Mexicans separately, after earlier censuses variously categorized them as white or mulatto. However, after the Mexican government and members of Congress from districts in Texas protested that Mexican Americans were white, the separate category was dropped.
5. See *Ex parte Shahid*, 1913, 205 F. 812 (E.D.S.C. 1913), 813. The Supreme Court similarly recognized deep ambiguity in defining races, even a decade later: "It may be . . . that a given group cannot be properly assigned to any of the enumerated grand racial divisions. The type may have been so changed by the intermixture of blood as to justify an intermediate classification" (*United States v. Bhagat Singh Thind*, 1923, 261 U.S. 204, 213).
6. Leonard Rhinelander v. Alice Rhinelander; 219 A.D. 189; 219 N.Y.S. 548; Supreme Court of New York, Appellate Division, Second Department (1927). See Lewis and Ardizzone 2001.
7. *United States v. Bhagat Singh Thind.*
8. Almost all Asians were excluded from the United States, so the ongoing muddle concerning Asian nationalities and "races" had little impact on American society in general. There is a separate, fascinating, story about racial classification of American Indians in the same period, but we save that for another day.
9. The legislature had to backtrack from this assertion of white racial purity, however, to accommodate the First Families that claimed descent from Pocahontas.
10. But not without a great deal of confusion:

    Between 1910 and 1924, for example, a mixed-race person less than one-fourth, who, before 1910, could marry only a white person—barred from marrying a "colored person" under penalty of indictment for a felony—could now marry only another person of color and, if marrying a white person, would be subject to prosecution for that choice. Two mixed-race people who, under the previous dispensation, might have legally married each other as white people (if, for example, each [was] seven-eighths European and one-eighth African), might now marry each other just as legally as non-white people (Wallenstein 1999, 572).

11. So did white poverty. Southern elites' commitment to keeping blacks poor through inadequate schooling, lack of access to public services, and economic peonage held the South in a state of deep economic underdevelopment, thus harming poor whites almost as much. White workers, sharecroppers, farm workers, and domestic servants were prevented from unionizing and deprived of most New Deal benefits either intentionally or as a side effect of repressing black workers (Katznelson 2005; Key 1949/1984; Reich 1981).

12. For example, when the census first allowed self-definition in 1960, there was no "noticeable fluctuation in the number of blacks, thus indicating that black Americans generally apply the one-drop rule to themselves" (Davis 2001, 7).

13. Although not immigrants, well over half of Native Americans marry outside their race, and that proportion also is rising (Lee and Edmonston 2005).

14. See Darryl Fears and Claudia Deane's "Biracial Couples Report Tolerance," a report of a survey sponsored by the *Washington Post*, the Henry J. Kaiser Family Foundation, and the Harvard University School of Public Health, July 5, 2001, accessed at http://www .washingtonpost.com/ac3/ContentServer?articlid=A19824- 2001Jul4&pagename=article.

15. Barack Obama refers to his African father and white American mother in many political speeches. For example, in his address to the Democratic National Convention in July 2004 he said: "I stand here today, grateful for the diversity of my heritage. . . . In no other country on earth is my story even possible" (Obama 2004). In an interview, he observed that his biracial background had "been entirely to my benefit. One of the things that I'm proud of is that I can move between many worlds and I think that's broadened my perspective" (Roach 2004, 23).

16. Boondocks comic strip reprinted with the permission of Universal Press Syndicate. Original comic from Mycomicspage.com, accessed on September 15, 2006.

17. Multiracialism will "grow" statistically if Hispanics are classified as a race on the United States census and other official forms, instead of being separately categorized as an ethnicity, as is now generally the case. Arguably, Hispanicity is itself a form of multiraciality, if it is understood as a culture and a heritage of *mestizaje*. In addition many Hispanics marry non-Hispanics, so their children would count as multiracial if Hispanics are deemed to be a race.

18. These results are based on one-way ANOVAS (analysis of variance). The differences in means are statistically significant, p = .01 (see also Edwards 1972; Keith and Herring 1991; Hunter 2002; Allen, Telles, and Hunter 2000; Seltzer and Smith 1991; Krieger, Sidney, and Coakley 1998).

    In the 1992–1994 Multi-City Study of Urban Inequality (MCSUI), dark-skinned blacks received on average 12.2 years of schooling; medium-skinned blacks received 12.5, and light-skinned blacks enjoyed 12.9 years of schooling. These results are based on one-way ANOVAS; p = .000 (for data, see Bobo et al. 2000).

19. p = .001 for blacks (see also Edwards 1972; Keith and Herring 1991; Seltzer and Smith 1991; Murguia and Telles 1996; Cotton 1997; Krieger, Sidney, and Coakley 1998; Hill 2000; Gomez 2000; Allen, Telles, and Hunter 2000; Hunter 2002; Bowman, Muhammad, and Ifatunji 2004).

    In MCSUI, the mean black family income rose from $23,191 for the dark-skinned to $24,773 for the medium-skinned to $25,886 for the light-skinned. That is, families of dark-skinned African Americans enjoyed about 90 percent of the income of families of light-skinned African Americans, in a year when the mean family income for blacks was 64 percent of that of whites. Based on one-way ANOVAs, for blacks, p = .114.

20. In MCSUI, for example, when asked if other blacks "treated them differently because of their color," the lightest set of blacks were most likely to say yes. Blacks of all shades were equally likely to say that whites treated them differently on the basis of color.

21. Roger Clegg (2002, 2), of the Center for Equal Opportunity, made a similar argument to the United States Commission on Civil Rights: "Insisting that people embrace a racial identity is bad for civil-rights progress and, therefore, bad for civil-rights enforcement. Discrimination is more likely to occur in a society in which people have strong racial identities and an us-them mentality."

22. Thanks to Lydia Saad of the Gallup Organization for providing the relevant cross-tabulations.

23. See also Fears and Deane 2001, note 14.

REFERENCES

Allen, Walter, Edward Telles, and Margaret Hunter. 2000. "Skin Color, Income and Education: A Comparison of African Americans and Mexican Americans." *National Journal of Sociology* 12(1): 129-80.

Beal, Anne, Shu-Chiung Chou, and R. Heather Palmer. 2006. "The Changing Face of Race: Risk Factors for Neonatal Hyperbilirubinemia." *Pediatrics* 117(5): 1618–25.

Bobo, Lawrence, James Johnson, Melvin Oliver, Reynolds Farley, Barry Bluestone, Irene Browne, Sheldon Danziger, Gary Green, Harry Holzer, Maria Krysan, Michael Massagli, and Camille Charles. 2000. Multi-City Study of Urban Inequality, 1992–1994 [Household Survey Data] [Computer file]. 3rd ICPSR version. Ann Arbor: University of Michigan, Inter-University Consortium for Political and Social Research. Accessed at http://www.icpsr.umich.edu/cocoon/ICPSR/STUDY/02535.xml.

Bodenhorn, Howard. 2003. "The Complexion Gap: The Economic Consequences of Color Among Free African Americans in the Rural Antebellum South." In *Advances in Agricultural Economic History*, Volume 2, edited by Kyle Kauffman. Amsterdam: Elsevier Science North-Holland.

———. 2006. "Colorism, Complexion Homogamy, and Household Wealth: Some Historical Evidence." *AEA Papers and Proceedings* 96(2): 256–60.

Bodenhorn, Howard, and Christopher Ruebeck. Forthcoming. "Colorism and African-American Wealth: Evidence from the Nineteenth-Century South." *Journal of Population Economics.*

Bowman, Phillip, Ray Muhammad, and Mosi Ifatunji. 2004. "Skin Tone, Class, and Racial Attitudes Among African Americans." In *Skin Deep: How Race and Complexion Matter in the "Color-Blind" Era*, edited by Cedric Herring, Verna Keith, and Hayward Horton. Chicago, Ill.: University of Illinois Press.

Brisbane, Robert. 1949. "His Excellency: The Provincial President of Africa." *Phylon* 10(3): 257–64.

Burch, Traci. 2005. "Skin Color and the Criminal Justice System: Beyond Black-White Disparities in Sentencing." Unpublished paper. Cambridge, Mass.: Department of Government, Harvard University.

Campbell, Angus, and Howard Schuman. 1997. Racial Attitudes in Fifteen American Cities, 1968 [Computer File]. 2nd ICPSR version. Ann Arbor, Mich.: Inter-university Consortium for Political and Social Research. Accessed at http://www.icpsr.umich.edu/cocoon/ICPSR/STUDY/03500.xml.

Chesnutt, Charles. 1898. *The Wife of His Youth and Other Stories of the Color Line and Selected Essays.* Accessed at http://manybooks.net/pages/chesnutt11051105711057-8/1.html.

Clegg, Roger. 2002. "Racial and Ethnic Data Collection by Government Agencies." Statement before the U.S. Commission on Civil Rights, May 17, 2002. Accessed at http://www.adversity.net/RPI/RPI_pages/3_news.htm.

Cohen, Cathy. 1999. *Boundaries of Blackness: AIDS and the Breakdown of Black Politics.* Chicago, Ill.: University of Chicago Press.

Cotton, Jeremiah. 1997. "Color or Culture? Wage Differences Among Non-Hispanic Black Males, Hispanic Black Males, and Hispanic White Males." In *African Americans and Post-Industrial Labor Markets*, edited by James Stewart. New Brunswick, N.J.: Transaction.

DaCosta, Kimberly. 2007. *Making Multiracials: State, Family, and Market in the Redrawing of the Color Line.* Palo Alto, Calif.: Stanford University Press.

Davis, F. James. 2001. *Who Is Black?: One Nation's Definition.* University Park, Penn.: Pennsylvania State University Press.

Douglas, J. Allen. 2003. "The 'Most Valuable Sort of Property': Constructing White Identity in American Law, 1880–1940." *San Diego Law Review* 40: 881–946.

Eberhardt, Jennifer, Paul Davies, Valerie Purdie-Vaughns, and Sheri Johnson. 2006. "Looking Deathworthy: Perceived Stereotypicality of Black Defendants Predicts Capital-Sentencing Outcomes." *Psychological Science* 17(5): 383–6.

Edmonston, Barry, and Jeffrey Passel. 1999. "How Immigration and Intermarriage Affect the Racial and Ethnic Composition of the U.S. Population." In *Immigration and Opportunity: Race,*

Ethnicity, and Employment in the United States, edited by Frank Bean and Stephanie Bell-Rose. New York: Russell Sage Foundation.

Edwards, Ozzie. 1972. "Skin Color as a Variable in Racial Attitudes of Black Urbanites." *Journal of Black Studies* 3(4): 473–83.

Elliott, Michael. 1999. "Telling the Difference: Nineteenth-Century Legal Narratives of Racial Taxonomy." *Law and Social Inquiry* 24(3): 611–36.

Fears, Darryl, and Claudia Deane. 2001. "Biracial Couples Report Tolerance." *Washington Post.* July 5, 2001. Accessed at www.washingtonpost.com/ac3/ ContentServer?articlid=A19824-2001 Jul4&pagename=article.

Finkelman, Paul. 1993. "The Crime of Color." *Tulane Law Review* 67: 2063–112.

Fletcher, Arthur. 1993. Testimony at Hearings on the Review of Federal Measurements of Race and Ethnicity. 103rd Congress, 1st session, House, Committee on Post Office and Civil Service, Subcommittee on Census, Statistics and Postal Personnel. November 3, 1993. Washington: U.S. Government Printing Office.

Ford, Christopher. 1994. "Administering Identity: The Determination of 'Race' in Race-Conscious Law." *California Law Review* 82: 1231–85.

Frazier, E. Franklin. 1957. *Black Bourgeoisie*. Glencoe, Ill.: Free Press.

Fryer, Roland. 2005. *Figures*. Cambridge, Mass.: Department of Economics, Harvard University.

———. 2007. "Guess Who's Been Coming to Dinner? Trends in Interracial Marriage over the 20th Century." *Economic Perspectives* 21(2): 71–90.

Gallup/CNN/*USA Today*. 2001. Poll, March Wave 1. March 9–11, 2001.

Garvey, Marcus. 1925/1969. *Philosophy and Opinions of Marcus Garvey.* 2 volumes. New York: Atheneum.

Gatewood, Willard. 1990. *Aristocrats of Color: The Black Elite, 1880-1920*. Bloomington, Ind.: Indiana University Press.

Gerstle, Gary. 1993. "The Working Class Goes to War." *Mid-America* 75(3): 303–22.

Gilanshah, Bijan. 1993. "Multiracial Minorities: Erasing the Color Line." *Law and Inequality Journal* 12: 183–204.

Gingrich, Newt. 1997. Statement at Hearings on Federal Measures of Race and Ethnicity and the Implications for the 2000 Census. 105th Congress, 1st Session, House, Committee on Government Reform and Oversight, Subcommittee on Government Management, Information and Technology. July 25, 1997. Washington: U.S. Government Printing Office.

Gitlin, Todd. 1995. *The Twilight of Common Dreams*. New York: Metropolitan Books.

Gomez, Christina. 2000. "The Continual Significance of Skin Color: An Exploratory Study of Latinos in the Northeast." *Hispanic Journal of Behavioral Sciences* 22(1): 94–103.

Gould, Benjamin. 1869. *Investigations in the Military and Anthropological Statistics of American Soldiers*. New York: Hurd and Houghton.

Graham, Hugh. 2002. *Collision Course: The Strange Convergence of Affirmative Action and Immigration Policy in America*. Oxford: Oxford University Press.

Graham, Lawrence. 2000. *Our Kind of People: Inside America's Black Upper Class*. New York: Harper-Collins.

Gross, Ariela. 1998. "Litigating Whiteness: Trials of Racial Determination in the Nineteenth-Century South." *Yale Law Journal* 108(1): 109–88.

Haines, Michael. 2006a. "Table Ab1-10: Fertility and Mortality, by Race: 1800–2000." In *Historical Statistics of the United States, Earliest Times to the Present*, edited by Richard Sutch and Susan Carter. Millennial Edition. New York: Cambridge University Press.

———. 2006b. "Table Ab704-911: Life table 1(x) Values at Selected Ages, by Sex and Race: 1850–1997." In *Historical Statistics of the United States, Earliest Times to the Present*, edited by Richard Sutch and Susan Carter. Millennial Edition. New York: Cambridge University Press.

Haney López, Ian. 1996. *White by Law: The Legal Construction of Race*. New York: New York University Press.

Hattam, Victoria. 2004. "Ethnicity: An American Genealogy." In *Not Just Black and White: Historical and Contemporary Perspectives on Immigration, Race, and Ethnicity in the United States*, edited by Nancy Foner and George Fredrickson. New York: Russell Sage Foundation.

———. Forthcoming. *Ethnic Shadows: Jews, Latinos, and Race Politics in the United States*. Cambridge, Mass.: Harvard University Press.

Higgenbotham, Jr., A. Leon, and Barbara Kopytoff. 1989. "Racial Purity and Interracial Sex in the Law of the Colonial and Antebellum Virginia." *Georgetown Law Journal* 77: 1967-2028.

Hill, Mark. 2000. "Color Differences in the Socioeconomic Status of African American Men: Results of a Longitudinal Study." *Social Forces* 78(4): 1437–60.

Hirschman, Albert. 1970. *Exit, Voice, and Loyalty*. Cambridge, Mass.: Harvard University Press.

Hochschild, Jennifer. 1995. *Facing Up to the American Dream: Race, Class, and the Soul of the Nation*. Princeton, N.J.: Princeton University Press.

———. 2005. "From Nominal to Ordinal: Reconceiving Racial and Ethnic Hierarchy in the United States." In *The Politics of Democratic Inclusion*, edited by Christina Wolbrecht and Rodney Hero. Philadelphia, Penn.: Temple University Press.

Hochschild, Jennifer, and Traci Burch. 2007. "Contingent Public Policies and Racial Hierarchy: Lessons from Immigration and Census Policies." In *Political Contingency: Studying the Unexpected, the Accidental, and the Unforeseen*, edited by Ian Shapiro and Sonu Bedu. New York: New York University Press.

Hochschild, Jennifer, and Brenna Powell. 2007. "Mulattos, Half-Breeds, Mixed Parentage, Hindoos, and the Mexican Race: Inventing Racial and Ethnic Classifications in the US Census 1850–1930." Unpublished paper. Cambridge, Mass.: Department of Government, Harvard University.

Hochschild, Jennifer, and Vesla Weaver. 2003. "From Race to Color: Does Skin Color Hierarchy Transform Racial Classification?" Paper presented at Harvard Color Lines Conference, Segregation and Integration in America's Present and Future. Cambridge, Mass., August 30-September 1, 2003.

———. 2007. "The Skin Color Paradox and the American Racial Order." Unpublished paper. Cambridge, Mass.: Department of Government, Harvard University.

Hodes, Martha. 2006. "Fractions and Fictions in the United States Census of 1890." In *Haunted by Empire: Race and Colonial Intimacies in North American History*, edited by Ann Laura Stoler. Durham, N.C.: Duke University Press.

Horowitz, Donald. 2000. *Ethnic Groups in Conflict*. Revised ed. Berkeley, Calif.: University of California Press.

Hunter, Margaret. 2002. "'If You're Light You're Alright': Light Skin Color as Social Capital for Women of Color." *Gender and Society* 16(2): 175–93.

Jackson, James, and Gerald Gurin. 1999. National Survey of Black Americans, 1979–1980 [computer file]. ICPSR ed. Ann Arbor, Mich.: University of Michigan, Inter-University Consortium for Political and Social Research. Accessed at http://www.icpsr.umich.edu/cocoon/ICPSR/STUDY/08512.xml.

Jacobson, Matthew. 1998. *Whiteness of a Different Color: European Immigrants and the Alchemy of Race*. Cambridge, Mass.: Harvard University Press.

Jones, Trina. 2000. "Shades of Brown: The Law of Skin Color." *Duke Law Journal* 49: 1487–557.

Katznelson, Ira. 2005. *When Affirmative Action Was White: An Untold History of Racial Inequality in Twentieth-Century America*. New York: Norton.

Keith, Verna, and Cedric Herring. 1991. "Skin Tone and Stratification in the Black Community." *American Journal of Sociology* 97(3): 760–78.

Kennedy, Randall. 2003. *Interracial Intimacies: Sex, Marriage, Identity, and Adoption*. New York: Pantheon Books.

Key, Vladimir Orlando. 1949/1984. *Southern Politics in State and Nation*. Nashville, Tenn.: University of Tennessee Press.

King, Desmond. 2000. *Making Americans: Immigration, Race, and the Origins of the Diverse Democracy*. Cambridge, Mass.: Harvard University Press.

Krieger, Nancy, Stephen Sidney, and Eugenie Coakley. 1998. "Racial Discrimination and Skin

Color in the CARDIA Study: Implications for Public Health Research." *American Journal of Public Health* 88(9): 1308–13.

Lee, Sharon, and Barry Edmonston. 2005. *New Marriages, New Families: U.S. Racial and Hispanic Intermarriage.* Washington: Population Reference Bureau.

Lewis, Earl, and Heidi Ardizzone. 2001. *Love on Trial: An American Scandal in Black and White.* New York: Norton.

Lieberman, Robert. 1998. *Shifting the Color Line: Race and the American Welfare State.* Cambridge, Mass.: Harvard University Press.

Mack, Kenneth. 1999. "Law, Society, Identity, and the Making of the Jim Crow South." *Law and Social Inquiry* 24(2): 377-409.

Maddox, Keith, and Stephanie Gray. 2002. "Cognitive Representations of Black Americans: Reexploring the Role of Skin Tone." *Personality and Social Psychology Bulletin* 28(2): 250–9.

Márquez, Benjamin. 1993. *LULAC: The Evolution of a Mexican American Political Organization.* Austin, Tex.: University of Texas Press.

Massey, Douglas, and Camille Charles. 2006. "National Longitudinal Survey of Freshmen." Report. Office of Population Research, Princeton University.

Matthews, Donald, and James Prothro. 1975. Negro Political Participation Study, 1961–1962 [computer file]. Conducted by the University of Michigan, Survey Research Center. ICPSR07255-v3. Ann Arbor, Mich.: Inter-university Consortium for Political and Social Research. Accessed at http://www.icpsr.umich.edu/cocoon/ICPSR/STUDY/07255.xml.

McDougall, Harold. 1997. Testimony at Hearings on Federal Measures of Race and Ethnicity and the Implications for the 2000 Census. 105th Congress, 1st Session, House, Committee on Government Reform and Oversight, Subcommittee on Government Management, Information and Technology. May 22, 1997. Washington: Government Printing Office.

Miller, Kelly. 1926. "Is the American Negro to Remain Black or Become Bleached?" *South Atlantic Quarterly* 25(3): 240–52.

Morgan, Edmund. 1975. *American Slavery, American Freedom: The Ordeal of Colonial Virginia.* New York: Norton.

Murguia, Edward, and Edward Telles. 1996. "Phenotype and Schooling Among Mexican Americans." *Sociology of Education* 69(4): 276–89.

Murray, Pauli. 1950/1997. *States' Laws on Race and Color.* Athens, Ga.: University of Georgia Press.

Newsweek. 1995. Newsweek Poll, February 1-3, 1995.

Nobles, Melissa. 2000. *Shades of Citizenship: Race and the Census in Modern Politics.* Palo Alto, Calif.: Stanford University Press.

Obama, Barack. 2004. "The Audacity of Hope." Speech to Democratic National Convention. Boston, Mass. July 27, 2004. Accessed at http://www.washingtonpost.com/wp-dyn/articles/A19751-2004Jul27.html.

Omi, Michael, and Howard Winant. 1994. *Racial Formation in the United States.* New York: Routledge.

Perlmann, Joel. 2001. "'Race or People': Federal Race Classifications for Europeans in America, 1898–1913." Unpublished paper. Levy Economics Institute, Bard College.

———. 2002. "The Intermingling of Peoples in the United States: Intermarriage and the Population History of Ethnic and Racial Groups since 1880." Unpublished paper. Levy Economics Institute, Bard College.

Quadagno, Jill. 1994. *The Color of Welfare: How Racism Undermined the War on Poverty.* New York: Oxford University Press.

Reich, Michael. 1981. *Racial Inequality: A Political-Economic Analysis.* Princeton, N.J.: Princeton University Press.

Reuter, Edward. 1917. "The Superiority of the Mulatto." *American Journal of Sociology* 23(1): 83–106.

Roach, Ronald. 2004. "Obama Rising." *Black Issues in Higher Education* October 7: 20–23.

Roediger, David. 2005. *Working Toward Whiteness.* New York: Basic Books.

Schor, Paul. 2000. "Changing Racial Categories: The United States Bureau of the Census and

Racial Minorities, 1900–1940." Paper presented at the annual meeting of the Organization of American Historians, St. Louis, Mo., March 30-April 2, 2000.

Seltzer, Richard, and Robert Smith. 1991. "Color Differences in the Afro-American Community and the Differences They Make." *Journal of Black Studies* 21(3): 279–86.

Shelby, Tommie. 2005. *We Who Are Dark: The Philosophical Foundations of Black Solidarity*. Cambridge, Mass.: Harvard University Press.

Sollors, Werner, editor. 1989. *The Invention of Ethnicity*. New York: Oxford University Press.

Stone, Alfred Holt. 1908. *Studies in the American Race Problem, with an Introduction and Three Papers by Walter F. Willcox*. New York: Doubleday, Page.

Tichenor, Daniel. 2002. *Dividing Lines: The Politics of Immigration Control in America*. Princeton, N.J.: Princeton University Press.

U.S. Census Bureau. 1918. *Negro Population 1790–1915*. Washington: U.S. Government Printing Office.

———. 1975. *Historical Statistics of the United States, Colonial Times to 1970*. Washington: Government Printing Office.

U.S. Census Office. 1864. *Population of the United States in 1860*. Washington: U.S. Government Printing Office.

U.S. Congress. 1911. *Reports of the Immigration Commission: Dictionary of Races or Peoples*. Washington: Goverment Printing Office.

Universal Press Syndicate. 1990. "The Boondocks." September 15, 1990.

Wallenstein, Peter. 1999. "Law and the Boundaries of Place and Race in Interracial Marriage: Interstate Comity, Racial Identity, and Miscegenation Laws in North Carolina, South Carolina, and Virginia, 1860s–1960s." *Akron Law Review* 32: 557–76.

Warren, Mark. 2001. *Dry Bones Rattling: Community Building to Revitalize American Democracy*. Princeton, N.J.: Princeton University Press.

Waterston, Adriana. 2004. *The Dawning of Multicultural America*. Larchmont, N.Y.: Horowitz Associates, Inc., and Surveys Unlimited.

Weaver, Vesla. 2005. "Race, Skin Color, and Candidate Preference." Paper presented at the annual meeting of the Midwest Political Science Association, Chicago, Ill., April 7-10, 2005.

———. 2007. *Dark Prison: Race, Rights, and the Politics of Punishment*. Ph.D. dissertation, Government and Social Policy Program, Harvard University.

Williams, Kim. 2006. *Mark One or More: Civil Rights in Multiracial America*. Ann Arbor, Mich.: University of Michigan Press.

Wilson, William J. 1999. *The Bridge over the Racial Divide: Rising Inequality and Coalition Politics*. Berkeley, Calif.: University of California Press.

Woodward, C. Vann. 1971. *The Strange Career of Jim Crow*. 2nd revised edition. Oxford and New York: Oxford University Press.

Wright, Carroll, and William Hunt. 1900. *The History and Growth of the United States Census*. Prepared for the Senate Committee on the Census. Washington: U.S. Government Printing Office.

Deborah Stone

Chapter 9

Welfare Policy and the Transformation of Care

By 2001, five years after "the end of welfare as we know it," reports from around the country were triumphal. Rolls had been cut—as much as 90 percent in some states. Millions of people once on the dole were now employed. The war on welfare was succeeding beyond anyone's wildest dreams. As one of many success stories, the New York Department of Human Services put forward Angel Martinez and Regla Belette, a couple with three children whose five-year time limit on welfare was fast approaching. The state told them they were no longer eligible for assistance and invited them to come in for an appointment "so you can discuss how you plan to manage your household expenses" (Bernstein 2001; all details and quotations in this family profile are from this source).

In a tiny gesture of resistance, Martinez and Belette told a *New York Times* reporter that they didn't count themselves as a success, despite what the city said. Although Mr. Martinez worked all the overtime he could get, he still couldn't pay the light bill *and* give his kids money for snacks. He summed up his feelings about the state's welfare program: "None of the those welfare bureaucrats' kids is going to go hungry and cry themselves to sleep. My kids are." Though they both held jobs, he as a warehouseman in the Brooklyn Navy Yard, she as a child-care worker, Mr. Martinez and Ms. Belette were still struggling to keep their family afloat—to pay the rent and keep hunger at bay. They were also trying to take care of each other in the way that families do, the way that usually involves little money and lots of personal attention—nurturing, nursing, teaching, protecting, loving. But thanks to New York City's welfare rules, Mr. Martinez and Ms. Belette were operating under a bizarre set of arrangements for family care.

In order to qualify for assistance, Ms. Belette had to be working for money, so instead of taking care of her *own* children, she was paid by the city to take care of her sister's three children while her sister worked in her workfare assignment. Presumably Ms. Belette and Mr. Martinez were either paying someone to look after their kids while they worked, or were getting a relative to do it for free, or asking their oldest child to look after the others, or just letting the children be on their own. The one child-care arrangement unacceptable to the city was taking care of their own kids. At some point in her time on public assistance, Ms. Belette went to Florida to take care of her sick father. While she was away, she missed some appointments with the welfare office, a transgression for which the family was penalized with loss of its Food Stamps and rent subsidies.

Since the 1996 Personal Responsibility and Work Opportunity Reconciliation Act, public policy expects almost all mothers to work outside the home for pay and to put their kids in child care. If a mother refuses to do this, she doesn't get benefits. In a strange and perverse twist, if a woman takes care of other people's children for money—as a baby-sitter or a family day-care provider—then welfare policy considers her to be doing some-

thing valuable and earning her keep as a citizen. We, her fellow citizens who are in a position to help her, will give her vouchers to purchase care for her children on the market,
but we will not help her, or even seem to reward her, to take care of her own kids. Likewise we will help her if she takes care of someone else's frail parents as a paid home
health aide or nursing-home assistant, but not if she takes care of her own parents out of
honor, loyalty, and love. As long as she exchanges her care for cash, we will help her if she
still earns too little to support her family.

The story of Angel Martinez and Regla Belette encapsulates the story of how American welfare policy makes a certain kind of politics. Policy creates incentives and disin-
centives for citizens to engage in some kinds of behavior and not others. In 1986, Charles
Murray launched the decisive battle in the war against Aid to Families with Dependent
Children (AFDC) with his argument about welfare's perverse incentives (Murray
1986/1996, 221–3). All social assistance, he declared, unintentionally but inevitably rewards people for being needy. So powerful and ineluctable was this effect that Murray described it as a natural law, calling it the Law of Unintended Rewards. Murray popularized
the idea that welfare "pays women to have babies" (Murray 1994, 30). Welfare policy, he
argued, tried to help children by helping their (single) mothers, but instead, it provided an
incentive for women to act badly: to have sex without protection, to decide to keep their
babies when they get pregnant, and to raise them in poverty instead of waiting to bear
children until they have achieved economic security.

If we were to follow Murray's logic and comb welfare policy for its "unintended rewards," we would have to conclude that current policy rewards people for putting the
family out on the market. As the Martinez-Belette story illustrates, welfare pays women
not to take care of their own children. The unintended reward—or perhaps it's really what
is intended—is a reward for hoarding one's own care and exchanging it for money. It is a
penalty on ordinary altruism, on caring for love instead of for money. It is a lesson in how
to live by raw economic self-interest.

Beyond creating incentives, policy shapes politics even more profoundly by providing
moral tutelage to citizens. In this era of conservative moral revival, government has con-
sciously defined its role in welfare policy as less the aid dispenser and more the moral
tutor. Yet it is hard to fathom how policymakers think they are inculcating virtue when
they require Ms. Belette to take care of her sister's children instead of her own and give
her a check for the job. How, one wonders, do policy rules teach Ms. Belette the meaning
of "responsibility" when they punish her for choosing to take care of her sick father instead of keeping an appointment with her government caseworker?

The morality encoded in current welfare policy reverses and rejects ordinary morality. The supreme laws of the universal human moral code might be stated as "Honor thy
parents," "Nurture thy children," and "Help thy neighbor." But in the new code book of
welfare policy (and arguably social policy more generally), "Earn thine own keep" has
become the first duty of adult citizens. And this is a third way that public policy shapes
politics. By pitting public morality against private morality, public policy sometimes
forces citizens to go underground and requires them to engage in behavior regarded as
immoral by the dominant morality, such as cheating, lying, and stealing. When people
must violate government laws in order to remain true to themselves, to fulfill their commitments to their deepest relationships, and to obey their understanding of higher law,
public policy risks fomenting disrespect for government and even civil disobedience.

Last, but not least, welfare policy has de facto reformed American notions of distributive justice, with scarcely any public deliberation about the profound transformation.
Most scholars of social policy in Western democracies, myself included, have regarded

work and need as the only politically recognized bases for economic distribution. Need, in turn, has been interpreted through demographic categories that describe valid reasons why people cannot work, typically old age, disability, illness, and childhood. These categories, by political consensus, render the people in them morally deserving of social aid (Stone 1984). In fact, as I will show in the next section, welfare policy historically recognized a third basis for social aid: caregiving responsibilities. But welfare reform has largely eradicated caregiving as a legitimate basis for redistribution. Meanwhile, politicians and policymakers give increasing attention to the importance of family caregiving and its tensions with market work among middle and upper-income citizens, and have enacted "work-family balance" policies to ease these tensions (Heymann 2006; Drago 2007). Thus, the moral basis for social redistribution differs for different economic classes. This hidden moral inequality among citizens, I would argue, threatens democracy far more than the economic inequality that currently garners political attention.

THE EVOLUTION OF FAMILY CARE IN WELFARE POLICY

Public policies toward families are caught in a tangle of conflicting visions. Policymakers have never been sure whether government help for economically struggling families should encourage mothers to work for wages or to stay home to care for their families. When forty states established mothers' pensions between 1910 and 1920, the surrounding rhetoric elevated motherhood to high heroism. "The pension," proclaimed the Illinois Congress of Mothers, as reported in the Illinois "State Report" published in *Child Welfare* in 1916, "removes the mother and her children from the disgrace of charity relief and places her in the class of public servants similar to army officers and school teachers" (Skocpol 1992, 475). Pensions, according to a 1914 article in *The Independent*, were "salaries for women who serve the state by giving all their time to rearing good citizens" (see Ladd-Taylor 1994, 144). The pensions were issued mostly to widows, but also to some women whose husbands had deserted them. If these destitute women could be paid for raising children, the thinking went, they wouldn't have to choose between caring for their children and earning a living, or between rearing their children in extreme poverty and placing them in an institution. This same vision—public support for family care—inspired what later came to be reviled as "welfare," but was more formally known first as Aid to Dependent Children and then as Aid to Families with Dependent Children (AFDC).

Yet political dissension about women's proper role made even the early public programs schizophrenic, snaring mothers in the same tangle of conflicting expectations that shaped the laws in the first place. Nominally, mothers' pensions enabled mothers to continue caring for their children in the absence of a male breadwinner, but most states effectively forced the mothers to work part-time by making sure their pensions were too low to live on. Mothers were supposed to contribute to their own standard of living and work their way out of dependence on aid, yet they weren't free, as men were, to seek out the best-paying work they could find. They were limited to jobs elite women deemed suitable for poor women, and these were usually just low-paying versions of the domestic work women otherwise did for nothing—laundry, cleaning, sewing, and taking in piece-work, in which they might also employ their children. No woman could achieve economic self-sufficiency on these kinds of jobs, but if a mother worked outside the prescribed occupations, she risked being declared an unsuitable mother or a disobedient pauper and having her pension taken away (Gordon 1994, 49–50; Skocpol 1992, 469–70; Mink 1995).

Another goal of mothers' pensions was to "Americanize" immigrant families, particularly by teaching immigrant mothers white, Anglo-American standards of homemaking and child rearing. These public-servant mothers were required to provide the proper homes and upbringing, but—a harbinger of things to come—few of them could maintain "suitable homes" and proper child-rearing practices on their meager allotments, with or without part-time work. And in yet another contradiction, although the programs prodded immigrant families to conform to white, middle-class standards of housekeeping and child rearing, many agencies figured that immigrant families needed less money to live on than white Anglo-Americans, and so gave them smaller grants (Gordon 1994, 47).

In all these ways, the internal contradictions in public aid programs translated into double binds for mothers. By the rules of public programs, it was virtually impossible for women to be good mothers and good providers. This double bind, perceived as unjust and oppressive by low-income women, catalyzed the welfare rights movement of the 1960s. Women's identities as mothers, with its fierce sense of moral duty, provided the political identity and sense of legitimacy necessary for an alternative form of political participation by low-income women (West 1981).

Confusion about the values of work and motherhood blurred welfare policy at every stage of its evolution. Until the late 1960s, work in the paid workforce remained highly suspect for women receiving public aid, even though paid work was the norm for low- and middle-income women generally. Under AFDC, women were not allowed to work for pay while receiving cash grants, or at least not to earn more than minimal amounts. If they did work, they were required to report their earnings, and when their earnings exceeded the tiny amounts allowed them, their welfare grants were cut back or cut off altogether. The vast majority of women on welfare have always worked for money and still do—but they do so under the table, forced to conceal their work in order to get state help (Edin and Lein 1997).

Significantly, while welfare policy before 1996 wasn't exactly munificent with mothers, it often treated family caregiving as honorable and something to be encouraged. In sharp contrast to current rhetoric, the moral ideal that suffused American family policy was women's dependence, not their independence. Women were supposed to be economically dependent on a husband-breadwinner. Economic independence was neither a virtue nor a proper aspiration for a woman. But starting with the so-called "welfare crisis" in the late 1960s, policy rhetoric about women, work, and motherhood began to fork along class lines.

First was the question of whether mothers of young children should work outside the home. It was a value question that became political, and as in all such issues, scientists weighed in with their opinions. Well into the 1990s, Benjamin Spock, T. Berry Brazelton, and Penelope Leach, child-rearing experts whose tomes appealed to well-educated readers, pressed full-time mothering as the healthiest route to child development. Good mothers, they advised, would be willing to buck the feminist trend and stay home for at least the first year, if not two or three, of their children's lives. They would regard raising a child, Leach said, as "more worthwhile than any other job" (Stone 1997, 79).

For low-income women, though, professional child-rearing wisdom clashed head-on with the growing political consensus according to which nothing was more worthwhile than a self-supporting job, or its equivalent, a supporting husband. Politicians and welfare reformers began to imagine child rearing as an obstacle to poor women's gainful employment, instead of a worthwhile dedication. With heightened concern about a welfare "explosion," and barely concealed racist assumptions that welfare and out-of-wedlock childbearing had become a way of life for African American women, Congress gave the states new leeway in operating welfare programs. Until 1967, Congress had insisted that mothers with young children not be forced to work out of the home. Starting in 1967, however, states could *require* mothers to work or accept job training in exchange for benefits. Even mothers with children under three years old could be sent to work if the states desired. Prodding and pushing women to go to work was helping them—helping them to achieve "self-sufficiency" by offering them "rehabilitation instead of relief," in the words of Senator Abraham Ribicoff (D-Conn.) (quoted in Michel 1999, 244).

The rhetoric surrounding the new work requirements in this and other welfare-reform legislation was the mirror image of Progressive-era rhetoric about work and family. Then, poor mothers were offered aid so that they could care for their children. Now, mothers were offered child care so they could stop receiving aid. Then, women were said to fulfill their citizenship obligations by rearing children, our future citizens. Now, they were said to fulfill their citizenship obligations by becoming economically self-sufficient. Then, they were expected to sacrifice any yearning for careers or high-paying occupations that were incompatible with motherhood. Now they were expected to sacrifice any yearning to care for their children that was incompatible with earning a living. Then, caring for one's own children was a moral duty and a calling. Now, caring for one's children was a luxury, merited only by those lucky enough to have a high-earning partner or an inheritance. To be sure, mothers' pensions were rarely implemented fully in the spirit of the political rhetoric that produced them (Ladd-Taylor 1994, 148–52), but still, the rhetorical ideals of welfare policy then and now stand in striking opposition.

Day care was the second issue on which public policy split along class lines. In the United States, there has never been much support for the kind of universal public day care common in Europe. In the late 1960s, Congress considered many proposals to expand day-care facilities using federal funds. But even as women at all economic levels were in the paid workforce and in dire need of day care, the only proposals that drew much political support were ones targeted to women on welfare. In 1971, President Nixon vetoed a child-care bill that would have created a vast network of federally supported child-care centers, saying it would undermine "parental authority and parental involvement with children" and would push the United States "to the side of communal approaches to child rearing over against the family-centered approach" (Michel 1999, 250). Three years later though, Congress quickly passed, and Nixon signed, title XX of the Social Security Act, a program targeting child care to welfare mothers and "at risk" children (Michel 1999, 251).

"At risk" is euphemistic policy-speak for "poor." Hidden between the lines in title XX was the extraordinary notion that poor children might be better off in "other care" than mother care. "The communal approach" might just be better for poor children than the all-American "family-centered approach." The same day care that was a form of deprivation to middle-class children was enrichment for poor children. The same day care that supposedly weakened middle-class family structure strengthened poor families. Here was the germ of an idea that would recur with even more bite in the run-up to passage of the Temporary Assistance for Needy Families (TANF) legislation.

Two years later, in 1976, Congress passed the most important new funding for day care in the Aid to Day Care Centers Act. Again, the funding was aimed at poor communities and day care was envisioned as an antipoverty strategy, not a pro-family strategy or a vehicle for equalizing women's work opportunities (Michel 1999, 251–53). Under the guise of a job creation program, the act also provided money to train welfare mothers to become a cadre of paid child-care providers to other people's children. Here were seeds of two more transformations that would reach full bloom in the TANF program—women could be paid by welfare to mind other people's children, but not their own; and child care was becoming a credentialed but low-education, low-skill, and low-paid occupation.

Balancing work and family was a third area where policy and politics split along class lines. The Family Support Act of 1988, another welfare reform measure, tightened work requirements for poor mothers still more, lowering the children's age at which the mothers could be required to work. Almost simultaneously, in 1989, Congress debated and then passed the Family and Medical Leave Act, the first glimmerings of a national parental leave policy. Wrapped in rhetoric of parental bonding and child development, the law required large employers to give new parents twelve weeks of leave without pay. Only dual-earner couples, and ones with at least one "family wage" at that, could afford to take it. Staying home with baby was at last permitted, even encouraged, for the well-off. In debates over the Family Support Act, stay-at-home (poor) moms were reviled as poor role models for their children, transmitters of a parasitic culture. But in debates over the Family and Medical Leave Act, a stay-at-home mom could be a perfectly good role model for children, as long as she had a high-earning husband by her side (Wexler 1997). The same double standard persisted through Bill Clinton's presidency. In 1999, three years after signing the welfare reform legislation that made family care nearly impossible for low-income women to obtain, Clinton proposed a tax credit to help middle-income women stay home with their young children (Chavkin 1999, 477).

A new idea about low-income motherhood animated all these debates. A life on welfare, Murray proclaimed, was "bad for children who need to be socialized into the world of work" (Murray 1994, 26). Poor women, especially nonworking women, were bad mothers. When Mickey Kaus proposed in 1992 that government should fund day care to enable low-income mothers to work, he was forthright about his motives: government ought to encourage day care, he wrote, "as part of an 'acculturation' campaign to get underclass kids out of the home and into classrooms at an early age." From the safe obscurity of a footnote he added: "It's not all clear that mothering by underclass mothers is better than day care." (Kaus 1992, 126, 252n. 21)

Poverty reformers, especially conservatives who seek to tighten social redistribution, have long emphasized personal deficiencies as the most important cause of poverty. From Oscar Lewis's "culture of poverty" to Daniel Patrick Moynihan's "pathology of the black family," poor people were said to have individual pathologies that, although transmitted through culture or community, were individual traits nonetheless (Lewis 1959; U.S. Department of Labor 1965). What was new in the 1990s was the emphasis on transmission of pathology from mothers to children. According to this mounting conservative critique, a mother's example as a "role model" for her children—even her infants, apparently—is more important than her taking care of them. As a role model, she could do more for them by being away from them than by being with them. No doubt Head Start and other good day-care programs are enriching and provide exposure to experiences that poor children don't get at home. But the idea that day care was better for these children than mother care was insulting and oppressive to poor families. It provided a professional, quasi-scientific rationale for requiring poor mothers to go to work even at the cost of not being able to care for their children. Day care, not they, would rescue their children from danger and tend to their well-being. The idea was an affront to the bond between mothers and children, no matter their income level. And, it sent a message to low-income families that harked back to the days of slavery, when black family life was disrespected and disrupted in a hundred ways.

HOW WELFARE POLICY SHAPED THE
POLITICS OF WELFARE REFORM

Welfare reform and the ideas that inspired it didn't spring full-blown from policy intellectuals' heads. Each iteration of welfare policy, from mothers' pensions to AFDC and its many revisions, contained structural features that overwhelmingly shaped the way intellectuals and ordinary citizens thought about welfare.

First, social redistribution always makes a weak, vulnerable, or disadvantaged group appear to be favored by policy, no matter how badly off the group. When government appears to treat any group favorably, no matter how stingy, stigmatizing, and unfavorable the actual treatment, the mere fact of positive treatment can make government appear to be treating its citizens unequally. Social Security Disability Insurance and disability rights legislation are cases in point. Never mind that few nondisabled people would wish themselves disabled; assistance to people with disabilities often generates enormous resentment and seems to threaten people's trust in fair competition (Krieger 2003). Affirmative action policies in universities and workplaces have generated the same sense that government, corporations, and schools discriminate against people in the nonfavored categories (Burstein 1993; Kennedy 1986). "Special" government help to any category of citizens almost invariably creates a backlash. Welfare policy is no exception. The mere existence of government help for some people invited others to ask themselves, "Why not for me, too?"

Second, all policies operate through rules that divide people and behavior into different categories (Stone 2002, 284–304). Rules are in effect boundaries; policy treats people on one side of a boundary one way, while people on the other side are treated differently. Such rules invite comparison of people on opposite sides of the boundary and inevitably raise the question of whether the difference between the two populations is significant enough to warrant different treatment. Welfare, as a means-tested program for single mothers (primarily), seemed to divide mothers into two categories: those who had to—or least did—enter the workforce to support their children and those who did not. From roughly the early 1970s on, two great changes in American life conspired to make this distinction seem wrong and unjust. As economic growth slowed, so did the growth of family income and wealth, and more and more two-parent families had to send women to work just to maintain their standard of living or get by. Add to these economic forces a cultural factor: the feminist campaign for gender equality succeeded in making employment outside the home a normal and even desirable life path for middle- and upper-class women. With nearly three-quarters of all mothers of young children in the labor force by 1990, the idea that government should pay poor women to stay home caring for their children came to seem (to many people) an outrage. Assistance for poor mothers seemed to insult the sense of justice, and it was easy to mobilize resentment among working women and two-earner families.

Third, the operation of welfare from its inception as mothers' pensions was predicated on inquiry into applicants' individual traits and circumstances. The eligibility structure based on individual examination sends a potent symbolic message to applicants, welfare workers, politicians, and citizens that the fact of poverty, as well as its cause, is to be discovered case by case, in individuals. The very eligibility structure, which is the face of the program to the public makes the problem of deficient family-keeping capacity appear to be personal, due to individual actions and traits, rather than structural, due, say, to larger economic forces. Welfare policy itself, then, focused everyone's attention on the wrong cause. In fact, the problem is largely systemic. Low-wage work simply doesn't pay enough to live on and care for children decently (Edin and Lein 1997), nor does it provide necessary health care, sick leave, unemployment compensation, and other forms of security for a family to survive (Hacker 2006). And the structure of market work is inherently incompatible with family keeping. Market work requires long hours away from home, when one is physically unable to watch and care for children. It typically also requires inflexible schedules that don't permit a parent to respond to the random, unpredictable needs of family members, anything from taking a child to a doctor to attending parent-teacher conferences. But the apparatus and procedures of individual examination at the heart of welfare administration became the lens through which most reformers saw the welfare problem, and that lens made it appear as a problem of deficient incentives rather than systemic forces.

POOR WORK AND POOR EDUCATION FOR POOR PEOPLE

In the national debates about welfare, taking care of family had come to be seen as the antithesis of work, almost a luxury or privilege that comes with already having earned enough to drop out of the workforce. Economics, casting its market lens on the family, transforms children into just another consumption item: "Having children is largely a voluntary choice, and may even be viewed as a matter of personal consumption preference from the point of view of parents," droned two economists (Slemrod and Bakija 1996). Touting the same idea, Elinor Burkett made a media sensation with her book, *The Baby Boon*, in which she portrayed child rearing as a luxury hobby and chastised those who wish to indulge in it without having the means (Burkett 2000). In this brave new world, staying home to care for the kids was now the adult equivalent of playing hooky.

Meanwhile, when reform advocates talk about wage work, they make it sound almost holy, and certainly redemptive, transformative, and character building. "Work is more than just a weekly paycheck," preached President Clinton, still stumping for his welfare reform in 1999. "It is, at heart, our way of life. Work lends purpose and dignity to our lives, instills in our children the basic values that built this nation" (DeParle 1999i). Sounding more like a parson than a state official, New York City's welfare commissioner, Jason Turner, explained why he planned to make work requirements so stringent: "Work is one's own gift to others, and when you sever that relationship with your fellow man, you're doing more than just harm to yourself economically. You're doing spiritual harm" (DeParle 1998a). Turner, according to the *New York Times*, harbored "an almost mystical belief in the power of work—not just as a source of income, but also as a redemptive force that can treat depression, order lives and stem moral disintegration" (DeParle 1998a). For Lawrence Mead, perhaps the leading academic voice in welfare reform, stringent work requirements help poor people by "enforc[ing] the values they already have and provid[ing] a control over their lives that benefits and services cannot give" (Mead 1992, 174). Work helps people be their best selves.

Thus, work for work's sake became the new mantra. When a study showed that Connecticut's welfare reform had indeed increased employment among recipients, but not their income, a state official explained why the program should still be counted a success: "We have to remember that the goal of the reform program was not to get people out of poverty, but to achieve financial independence, to get off welfare" (Flanders 2001). In 2000, when a study found that poverty among New York City families with children had risen sharply despite the economic boom of the late 1990s, Lawrence Mead told a reporter that the drop in the welfare rolls was more important than the rise in poverty, and that families are better off when they earn money rather than get it from welfare, even if their income drops (Bernstein 2000). "Work first," the national slogan of welfare reform, is shorthand for the new philosophy. It's better to take whatever job you're qualified for *now*, no matter how bad the job or the pay, than to put off working while you acquire skills for a better life (Boris 1999, 41). "Any job is a good job," sing posters in Massachusetts welfare offices (Albelda 1999).

Welfare reform's cardinal principle was putting welfare recipients and would-be recipients to work, and to do this, the reform created some new categories of work and some strange relationships between care work and wage work. Federal pressure on states comes in the form of work quotas, or what are called participation rates; the federal government ties state grants to the percentage of welfare recipients engaged in work. And here's where things get murky, because states are allowed to count as work a broad range of "work-related activities." Among these are various kinds of subsidized public and private employment, nonpaid work experiences, on-the-job training, job searching and job readiness classes, certain education programs, community service programs, and—notably—providing child care to a person who is participating in community service.

And so welfare reform has created a strange world of Orwellian euphemisms and Potemkin workshops whose purpose is to baptize people as workers. Caseworkers have been renamed with titles such as financial planner, employment specialist, or in some places, double-duty financial and employment planner. Clients who aren't capable of getting a real job get "work experience" placements, subsidized jobs, trial jobs, or mock jobs. One of the private agencies that runs Milwaukee's welfare program owns and operates an entire plastics plant to train welfare recipients as workers (DeParle 1999c). Wisconsin has "transition jobs," with shorter hours and state-paid supervisors. In one such job, a woman packs cartons with books or calendars for four hours a day under close supervision (DeParle 1999g). In most states, welfare clients who aren't ready for real work are put to work with "job coaches," "mentors," or "buddies" by their side. All these pretend-workers are kept in place—"job retention" is the euphemism—with an array of "supportive services" such as child care, transportation, and on-site meetings with caseworkers. To get them through their lives while they're not on the job, they get "wrap-around services" such as more child care, drug treatment, and case management (DeParle 1998b; Furchtgott 1998). Despite all these kinds of soft work, make-work, and pretend work, caring for one's family doesn't count as work in the eyes of welfare policy.

Given the cost of supervision and coaching, these transitional workers can't be terribly productive, but that doesn't matter. What matters is that they are imitating what real workers do. In effect, state program rules make everybody pretend to work in some way. It's not clear how many of these people who require a double to get them through their work day will ever be able to work on their own. But pretend work sustains the fiction that everyone can and will become a real worker—a worker who is productive and can support a family. And if work is redemptive, just going through the motions and imitating work is more important than what people actually do, whether or not they are productive.

Welfare policy also has a system of education that is parallel but not equal to education for citizens lucky enough to escape welfare's net. Recipients and would-be recipients are allowed to count education and training as meeting their work requirements, but the system limits what kind and length of education people can pursue before taking a paying job. Under the "Work first" philosophy, clients are pushed to take whatever job they can get with whatever abilities they have. Training and education for a better job will have to come later, which usually means never. After welfare reform, college is no longer a proper aspiration for clients. In Massachusetts and New York, students have been forced to abandon their studies and get a real job. But it's not just college that's off limits to welfare clients. In Boston, a survivor of Vietnamese refugee camps who had no skills to earn more than minimum wage was denied the chance to attend an eight-month training program tailored to immigrants. Graduates of the program find jobs with average wages of $10.32 an hour, a lot better than the $8.00 an hour the state welfare department finds for people who leave its rolls directly for work, and a far bigger jump than most workers starting at $8.00 would ever be able to garner in eight months. Massachusetts wouldn't tolerate the woman lingering in a training program, though, and rejected her request. Why? "At some point these people have to go to work and it's her time," the welfare department spokesperson explained. "Work is work; it's not job training" (McNamara 2000).

In place of real education, welfare clients are offered courses in good manners and behavior, masquerading behind high-flying titles like Milwaukee's "Academy of Excellence." The academy is not, as its name cheerily suggests, a prep school with a liberal arts curriculum, nor is it an exam school for the talented. In the Academy of Excellence, students get motivational talks and two weeks of classes on "life's basic arts—negotiating with the gas company, avoiding domestic violence, and securing birth control" (DeParle 1999e; 1999h). (Presumably they learn how to negotiate for extended credit when their paycheck is insufficient to cover the utilities, how to escape domestic violence now that they have no independent means of shelter and food, and how to get birth control once they are cut off from Medicaid, either intentionally or in bureaucratic error.) In classes on "Job Search," students get motivational talks, lessons on interviewing ("Make eye contact"), and tutoring in the rudiments of grooming, such as, "Don't go in there with body odor on you" (DeParle 1999f).

In New York, welfare clients are offered the advice of "financial planners." These are not your father's financial planners, the folks at Fidelity Investments, say. These planners advise welfare clients how to obtain enough money by relying on relatives or sticking out a job they loathe. The goal of welfare's financial planners, employment planners, social-service planners, whatever kind of planner, one office frankly admits, is "to redirect the participant to another source other than Temporary Assistance" (DeParle 1998b). Translation: Mooch, beg, whatever you do, ask somebody else for help, not us. At one time, Oregon's welfare recipients got financial planning advice in the form of a "tip sheet" with ideas for saving money, including shopping at thrift stores (as if they didn't know), clipping coupons (as if they could afford newspapers and magazines), and "Check the dump and residential/business Dumpsters" (Verhovek 2001). The sheet was withdrawn when several recipients said they felt demeaned by its advice to pick garbage—but it captures the spirit of so-called financial advice for the poor.

More often than not, welfare clients don't even get the pretense of financial planning help. Instead, they get glib advice from their caseworkers or politicians. When they don't have enough money to buy food or pay the rent, they are told to get more adept at budgeting. Asked whether he would consider offering money management classes to welfare clients, Jason Turner, the New York City welfare commissioner, demurred. The real way to learn, he said, was just do it: "Live on what you get, and if you run out, figure out what to do until your next paycheck" (DeParle 1998b). And as the five-year deadline loomed and clients like Angel Martinez and Regla Belette were unable to make ends meet even *with* federal assistance, Turner offered this reassurance: "Individuals should use the five-year milestone as an important opportunity to reassess their lives and their progress toward achieving self-sufficiency" (Bernstein 2001). For sheer cynicism, though, it's hard to beat this: in Chicago, a young mother of an infant named Jessilean sought her case-worker's help when she had no money to buy formula. The caseworker suggested she fast (DeParle 1999a).

The nominal goal of welfare reform is to put low-income people on a par with every-one else. By holding poor people to the same expectations of personal responsibility and self-sufficiency, and by nudging them, even forcing them, into honest paying jobs, welfare reform promised to stop condescending to the poor, stop oppressing them as dependents, and finally grant them genuine equality in dignity and social integration (Mead 1986). In fact, the new welfare policy inscribes different expectations for the poor and everyone else. Behind welfare's façade of employment training and actual work, poor people get education, training, and jobs of a distinctly lower caliber than what middle- and upper-class people receive.

CAREGIVING DENIED

Welfare reform shrank the space for family care in low-income women's lives. States were allowed by the federal government to set their own program rules within certain parame-ters. Exempting women with young children was one of those parameters. By the year 2000, forty-four states exempted adult recipients from work requirements if they were caring for a young child, but only five of these exempted parents with a child older than one year. Twenty-three states required recipients to work when their child reached age one, and sixteen states set the age for exemption at younger than one year (State Policy Documentation Project 2000).

In current welfare policy, family caregiving has largely receded into a private realm, akin to personal grooming or bodily needs that people should take care of before they go to work. Nevertheless, caregiving has reentered welfare policy through the new category of "barriers to work." According to federal rules, some people cannot reasonably be ex-pected to perform wage work because they have personal barriers to working. Those peo-ple can be counted as working if they are "addressing their barriers." Two common bar-riers to work are substance abuse and mental illness. Welfare recipients with these barriers count as being in a work-related activity if they participate in rehab programs, psycholog-ical counseling, or mental health treatment. In the moral map of welfare policy, two other common barriers to work are "having an infant" and "having a disabled child." If a state, such as Wisconsin, deems having a seriously disabled child a barrier to work, then taking care of the child becomes a work activity, because in caring for her child, the mother is trying to overcome her barrier to work (Meyer 2001). Similarly, if having an infant is de-fined as a legitimate barrier to its parent's wage work, then permitting the parent to care for the infant doesn't upset the state's philosophical system in which wage work is the only morally worthy activity.

These bureaucratic definitions conceal an astounding bit of moral reasoning: caring for your own children is morally worthy only if they are considered obstacles to your per-sonal advancement along the road to economic self-sufficiency. Beyond the grotesque transformation of children into barriers to personal advancement, policies like these raise interesting philosophical questions. Why is a disabled child a barrier to work, but not an ordinary child? Why aren't two children a barrier to work, or three or four? Why is caring for an infant or a disabled child worklike activity while caring for other children is lazy nonwork? Why isn't caring for a disabled spouse, parent, aunt, or grandparent valid work? And why isn't caregiving, period, valid work?

The philosophical basis and the administrative rules of welfare reform teach mothers, and all citizens, some perverse moral lessons:

Lesson 1: Taking care of your children is a legitimate dedication only when they are barriers to your self-advancement.

Lesson 2: Caring for them just because you love them and want them to have a good life is personal indulgence.

Lesson 3: Caring for your infant or disabled child isn't virtuous because you are generous and loving and giving, but because by taking care of him or her, you are battling an obstacle that prevents you from getting ahead.

Lesson 4: Society regards caregiving as valuable and worthy only when you do it for material reasons.

Lesson 5: Society won't help you care for the people you love, but will help you pay someone else to do it while you go out and earn a living, perhaps taking care of people somebody else loves.

Many states are using money from their federal welfare grants to train mothers how to market their caregiving. Women who want aid can learn to provide child care in their homes or in day-care centers, or to be licensed home health aides and nursing home assistants. According to one reporter who investigated welfare in Washington, D.C., "[I]t is possible to see welfare reform as a Ponzi scheme whose currency is children. You put your children in day care so that you can work, but the only work you may be qualified for, after years of being a full-time mother, is in a day-care center. There you take care of the children of other poor women, many of whom now spend their days working at other day care centers" (Boo 2001, 100).

At the extremes, the new welfare rules pressure women to shed their kids when they pose too big a barrier to self-sufficiency. One Michigan mother of three described her desperate search for housing with a $310 voucher from the social services department. "I could find a two-bedroom that fit that, but not a three-bedroom, and with three kids they said I couldn't live there. They said, if you can do something about one of your kids. . . . Well, what do you want me to do—get rid of one of my kids?" (Polakow 1994, 29). Newt Gingrich famously suggested just that—that government should help poor women care for their kids by paying for the kids to live in orphanages (Van Biena 1994).

In all these ways, public policy has transformed family keeping, the most elemental form of social cooperation. Through welfare reform, government has elevated the civic obligation to be economically self-sufficient above the human obligation to care for one another. Government tells citizens that it prefers to deliver care as an economic commodity rather than to allow people to care as human expression. A century ago, Jane Addams trained women to mother their own children and nurse their own families. The new welfare trains women how to turn their caring into a business—to be economic agents first, mothers and daughters second.

Family keeping is a near-universal human aspiration. By denigrating family caregiving vis-à-vis other kinds of work and refusing to let caregiving earn entitlements to social aid and public respect, the new welfare policy dismisses low-income people's private lives and their rights to share in a precious and fundamental moral good.

THE NEW MORAL ECONOMY OF FAMILY CARE

According to the market view of human motivation, poor women (like everyone else) are moved by economic motives. This was Murray's great transformation in how policymakers understood welfare, and from this vision came one goal of welfare reform: to make paid work more lucrative than welfare.

But mothers for the most part do not choose between work and welfare. They choose between different ways of caring for their families. More often than not, they must choose between bad ways of caring, because they have no good choices. The harshness of life at the bottom forces brutal choices on parents, and on anyone who has family members they love. Poor people have to choose between buying food and paying for heat, or between food and medicine. Between getting to work on time or making sure their children are in safekeeping. Between showing up for work or taking care of a sick baby. Between being a responsible employee or a responsible mother. Between risking their job or risking their children. And ultimately, they have to choose between becoming cheaters and lawbreakers or watching their children starve and suffer.

These are moral choices as well as economic ones. And this is what we know about poor women: they often choose care. They choose to put somebody else's welfare ahead of their own. The tradeoffs they make show how differently they think from *Homo economicus*. They sometimes choose homelessness over public housing because they believe public housing is a worse threat to their children. Some are willing to go without medical care to avoid living in the projects, where their children will be vulnerable to gangs, drugs, squalor, and despair. Sometimes, they give up their children to foster care rather than take them into the projects or subject them to medical and economic deprivation (Edin and Lein 1997, 116–17). And when they choose welfare over paid work, they usually do it because it is the least bad way for them to care for somebody else, not because it is the most lucrative way to live for themselves.

Furthermore, it turns out that low-income mothers are often shrewd economists after all. Kathryn Edin and Laura Lein interviewed several hundred low-income mothers, some on welfare, some working (Edin and Lein 1997, 63–65). Most of them, even the ones who weren't currently working, could tick off the added expenses of working. Some pulled out envelopes or scraps of paper with the calculations they'd already done for themselves. The truth, as the women know, is that they get a better net return from welfare than from working in the kinds of low-wage, no-benefit jobs available to them. Working is "not worth it," one woman told Edin and Lein. "It's not worth it 'cause you have kids and then they gonna be sick and you gonna have to go to the doctor and you gonna have to pay hundreds of dollars and that's why" (Edin and Lein 1997, 66). It's not worth working, even for extra money, if you can't afford to take your kids to the doctor. On welfare, you get a Medicaid card. On welfare, you can often take better care of your kids.

The low-income women in Edin and Lein's study—and every other sociological study that takes the trouble to talk with women instead of totting up numbers in a large survey database—defy the model of economic man. In economic models, mothers calculate the return-to-self from each of their actions. Real mothers, for the most part, don't think of their jobs as providing an income for themselves. They think of a job as a resource for giving. They ask themselves, "How will this job enable me to take care of my family and to give them what they need?"

When mothers calculate that working isn't "worth it," they're often using figures that economists omit. Not just "Can I afford to take my child to the doctor or the hospital?"

but "Can I get the time off to take my child to a doctor?" Not only "Can I buy sneakers for my boy?" but also "Can I be around enough to keep him safe?" Real women don't read just the bottom line. They consider how different strategies for getting income might help or hinder their caretaking. Does it give them time with their children? Time to talk with teachers and wait in doctors' offices? Time to listen and watch so they know what's going on in their kids' lives? Time to invest in their children's future? Time to care in the ways they deem decent?

And so mothers often sacrifice their own stature and income in the work world to gain greater power in the care world. "I don't think I could accept a promotion," one mother told Edin and Lein. "I mean they have talked to me before about being a manager, but I need the availability" (Edin and Lein 1997, 95). Some women leave better-paying jobs for ones with lower pay but health insurance for their kids. One woman left a job as a bookkeeper in a health clinic for a job with a dry cleaner because the health clinic, of all places, didn't provide health insurance (Edin and Lein 1997, 96–97).

On this score, mothers are no different from family caregivers in general. Caregivers often reduce their paid work and sacrifice their income, even sometimes their careers, to accommodate their caregiving responsibilities. The National Alliance for Caregiving surveyed caregivers to the elderly and disabled. Of the two-thirds who were (or had been) in the paid workforce, more than half had changed their daily schedules, taken leaves of absence, worked fewer hours, taken less demanding jobs, turned down promotions, taken early retirement, or left paid work altogether, all in order to devote more of themselves to caregiving (National Alliance for Caregiving 1997).

It's not just money and promotions women sacrifice to care for their families. Mothers also orient their political participation in welfare around the primacy of their caregiving role, sometimes sacrificing their autonomy by silencing themselves, and other times sacrificing their security by taking risks with their caseworkers. Several welfare clients who took a decidedly passive role with their caseworkers explained to Joe Soss why they thought this was the best way to support their children. "I figure if I say something back, they know a way of getting me cut off of AFDC. And then I wouldn't have anything for me and my kids" (Soss 2000, 129). Explaining why "we all fear our caseworkers," another client stated, "Your life is in their [the caseworker's] hands. Your kid's life is in their hands" (Soss 2000, 134). And among the smaller number of welfare clients who were willing to express grievances and stand up to their caseworkers, Soss found that they "described taking a stand as a duty growing out of the obligation to protect their children" (Soss 2000, 138).

In the welfare office, mothers will sacrifice their pride and their reputation if they must. The sociologist Lisa Dodson tells this story she learned from a social worker. A young white woman came into a welfare office with her baby drinking coke out of a baby bottle. The social worker cajoled and encouraged her to enroll her son in a preschool program for special-needs children. The mother remained blank-faced, passive, so much so that the social worker was convinced she was retarded and all but filled out the forms for her. At the end of the day, the social worker stopped for pizza. She recognized her "slow" client, now talking animatedly with some friends. The baby was drinking milk with a straw. The young mother was telling her friends about the preschool her son would attend. "She was saying something like, 'If you act *really* dumb, they figure you really need the help and they *see* those forms are in proper order'" (Dodson 1998 139–40).

A twenty-year-old mother told Dodson of an even greater sacrifice she made to get help from welfare officials. Luscious (as Dodson calls her) received a great deal of support and kindness from her child's father, and his parents gave her their succor and a lot of child care as well. So Luscious agreed to keep the father's identity from the welfare officials. She hated the lie, but explained, "If I'd of told on Lennie, it would have ruined everything." Protecting the extended family relationships meant saying that "I didn't know who the father was . . . like I was so loose I didn't know who I'd had sex with." Dodson comments, "This deceit was antithetical to everything Luscious had been raised to believe and value. It meant accepting the most disrespectful label a woman can have" (Dodson 1998, 137–38).

It doesn't matter whether work is more lucrative than welfare or if it endows women with an official stamp of approval. When work puts women in moral double binds, they are likely to break the work rules rather than their own care ethic. They show up late for work if the baby-sitter doesn't come and being on time would mean leaving the children alone. They skip work when a child spikes a fever and going to work would mean not taking the child to a doctor. They cut back from two or three jobs to one when they fear for their children's safety unless they can meet the school bus or shoo away the rats from the crib at night. They turn down promotions and new assignments that offer more money but less flexibility to care for their children. They disappear from work for weeks at a time to care for a sick parent, knowing full well that they probably won't have a job when they come back. Perhaps they lie for as long as they can get away with it, because they know their employer won't take caregiving for an excuse.

Welfare officials observe such behavior and think the women need a dose of job-readiness training, so they herd these "irresponsible" women into classes to learn about the work ethic and the almighty importance of showing up every day, on time. Surely some need these lessons. But blackboard lessons in punctuality and reliability don't sink in with people whose loyalties to kin are stronger than to clocks or cash.

"Family bonds are more powerful than policymakers understand," wrote Jason DeParle in one of his characteristic understatements about poverty and welfare. He was trying to explain why Lashanda Washington, one of Wisconsin's problem cases, has trouble living by the textbook work ethic. Ms. Washington puts safeguarding her alcoholic, disturbed, sometimes abusive mother above most everything else. On the day she was supposed to start training as a nursing assistant, she spent the morning caring for her mother instead, getting her sober, tending her bruises. "Skipping work to keep watch at home, Lashanda has found herself trapped in irreconcilable roles: breadwinner, daughter, confidante, playmate, social worker, nurse, and cop," DeParle wrote. Caring for her mother was a job ten times over. Ms. Washington could probably teach an advanced graduate seminar on the work ethic for caregivers. But there's not much call for her expertise. Most policymakers don't respect it, or even recognize it. Besides, most of the other people in her position have already learned the same way she did—on-the-job training. As DeParle puts it, "Addicted sisters, imprisoned brothers, needy cousins and aunts—the great national drive from welfare to work winds through a forest of familial distractions" (DeParle 1999e).

"Familial distractions" is putting it mildly, another of DeParle's understatements. But that's just what welfare officials would like to believe about these cataclysmic clashes between one person's meltdown and another's yearning for family connection. The system can't afford to admit the truth: The yearning is so powerful that no Harvard, let alone an Academy of Excellence or a Draconian threat, can ever eradicate it. The yearning starts young. Ten-year-old Tremayne Franks was abandoned by his father (in prison) and his mother (gone South to work as a stripper, not heard from since). His grandmother worked the night shift as a hospital housekeeper and during the days, had no energy and even less use for Tremayne. Tremayne hung out at a neighborhood grocery store and pretended to work for the owner. "Dude, it ain't the money," he explained to a reporter. "I just like to have someplace to go." At ten, Tremayne wanted to be a lawyer so he could "make a lot of money so I can take care of my dad, and if she comes back, my mom" (DeParle 1999d).

Until 1996, welfare permitted mothers a great deal of discretion in managing their families. There were work requirements, to be sure, but when a woman decided to punt on work in order to do what she thought necessary for her children, she wasn't thrown off the rolls, usually. It was precisely this maternal discretion that welfare reformers wanted to eliminate, and did, by setting lifetime limits on welfare and tough, unbendable work requirements for the short few years that welfare was still on offer (Oliker 2000a, 2000b).

What is likely to happen when yearning meets rules? The new system violates a basic human urge. People cheat, lie, and steal to care for their families. When work rules conflict with their caregiving, they choose care. Likewise, with government rules. They'd sooner break the law than violate their own ethic of care.

Virtually every person on welfare cheats. They have to in order to survive because it is not possible to live on the income from welfare (Edin and Lein 1997; Dodson 1998). Most work off the books, doing things legal and illegal. Some pay professional shoplifters to get clothes for their kids. Some use false ID cards to get food, and, more often, health care. Doctors and clinics sometimes abet these families, looking the other way or even suggesting that Mom bring in Tommy under cousin Johnny's Medicaid card (Finkelstein 2000).

Many women receive goods and money from their children's fathers or grandparents. They don't report these gifts, as they are required to do. They lie to caseworkers about the identity and whereabouts of their children's fathers. In effect, they build their own child support systems, because the official one would confiscate all but a smattering of any child support fathers paid, instead of using it to support the children.

Mothers collaborate with their children's fathers to maximize benefits from the Earned Income Tax Credit. To get this rebate at tax time, a parent has to have worked (and earned income) and has to have had children living with him or her for at last half the year. If the mother has custody of the children but doesn't work, and the father works but doesn't have custody, the family loses out on the benefit. If they report that the children live with him, however, everyone benefits. When asked a hypothetical question, Deborah Morton, a cashier at a discount store, saw nothing wrong with letting her daughter's father claim the child lived with him, even though he lived in another city. She explained what was to her a simple moral calculus: "She is his child and he helps me with her" (DeParle 1999b).

These people see themselves as virtuous—indeed, as hewing to a higher moral code than what the government asks of them. In order to meet their own sense of moral duty, they must violate what they see as lesser standards, such as telling the truth, following rules, being on time, and being a reliable worker. Thus, policy rules encourage and sometimes demand that they engage in the very behavior that stigmatizes them in the eyes of elites (Schneider and Ingram 1993).

Nemesis, another of Lisa Dodson's informants, recalls the time when she was eleven and the police raided her mother's apartment. Her father had been an alcoholic and a batterer, and her mother had thrown him out. Her mother, unable and unwilling to live "on the dole," ran a gambling parlor, and kept the proceeds in a box of tissues. As the police were arresting her mother and the children were being taken off to relatives, Nemesis's mother handed her the tissue box and told her to take care of the other children and wipe their faces. Later, Nemesis's mother talked to her children about the law and breaking rules. "My mother said it was wrong to tell lies and to cheat and to break the law. But she said there were bigger wrongs. Having hungry children, being dependent on people who abuse you, are bigger wrongs. She said that you feed your children first. You belong to nobody. The other comes later" (Dodson 1998, 194–95.) Twenty-three-year-old Carmelina Smith, with two kids to support, thought she'd supplement her meager wages with a cashier's job at a university bookstore. She pilfered $11,000 from the cash register and wound up in jail. "I couldn't buy my kids milk and Pampers—that's why I did what I did," she told the *New York Times*. "I wasn't able to put clothes on their back the way I should have." Did she feel like a criminal? Not hardly, Jason DeParle reports: "Ms. Smith recalls the moment as a rare time of inner peace. 'It felt good. I felt like now I can take care of my kids the way I want to'" (DeParle 1998a).

In one way of looking at things, Nemesis's mother and Carmelina Smith were ordinary criminals. In another way of looking at things, each is a modern Antigone, the heroine of Sophocles' play about civil disobedience. The play opens when Antigone's brother has died in battle, fighting against King Creon in a civil war. King Creon forbids anyone to bury him, on pain of death. According to ancient Greek beliefs, without a burial, the soul of the dead person could never join with other departed souls and find peace. Antigone buries her brother and defiantly tells Creon she is guilty of following a higher law. Sophocles' *Antigone* stands for an essentially personal kind of civil disobedience. Her defiance was not about abstractions or grand principles like freedom, patriotism, or peace. It was about simple loyalty to kin and the right to care for people we love.

WELFARE POLICY AS MORAL TUTELAGE FOR CITIZENSHIP

This reading of welfare policy suggests several ways that policy feedback can be detrimental to democratic politics. Families are the building blocks of society. They are the schools for democracy, the place where citizens learn moral values and attitudes toward other people as well as toward government. Current welfare policy elevates self-sufficiency through paid work above all other virtues. By pushing poor people into jobs that cannot possibly support them and their families, welfare policy undermines their ability to care for their families. To a large degree, the rules transform family care into paid work. These policies divide families, so that parents, usually women, find jobs caring for other people's parents and children while being forced, through strict exemptions from paid work, to put their own families out onto the market to be cared for. The only way the state will help them care for their own family is by providing child-care vouchers in exchange for paid work, or Medicaid coverage of nursing home care. If ever children were regarded by welfare policy as future citizens, to be nurtured, educated, and trained to think of the common good, current policy redefines them as barriers to their parents' employment (if they are very young or very disabled) or as business opportunities for adults other than their own parents.

Families are the place where we learn about altruism, about taking into consideration the well-being of others as we make our decisions. Families are where almost every person first experiences being cared for and gains a sense that care for others is the essential glue and lifeblood. But welfare policy denigrates family care done out of love and loyalty, in preference to care done to earn money. Moreover, public laws create different pathways and different lessons for low-income and upper-income families. As we have seen, reforms in 1988 and 1989 toughened work requirements for low-income parents but promoted work-leaves for middle-class parents.

Families are where early political socialization takes place. Children learn by observing their parents whether government is something one can turn to for help or whether it is a dangerous part of one's environment. In families on welfare, children learn very young that the government is not helpful and that deception and strategic avoidance are necessary to their family's survival. In low-income families, parents have to buck welfare rules in order to survive, and they often have to violate their own moral rules, such as not lying, cheating, or stealing. Thus, they end up teaching their children to disdain government rather than to respect it. Like Nemesis's mother, they school their children in civil disobedience and the finer points of higher law.

It shouldn't be so hard to reconcile family care and market work. The issue has played out largely as a women's issue, and consequently seems caught in an inevitable tension between women's demand for independence and equality on the one side and their desires to care for family on the other. But family care shouldn't be a women's issue. It should be, and is, a social issue. It would be easier to recognize family care as real work, worthy of social support, if policymakers started with the assumption that family keeping is every bit as important to our civic well-being as national defense, universal education, and law and order.

From such a social vantage point, a few policy directions are obvious. Family care is incompatible with full-time paid work, sometimes even part-time paid work. For starters, it's impossible to take care of people if you are not physically in the same place with them. It's also hard to mesh two different schedules, a work schedule that calls for predictability and long-term planning and a care schedule that calls for spontaneity in responding to erratic needs. But policies can go a long way toward helping people cope with these irreconcilable demands. Flexible, care-sensitive work rules can modify the paid-work side of the equation. Public support for an infrastructure of short-term care organizations, such as day-care and respite-care centers and home health care, can modify the family side of the equation. Most of all, though, a polity founded on the ideal of equality ought not promote different family systems and moral values for citizens depending on their income. If there is any hope for a democratic politics, it starts with rearing citizens who care for others besides themselves and who trust government to treat all its citizens with equal respect.

REFERENCES

Albelda, Randy. 1999. "Now We Know: 'Work First' Hasn't Worked." *Boston Globe*, May 24, 1999, 23.

Bernstein, Nina. 2000. "Poverty Snaring Families Once Thought Immune." *New York Times*, April 20, 2000, A25.

———. 2001. "As Welfare Deadline Looms, Answers Don't Seem So Easy." *New York Times*, June 25, 2001, A1.

Boo, Katherine. 2001. "After Welfare." *The New Yorker*, April 9, 2001, 93–107.

Boris, Eileen. 1999. "When Work Is Slavery." In *Whose Welfare?* edited by Gwendolyn Mink. Ithaca, N.Y.: Cornell University Press.

Burkett, Elinor. 2000. *The Baby Boon: How Family Friendly America Cheats the Childless.* New York: Free Press.

Burstein, Paul. 1993. "Affirmative Action and the Rhetoric of Reaction." *The American Prospect*, 4(14) 136–47.

Chavkin, Wendy. 1999. "Editorial: What's a Mother to Do? Welfare, Work, and Family." *American Journal of Public Health* 89(4): 477–9.

DeParle, Jason. 1998a. "Faith in a Moral Motive for Work: The Man Who Redesigned Welfare in Wisconsin Is Coming." *New York Times*, January 20, 1998, B1.

————. 1998b. "What Welfare-to-Work Really Means." *The New York Times Magazine,* December 20, 1998, 50–80.

————. 1999a. "The Grandmothers: As Welfare Rolls Shrink, Load on Relatives Grows." *New York Times,* February 21, 1999, A1.

————. 1999b. "First Time Filers: On a Once Forlorn Avenue, Tax Preparers Now Flourish." *New York Times,* March 21, 1999, A1.

————. 1999c. "Symbol of Welfare Reform, Still Struggling." *New York Times,* April 20, 1999, A1.

————. 1999d. "One Child's Story: For Two Improbable Pals, a Few Notable Weeks." *New York Times,* May 25, 1999, A18

————. 1999e. "Conflicts at Home Mine the Road to Independence." *New York Times,* July 4, 1999, A1

————. 1999f. "Spending the Savings: Leftover Money for Welfare Baffles, or Inspires, States." *New York Times,* August 29, 1999, A1.

————. 1999g. "As Benefits Expire, the Experts Worry." *New York Times,* October 10, 1999, A1.

————. 1999h. "Early Sex Abuse Hinders Many Women on Welfare." *New York Times,* November 29, 1999, A1.

————. 1999i. "Bold Effort Leaves Much Unchanged for the Poor." *New York Times,* December 30, 1999, A1.

Dodson, Lisa. 1998. *Don't Call Us Out of Name: The Untold Lives of Women and Girls in Poor America.* Boston, Mass.: Beacon Press.

Drago, Robert W. 2007. *Striking a Balance: Work, Family, Life.* Boston, Mass.: Dollars and Sense.

Edin, Kathryn, and Laura Lein. 1997. *Making Ends Meet.* New York: Russell Sage Foundation.

Finkelstein, Katherine Eban. 2000. "Medical Rebels: When Caring for Patients Means Breaking the Rules." *The Nation,* February 21, 11–17.

Flanders, Stephanie. 2001. "Influential Connecticut Welfare Plan Is Tested in Hard Times." *New York Times,* August 13, 2001, B1.

Furchtgott, Roy. 1998. "UPS's Package Deal for Workers." *Business Week,* June 1, 105.

Gordon, Linda. 1994. *Pitied but Not Entitled: Single Mothers and the History of Welfare.* New York: Free Press.

Hacker, Jacob. 2006. *The Great Risk Shift.* New York: Oxford University Press.

Heymann, Jody. 2006. *Forgotten Families: Ending the Growing Crisis Confronting Children and Working Parents in the Global Economy.* New York: Oxford University Press.

Kaus, Mickey. 1992. *The End of Equality.* New York: Basic Books.

Kennedy, Randall. 1986. "Persuasion and Distrust: A Comment on the Affirmative Action Debate." *Harvard Law Review* 99: 1327-46.

Krieger, Linda Hamilton, editor. 2003. *Backlash Against the ADA: Reinterpreting Disability Rights.* Ann Arbor, Mich.: University of Michigan Press.

Ladd-Taylor, Molly. 1994. *Mother-Work: Women, Child Welfare and the State, 1890-1930.* Urbana, Ill.: University of Illinois Press.

Lewis, Oscar. 1959. *Five Families: Mexican Case Studies in the Culture of Poverty.* New York: Basic Books.

McNamara, Eileen. 2000. "Welfare Rules Holding Her Back." *Boston Globe,* August 16, 2000, p. B1.

Mead, Lawrence M. 1986. *Beyond Entitlement: The Social Obligations of Citizenship.* New York: Free Press.

————. 1992. *The New Politics of Poverty: The Nonworking Poor in America.* New York: Basic Books.

Meyer, Daniel. 2001. "Income Support for Children in the United States." *Focus* 21(3): 38–43.

Michel, Sonya. 1999. *Children's Interest/Mothers' Rights: The Shaping of America's Child Care Policy.* New Haven, Conn.: Yale University Press.

Mink, Gwendolyn. 1995. *The Wages of Motherhood.* Ithaca, N.Y.: Cornell University Press.

Murray, Charles. 1986/1996. *Losing Ground.* Revised edition. New York: Basic Books.

————. 1994. "What to Do About Welfare." *Commentary* (December): 26-34.

National Alliance for Caregiving. 1997. *Family Caregiving in the U.S.: Findings from a National Survey.* Washington: National Alliance for Caregiving.

Oliker, Stacy. 2000a. "Family Care After Welfare Ends." *National Forum* 80(3): 29–33.

———. 2000b. "Challenges for Studying Care after AFDC." *Qualitative Sociology* 23(4): 453–66.

Polakow, Valerie. 1994. "Welfare Reform and the Assault on Daily Life: Targeting Single Mothers and their Children." *Social Justice* 21(1): 27–32.

Schneider, Anne, and Helen Ingram. 1993. "Social Construction of Target Populations: Implications for Politics and Policy." *American Political Science Review* 87(2): 334–47.

Skocpol, Theda. 1992. *Protecting Soldiers and Mothers*. Cambridge, Mass.: Harvard University Press.

Slemrod, Joel, and Jon Bakija. 1996. *Taxing Ourselves*. Cambridge, Mass.: MIT Press.

Soss, Joe. 2000. *Unwanted Claims: The Politics of Participation in the U.S. Welfare System*. Ann Arbor, Mich.: University of Michigan Press.

State Policy Documentation Project. 2000. "State Policies Regarding TANF Work Activities and Requirements." Accessed at http://www.spdp.org/tanf/work/worksumm.htm.

Stone, Deborah. 1984. *The Disabled State*. Philadelphia, Penn.: Temple University Press.

———. 1997. "Work and the Moral Woman." *The American Prospect* 8(35): 78–86.

———. 2002. *Policy Paradox: The Art of Political Decision Making*. New York: Norton.

U.S. Department of Labor, Office of Policy Planning and Research. 1965. "The Negro Family: The Case for National Action" (the "Moynihan Report"). Washington: U.S. Department of Labor, Office of Policy Planning and Research.

Van Biena, David. 1994. "The Storm over Orphanages." *Time*, December 12, 1994, 12.

Verhovek, Sam Howe. 2001. "National Briefing Northwest: Oregon: Welfare Agency Recalls Advice." *New York Times*, May 12, 2001, A11.

West, Guida. 1981. *The National Welfare Rights Movement: The Social Politics of Poor Women*. New York: Praeger.

Wexler, Sherry. 1997. "To Work and to Mother: The Politics of Family Support and Family Leave." Ph.D. dissertation, Heller School of Social Policy and Management, Brandeis University.

Part VI

The State's New Look:
Decentralization, Inequality, and
Social Control

Richard B. Freeman and Joel Rogers

Chapter 10

The Promise of Progressive Federalism

American progressives are generally suspicious of federalism and the authority it gives state and local governments to make social and economic policy decisions. They would prefer the country run by a capable national government that supports their political goals. Progressives believe that only national power can lessen inequalities and fear that competition among states leads to reduced labor standards and social expenditures. They know that throughout United States history "states rights" has been associated with the suppression of African Americans in the South and that many of the achievements of twentieth-century American democracy—civil rights, the New Deal, and the extension of social benefits and protection to all Americans—required national action. Over the past few decades, as American national politics has withdrawn from many of the commitments of the New Deal, many progressives have decried the devolution of national responsibilities to states. They see the lessons of history on federalism as clear. More power to the states means more inequality, weaker civil rights, less popular organization, greater business influence on government decisions.

In this chapter we argue that the progressive disposition against federalism is outmoded. States are too important and enduring a part of the American national political system to be treated as some minor afterthought in policy debate. The current economy and attitudes on civil rights are different from those of the 1930s or 1960s. An exclusively national focus of policy initiatives also reflects an unreal vision of the nature of modern government and politics. The devolution of governmental authority to levels closer to the persons it affects is a worldwide phenomenon.[1]

States also have the power to enact policies that improve the lives of ordinary citizens. Responding to national political failure to deal with social and economic problems in the 1990s and 2000s, many states have adopted policies that advance individual freedom, protect public goods such as the environment, or strengthen local protection of the interests of workers and the poor. Although some states favor more conservative policies, enough have chosen progressive policies to belie any general race to the bottom in state policies. The wide variation in policies across states shows, moreover, the utility of one-size-fits-all politics. Regardless of their political coloration, the willingness of states to experiment with new approaches and serve as "laboratories of democracy" is welcome in a time of uncertainty about successor institutions to those of the New Deal and Great Society.[2]

A NEW VIEW OF FEDERALISM

Accepting these changes in American politics and the state contribution to national democracy, we argue that progressives should embrace federalism and work to improve it. The "progressive federalism" of our title gives one vision of such improvement. This new federalism does not turn on the distinction, popular with the Supreme Court, between "truly local" and "truly national" areas of activity. Nor does it reserve economic regulation to national government while assigning social regulation to the states. It aims instead to manage the slowly evolving terms of national democratic consensus, and differing state efforts to improve citizen well-being in ways that promote collective democratic advance and learning.

Progressive federalism has three features.

The first concerns rights and standards. We suggest that the national government should set and enforce basic minima below which no locality can go, but should let states choose alternative enforcement mechanisms and standards above the national minimum. This "floors, not ceilings" approach to national preemption of state activities is meant to ensure protections of constitutional rights and national agreement on statutory regulation and protections, while removing barriers to the states to experiment beyond them. At present, in a variety of areas—labor regulation, environmental protections, consumer protection, and social insurance—many states want to undertake more progressive action, but they are preempted by national law or its interpretation by the Supreme Court. We want to loosen this constraint.

A second feature of progressive federalism concerns taxes and spending. Recognizing the continued variation in state individual incomes, which makes it difficult for lower-income states to provide some goods and services to citizens, and the pressures on states of meeting unfunded congressional mandates, we suggest some tax harmonization among states, a renewed federal commitment to an equalizing fiscal federalism, and an end to unfunded mandates. The goal is a more sensible balance between state taxing capacities and responsibilities—a different sort of floor from which states would be free to compete—and a more honest accounting of the costs of meeting national commitments.

A third feature of progressive federalism concerns state experimentation and learning. We recommend more systematic benchmarking and evaluation of state experiments and national promotion of results. The aim is to improve the role of states as "laboratories of democracy" and to speed up the diffusion of successful practices.[3]

Too often, views on federalism seem to change with change in the party that controls the national government. On the right, the Bush administration largely abandoned respect for states rights and decentralized federalism once it assumed control of Washington. On the left, some progressives have looked more favorably on states as their governments addressed issues such as global warming, health-care access, minimum wages, and stem-cell research, which the national government failed to address. Perhaps the recent switch in party dominance in Congress, or a Democratic presidential win in 2008, will restore the historic division of attitudes and lead progressives once again to place all of their eggs in the national government basket, but in our analysis this would be shortsighted. Regardless of which party is in power in Washington, states will remain, and they will have enormous powers to do good or ill. Within the limits of our Constitution, moreover, many federalisms are possible. Progressives should be thinking about the one they want, with a longer perspective than the next election cycle.

How does this essay fit in the present volume? This chapter gives more attention to consequences of the choice of the locus of policy authority, and less to the content of policies themselves. But that choice is itself a political one, and is particularly fair game for a "policy-centered perspective" (see chapter 1, this volume) concerned with how political outcomes structure future conflict. Just as the "new institutionalism" (March and Olsen 1984) treated institutions as causes of the interests of social actors as well as the consequence of those interests, the editors of this volume argue that policy decisions should be considered not just as outcomes of conflict but as constitutive of its next terms. Certainly this is true of choices regarding federalism. Few institutions have been so continuously adjusted through United States history. Each decision to move the locus of decisionmaking up or down the chain of government, to describe and enforce new boundaries between states and federal authority, or to set new rules for their interaction, has both reflected conflict and helped organize interests and resources for its next round. Along with its high stakes and permanent institutional players, this continuing adjustment is what makes federalism "America's endless argument" (Donahue 1997). At this point in that argument, we think that states and federalism are better considered as part of the solution to our national failure to address growing economic and political inequalities than as part of the problem.

STATE POWERS AND INNOVATION

The United States Constitution establishes a federated government, not a unitary one. National government powers are restricted to those enumerated in the Constitution; the reserve powers of states are assumed as plenary. The "supremacy clause" of Article VI resolves conflict between federal and state law in favor of the former and the Fourteenth Amendment requires that states accord all "persons" (not only citizens) within their territories due process and equal protection of the law. Consistent with respect for individual rights and the supremacy of any contrary federal law, states are free to do what they please, making the United States indeed a strongly decentralized federal system. Around this basic design, two centuries of political custom have given states and the local governments they create a privileged role in implementing and enforcing much federal law.

The result is that states do by far the largest share of governing in America. They write most law and implement much national legislation. Most government action that affects citizens in their everyday lives runs through the states.[4] Critically, states also control the election system, from voter regulation to campaign finance to the way votes are counted to the boundaries of most election districts, including congressional districts. State electorates choose the members of the Electoral College, which selects the president. Over the past two decades, successive waves of "new federalism" have given states more discretion in using their powers. New national programs in education and training, housing, transportation, and economic development have been decentralized from the start. And state waivers from federal guidelines have become the norm.

For its part, the federal government controls the currency, domestic macroeconomic policy, trade with foreign nations, the military, and the major social insurance programs like Social Security. It collects more taxes—in 2004, 1.88 trillion dollars for the national government vs. 1.59 trillion dollars for state and local government (U.S. Census Bureau 2006, tables 459, 424). But most federal spending is for the military, transfer payments to individuals, and debt service. Excluding these categories, the federal government spent only 2.2 percent of GDP in 2005. State and local governments spent 11.1 percent, or five times as much (Office of Management and Budget 2007, table 15.5). Reflecting their greater role in delivering services, state and local civilian public employment was six times national civilian public employment and state and local nonmilitary government investment and consumption was five times that of federal nonmilitary government investment and consumption (U.S. Census Bureau 2006, figure 8.3, table 420). Finally, state economies are large on a global scale. If one rank-orders all non-United States economies in the world by gross product and admits individual American states to the list, three states (California, Texas, and New York) are among the top dozen, and twenty-two others are among the top fifty.[5] State and local government pension funds, uniquely regulated by states, are worth $2.7 trillion, making them huge players in capital markets.

Globalization and State Powers

Some think that globalization has shifted economic decisionmaking beyond the reach of nations, much less states, and thus has made geography and place largely irrelevant to economic activity. Surely if wages and working conditions in Des Moines are effectively set in Bangalore or Beijing, there is nothing the Iowa state legislature can do to improve the economic situation of resident Hawkeyes, no matter how hard it tries.

But both opponents and proponents of globalization exaggerate the impact of trade treaties, immigration, and global capital flows on economic outcomes (Freeman 2004, 2006b). The view that globalization trumps other economic forces does not capture modern economic realities, where increased concentration of activity in urban areas proceeds along with global outsourcing. Place continues to matter in economies because spatial density of related firms and skills can create external economies of scale ("agglomeration effects"), as in Silicon Valley. The importance of place is also reflected in home bias and home market effects in consumption and investment—that is, the tendency for citizens to spend their money and invest assets in their immediate location more than pecuniary calculations suggest they should. Place also matters in labor markets, where better-skilled workers are willing to sacrifice market earning for better public goods or more future opportunity. It matters in trade because of transportation costs and the premium customers put on delivery speed. It matters in production because of the importance of direct exchange among networks of like or complementary producers.[6]

For the present argument, the strongest evidence that place matters is within the United States itself, where states with different income levels and wages compete with completely free flows of goods, people, and capital. The surprising fact about American economic development is that although the relative incomes of the nation's regions and states are slowly converging, absolute income differences have actually increased. Table 10.1 shows regional per capita income in constant 2004 dollars for the Bureau of Economic Analysis's eight multistate regions over the past generation, reporting endpoints of 1969 and 2004.[7] While the ratio of poorest-to-richest regional incomes increased over the period, from 70 to 75 percent, absolute income differences between them rose two-thirds, from a bit under $6,000 to over $10,000.[8] Across all regions, the standard deviation in their per capita incomes also increased 68 percent. Individual state data over the period, not reported in table 10.1, show the same pattern.[9] All regions except one (the far West) experienced higher variation of state per capita incomes within them, and across all states the standard deviation of state per capita incomes nearly doubled, rising 96 percent.[10]

To make this concrete, consider the comparative income trends of Mississippi, the poorest state in the nation, and Connecticut, one of the richest, over the same period. Again using constant 2004 dollars, Mississippi's real per capita income increased 127 percent, from $10,549 to $23,943; Connecticut's increased a slower 113 percent, from $21,346 to $45,412. In relative terms, Mississippi's income grew from 49 to 53 percent of Connecticut's. But at that rate it won't actually catch up to Connecticut for several hundred years, and in the meantime Connecticut's absolute income advantage doubled.[11] The bottom line is that Mississippi hasn't brought living standards in Connecticut down and shows no signs of doing so.

TABLE 10.1   Regional Differences in Per Capita Personal Income, 1969 to
2004 (2004 Dollars)

Bureau of Economic Analysis Regions	1969	2004	Annualized Growth
New England	$18,480	$40,059	2.34%
Mideast	$19,067	$38,023	1.99%
Great Lakes	$17,840	$32,171	1.70%
Plains	$15,830	$32,164	2.05%
Southeast	$13,561	$29,927	2.29%
Southwest	$14,660	$29,919	2.06%
Rocky Mountains	$15,137	$31,416	2.11%
Far West	$19,469	$34,741	1.67%

Source: U.S. Department of Commerce Bureau of Economic Analysis and authors' calculations.

Competition with China and India and other low-wage countries changes the economic environment of states, but it does not make state policies irrelevant to economic outcomes any more than competition between Mississippi and Connecticut has invalidated the policies of those states. Indeed, if anything, the powers of states are probably less dramatically affected by the changes wrought by globalization than are those of the nation. The latter has surrendered some control of its domestic market, its ability to steer that market through macroeconomic policy, and the value of its currency. But states never had control of these things. So as actors they are less affected.

The net of all this is that states indeed have power, and room to maneuver in its application.

State Innovation

States use their power in all sorts of initiatives and legislation. Indeed, for every law passed by Congress, state legislatures pass several hundred. Unfortunately there is no easily accessed public database on this welter of activity. Nor is there precise tracking of the sorts of legislation of greatest relevance to this chapter, namely, state laws or initiatives that move above and beyond national standards and protections. Here, however, is a small sampling of recent innovative legislation at the state level.

Environment. This is an active area of state reform. Thirteen states have adopted or are in the process of adopting California fuel emissions standards, more stringent than national ones; twenty-three have enacted "renewable portfolio standards" requiring that a certain share of state energy needs be satisfied by renewable sources; eleven have adopted their own appliance efficiency standards, again above federal levels; twenty-nine have completed comprehensive Climate Action Plans, specifying steps to slow global warming; twelve have set greenhouse gas emissions targets.[12] In an early move toward applying the principle of "extended producer responsibility," thirty-two states now require the removal of mercury switches from automobiles and a growing number require manufacturers of computers and other consumer electronics to offer customers take-back provisions at end of use to ensure appropriate recycling or disposal.[13] Most states have also passed some version of "smart growth" legislation. The aim of such legislation is to discourage sprawl by forcing developers to internalize more of its costs, and to encourage local governments to develop higher-density and more inclusive development plans and preserve or promote open space.[14]

Education and Training. One of the most important activities reserved primarily to states is education and training. In recent years, the mandatory testing requirements of the No Child Left Behind Act (NCLB) have gotten most of the headlines, but the most education reforms have come from the states on their own initiative.[15]

Health. State-initiated innovations in dealing with rising costs and declining coverage in health care have been sufficiently successful to become standard fare in national reform proposals. Some examples: "reinsurance" funds to protect insurers or employers against risk; mandates for individuals to purchase insurance; state "basic plans" that extend Medicaid coverage to lower-income groups; and experimentation with community clinics to deliver advanced services. The health-care plans of Maine, Massachusetts, Vermont, and California are important models for national policy. And many states have done more than the national government in protecting patients' rights to sue health maintenance organization's (HMOs) and insurance companies for denying medical treatment. Sixteen states have developed Health Information Technology/Health Information Exchange reforms in their publicly supported health-care systems; twenty-two states ban smoking in nearly all indoor workplaces, with a few still exempting bars (Center for Policy Alternatives 2006, 217, 232). States brought the lawsuit against Big Tobacco that was settled in 1998 with a $250 billion award.

Election and Voting Reform. States are reforming campaign finance rules. Three states (Arizona, Connecticut, and Maine) have now adopted full public financing for statewide and legislative offices, with another four (North Carolina, New Jersey, New Mexico, and Vermont) applying those rules to some public offices.[16] Most now provide at least some public match for private campaign contributions. States have also tried to make voting easier and more reliable. Many states, inspired by Oregon's successful switch in 1998 all-mail voting, have extended the time available for absentee balloting and removed other barriers to their use. Thirty-five states require paper ballot trails, with thirteen having audits of those trails. Finally, states are expanding the franchise, for instance for persons with felony records. Since 1997, sixteen states have changed their laws to permit voting by those with such records (Center for Policy Alternatives 2006, 161, 167).

Reproductive Rights and Sexual Orientation. Sixteen states have acted, ten through amendment of their own constitutions, the other six by legislation, to guarantee a woman's state-based right to abortion, in anticipation of possible Supreme Court reversal of Roe v. Wade (Center for Policy Alternatives 2006, 213). Twenty-three states have passed laws requiring insurers to cover the costs of contraception.[17] Another seventeen states have passed laws barring discrimination based on sexual orientation (Center for Policy Alternatives 2006, 60).

Government Reform. Along with innovations in policy, states and local governments have sought to reform their own operations and delivery of services, in some cases borrowing techniques from the private sector and applying them to public bodies. States make great use of outcome-based performance measures, benchmarking, total quality management, and information technology to improve the quality and productivity of traditional services. They have developed functionally integrated agencies, with more autonomy and knowledge in line personnel and have improved delivery of services to diverse populations: poor children in urban schools, those in child protective services, juvenile delinquents, drug addicts, the frail at-home elderly. New York City school reforms, Utah innovations in child protective services, Missouri programs for juvenile delinquent homes, Salt Lake City's "harm reduction" approach to addiction, San Francisco's treat-ment of the homeless, and Arkansas programs for elder-care are examples of this new work.

Subsidy and Tax Reform. At least nine states now have some advance disclosure re-quirement for economic development subsidies; forty-three states have standards on some public programs; eighteen have clawback provisions when recipient firms fail to perform. Texas has adopted a unified economic development budget, requiring reporting on all tax expenditures as well as direct appropriations for development, and this reform is now under consideration in several other states.[18] Fourteen states with estate taxes pre-viously tied to the federal estate tax are in process of decoupling from it; thirty have de-coupled from the "bonus depreciation rules" that the Bush administration passed shortly after the September 11 attacks; and eighteen have disallowed the massive qualified pro-duction activities income corporate tax break of 2004. To avoid corporate gaming of dif-ferences in their tax systems, seventeen states have also now adopted combined reporting requirements on corporate tax filings (Center for Policy Alternatives 2006, 3–5).

In sum, many states are experimenting with new and broadly progressive policy that goes beyond the requirements of federal law and that often is in direct opposition to its re-cent direction. When federalism presents an open door to progressive responses, many states step through it. If that door were more ajar, they can be expected to step farther.

STATE POLICIES TOWARD LABOR

Would greater power to the states help workers on economic matters? To answer this question, we examine seven policy areas where states have the ability to do more for workers than federal law requires or are unrestricted by federal legislation in their poli-cies: state-level minimum wages above the federal level; Medicaid eligibility at levels at or above the federal poverty line; supplemental postsecondary aid to students (at or above 40 percent of the federal Pell Grant); a transitional Food Stamp option for families leaving welfare; prevailing wage laws on state government construction projects; a state supple-ment to the federal Earned Income Tax Credit; and collective-bargaining rights for pub-lic-sector workers. We chose this set of policy areas because it is easy to determine their pro-worker character and to find data on them.

Table 10.2 shows the states that have enacted laws in the seven areas. The first entry in the left-hand column, "minimum wages above federal level," shows the thirty states that have state minimum wages above the federal minimum. The next entry down shows the thirteen states that offered Medicaid eligibility to workers with earnings at or above the poverty line instead of the lower levels permitted federally. And so on. Although the effectiveness and impact of these laws can vary greatly, we take state adoption of them as a reasonable indicator of state intentions to help workers, even if success in realizing those intentions is uneven.

There are three messages in the table 10.2 statistics. First, taking all of the laws to-gether, there is wide variation in state adoption of these pro-labor laws. Of 350 possible instances of the laws (seven laws times the number of states), states have enacted 151, or 43 percent. Second, across the laws, the number of state adoptions varies considerably, ranging from thirteen to thirty-one. Third, across the states, there is significant clustering of states in their enactment of the laws. For instance, New York and Wisconsin are listed under each law, and California is listed under six laws. But a number of states are missing altogether, or only present for one law. This confirms the diversity in state preferences that we would expect from any federalist system. Judging by their political culture, we would

TABLE 10.2   Seven Pro-Worker Laws in States

Law	Number of States with Law	Names of States
State minimum wage is more than federal minimum wage[a]	30	AK, AZ, AR, CA, CO, CT, DE, FL, HI, IL, IA, ME, MD, MA, MI, MN, MO, MT, NV, NJ, NY, NC, OH, OR, PA, RI, VT, WA, WI, WV
Medicaid income eligibility level for working parents equal to or greater than the federal poverty line[b]	13	AZ, CA, CT, DE, IL, ME, MA, MN, NM, NY, RI, VT, WI
Postsecondary scholarship aid to low-income families equal to or greater than 40 percent of Federal Pell Grant aid[c]	15	CA, CT, DE, IL, IN, KY, MD, MA, MN, NJ, NY, PA, VT, WA, WI
Transitional Food Stamp option for families leaving welfare[d]	17	AZ, CA, CO, IL, MD, MA, NE, NH, NM, NY, NC, OR, PA, TN, VA, WA, WI
Prevailing wage for state construction projects[e]	31	AK, AR, CA, CT, DE, HI, IL, IN, KY, ME, MD, MA, MI, MN, MO, MT, NE, NV, NJ, NM, NY, OH, OR, PA, RI, TN, TX, WA, WV, WI, WY
State supplement to federal Earned Income Tax Credit[f]	18	CO, DE, IL, IN, IA, KS, ME, MD, MA, MN, NJ, NY, OK, OR, RI, VT, VA, WI
Public sector collective bargaining[g]	27	AK, CA, CT, DE, FL, HI, IL, IA, ME, MD, MA, MI, MN, MT, NE, NH, NJ, NM, NY, OH, OR, PA, RI, SD, VT, WA, WI

Source: Authors' compilation.
Note: (1) actual/possible number of pro-labor laws: 151/350; (2) average/weighted probability of a state having a law: 0.43/.52; (3) average/weighted number of such laws *per* state: 3.0/3.6; (4) standard deviation of random (multinomial)/actual distribution of laws by state: 1.25/2.18.
a. See U. S. Department of Labor, "Minimum Wage Laws in the States," http://www.dol.gov/esa/minwage/america.htm.
b. See Kaiser Commission on Medicaid and the Uninsured, "In a Time of Growing Need: State Choices Influence Health Coverage Access for Children and Families" (2005, figure 9).
c. See National Center for Public Policy and Higher Education, *Measuring Up 2006: The National Report Card on Higher Education*, "About *Measuring Up*: *Measuring Up 2006* Database" http://measuringup.higher education.org/about/database.cfm (see "Affordability 2006").
d. See U. S. Department of Agriculture, "Transitional Benefits," http://www.fns.usda.gov/fsp/rules/Memo/Support/State_Options/fifth/transitional-benefits.pdf.
e. See National Alliance for Fair Contracting, "Prevailing Wage Law Answers," http://www.fair contracting.org/NAFCnewsite/prevlawquestions/prevwagestates.htm.
f. See Nagle and Johnson (2006).
g. From Brian Klopp, American Federation of State, County, and Municipal Employees, personal communication, 4/7/06.

expect New York, Wisconsin, and California to enact more labor-friendly policies than Alabama, Mississippi, and South Carolina, which are some of those missing from the list.

Table 10.3 analyzes this clustering by listing all states by the number of our seven laws that they have passed. Thirteen states (Alabama, Georgia, Indiana, Kansas, Louisiana, Mississippi, North Dakota, Oklahoma, South Carolina, South Dakota, Texas, Utah, and Wyoming), disproportionately southern and with lower average incomes, have none or only one. Sixteen states (California, Connecticut, Delaware, Illinois, Maine, Maryland, Massachusetts, Minnesota, New Jersey, New Mexico, New York, Oregon, Rhode Island, Vermont, Washington, and Wisconsin), disproportionately northern and coastal, with higher average incomes, have passed five or more of them. In current political jargon, most in the first set are "red" states and most in the second set are "blue" states.

We can also express the differential propensity of states to enact pro-labor laws by comparing the actual distribution of such laws to what we would expect from a random distribution. The bottom of table 10.2 shows that the chance of a state's having some pro-labor law from the 350 possible instances of the seven laws is 151/350, or 0.43, and that the average number of laws per state is seven times that, or 3.01. If states repeatedly drew laws randomly from an urn, with the average proportion of 0.43, the distribution of pro-labor laws across states would be binomial, with a standard deviation of 1.29. More properly, given that different laws vary in the frequency of their enactment, the random distribution would be a multinomial in which each state drew randomly from each of seven urns, with different probabilities depending on the frequency of each law. In this case, the standard deviation of the distribution of pro-labor laws would be slightly smaller, 1.25. The actual distribution of laws diverges greatly from the distributions that would arise from either the binomial and multinomial models. The standard deviation of the actual distribution of laws is 2.18.

Figure 10.1 shows the difference graphically, comparing the hypothetical multinomial distribution to the actual one. The greater dispersion of the actual distribution is evident from the higher number of states represented in its tails. Many more states than would be expected by chance have a lot of the seven laws. Many more than would be expected by chance have none or just one law.

TABLE 10.3   States with One to Seven Pro-Worker Laws

Number of Laws	States
0	AL, GA, ID, LA, MS, ND, SC, UT
1	KS, OK, SD, TX, WY
2	AK, FL, KY, MO, NV, NH, NC, TN, VA, WV
3	AK, AZ, CO, HI, IN, IA, MI, MT, NE, OH
4	NM
5	CT, ME, NJ, OR, PA, RI, VT, WA
6	CA, DE, MD, MN
7	IL, MA, NY, WI

Source: Authors' compilation.

FIGURE 10.1   Multinomial Versus Actual Distribution of Pro-Worker Laws, by States

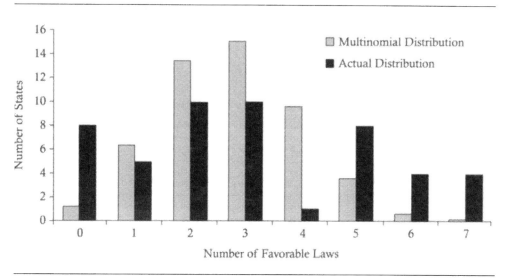

Source: Authors' compilation.

Since states vary greatly in population, we also calculated the weighted average of the probability of having a pro-labor law, with the population of the state as the weight. If more populous states were more favorable to pro-labor legislation, the weighted probability would exceed the 0.43 average. As the second calculation at the bottom of table 10.2 shows, this weighted probability is 0.52. The more populous states are more pro-labor. The nature of the Congress, with all states having two votes in the Senate irrespective of population, enables smaller states to block pro-labor legislation supported by bigger states and national majorities. At the same time, these more populous states' ability to change their local laws in pro-labor ways is commonly preempted by existing national law. These states would be better able to represent their residents under a progressive federalist system which gave them greater freedom to set labor laws.

Of course, under a more decentralized scheme for labor regulation, states with less labor-friendly orientations would also be freer to set labor laws less favorable to labor, albeit short of violating individual rights or whatever new national consensus is reached as to the labor rights floor.[19] The result would be increased geographic diversity of policies toward workers—at least before some laws proved to be so much better or worse for citizens that more and more states would adopt or reject them. So the question becomes: Would such increased diversity likely be a net good or net bad for workers?

Federal Versus State Regulation of Collective Bargaining Law

The ideal way to determine whether states would produce more or less progressive policies than the national government in a given area would be to compare how the United

States Congress sets policy in that area with how fifty state governments independently set policy in that area. There are many areas where both the federal government and state government operate, and make different policy judgments. But there are none where they both have laws that are fundamentally different or contradictory, for that would violate the "supremacy clause" of Article VI.

There is, however, one area of legislation regarding labor that approaches the ideal test of how the states and federal government would legislate in the same area: collective bargaining. In the private sector, the federal Labor Management Relations Act (LMRA) governs union elections, unfair labor practices, and collective bargaining. It preempts state and local regulation, with the exception of allowing states to ban union security clauses.[20] For state and local public employees, however, there is no federal law. States are free to set the rules themselves. Thus, in every state there are private-sector workers covered by federal legislation and enforcement and public-sector workers covered by state legislation and enforcement.

As table 10.4 shows, twenty-seven states have enacted laws favorable to bargaining by state and local government employees. The remaining twenty-three states have not enacted such laws, and some of those ban collective bargaining altogether for some groups of workers. Table 10.4 examines the link between these laws and other pro-worker legislation on our list. We sort states into two categories, on the basis of their positive or negative public-sector labor law (+ or − PSLL). We then report in each row of the table how many states in each category have any of our remaining six pro-worker policies. In parentheses, we also report the percentage of states in that category that this number represents, and the percentage of national incidence of the law that it represents. For example, row 1 shows that among states with favorable public-sector labor laws (PSLL), 23 have minimum wages higher than the national, and (in parentheses) that those 17 represent 85 percent of the PSLL states and 77 percent of the national population of such laws. The summary tabs at the bottom of the table indicate that the 27 states with positive PSLL account for 123 of the total 151 pro-worker laws, or 81 percent of the national total, and average 4.6 pro-worker laws out of the seven available. States with negative PSLL, by contrast, average just 1.2 pro-labor laws apiece. That is a huge difference.

Do state laws favorable to public-sector bargaining actually affect unionization in the public sector? Studies of public-sector unionization before and after changes in state labor laws in the 1970s and 1980s show that favorable laws had a positive independent effect on public unionization, or at least on the timing of public-sector union growth (Farber 1988; Saltzman 1988; Valletta and Freeman 1988). Ensuing examination of within-state variation in collective-bargaining laws by type of worker shows a similar pattern: stronger laws produce more collective bargaining (Farber 2005). Although in all states public-sector workers are more highly organized than private-sector ones, their advantage in unionization is much greater in states with laws favorable to public-sector bargaining. Richard B. Freeman (2006a) shows that union density in the public sector exceeds union density in the private sector by thirty-nine percentage points in states with favorable laws as compared to eighteen percentage points in states without the laws. The standard deviation in public-sector collective-bargaining coverage across states is 2.44 times the standard deviation from a binomial distribution based on the national average rate of coverage. By contrast, for the private sector, covered by the same national law, the actual standard deviation is nearly identical to the expected one.

How, then, might giving to the states the rights to regulate collective bargaining in the private sector affect unionization? Presumably, states hostile to workers would make it more difficult to organize than it now is (though presumably without banning unions or

TABLE 10.4   Pro-Worker Laws by Positive or Negative Public-Sector Labor Law

Pro-Worker Law	Positive Public-Sector Labor Laws N = 27			Negative Public-Sector Labor Laws N = 23		
	Number of Laws	Percentage of States That Have	Percentage of National	Number of Laws	Percentage of States That Have	Percentage of National
Minimum wage is above the federal minimum wage	23	85	77	7	30	23
Medicaid income eligibility level for working parents is 100 percent of federal poverty line	12	44	92	1	4	8
Postsecondary need-based aid is 40 percent of federal Pell Grant	13	48	87	2	9	13
Transitional Food Stamp option for families leaving welfare	12	44	71	5	22	29
Prevailing wage law for state construction projects	22	81	71	9	39	29
State supplement to federal Earned Income Tax Credit	14	52	78	4	17	22
Total pro-worker laws	123			28		
Average per state	4.6			1.2		
Share of national	81%			19%		

Source: Authors' compilation.

bargaining altogether), whereas states favorable to workers would pass laws to make it easier. But the states unfavorable to labor, most easily marked as those that have not enacted collective-bargaining laws for the public sector, are less populous and have lower private-sector union density than other states. If they had laws less favorable than the federal law, they would presumably lower total national private-sector unionization, but not by much. By contrast, the states that are more favorably inclined to labor, with larger populations, would be expected to increase unionization in the private sector, and by a larger amount. A regression equation of the determinants of public-sector unionization gives a response of 0.5 ln points to the presence of a favorable law (Freeman 2006a). That is, moving from an unfavorable law to a favorable one changes density by that amount. Applying the 0.5 ln (65 percent) response parameter to the private sector, Freeman estimates that labor would lose about 0.5 million members in labor-unfriendly states, but gain about 4 million in labor-friendly ones, for a net addition of 3.5 million union members.

To be sure, public- and private-sector union density diverge for reasons beyond the legal regime. The profit motive induces private-sector employers to be more opposed to unions than public-sector employers, for whom union members and their allies can be an important part of the electorate. Workers may also have different desires for unions in the two sectors, depending on lengths of employment, civil service regulations, and political pressures. Even if some states enacted and enforced labor laws more favorable to private-sector organizing, private-sector density of union membership is unlikely to rise to public-sector levels, absent some change in understanding what private-sector unionism itself should look like. The hypothetical exercise discussed previously is only that, hypothetical. Still, there is no mistaking the direction of effect. The closest we can get to an ideal test of whether federalism would produce policies more or less favorable to workers than national legislation comes down in favor of federalism. And while this need not apply to other outcomes or labor laws, we conjecture that in fact it is more representative of the social world than the alternative view that federalism will harm workers.

We note, finally, that the labor movement, long focused on national politics, has barely begun to explore the possibility of using state political power to promote its broad goals. If labor did focus more attention on the states, we suspect that it would uncover diverse state and local policies that strengthen unionism while also promoting the general welfare and winning popular majorities. For a fraction of what it spends on national election campaigns, labor unions might be able to win sizable reforms in a limited number of states, and then promote them as models for others.

FEDERALISM: THE CASE AGAINST THE CASE AGAINST

In the "endless argument" over federalism, there are certain classic arguments for and against. The case for federalism has always rested on the potential benefits of policies more attuned to local preferences, the gains to efficiency and accountability in subnational government that come from competition among its units, and the learning that comes from natural or deliberate policy experiments in states.[21] Although there is disagreement about the magnitude of these gains, there is little disagreement that they exist, and the gains from them are endorsed across the political spectrum. In addition, conservatives have favored federalism because it provides a check on concentrated governmental power and because it pressures states against taxing for anything beyond the public goods that local citizens and business determine to be of use to them.

The arguments against federalism divide along ideological lines. Conservatives going back to Alexander Hamilton have been concerned about the potential irresponsibility of states in spending or borrowing beyond their taxing powers (Ferejohn and Weingast 1997; Rodden 2006). But the near absence of redistributive fiscal federalism in the United States, state constitutional bars on deficit spending, and the relative efficiency of American capital markets in disciplining state borrowing all limit the force of these concerns in the United States. Thus, it is the arguments against federalism on the left that deserve most attention here. Their objection is that federalism promotes inequality: social exclusion and local domination, a race to the bottom in standards, and limits on national efforts to redistribute income from the rich to the poor. We do not find these objections persuasive.

Social Exclusion and Local Domination

As noted in the introduction, one reason many progressives oppose increased federalism is because "states' rights" has a long association with racism. We believe that the risk that allowing states a freer hand in government would lead to the old abuses is exceedingly small in today's society. One reason is that exclusionist discriminatory practices of the type that have shamed the country in the past no longer enjoy much popular support. Without minimizing the problems created by individuals or firms discriminating against particular groups, we assert that the civil rights revolution effectively ended the notion that the government can engage in such practices. Americans disagree strongly about the nuances of gay marriage, immigrant rights, and unregulated abortion. They disagree about the best means of redressing past racial wrongs, or whether they have a responsibility to redress them at all. But analyses of social and political attitudes consistently show that Americans are qualitatively more tolerant toward diverse groups than they were a generation or two ago. In survey after survey, white attitudes toward blacks, men toward women, straights toward gays, and adherents of different religious faiths toward each other all show increased acceptance of diversity (among other surveys, see Page and Shapiro 1992; Mayer 1993; Fiorina 2005; McCarty, Poole, and Rosenthal 2006). For overwhelming majorities of the public, the notion that public power should be used to constrain opportunity on the basis of race or sex or sexual orientation is simply no longer accepted.

A second reason why allowing states a freer hand in government is unlikely to lead to the old abuses is that the geographic bases of domination are no longer secure. The idea of a culture war in America may be overdrawn and misleading, but the idea that the sides in that war match state boundaries is preposterous. Almost all communities in the United States are more diverse now than they were fifty years ago. Greater personal mobility, a more integrated national and increasingly international market, the greater role of multistate and multinational firms, national media, increased immigration, and the urbanization of American life have all helped produce this within-community diversity. And that means the likelihood of assembling stable oppressive voter majorities is much smaller than it once was. The same forces have also reduced the ability of any single uncontested employer or small group of employers to have a stranglehold on local political life. Americans have not enjoyed increases in real wages commensurate with the growth of productivity, but the reason for this is not that they are locked into company towns with little opportunity to switch employers. The backwaters of racist reaction, and company towns, are largely a thing of the past.

But assuming for the sake of argument that some state or group of employers in fact sought to suppress individual rights, our proposed progressive federalism would arrest any such effort. That is the point of having a floor of individual constitutional rights and other statutory minima. Under progressive federalism, if states conspicuously violate the

Fourteenth Amendment or national civil rights law or other specified national rights, the national government would have the duty to protect those floors, using federal marshals if necessary, as in the past.

The Race to the Bottom

A stronger argument from the left against federalism is that it opens the door to competition among states which will inevitably pressure states to reduce taxes, labor standards, and public goods in hopes of attracting business. Indeed, whenever states try to pass progressive legislation or tax the wealthy for public goods, some firms or wealthy persons inevitably threaten to move to areas with more favorable business or tax regulations. Business has always played states off against each other to block or roll back progressive legislation, at least until enough states pass their own but differing laws so that business ends up preferring nationalization to the multiplicity of laws (Robertson 1989; Robertson and Judd 1989; Gordon 1994; Hacker and Pierson 2002). States have sometimes been complicit in this game, exchanging autonomy and control of legislation for inequality-compounding weakness in its terms (Mettler 1998). Despite the fact that there is no systemic relation between state taxation and long-run trends in state growth, and little effect of differences in state taxation on corporate profitability, business concerns over taxes and regulation are almost always central to state political debate.[22] As a political fact, state competition for capital is real.

Despite the political and rhetorical jostling, however, there is in fact little evidence that states are on a policy road to the bottom, with most states mimicking the practices of those least restrictive of business. If that were true, we'd expect substantial convergence of state regulatory legislation at the lowest possible level, but we have just seen that this is not the case. We'd also expect convergence in taxes and fees collected as a share of income, but instead we see an ongoing 50 percent difference in "tax" burden (state own source revenues as share of personal income) between low-taxing states such as New Hampshire and high-taxing ones such as New York.

Why is this? One reason for this is that states' inherited differences in wealth, and the power of the private economy relative to government spending and effort, overwhelm any race-to-the-bottom effect in public policy that might exist. Another reason is that most states can afford taxes for public goods that are useful to business and wealth accumulation. A well-run public education and training system improves the skills of the bulk of the population, which helps business. A functioning transit infrastructure, which gets workers to work on time without their having to go mad in traffic helps business. An efficient local government and clear regulatory climate is more important to most businesses than small differences in standards imposed, or the costs of paying for that government efficiency. Most skilled workers and managers also want to live in a community where they can be free of pollution and crime, and have good schools, recreational opportunities, and cultural amenities available to them. Business, often more than individual citizens, knows that to attract high-quality labor they need to support livable communities. This is why states such as Minnesota and Connecticut continue to prosper despite greater worker protection, higher wages, and more taxes, and states such as South Dakota and Mississippi, lacking these types of laws, continue to be poor.

So the pressures through cross-state competition to pay attention to business concerns, while real, have not resulted in effective equalization of states' regulation, taxation, and incomes. There is space for constructive policy intervention. The race-to-the-bottom is not the nine-hundred-pound gorilla that opponents of federalism fear it to be.

DISABLING NATIONAL REDISTRIBUTION

Another argument from the left is that federalism inevitably weakens national efforts to redistribute income from the wealthy to the poor and thus limits the reduction of poverty. The combination of competition among states and the complexity they introduce in any national legislation disables efficient redistribution. Many scholars have pointed out that the historic dominance of state politics over national, and the domination of state and local governments in the United States by local elites reduced the impulse toward ambitious class-based political activity or drained it off into finally barren local initiatives (Lowi 1984; Pierson 1995; Robertson 1989; Robertson and Judd 1989).

Without doubting the veracity of this history, we doubt its relevance today. The establishment of a national affirmative state, no less than the civil rights revolution, is a permanent achievement. Citizens are not likely to forget its existence, and availability as a vehicle for reform. The failure of the national government to deal with problems such as income inequality, persistent poverty, the crisis in health-care delivery, and problems with the private pension system cannot plausibly be blamed on state resistance. National politics is dominated by money organized by industry, not by quarreling blocs of states. It's not Kentucky but K Street that has blocked national health insurance, delayed response to global warming, forced regressive changes in federal tax rules, and so forth.

As a general matter, moreover, it is not clear that federalism per se inhibits national redistribution. Analysts in comparative politics once held that federalism both slowed welfare state formation and inhibited its development. But closer recent inspection, in part fueled by worldwide devolution, has led to changes in that view. Most scholars still think that federalism delayed early welfare state formation, but most now believe that it imposed few barriers to consolidation and growth of social protections thereafter. In the current period of welfare state retrenchment, the "veto politics" (Tsebelis 2002) that federalism encourages appears to slow the rate of retrenchment. The emerging consensus is that the effect of federalism on redistribution "in good economic times . . . appears to be negligible . . . and, when times are not so good, may even be positive, with federal institutions serving not only to keep the peace but also to preserve the existing state of welfare" (Leibfried, Castles, and Obinger 2005, 338–39).

The experience of federal systems in advanced countries outside the United States (e.g., Canada and Germany), which are invariably more egalitarian than our own, is also telling. Unlike the United States, they have adopted some explicit form of redistributive "fiscal federalism," in which the national government compensates for cross-regional or within-region inequalities. This brings its own problems. The enhanced national government role makes it more difficult for subnational units to maintain the autonomy needed to capture fully the information and other advantages of local decisionmaking and raises the risk that those units might be irresponsible in their borrowing and spending (Rodden 2006). But the experience of other federations shows that federalism per se is not a barrier to greater efforts to reduce poverty and inequality.

The reason some national governments are more redistributive than others appears to lie in the specifics of voting rules rather than federalist governmental structures. Political systems that permit proportional representation are more redistributive than those that do not (Persson and Tabellini 2003; Iversen and Soskice 2006). They are more encouraging to class-based politics (often first expressed through the activities of small, new parties), and give fairer weight to geographically concentrated progressive voters, like those found frequently in cities, than do American-style single-member districts with "winner-take-all" election rules. That the American electoral system sometimes produces electoral victories for presidential candidates or majorities in Congress that fail to reflect the will of voters nationally is undesirable, but it is not the fault of federalism.

Does Federalism Mean Inequality?

In a posthumous collection of his writings on federalism, Aaron Wildavsky (1998, 39–54) titled one chapter "Federalism Means Inequality." Wildavsky, a lifelong New Deal Democrat and a great fan of federalism, meant that federalism's admission of political variation and choice, its firm rejection of one-size-fits-all politics, inevitably disappoints those who would mandate equality of outcomes. This is true. If federalism meant inequalities of opportunity, this would be a major cause for concern. If federalism barred national redistribution to alleviate poverty, it would be as well. But in fact it does neither. Federalism generates two types of inequality. The first inequality is a reflection of differences across geographic areas in preferences and local politics—such as those, discussed previously, that we expect would occur if national labor law gave greater discretion to states to deal with private-sector firms and employees. The second inequality reflects differences in the development of successful policy innovations, such as innovative legislation in one state that takes time to spread to others. Since it is hard to imagine that people's preferences would be geographically consistent, or that progress in policy can take place without someone being the first mover, progressives should have no objection to either of these forms of inequality.

MAKING A PROGRESSIVE FEDERALISM

Our vision of progressive federalism includes vigorous enforcement and adequate funding of minimum standards and rights determined nationally, a national commitment to fiscal federalism and interstate tax harmonization, and the more deliberate harnessing of state experiments within them. This is a different compact between states and the federal government than now exists. Here we briefly describe the changes that could encourage the development of this new compact.

Preemption

Perhaps the most important change implied by progressive federalism is the "floors, not ceilings" approach we recommend for preemption, across all areas of economic and social rights and regulation. Unlike the Rehnquist and Roberts Supreme Courts, we would not seek to shield the states from the obligation to meet national standards or to prevent citizens from suing states for nonenforcement of national rights or standards. We also see no purpose in distinguishing sharply between social and economic regulation. In our vision of progressive federalism, the country would debate what national minimal standards should be in place, and then give the states freedom to surpass them. Over time, based on experience and new problems, the country would presumably develop new standards in certain areas. But states should always have the right to try new initiatives as long as they did not contravene national standards. Legal niceties aside, this amounts to a recommendation that most federal law be written with a conclusion along the lines of: "nothing in this act shall bar the states from exceeding the federal requirements declared here, or from acting in ways other than those specified here to further its declared aims." More regulation would look like the minimum wage requirements of the Fair Labor Standards Act, where states are free to go above national standards, and less like the Labor

Management Relations Act, where states have been prevented from experimenting with new ways for workers to organize unions, new ways to penalize firms that break the national law, and, until recently, even from keeping employers from using state funds to undermine the principles furthered by the act.[23]

In recent years, when Congress has regulated business or guaranteed more rights than states were prepared to do, the Court sought to narrow the permissible "enumerated powers" grounds of congressional action or has argued that Congress could not compel state enforcement of good law or given states immunity from damages arising from their violation of it, while also limiting direct federal enforcement under the Fourteenth Amendment. On the other side, where states threatened to regulate business more than Congress was prepared to, the Court has routinely preempted their activity. Progressive federalism would have counseled the opposite on all these matters, for substantive reasons and legal coherence. States should be allowed to go above federal minima on regulation, with competition among them deciding if those innovations prove sustainable or worthy of wider replication. But existing law should be enforced, not consigned to a no-man's-land of unpredictable enforcement.

To empower progressive federalism to do its job, we would strengthen the Fourteenth Amendment obligations of the states to ensure equal protection of the law, and federal power to enforce the Amendment. But we concur with the Supreme Court's seeming weariness of congressional straining since Wickard v. Filburn (317 U.S. 111, 1942) to justify any sensible regulation under the commerce clause. For textualists concerned with the matter, more suitable language can be found for congressional activity in other areas (the Fourteenth Amendment again), or should simply be made through a constitutional amendment.

We recognize that a change in the Supreme Court's views on federalism, if it ever arrives, will take time to come about. But we note too that such a change could just as readily come from a conservative Court that takes a narrow constructionist view as from a more freely interpretive one. Certainly, our proposed "floors, not ceilings" approach to preemption has as secure a constitutional foundation as current doctrine, and a good deal more force as a view of legislation. The Constitution does not declare what areas of law should have a floor mandate and which a ceiling. That is a political choice, and there is no legal reason why we cannot choose to make floors a general presumption. Almost everything we know about the competence of Congress, the diversity of views within it, local variation in the sites where national regulation is to be applied, and the possibilities of learning also recommends specifying goals and outcome minima rather than specifying a detailed process for achieving artificially capped results.

The 110th and future Congresses can also act to stimulate progressive federalist policies by undoing the efforts of the Republican 107th to 109th Congresses to undermine state independence by expanding federal preemption of progressive state initiatives. The 107th to 109th invalidated hundreds of state laws protecting workers, consumers, and the environment, often reaching far into traditional preserves of the states such as tort law, health and safety inspections, land use, and local social conventions to do so. A recent congressional report expressively sorts this overreaching into four categories: "usurping state choices on social polices . . . preventing states from protecting health, safety, and the environment . . . overriding state consumer protection laws . . . seizing power from state courts" (U.S. Congress, House of Representatives, Committee on Government Reform-Minority Staff Special Investigations Division 2006, 2). The first task of progressive federalism is thus clear: undo this bad work and its excessive concentration of power in Washington. A second step would be to add the language previously suggested to legislation designed to protect workers and citizens broadly. Third, where Congress cannot reach consensus on reform or the President successfully vetoes a bill, proponents of reform should offer legislation giving states the power to act where the nation is not prepared to do so. Assume for example that the Employee Free Choice Act—which would allow workers to form unions under the Labor Management Relations Act by obtaining majority support through card checks as an alternative to winning National Labor Relations Board elections, and would require arbitration of first contracts and impose larger damages on employer violators of the LMRA—goes down to defeat. Unsuccessful proponents should next propose offering states the option of adopting its terms.

Taxes and Unfunded Mandates

States cannot become real laboratories of democracy if they cannot afford to invest in desired public goods, nor can low-income states reasonably be expected to compensate for poverty and inequality within them. Given the sizable differences in state incomes noted earlier and the federal government's greater capacity to generate revenue, progressive federalism would recommend greater coordination among states, and between them and the federal government, in taxes and redistribution. We should align ourselves with other national systems by instituting greater harmonization of state tax systems—with some common taxes collected in all, and perhaps repatriated to all on a per capita basis (Rivlin 1992)—and explicit guidelines for redistribution to poorer states. We should also create funding for the currently unfunded mandates that the federal government has imposed on states.[24] If the national government declares a national responsibility to the poor, or to equality in educational opportunity, or to the disabled, or to anything else, the nation should assume the costs of meeting such responsibilities. In a progressive federalism, such substantive national floors should be funded by the national government, with states free to use their resources to exceed minimums.

Improving the Laboratories

If states were in these ways freed of unwarranted legal and fiscal constraints, they would presumably undertake more experiments in policy. It is important that they do this with the best information available, and that we collectively learn from what they find out. This suggests a natural role for national government. As the primary collector of data on American society, the federal government could help collect and standardize new data to enable states to make more intelligent decisions about local policy. It could also do a much better job of disseminating the results of state initiatives to all of the states. It could relieve some of the local costs of policy experiments, or improve their design by facilitating participation by additional states. The federal government might usefully create and fund a specific agency—call it, for the sake of discussion, the Office of State Innovation (OSI)—to undertake evaluation studies of state innovations, just as the Government Accounting Office or private firms such as RAND routinely do for Congress or federal agencies. The key is to keep track of innovation, measure and benchmark constantly, and actively disseminate results to state-level decisionmakers and others around the country. Given recent advances in knowledge and vastly lowered communication costs, this is something that we can now do more effectively than in the past. We should do it.

CONCLUSION

States have the power, and often the will, to meet the needs of citizens in progressive ways. They have shown that repeatedly in recent years. There is nothing intrinsic to federalism that justifies progressive opposition to giving states leeway to do more. There is much in federalism that should excite anyone seeking the variety, experimentation, and learning that states can bring to finding solutions to national problems. Progressive federalism seeks to harness this potential state contribution to our national democracy without retreating from civil rights and a national affirmative state. It seeks to reform current preemption doctrine to invite constructive experiment, to bring state government financing in line with other contemporary federalisms, and, by means of current technology and technique, to update and give content to the metaphor of states as "laboratories for democracy." Progressive federalism does not propose handing all government over to states. It does propose making more policy in the state capitals we all memorized in grade school—Juneau and Pierre, Helena and Frankfort, Albany and Topeka, Lincoln and Lansing, Sacramento and Springfield—and less in the K Street suites of Jack Abramoff and his kind, or in secret Executive Office Building meetings with Big Oil, Big Pharma, and their ilk, which we have latterly come to know all too well.

Who can seriously object to that?

NOTES

1. As Jonathan A. Rodden (2002, 670) puts it: "A rapid growth in the autonomy and responsibility of state and local governments is one of the most noteworthy trends in governance around the world in recent decades."
2. See J. Louis Brandeis's dissenting opinion in New State Ice Co. v. Liebmann, 285 U.S. 262 (1932). "It is one of the happy incidents of the federal system that a single courageous state may, if its citizens choose, serve as a laboratory; and try novel social and economic experiments without risk to the rest of the country" (311).
3. Though states are making substantial progress, we agree with John D. Donahue's (1997, 45) observation:

   [States are] laboratories for national policy in much the same way as a rain forest, say, is a laboratory for the biological sciences. There is a lot going on. Much of it has great potential relevance for improving the state of the art. But the rain forest's drama of predator and prey, its roiling interplay of survival strategies, are not set in motion to test hypotheses or to speed the progress of theory. A great deal of this ferment of [state] activity, moreover, goes unobserved, doing little or nothing to advance best practice.

4. Education and training, housing, land use, construction, transportation, marriage and the family, prisons, public safety, consumer protection, private insurance, abortion access, drug use, public health, sanitation, health and safety, environment, tort law, economic development, licensing, inspections, other business regulation, and non-federalized civil rights and discrimination law are just some of the areas where states have primary responsibility in setting law, or a particularly decisive one in enforcement of national law.
5. For state product see http://www.bea.gov/regional/ index.htm#GSP. For country GDP, see World Bank Statistics at http://www.nationmaster.com.
6. For introductions to the economics and politics of regions, see Masahisa Fujita, Paul Krugman, and Anthony J. Venables (2001) and Allen J. Scott (2001). Note as well the view of Ronald W. Jones and Hnryk Kierzkowski (2003), which emphasizes the capacity for decoupling in most modern production systems. This reduces the needed scale of well-organized places and increases the number of opportunities to create them, strengthening the applicability of our argument.

7. These regions are: New England (Connecticut, Maine, Massachusetts, New Hampshire, Vermont, Rhode Island), Mideast (Delaware, District of Columbia, Maryland, New Jersey, New York, Pennsylvania), Great Lakes (Illinois, Indiana, Michigan, Ohio, Wisconsin), Plains (Iowa, Kansas, Minnesota, Missouri, Nebraska, North Dakota, South Dakota), Southeast (Alabama, Arkansas, Florida, Georgia, Kentucky, Louisiana, Mississippi, North Carolina, South Carolina, Tennessee, Virginia, West Virginia), Southwest (Arizona, New Mexico, Oklahoma, Texas), Rocky Mountain (Colorado, Idaho, Montana, Utah, Wyoming), and Far West (Alaska, California, Hawaii, Nevada, Oregon).

8. The poorest region at both times was the Southeast; the richest changed from the Far West to the Northeast. The figures reported in the text are first the ratio of Southeast to Far West and Southeast to Northeast, and then their absolute differences.

9. All data are from the State Annual Personal Income series, at http://www.bea.gov/regional/spi/.

10. Within BEA regions, the increase in standard deviation of state per capita incomes were: New England (125 percent), Mideast (435 percent); Great Lakes (47 percent); Plains (75 percent); Southeast (106 percent); Southwest (54 percent); Rocky Mountain (330 percent), Far West (10 percent).

11. Over the last decade, in fact, Connecticut's rate of growth in per capita income exceeded that of Mississippi, so there was no catching up at all.

12. State maps on these and other state environmental policies are available from the Pew Center on Global Climate Change, at http://www.pewclimate.org/whatsbeing-done/in_the_states/state_action_maps.cfm.

13. See the website of End of Life Vehicle Solution (ELVS), an auto-industry sponsored program, at http://www.elvsolutions.org/ index.htm. See also reporting from the National Caucus of Environmental Legislators at its website, in particular the useful early 2006 update at http://ncel.net/newsmanager/ news_article.cgi?news_id=140.

14. For reviews of current practices and the welter of state innovations in this area, see Smart Growth America (http://www.smartgrowthamerica.org), PolicyLink (http://www.policylink.org), the Center for Neighborhood Technology (http://www.cnt.org), and links therein.

15. Here are some: the charter schools first pioneered by Minnesota in the early 1990s, universal pre-kindergarten programs, longer school days and years, more demanding teacher certification programs, greater principal autonomy and accountability in school systems, unified records of students as they pass through different schools, student-based school funding formulae, better customization of social services to the families of at-risk students, the integration of high school and community and technical college training, state guarantees of access to higher education, increased ease of movement between two- and four-year colleges, wider use of skill certification upon exiting the system, more deliberate use of customized training for adults, sectoral consortia of multiple employers involving in further skill upgrading, compensation systems rewarding skill advancement.

16. See the website of Public Campaign, at http://www.publicampaign.org/clean123.

17. Progressive States Network at http://www.progressivestates.org.

18. See Anna Puriton (2003) for a summary and Good Jobs First (http://www.goodjobsfirst.org) for later developments.

19. Here we make the conservative assumption that whatever the new level of national consensus is on labor regulation, it is probably lower than in 1935 or 1947, when the Labor Management Relations Act, our basic private-sector labor law, was established. Of course, this conservative assumption may be wrong. Certainly the public favors better protection of labor, including unions. See polls cited in Freeman and Rogers (2006).

20. This is paragraph 14(b) of the Labor Management Relations Act, its "right-to-work" provision, which allows states to prohibit a "union security clause" for citizens of that state. This is a clause in a collective-bargaining agreement that requires members of the bargaining unit to join and pay dues to the union that does bargaining for them. It is a way of securing money for the union's operation, and some measure of solidarity in the unit.

21. Donahue (1997) and Rodden (2006) both provide good reviews of debates.

22.   This is presumably in part because state and local taxes are a small cost of doing business, accounting in 2000 for only 0.7 percent of revenues and 0.8 percent of costs (Lynch 2004).
23.   In Chamber of Commerce v. Lockyer, 463 F.3d 1076 (9th Cir. 2006), the 9th Circuit Court of Appeals finally upheld the provision of California's 2000 "Cedillo Law" (AB 1889, subsequently codified in California Government Code §§16645-16649), which bars employers receiving ten thousand dollars or more in state contract funds from using any of them to "assist, promote, or deter union organizing." The case will almost certainly be taken up for review by the Supreme Court.
24.   These include regulations covering compliance with the Americans with Disabilities Act, the new guidelines under No Child Left Behind, the child-care provisions of Temporary Assistance for Needy Families, changes in Medicaid reimbursement, and the new requirement that states bail out the federal government to reimburse expenses covered under Medicare.

REFERENCES

Center for Policy Alternatives. 2006. *Progressive Agenda for the States 2007: Values and Vision for America*. Washington: CPA.

Donahue, John D. 1997. *Disunited States*. New York: Basic Books.

Farber, Henry S. 1988. "The Evolution of Public Sector Bargaining Laws." In *When Public Sector Employees Unionize*, edited by Richard B. Freeman and Casey Ichniowski. Chicago, Ill.: University of Chicago Press.

———. 2005. "Union Membership in the United States: The Divergence Between the Public and Private Sectors." Working Paper No. 503. Princeton, N.J.: Princeton University Industrial Relations Section.

Ferejohn, John A., and Barry M. Weingast. 1997. *The New Federalism: Can the States Be Trusted?* Palo Alto, Calif.: Hoover Institution Press.

Fiorina, Morris P. 2005. *Culture War? The Myth of a Polarized America*. New York: Pearson Education.

Freeman, Richard B. 2004 "Trade Wars: The Exaggerated Impact of Trade in Economic Debate." *The World Economy* 27(1): 1–23

———. 2006a. "Will Labor Fare Better Under State Labor Relations Law?" LERA Meetings.

———. 2006b. "People Flows." *Journal of Economic Perspectives* 20(3): 145-70.

Freeman, Richard B., and Joel Rogers. 2006. *What Workers Want*, 2nd edition. Ithaca, N.Y.: Cornell University Press.

Fujita, Masahisa, Paul Krugman, and Anthony J. Venables. 2001. *The Spatial Economy: Cities, Regions, and International Trade*. Cambridge, Mass.: MIT Press.

Gordon, Colin. 1994. *New Deals: Business, Labor, and Politics in America, 1920-1935*. Cambridge: Cambridge University Press.

Hacker, Jacob S., and Paul Pierson. 2002. "Business Power and Social Policy: Employers and the Formation of the American Welfare State." *Politics and Society* 30(2): 277–335.

Iversen, Torsten, and David Soskice. 2006. "Electoral Institutions, Parties, and the Politics of Class: Why Some Democracies Redistribute More Than Others." *American Political Science Review* 100(2): 165–81.

Jones, Ronald W., and Hnryk Kierzkowski. 2003. "International Trade and Agglomeration: An Alternative Framework." Unpublished paper. University of Rochester and Graduate Institute of International Studies, Geneva. Accessed at http://www.econrochester.edu/Faculty/jones/Jones-Kierzkowski%20paper.pdf.

Kaiser Commission on Medicaid and the Uninsured. 2005. "In a Time of Growing Need: State Choices Influence Health Coverage Access for Children and Families." Survey and report. Accessed at http://www.kff.org/medicaid/7393.cfm.

Leibfried, Stephan, Francis. G. Castles, and Herbert Obinger. 2005. "'Old' and 'New Politics' in Federal Welfare States." In *Federalism and the Welfare State: New World and European Experiences*, edited by Herbert Obinger, Stephan Leibfried, and Francis. G. Castles. New York: Cambridge University Press.

Lowi, Theodore. 1984. "Why Is There No Socialism in the United States? A Federal Analysis." In

The Costs of Federalism, edited by Robert T. Golembiewski and Aaron Wildavsky. New Brunswick, N.J.: Transaction.

Lynch, Robert G. 2004. *Rethinking Growth Strategies: How States and Local Taxes and Services Affect Economic Development.* Washington: Economic Policy Institute.

March, James G., and Johan P. Olsen. 1984. "The New Institutionalism: Organizational Factors in Political Life." *American Political Science Review* 78(3): 734–49.

Mayer, William G. 1993. *The Changing American Mind: How and Why American Public Opinion Changed between 1960 and 1988.* Ann Arbor, Mich.: University of Michigan Press.

McCarty, Nolan, Keith T. Poole, and Howard Rosenthal. 2006. *Polarized America: The Dance of Ideology and Unequal Riches.* Cambridge, Mass.: MIT Press.

Mettler, Suzanne. 1998. *Dividing Citizens: Gender and Federalism in New Deal Public Policy.* Ithaca, N.Y.: Cornell University Press.

Nagle, Amy, and Nicholas Johnson. 2006. "A Hand Up: How State Earned Income Tax Credits Help Working Families Escape Poverty in 2006." Center on Budget and Policy Priorities. Accessed at http://www.cbpp.org/3-8-06sfp.htm.

National Center for Public Policy and Higher Education. 2006. "Measuring Up 2006: The National Report Card on Higher Education." Survey. Accessed at http://measuringup.highereducation .org.

Office of Management and Budget. 2007. *The Budget for Fiscal Year 2007, Historical Tables.* Washington: Government Printing Office.

Page, Benjamin I. and Robert Y. Shapiro. 1992. *The Rational Public: Fifty Years of Trends in Americans' Policy Preferences.* Chicago, Ill.: University of Chicago Press.

Persson, Torsten, and Guido Tabellini. 2003. *The Economic Effects of Constitutions.* Cambridge, Mass.: MIT Press.

Pierson, Paul. 1995. "Fragmented Welfare States: Federal Institutions and the Development of Social Policy." *Governance: An international Journal of Policy and Administration* 8(4): 449–78.

Puriton, Anna. 2003. *The Policy Shift to Good Jobs.* Washington: Good Jobs First.

Rivlin, Alice M. 1992. *Reviving the American Dream: The Economy, the States, and the Federal Government.* Washington: Brookings Institution.

Robertson, David Brion. 1989. "The Bias of American Federalism: The Limits of Welfare-State Development in the Progressive Era." *Journal of Policy History* 1(3): 261–91.

Robertson, David Brion, and Dennis R. Judd. 1989. *The Development of American Public Policy: The Structure of Policy Restraint.* Glenview, Ill.: Scott Foresman.

Rodden, Jonathan A. 2002. "The Dilemma of Fiscal Federalism: Grants and Fiscal Performance Around the World." *American Journal of Political Science* 46(3): 670–87.

———. 2006. *Hamilton's Paradox: The Promise and Peril of Fiscal Federalism.* New York: Cambridge University Press.

Saltzman, Gregory M. 1988. "Public Sector Bargaining Laws Really Matter: Evidence from Ohio and Illinois." In *When Public Sector Employees Unionize,* edited by Richard B. Freeman and Casey Ichniowski. Chicago, Ill.: University of Chicago Press.

Scott, Allen J., editor. 2001. *Global City Regions: Trends, Theory, Policy.* New York: Oxford University Press.

Tsebelis, George. 2002. *Veto Players: How Political Institutions Work.* Princeton, N.J.: Princeton University Press.

U.S. Census Bureau. 2006. *Statistical Abstract of the United States.* Washington: Government Printing Office.

U.S. Congress, House of Representatives, Committee on Government Reform-Minority Staff Special Investigations Division. 2006. *Congressional Preemption of State Laws and Regulation.* Prepared for Henry Waxman.

Valletta, Robert G., and Richard B. Freeman. 1988. "The Effects of Public Sector Labor Laws on Labor Market Institutions and Outcomes." In *When Public Sector Employees Unionize,* edited by Richard B. Freeman and Casey Ichniowski. Chicago, Ill.: University of Chicago Press.

Wildavsky, Aaron. 1998. *Federalism and Political Culture.* Edited by David Schleicher and Brendon Swedlow. New Brunswick, N.J.: Transaction.

Joshua Guetzkow and Bruce Western

Chapter 11

The Political Consequences of Mass Imprisonment

With more than 2 million people behind bars and another 4 million under some form of correctional supervision, the scale of imprisonment in the United States is now unequaled in the world. Imprisonment has become a routine life event for the young, low-education, mostly minority men who fill the nation's prisons and jails. The development of mass imprisonment also involved a significant shift in public resources. By 2001, public spending on prisons and jails totaled $60.3 billion, equal to federal antipoverty spending on Temporary Assistance for Needy Families and the Earned Income Tax Credit. At the state level, prisons and jails consume over 3 percent of expenditures on average, more than double their share in 1970.

The growth of the American penal system has had far-reaching effects on the poor urban communities that supply most of the nation's prison and jail inmates. The rapid rise in the incarceration rate has contributed a little to reducing crime in poor neighborhoods, but mass imprisonment also carries a significant social cost in the form of family disruption and diminished economic opportunity. Rather than integrate the most disadvantaged into the American mainstream, the growth of the penal system has functioned to divide society's outcasts—particularly young African American men with little schooling—from the commonwealth.

Although trends in crime helped set the stage for mass imprisonment, the growth in incarceration rates was fundamentally a political development. From the late 1960s, the Republican Party developed law-and-order appeals as part of a new style of conservative politics that attempted to divide blue-collar whites from black voters. The right turn in Republican politics contributed to a realignment in which the GOP by the 1990s became the dominant party at the state and the national levels. The politics of law and order and the electoral success of the Republican Party transformed American criminal justice. The ideal of rehabilitation was discredited and retribution became a legitimate objective of penal policy. Prisons and jails were assigned the tasks of incapacitation and deterrence. As a consequence, control over criminal sentencing shifted from judges to legislatures, and tough new sentences were introduced for drug crimes and repeat offenders.

Just as the prison boom emerged from a partisan realignment and a repudiation of government's rehabilitative role in the lives of the poor, the political consequences of the boom and the policies associated with it may be likewise fundamental. In this chapter, we situate the prison boom within the policy-centered perspective in three ways. First, we describe the political origins of mass incarceration, highlighting how the shift from indeterminate to determinate sentencing policies has altered the politics of crime and punishment. Second, we discuss how incarceration has eroded the economic and civic standing of the disadvantaged individuals, families, and communities that are disproportionately affected by the prison boom. Finally, we examine whether spending on state programs has been curtailed in the face of expanding prison budgets.

THE POLITICS OF MASS IMPRISONMENT

High rates of incarceration at the end of the 1990s were largely the products of policy choice. American criminal justice was transformed in the 1970s. Two political projects, the war on crime and the war on drugs, generated a new role for prisons, and a new array of offenses and procedures for criminal processing (Beckett 1997). In a time of rising crime and skepticism about rehabilitative programs, prisons were enlisted in their more punitive function—to incapacitate criminals who would otherwise be on the streets, and to deter those who are tempted to offend.

If the wars on crime and drugs were the means, the key agent of change was the Republican Party. Nixon's "Southern Strategy" in 1968 pioneered the law-and-order appeals that peeled off traditional Democratic constituencies disaffected by civil rights reforms and the disorder of social protest. Political support for "tough-on-crime" policy galvanized opposition to the rehabilitative ideal. In the 1970s these political currents eroded long-standing rules of indeterminate criminal sentencing, which gave judges and parole boards control over punishment. The new model of "determinate sentencing" shifted control to legislatures, ensuring that criminal-justice policy would remain a significant issue in state political campaigns as candidates were forced to be more responsive to popular sentiment about crime.

The Republican Party, Voter Realignment, and Mass Imprisonment

Although the prison boom moved into high gear only in the 1980s, its political origins are often traced to Barry Goldwater's presidential run in 1964 (Beckett 1997; Gest 2001). Goldwater, in accepting the Republican nomination, warned of "the growing menace in our country . . . to personal safety, to life, to limb, and property." Crime and disorder were a threat to human freedom, and, to Goldwater conservatives, "only the strong can remain free" and "only the strong can keep the peace." The Republican campaign of 1964 linked the problem of street crime to civil rights protest, and desegregationists, more in evidence than criminals, threatened the peace. Although Goldwater was defeated by Lyndon Johnson, conservatives within the GOP introduced a new kind of politics that established Republicans as the party of law and order. Historically, responsibilities for crime control were divided mostly between state and local agencies. The Republicans now placed the issue of crime squarely on the national agenda. What's more, by treating civil rights protest as a strain of social disorder, veiled connections were drawn between the crime problem on the one hand and political progressives and African Americans on the other.

Despite Goldwater's defeat, the law-and-order message resonated, particularly among white working-class men in the Midwest and the South, who by some accounts were turning away from the Democratic Party in the 1970s (Edsall and Edsall 1991; though see Bartels 2006; Brewer and Stonecash 2007). No longer a social construction, the problem of crime had become a reality as rates of murder and other violence escalated in the decade following the 1964 election. Through the 1960s urban riots in Los Angeles, New York, Newark, and Detroit fueled the racial anxieties of many whites, already discomfited by desegregation, black voting rights, and other civil rights victories.

Elevated crime rates and the realigned race relations of the post–Civil Rights period provided a receptive context for the law-and-order themes of the national Republican Party. The message was refined and sharpened by Republican presidential candidates in each electoral season over the next twenty years. In his 1970 State of the Union address, Richard Nixon declared war on "the criminal elements which increasingly threaten our cities, our homes, and our lives." In 1982, Ronald Reagan extended the campaign against crime to a war on drugs. In the 1988 contest, the Republican candidate, George Bush, declared his strong support for the death penalty and charged his opponent, Michael Dukakis, with coddling dangerous criminals. The soft-on-crime charge was leveled in a famously effective campaign commercial that described the case of convicted murderer, Willie Horton (Mendelberg 2001). Like the Goldwater campaign two decades earlier, Bush, in the Willie Horton advertising spot, signaled Democrats' quiescence and complicity in black criminality.

Presidential politics illustrate the hardening of Republican crime policy, but governors and state legislators were the ones who led the effort to rebuild the penal system. The law-and-order politics of the state Republican parties can be seen in Joseph Davey's (1998) comparison of imprisonment trends in adjacent states in the 1980s and early 1990s. Five out of six states with the highest rates of imprisonment growth were governed by Republicans when state prison populations were growing most rapidly. Republican governors presided in fewer than half of the comparison states where incarceration rates changed little.

The clearest examples of aggressive law-and-order politics were provided by Governors John Ashcroft of Missouri (later President George W. Bush's attorney general) and Carroll Campbell of South Carolina. From 1985 to 1993, when Ashcroft was governor, the Missouri imprisonment rate increased by 80 percent. During his two terms, Ashcroft cut state services by over $1 billion, but spent $115 million on new prisons and increased the annual correctional budget from $87 million to $208 million. The Missouri legislature passed a range of tough penalties for criminal offenders, and Ashcroft pursued sentence enhancements for drug offenders (Davey 1998, 56–57). In South Carolina, Governor Campbell oversaw a 39 percent increase in imprisonment from 1986 to 1990. Like Ashcroft, Campbell supported tough sentences for drug offenders. No-parole and mandatory minimum prison sentences for drug crimes were adopted during Campbell's tenure.

To be sure, Democrats also participated in the punitive transformation of criminal justice (Murakawa 2004). For example, incarceration rates in Texas grew more quickly under Governor Ann Richards, a Democrat, than they did under her Republican successor, George W. Bush. Mario Cuomo, the liberal Democratic governor from New York, oversaw a massive increase in prison capacity, and incarceration rates grew strongly (Greenberg and West 2001, 625). In short, Democrats also joined in the rejection of penal welfarism, although they may have come later and with less enthusiasm to punitive criminal-justice policy. In analyses not shown, but available from the authors, using annual data on states from 1970 to 2003, we found that states spent more on corrections under Republican governors than Democratic ones, with no evidence of convergence between the parties on prison spending over time.

The law-and-order message would have had little force if not for its perceived success in helping establish the Republicans as the dominant party of the post–Civil Rights period. By the time of President Nixon's election in 1968, only Eisenhower had represented the GOP since Herbert Hoover. From 1968, Republicans won seven of the next ten elections, reversed the Democrats' historic majority in the House in 1994, and held a majority in the Senate for fourteen of the twenty-four years since 1981. The Republican realignment in national politics, and the conversion of the South into a Republican constituency, has been analyzed at length (see Edsall and Edsall 1991; Manza and Brooks 1999). At the state level, key for criminal-justice policy, Democrats lost ground around the country. In 1975, thirty-six governors were Democrats. By 2001, Democratic governors would be found in just twenty-one states. In the South and the West, Democratic governors represented twenty-two out of twenty-seven states in 1975, but by 2001, the number had dropped to eleven. A similar transfer of power can be seen among state legislators. In short, the new tough-on-crime message was advanced by a Republican Party whose electoral strength increasingly commanded state legislatures and executives. Although the actual role of the "tough-on-crime" message in helping to secure Republican victories is a matter for further investigation, being labeled "soft on crime" became a severe political liability.

The Repudiation of Rehabilitation, and Institutional Control of Sentencing

Where would the new law-and-order politics focus its efforts? The legal framework for criminal processing, the system of sentencing and parole release, was a visible and vulnerable target. For most of the twentieth century, the official objective of criminal justice was correction (Blomberg and Lucken 2002, 99–116; Garland 2001; Rothman 1980/2002). Correction was obtained by tailoring sentencing and treatment to individual cases. Judges were given wide latitude to decide whether an offender should go to prison. Conviction would often not result in incarceration. Instead, criminal offenders were assigned to community supervision and allowed to reenter society under the charge of a probation officer. If sentenced to prison, the offender's release was typically decided by a parole board that would consider the circumstances of an individual's crime, criminal history, and measure the potential for rehabilitation (Rothman 1980/2002, 165–74). Parole supervision itself was intended to reintegrate criminal offenders back into society (Petersilia 1999). Parole officers often resembled social workers, connecting their parolees to social services and job opportunities. This combination of sentencing, corrections, and community supervision constituted a type of "penal welfarism" (Garland 1990). Ideologically, at least, the criminal-justice system was an extension of the welfare state—a government-sponsored effort to provide opportunity and lift society's failures back into the mainstream.

In practice, judges and prison wardens adapted the ideals of penal welfarism to the realities of criminal processing, and the goal of rehabilitation was regularly compromised (Rothman 1980/2002). Still, the principles of individualized treatment and rehabilitation were embodied by indeterminate sentencing and parole. Prison was not yet the default punishment for convicted felons, and penal confinement was reserved for the most dangerous and incorrigible.

By the end of the 1960s, the discretion of judges and parole boards was being assailed from the left and the right. Left-wing critics charged that police and judicial discretion enabled racial and class bias (Somer 1976). In California, prisoners petitioned Governor Jerry Brown to end indeterminate sentencing, citing their psychological torment in facing uncertain release at the hands of capricious parole officials. The American Friends Service Committee in its report *The Struggle for Justice* (1971, 124) argued that "many distortions and corruptions of justice—such as the discriminatory use of penal sanctions . . . depend on the existence of wide margins of discretionary power." To remedy the abuse of discretion, they recommended short fixed sentences, the abolition of parole, and unsupervised street release. While activists on the left were concerned that judicial discretion resulted in excessive incarceration, conservatives feared that incarceration was used too sparingly. James Q. Wilson made the case in his book, *Thinking About Crime* (1975). Wilson's criminals were not made in the poor and broken homes that dotted orthodox criminology; Wilson's criminals were born into the world wicked and covetous. Rehabilitation was a sentimental delusion for this tough-minded analysis. Incarceration could reduce crime only by locking away the hard cases and by deterring the opportunists (Wilson 1975, 172). To deter, punishment had to be certain and not left to the vagaries of the sentencing judge and the parole hearing.

The earliest efforts at sentencing reform aimed to reduce racial and gender disparities. In 1978, lawmakers in Minnesota and Pennsylvania established the first sentencing commissions that developed guidelines for judges. Arbitrary punishment was to be minimized by a grid that specified the sentence using only information about the crime, and the offender's criminal history. Twenty more states adopted sentencing guidelines over the next fifteen years. Narrowing the criteria for sentencing may have reduced disparities in the early years of reform (Tonry 1996, 41), but guidelines also operated to increase the severity of sentences. Judges were forced to ignore many of the mitigating factors—such as employment and family connections—that would have reduced prison time under the indeterminate scheme. Those with long criminal histories were also given longer sentences (Tonry 1996, 49–59). Although guidelines were typically drafted at the outset by a specially appointed committee of experts, their terms were subsequently subject to the input, revision, or direct control of legislatures who often saw fit to raise, repeatedly, sentence lengths under the grid.

Guidelines were sometimes introduced as one piece of a two-part reform that also abolished early release through parole. As in the case of sentencing guidelines, early-parole abolitionists were motivated to prevent unfair treatment particularly for minority defendants. Maine disbanded its parole board in 1975 and fourteen states followed over the next twenty years. Another five states rescinded parole release just for violent or personal crimes (Bureau of Justice Statistics 1999, 3). Parole supervision was also transformed through the 1990s. Whereas historically parole officers had functioned something like social workers, connecting ex-offenders to job opportunities and social services, increasingly parole officers resembled law enforcement officers (Simon 1993). Carrying sidearms and charged with regular drug testing, parole officers in the 1990s sharply increased the rate of revocation for technical violations. In 1980, fewer than one in seven offenders entering prison were parole violators; by 1998 it was one in four (Rice and Harrison 2000; Petersilia 2003, 150–53).

New mandatory minimum sentences also affected prison release. Mandatory minimums require offenders to serve a fixed period before the possibility of early release. Although mandatory minimum sentences were on the books in many states before 1970, they were disliked by judges and few appeared to comply with the mandate (Tonry 1996, 145–46). From the 1970s, mandatory sentencing became popular among lawmakers eager to show their tough-on-crime credentials. The trend to mandatory sentencing was initiated by Governor Nelson Rockefeller of New York. In 1973, he proposed mandatory life prison sentences for anyone selling or conspiring to sell heroin, amphetamines, LSD, or other hard drugs. Life sentences were not confined to drug dealers. Possession of more than an ounce of heroin or cocaine would also earn life in prison (Griset 1991). By the mid-1990s, thirty-five other states had adopted mandatory minimums for drug possession or trafficking (Bureau of Justice Assistance 1996, 6–7), though the New York laws remained the toughest.

Mandatory minimum sentences were also widely adopted for repeat offenders. California's three-strikes law, passed in 1994, is the best-known example. Three-strikes, however, is a misnomer. The Californian law doubles sentences for serious second-time felony offenders. The third strike carries life in prison. The burden of the sentence enhancements has fallen mostly on second-time offenders. A year after the law was passed, about 65 percent of those eligible, about ten thousand California prisoners, were estimated to be sentenced under the second-strike provision (Zimring, Hawkins, and Kamin 2001, 64). By adding time to the sentences of large numbers of defendants with just a single felony conviction, the California three-strikes law is probably the most severe. Still, many other states also adopted some version of these provisions and by the mid-1990s, forty states had passed some type of mandatory sentence for repeat offenders, outnumbering states with mandatory minimum drug sentences.

Another mechanism that limited early release was the requirement that offenders serve a substantial portion of the prison sentence. These so-called truth-in-sentencing measures usually apply to violent crimes, although in Florida, Mississippi, and Ohio the measure applies to all prisoners (Bureau of Justice Statistics 1999, 3). The earliest truth-in-sentencing scheme was introduced in Washington State in 1984. Truth-in-sentencing proliferated after a federal law in 1994 authorized funding for additional prisons and jails for states mandating 85 percent of time served for serious violent crimes. By 1998, twenty-five states had adopted truth-in-sentencing measures. Another seven states require that at least half the sentence be served (Bureau of Justice Statistics 1999, 2).

Broad trends in criminal sentencing can be gauged by an index that records whether a state has sentencing guidelines, parole release, three-strikes laws, and truth-in-sentencing laws (table 11.1). Parole abolition was adopted most widely at an early stage, in seventeen states by 1980. Innovations such as three-strikes and truth-in-sentencing were only widely adopted through the 1990s. The table shows that legislatures—by mandating minimum prison sentences and limiting the role of judges and parole boards—increasingly controlled criminal punishment. In the courtroom, much of the power to incarcerate moved from judges to prosecutors. By choosing which charges to bring, prosecutors largely determined a defendant's chances of going to jail.

The Republican Party's law-and-order politics, the electoral decline of the Democratic Party through the 1980s and 1990s, and the establishment of tough new criminal sentences for drug crimes and repeat offenders amounted to a fundamental rejection of the correctional philosophy. The institutions of criminal justice were given new functions, to incapacitate the incorrigible and deter the covetous. At the same time, determinate sentencing policies, in part a product of law-and-order politics, have cemented and

TABLE 11.1 Number of States with Selected Determinate Sentencing Provisions, 1980, 1990, and 2000

Sentencing Provision	1980	1990	2000
Sentencing guidelines	2	10	17
Abolished or limited parole	17	21	33
Three-strikes laws	0	0	24
Truth-in-sentencing laws	3	7	40

Source: Authors' compilation.

institutionalized the perennial politicization of punishment practices by shifting responsibility for sentencing decisions from the judiciary to the legislature, from experts to the
polity. Now that the question of whom to punish—and for how long—falls more squarely
and visibly on the shoulders of legislators rather than judges and parole boards, sentencing practices are more exposed to populist, retributive sentiment (Savelsberg 1994), and
politicians can be held accountable for whether they are sufficiently "tough on crime."

INEQUALITY, CITIZENSHIP AND MASS IMPRISONMENT

David Garland coined the term "mass imprisonment" to refer to the high rate of incarceration in the contemporary United States. He argues that the scale and demographic
concentration of imprisonment produces the "systematic imprisonment of whole groups
of the population" (Garland 2000, 2). Because confinement has become a routine life
event among some populations, incarceration—which imposes long-lasting civic and economic penalties—has broader political repercussions while at the same time eroding the
quality of citizenship for certain social groups. By citizenship, we mean not just the possession of rights, like the right to vote (which ex-felons lose in many states), but also social standing, which can be thought of as access to a dignified standard of living by virtue
of being a member of a particular society (Shklar 1991; see also Katzenstein 2005). Here
we describe the scope of confinement and its implications for citizenship.

The Scope of Confinement

Table 11.2 shows the percentage of men aged twenty to forty behind bars in prison or jail
in 1980 and 2000. Among men with just a high school education, incarceration rates increased threefold in the two decades after 1980. By 2000, nearly 20 percent of young
black non-college-educated men were incarcerated, compared to 5.5 percent of Hispanics
and 3.2 percent of whites. Incarceration was even more common among high school
dropouts. One out of three young black male high school dropouts were incarcerated by
2000, compared to one out of nine, twenty years earlier. By the end of the 1990s, young
black, low-education men are more likely to be incarcerated than enrolled in some type of
welfare or training program.

   We can also measure the prevalence of incarceration by asking what proportion of
men have ever served time in prison by, say, their mid-thirties. In this case, we are focusing
just on imprisonment—at least twelve months' incarceration for a felony conviction, and a
median of about twenty-two months of time served. Becky Pettit and Bruce Western (2004)
calculated these figures for one birth cohort born just after World War II, 1945 to 1949, that
grew up before the prison boom, and another born in the late 1960s, whose members passed
into midlife in the mass imprisonment era. The likelihood of imprisonment had increased
significantly for low-education white men, from 2.1 to 5.3 percent, and for young black
men, serving prison time had become a routine life event. One in three young non-college-
educated black men reaching their mid-thirties at the end of the 1990s were estimated to
have served time in prison. Among high school dropouts the figure was 58 percent. Young
black men born in the late 1960s were more likely to have a prison record than to have obtained a four-year degree or served in the military (Pettit and Western 2004, 164).

   Significant increases in the risks of imprisonment were confined to just those with
only a high school education. While incarceration rates generally increased 300 percent
over the last two decades of the twentieth century, the imprisonment rate for young black
men with any college education increased from just 1.5 to 1.7 percent. The cumulative risk

TABLE 11.2   Incarceration Rates and Cumulative Risk of Imprisonment Among Young Men, by Education Level and Race and Ethnicity, 1980 and 2000 (Percentage)

	1980	2000
Noncollege men, twenty to forty, in prison or jail		
White	.9	3.2
Hispanic	2.6	5.5
Black	6.0	17.0
Male high school dropouts, twenty to forty, in prison or jail		
White	2.1	6.7
Hispanic	3.2	6.0
Black	10.7	32.4
Noncollege men's risk of imprisonment by age thirty to thirty-four		
White	2.1	5.3
Black	12.0	30.2
Male high school dropouts' risk of imprisonment by age thirty to thirty-four		
White	4.0	11.2
Black	17.1	58.9

Source: Pettit and Western (2004).
Note: Prison and jail incarceration rates are estimated by the authors; cumulative risks of imprisonment are calculated for birth cohorts born 1945 to 1949 and 1965 to 1969, as reported by Pettit and Western (2004).

of imprisonment for college-educated black men in their mid-thirties was estimated to have fallen between 1979 and 1999, from 5.9 to 4.9 percent (Pettit and Western 2004, 162). In short, mass imprisonment is characterized by greater class inequality in incarceration.

Imprisonment and Citizenship

At the most basic level, imprisonment constricts citizenship by taking away the right to vote. In only two states are prisoners allowed to vote, and fourteen states impose a permanent voting ban on those with a felony conviction. In their study of felon disenfranchisement laws, Jeff Manza and Christopher Uggen (2006) have estimated that there were 5.3 million felons barred from voting on Election Day in November 2004, or about 2.5 percent of the voting-age population. Of this, just over 2 million were ex-felons who had completed their sentence and were no longer under any correctional supervision. As with incarceration, disenfranchisement falls disproportionately on African American men: at least one in seven black American men has lost the right to vote, and as many as one in four in states with the highest rates of African American disenfranchisement (Mauer and Fellner 1998).

Have high levels of voter disenfranchisement had political repercussions? The answer is complicated, because it is difficult to estimate what proportion of disenfranchised felons would have voted, and for whom. Manza and Uggen (2006, chapters 7 and 8) estimate that between 24 and 35 percent of disenfranchised felons would vote if they could, with 70 to 80 percent of them voting Democratic. Overall, the impact of disenfranchisement on national politics appears to be marginal, mattering only when votes for Republicans barely outnumber votes for Democrats. For example, Manza and Uggen estimate that about six Senate elections since 1978 would have gone to Democrats instead of Republicans, which is less than 2 percent of the over four hundred Senate elections during the period. Making even more conservative assumptions, they calculate that in 2000, the vote in Florida—and hence the election—would have gone to Al Gore if Florida permitted ex-felons to vote (Manza and Uggen 2006, 192). Perhaps more significant is the way in which disenfranchisement works, along with a host of other civic penalties, to dilute the civic status of felons long after they have been released. In addition to losing the right to vote, these "civil disabilities" limit former offenders' access to welfare, public housing, licensed occupations, and educational grants (U.S. Department of Justice, Office of the Pardon Attorney 1996; Legal Action Center 2004).

The effects of incarceration also extend into the spheres of employment and the family (Patillo, Weiman, and Western 2004). In a purely accounting sense, high rates of incarceration affect our measure of the economic well-being of those at highest risk of imprisonment. Because so many young black men are in prison and jail, standard labor-force statistics understate the numbers of the jobless because those statistics do not include institutionalized populations. By 2000, standard labor-force surveys indicated that 30 percent of young noncollege black men were out of work, but the true figure exceeded 40 percent once prison and jail inmates were included in the population (Western 2006).

The effects of imprisonment also extend after release. Analysis of survey data shows that a prison record is associated with a 15 percent reduction in the level of hourly wages. The rate of wage growth over the life course is about two-thirds that of similar men without prison records (Freeman 1992; Western 2002). Much of this negative effect of imprisonment appears to be due to the stigma of incarceration. Experimental audit studies show that employers are one-third to one-half as likely to call back job applicants with conviction records than otherwise identical applicants without records (Pager 2003). The effects of incarceration on families are similarly large. Few families remain intact following the incarceration of a male household head (Western, Lopoo, and McLanahan 2004; Braman 2002). Prospects for finding marriage partners and achieving domestic stability are also reduced: unmarried women, like employers, express great reluctance at forming partnerships with men who have a history of criminal involvement (Edin 2000; Holzer 1999).

Because of the deep concentration of incarceration among low-education, young African American men, the collective experience of poor urban minorities has taken a uniquely disadvantaged and stigmatized form. Far more than simply the withdrawal of programs aimed at rehabilitation and reintegration, the myriad penalties faced by people who have been incarcerated serves to stoke recidivism and deepen their disconnection from the polity. Incarceration imposes civic penalties, disrupts family life, and creates long-lasting labor-market disadvantage for convicts long after they have served their time. In this way, mass imprisonment serves to constrict the citizenship, in terms of both civil rights and social standing, of large segments of the American population.

FIGURE 11.1   Box and Whisker Plot of Correctional Spending as a
Percentage of Total State Spending in Fifty States,
1971 to 2003

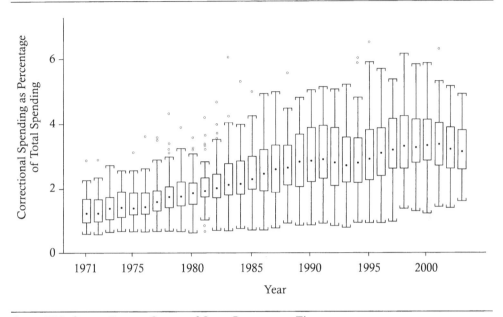

Source: U.S. Census Bureau, Survey of State Government Finances.

The Collateral Budgetary Consequences of Correctional Spending

The recession of 2001 brought into sharp relief the extent to which correctional outlays had become a significant part of state budgets. Whereas in 1970 states spent an average of $23 per capita on corrections, or a little over 1 percent of all budget outlays, by 2001 they spent an average of $125, or 3.5 percent of general expenditures (expressed in constant 2002 dollars). The fiscal pressure of correctional budgets is illustrated by figure 11.1, which shows the distribution across the fifty states of spending on corrections as a proportion of all general expenditures. By the end of the 1990s, big spenders such as Florida, Texas, and Colorado were spending between 5 and 6 percent of their state budgets on corrections.

Growing correctional budgets must be financed either by raising taxes or by cuts to other services. As states searched for ways to reduce budget shortfalls, calls for reduced prison spending were widespread. In one prominent example, Governor Paul Patton, a Democrat, released over five hundred prisoners to help stem Kentucky's budget deficit. However, fear of the soft-on-crime accusation may prevent Democrats generally from taking the lead in cutting correctional budgets. Many observers saw a softening of the tough-on-crime party line among Republicans, who may be as reluctant to cut popular programs (because corrections has used up the funds) as they are to raise taxes. Governor Arnold Schwarzenegger's support for reform of California's three-strikes laws and

President Bush's proposal in the 2004 State of the Union address for job training and housing for released prisoners are two prominent examples. If Republicans are the only party that can afford the political risk of cutting correctional spending in response to budget shortfalls—something like Nixon's going to China—we see little evidence of this effect in states' annual spending through the 1990s and early 2000s. However, our multivariate regression analysis of annual state spending on prisons from 1970 to 2003 indicates no significant spending difference between Democrat and Republican governors in the face of a budget gap in recent years (full results available from the authors upon request).

In fact, prison spending has remained largely immune from fiscal pressures: from 2001 to 2003, the average rate of growth in prison spending outpaced that of all other expenditures combined, something that had happened in only two out of the previous thirty years. It would appear that the politics of crime and punishment have created a climate where correctional expenditures are sacrosanct in the budgetary decisionmaking process. This suggests the possibility that, in a zero-sum game of state budget decisionmaking, outlays for prisons may come at the expense of spending on other programs. Spending on prisons may thus function similarly to the kinds of tax policies discussed in chapter 2 of this volume, by Kimberly Morgan, which act as constraints on the growth of social programs. Here we examine the repercussions of correctional budgets on spending for welfare, health, and education.

Figure 11.2 shows scatter plots of the growth in per capita state spending on corrections against growth in per capita welfare (plot a), health (plot b), and education (plot c) spending between 1980 and 2000, with bivariate regression slopes overlaid. These plots indicate a budgetary trade-off only for welfare: states with larger growth in correctional spending appear to have had smaller growth in welfare expenditures. There is only a weak, and statistically insignificant, positive correlation between the growth of correctional spending and its effect on health and education spending. A more rigorous analysis of trends in state spending, using annual spending data from the forty-eight continental states from 1970 to 2001, confirms the trade-off between corrections and welfare spending shown in figure 11.2, but suggests somewhat different results for health and education spending. Our analysis controls for the party of governor, the index crime rate, the poverty rate, total expenditures, and population size, and we include state and year fixed effects. The positive relationship between correctional and health spending depicted in the scatter plot proves to be robust: greater state spending on corrections was associated with more, not less, spending on health over this period—even after using year fixed effects to control for temporal variation common to all states, such as changing presidential regimes and increasing health care costs throughout the period.

In contrast to the data shown in figure 2(c), our regression results indicate the existence of a trade-off between education and correctional spending, but this trade-off is not only less robust but also much smaller than that for welfare: whereas 10 percent more corrections spending is associated with 2 percent less welfare spending, it is only associated with 0.5 percent less education. (Because the magnitude of education spending is much greater than that of welfare spending in absolute terms, these coefficients translate into larger dollar amounts for education than for welfare.) If bloated correctional spending has had any impact on resource allocation within state budgets, it has primarily siphoned funds from welfare expenditures. However, it remains unclear whether this trade-off results from the reallocation of funds due to the increased burden posed by correctional spending or from the reconfiguration of policy responses to marginalized populations. That benefits for the "undeserving" poor are most affected, rather than broad-based pro-

FIGURE 11.2   Growth in Per Capita State Spending on Welfare, Health, and Education Plotted Against Growth in Per Capita Corrections Spending, 1980 to 2000

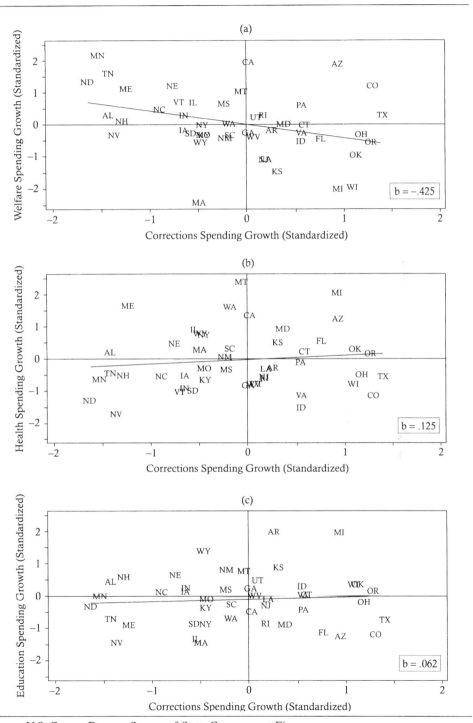

Source: U.S. Census Bureau, Survey of State Government Finances.

Note: Standardized Values with Bivariate Regression line. Plots include forty-eight contiguous states; plots (a) and (b) exclude Delaware; plot (c) excludes Delaware and Vermont.

grams aimed at more "deserving" populations, suggests that the trade-off is evidence of the extent to which the politics of crime and punishment have helped usher in a punitive approach to dealing with poverty and the governance of marginalized populations (Beckett and Western 2001; Guetzkow 2004; Wacquant 2001; Young 1999).

CONCLUSION

In this chapter we have explored the political implications of mass imprisonment and the policy changes wrought by law-and-order politics. This exploration began with a description of how the Republican Party has tried to use a tough-on-crime stand to gain support among white voters, in particular more conservative, working-class Democrats. Among the policy changes that are a by-product of law-and-order politics and that are of particular importance for the policy-centered perspective was the move toward determinate sentencing schemes designed to bring sentencing practices under the control and responsibility of state legislatures. This shift has helped to expose sentencing policy to perennial populist posturing.

Next, we discussed the consequences of mass imprisonment for ex-inmates, their families, and their communities; we reviewed evidence on incarceration's desultory impacts on citizenship, labor-market outcomes, and family life. The best evidence to date suggests that direct effects of felon disenfranchisement on elections are marginal. However, because of the scope of confinement and the high concentration of incarceration among young black men with little education, mass imprisonment has eroded the citizenship and social standing of whole segments of the population.

Finally, we provided evidence that spending on prisons has come at the cost of spending on social programs: when states devote a larger portion of their budget to corrections, they have then tended to spend less on means-tested income-transfer programs. Furthermore, state correctional budgets do not appear to have been affected by recent budget shortfalls. Despite anecdotal evidence to the contrary, the political climate created by law-and-order politics—where being perceived as "soft on crime" is the equivalent of political suicide—is alive and well. The secure position of correctional budgets may also be due in part to the relatively small—albeit rising—share of state budgets devoted to corrections, especially when compared with other areas such as education and Medicaid. State officials may feel they can get bigger savings by cutting into other programs. Corrections' budget security is also likely due in part to the institutionalization of state prison systems, which has created, among other things, a set of vested interests, including the multi-billion-dollar corrections prison construction and contracting industry, that works to preserve and expand correctional budgets. Whatever the explanation, the conditions that produced the prison boom still seem to be strongly at work.

The prison boom may also help us understand broader changes in conservative politics. Proponents of mass imprisonment support an active but coercive role for the government. More properly called authoritarian than conservative, these politics have taken a punitive attitude to social welfare, immigration, and, perhaps, foreign policy, as well as criminal justice. In all these spheres, authoritarian politics views government as having a legitimate and active role in coercing moral behavior from the poor, fortifying the borders, and projecting American power abroad. Although the long-term objectives are different, authoritarian politics shares with American liberalism a faith in the state as the key agent of social change. Both liberalism and authoritarianism reject the traditional conservatism of limited government and minimal taxation. From this perspective, mass imprisonment is just one piece of a broader transformation of the American politics of inequality.

REFERENCES

American Friends Service Committee. 1971. *Struggle for Justice. A Report on Crime and Punishment in America*. New York: Hill & Wang.

Bartels, Larry. 2006. "What's the Matter with *What's the Matter with Kansas?*" *Quarterly Journal of Political Science* 1(1): 201–26.

Beckett, Katherine. 1997. *Making Crime Pay: Law and Order in Contemporary American Politics*. New York: Oxford University Press.

Beckett, Katherine, and Bruce Western. 2001. "Governing Social Maginality: Welfare, Incarceration, and the Transformation of State Policy." *Punishment and Society* 3(1): 43-59.

Blomberg, Thomas, and Karol Lucken. 2002. *American Penology: A History of Control*. Hawthorne, N.Y.: Aldine de Gruyter.

Braman, Donald. 2002. "Families and Incarceration." In *Invisible Punishment: The Collateral Consequences of Mass Imprisonment*, edited by Marc Mauer and Meda Chesney-Lind. New York: Norton.

Brewer, Mark D., and Jeffrey M. Stonecash. 2007. *Split: Class and Cultural Divides in American Politics*. Washington: Congressional Quarterly Press.

Bureau of Justice Assistance. 1996. *1996 National Survey of State Sentencing Structures*. Washington: U.S. Department of Justice.

Bureau of Justice Statistics. 1999. *Truth in Sentencing in State Prisons*. BJS report, NCJ 170032. Washington: U.S. Department of Justice.

Davey, Joseph D. 1998. *The Politics of Prison Expansion: Winning Elections by Waging War on Crime*. Westport, Conn.: Praeger.

Edin, Kathryn. 2000. "Few Good Men: Why Poor Mothers Don't Marry or Remarry." *American Prospect* 11(4): 26–31.

Edsall, Thomas B., and Mary D. Edsall. 1991. *Chain Reaction: The Impact of Race, Rights, and Taxes on American Politics*. New York: Norton.

Freeman, Richard B. 1992. "Crime and the Employment of Disadvantaged Youth." In *Urban Labor Markets and Job Opportunity*, edited by George E. Peterson and Wayne Vroman. Washington: Urban Institute Press.

Garland, David. 1990. *Punishment and Modern Society: A Study in Social Theory*. Chicago, Ill.: University of Chicago Press.

———. 2000. "The Meaning of Mass Imprisonment." In *Mass Imprisonment: Social Causes and Consequences*. Thousand Oaks, Calif.: Sage.

———. 2001. *The Culture of Control: Crime and Social Order in Contemporary Society*. Chicago, Ill.: University of Chicago Press.

Gest, Ted. 2001. *Crime and Politics: Big Government's Erratic Campaign for Law and Order*. New York: Oxford University Press.

Greenberg, David F., and Valerie West. 2001. "State Prison Populations and Their Growth, 1971–1991." *Criminology* 39(3): 615–54.

Griset, Pamala. 1991. *Determinate Sentencing: The Promise and Reliability of Retributive Justice*. Albany, N.Y.: State University of New York.

Guetzkow, Joshua. 2004. "The Carrot and the Stick: An Inquiry into the Relationship Between Welfare and Criminal Justice." Ph.D. dissertation, Princeton University.

Holzer, Harry. 1999. *What Employers Want: Job Prospects for Less-Educated Workers*. New York: Russell Sage Foundation.

Katzenstein, Mary F. 2005. "Rights Without Citizenship: Activist Politics and Prison Reform in the United States." In *Routing the Opposition: Social Movements, Public Policy, and Democracy*, edited by David S. Meyer, Valerie Jenness, and Helen Ingram. Minneapolis, Minn.: University of Minnesota Press.

Legal Action Center. 2004. *After Prison: Roadblocks to Re-Entry. A State by State Report Card.* New York: Legal Action Center.

Manza, Jeff, and Clem Brooks. 1999. *Social Cleavages and Political Change: Voter Alignments and U.S. Party Coalitions.* New York: Oxford University Press.

Manza, Jeff, and Christopher Uggen. 2006. *Locked Out: Felon Disenfranchisement and American Democracy.* New York: Oxford University Press.

Mauer, Marc, and Jamie Fellner. 1998. *Losing the Vote: The Impact of Felony Disenfranchisement Laws in the United States.* New York: Human Rights Watch.

Mendelberg, Tali. 2001. *The Race Card: Campaign Strategy, Implicit Messages, and the Norm of Equality.* Princeton, N.J.: Princeton University Press.

Murakawa, Naomi. 2004. "Electing to Punish: Congress, Race, and the Rise of the American Criminal Justice State." Ph.D. dissertation, Yale University.

Pager, Devah. 2003. "The Mark of a Criminal Record." *American Journal of Sociology* 108(5): 937–75.

Patillo, Mary, David Weiman, and Bruce Western, editors. 2004. *Imprisoning America: The Social Effects of Mass Incarceration.* New York: Russell Sage Foundation.

Petersilia, Joan. 1999. "Parole and Prisoner Re-Entry in the United States." *Crime and Justice* 21: 479–530.

————. 2003. *When Prisoners Come Home: Parole and Prisoner Reentry.* Oxford: Oxford University Press.

Pettit, Becky, and Bruce Western. 2004. "Mass Imprisonment and the Life Course: Race and Class Inequality in U.S. Incarceration." *American Sociological Review* 69(2): 151–69.

Rice, Coliece, and Paige Harrison. 2000. "Conditional Release Violators Returned to State or Federal Jurisdiction, 1977–98." Bureau of Justice, National Prisoner Statistics data series (NPS-1). Accessed at http://www.ojp.usdoj.gov/bjs/ data/corpop15.wk1.

Rothman, David. 1980/2002. *Conscience and Convenience: The Asylum and Its Alternatives in Progressive America.* New York: Aldine de Gruyter.

Savelsberg, Joachim. 1994. "Knowledge, Domination, and Criminal Punishment." *American Journal of Sociology* 99(4): 911–43.

Shklar, Judith. 1991. *American Citizenship: The Quest for Inclusion.* Tanner Lectures on Human Values. Cambridge, Mass.: Harvard University Press.

Simon, Jonathan. 1993. *Poor Discipline: Parole and the Social Control of the Underclass.* Chicago, Ill.: University of Chicago Press.

Somer, Robert. 1976. *The End of Imprisonment.* New York: Oxford University Press.

Tonry, Michael. 1996. *Sentencing Matters.* New York: Oxford University Press.

U.S. Department of Justice, Office of the Pardon Attorney. 1996. *Civil Disabilities of Convicted Felons: A State-by-State Survey.* Washington: U.S. Department of Justice.

Wacquant, Loic. 2001. "The Penalization of Poverty and the Rise of Neoliberalism." *European Journal on Criminal Policy and Research* (special issue on Criminal Justice and Social Policy) 9(4): 401–12.

Western, Bruce. 2002. "The Impact of Incarceration on Wage Mobility and Inequality." *American Sociological Review* 67(4): 526-46.

————. 2006. *Punishment and Inequality in America.* New York: Russell Sage Foundation.

Western, Bruce, Len Lopoo, and Sara McLanahan. 2004. "Incarceration and the Bonds Between Parents in Fragile Families." In *Imprisoning America: The Social Effects of Mass Incarceration*, edited by Mary Patillo, David Weiman, and Bruce Western. New York: Russell Sage Foundation.

Wilson, James Q. 1975. *Thinking About Crime.* New York: Vintage Books.

Young, Jock. 1999. *The Exclusive Society: Social Exclusion, Crime and Difference in Late Modernity.* Thousand Oaks, Calif.: Sage.

Zimring, Franklin E., Gordon Hawkins, and Sam Kamin. 2001. *Punishment and Democracy: Three Strikes and You're Out in California.* New York: Oxford University Press.

Part VII

Putting the Pieces Together:
Constructivist and
Institutionalist Perspectives

Chapter 12

Poverty, Policy, and the Social Construction of Target Groups

Poverty, policy, and the shape of American democracy are related in many, often unexpected, ways. More than forty years after the nation declared a "war on poverty" and passed a multitude of policies aimed at its eradication, poverty persists and has become more intractable. Public policy itself is a significant part of the poverty problem. Not only are these public policies counterproductive, they also distance and alienate the poor from the very political processes that are supposed to remedy social and economic problems.

The first of the two major accomplishments of this book is to direct attention to the political consequences of policies that reduce government's role as a source of opportunity and security for the poor while expanding the scope and size of benefits for the well off. Rather than alleviating poverty, such policies of government are powerful perpetrators of inequality and creators of an "underclass." Part of the poverty story, as explained by the editors of this book (chapter 1, this volume), is rising inequality, where 1 percent of the population controls a substantial and growing portion of the nation's wealth. At the same time earnings of the middle- and lower-income families are stagnant or falling. There is growing insecurity among Americans as larger numbers spend some of the years of their lifetime in poverty. Poverty is perpetuated and deepened by many forces, including structural problems with capitalism, global markets, transition of the United States to a service economy, racial and gender prejudices, change in the family structure, and a deep-seated culture of individualism that honors self-reliance and abhors dependence. To be sure, poverty has many causes, but current public policy animates, reflects, and carries poverty forward. I have long been persuaded that the historic and contemporary designs of social-welfare policy contribute importantly to perpetuating poverty (Lieberman 1995; Ingram and Schneider 1995), and most of the chapters in this book have reinforced that view.

Democratic theory suggests that citizens who are affected by policy in ways they do not like are able to take corrective action. They can form themselves into interest groups that can bring pressure for change. Yet, as the chapters in this book have demonstrated, public policies have thwarted the operation of accountability and responsiveness mechanisms that are supposed to correct for failing policies. Rather than mobilizing their great numbers to reverse hurtful policies, the poor are mainly quiescent and surprisingly accepting. The tools embedded in policy designs deny the poor necessary capacity to challenge prevailing policies and discourage political mobilization to confront the systemic causes of poverty. For example, poor African American youths, a constituency I discuss in this chapter, are incarcerated in astounding numbers and thus cannot use the tools of political participation to help themselves. The failure of others disadvantaged by policy, such as the medically uninsured, to fight back politically has a much more subtle explanation discussed in many chapters of this book, and I intend to pursue this subject further here, as well.

The second major achievement of this book is to advance the "policy-centered perspective" in examining the linkage between democratic citizenship, patterns of politics, and public policy. For the editors and authors in this volume, public policy is treated as the "fulcrum" connecting changes in American politics to trends in inequality and insecurity. Some political scientists and public policy scholars have pursued a policy-centric approach since Harold Lasswell (1936), a pioneer in the field of policy sciences, first asserted that the study of politics should serve the public welfare (Ingram and Smith 1993; Schneider and Ingram 1997; Goodin, Rein, and Moran 2006). In general, however, an active examination of the content and consequences of public policy has been sidelined in political science in favor of a better understanding of political behavior and institutions, and in policy science by utilitarian mean-ends analysis (deLeon 1997). The editors and authors in this volume see public policies as strategies for achieving political goals, structures shaping political exchanges, and symbolic objects conveying status and identity.

Paul Pierson and I both celebrate the policy-centric approach of this volume, but we respond to the book differently. I stress what this book has to offer toward unraveling the symbols or social constructions embedded in public policy. I will argue that these constructions not only constitute very significant burdens on the poor and underserved but also undercut their inclinations toward political participation. Whereas Pierson augments the content of the book by taking a macro approach covering policymaking over a range of issues in a long time frame, I choose to focus much more narrowly on public policy and social constructions. I begin with the creation and perpetuation of negative stereotypes of the poor. A brief explanation of the social constructions framework that Anne Schneider and I have worked on for the past decade or so is provided, using examples from chapters in this book. I then focus on the many aspects of policy design that individualize and atomize policy recipients or targets so that they fail to recognize their own deservedness, their shared group interests, and their ability to mobilize. Next, I will reflect on what this volume has taught me about how social constructions of target groups change, and why the creation of more positive images has turned out to be so difficult. Finally, I conclude with some reflections about public policy, democracy, and citizenship.

PUBLIC POLICY AND SOCIAL CONSTRUCTIONS

Public policies send powerful messages about who really matters in politics, what kind of game politics is, and whether groups with certain identities can expect to receive anything positive from government. Paul Pierson distinguishes between two types of policy effects. Interpretive effects are those associated with symbolic messages about social status, citizenship, and standing, whereas resource effects relate to material benefits and costs of various kinds, including economic and institutional impacts, and are enforced with political authority (Pierson 1993). In Anne Schneider's and my work, we make no distinction between material, resource, hortatory, or symbolic messages and effects associated with public policies, since almost all material impacts carry significant symbolic messages (Ingram and Schneider 2006). The emphasis of our work, and my emphasis in this chapter, is upon the ways in which public policies implicitly, through their portrayal of different kinds of groups, shape participation and the nature of social and economic citizenship.

This is a complementary but different focus from the institutional and interest-group relationship to public policy that Pierson emphasizes.

THE SOCIAL CONSTRUCTION OF TARGET GROUPS

Public policies operate through the creation of categories, groupings of persons distinguished as eligible for benefits and burdens designed to change behavior or serve some public-policy goal (Stone 2005). The term "target group" or "target population" identifies groups chosen to receive benefits and burdens through policy design. Different target groups are treated differently, with some receiving benefits and others costs, according to their political power and social construction. In consequence and over time, some categories of people are made much better off and more able to exert influence over government policy than some others, mainly the bearers of costs, who fall further behind. In such cases, public policy becomes an engine of hierarchical social order and a perpetuator of poverty.

The broad outlines of a framework for the social construction of target groups and the position of various groups are laid out in figure 12.1. The vertical dimension reflects level of political power as it is conventionally portrayed and includes such attributes as control over elected and appointed offices, size of constituency, amount available for campaign contributions, and the like. In the figure, employers are portrayed as more powerful than Medicare beneficiaries, who in turn have considerably more power than welfare mothers. The horizontal dimension indicates the social construction of deservedness or positive-negative valence afforded different target groups by the policymaking processes, discourses, and contents. For instance, feminists may have about the same level of political power as mothers, but feminists are socially constructed very negatively, as illustrated by their placement at the far right of the figure. Target groups that are powerful and deserving are placed closest to the upper-left, or advantaged, quadrant. Powerful but negatively constructed groups are in the upper-right, or contender, space. Powerless but relatively positively constructed groups who elicit sympathy or pity, such as dependents, are located in the lower-left quadrant. Powerless and undeserving groups, such as deviants, are positioned in the lower-right quadrant (Schneider and Ingram 1993, 1997, 2005; Ingram and Schneider 2006; Ingram, Schneider, and deLeon 2007). The placement of groups in this figure is derived from evidence provided in the chapters of this book. The exact positioning of some groups is open to question, and in any case can shift over time. Because the book's subject is inequality, the "Dependents" and "Deviants" categories are more completely populated than "Advantaged" or "Contender."

Neither political power nor social constructions are static, and the policy treatment of target groups can change. For example, immigrants, particularly undocumented "illegal" immigrants, were regarded much more positively a decade or so ago than they are now. There is a continuing struggle in policy processes to gain acceptance of particular constructions and their consequences. Some constructions tend to become so hegemonic that they are viewed as "natural" conditions and are seldom questioned. For example, the divergent and solidified positive social constructions of the "employed" and negative stereotype of "welfare recipients" is illustrated in Frances Fox Piven's discussion of the welfare rights movement of the 1960s (chapter 7, this volume). Many critics believed the movement should focus on jobs, not welfare, and Piven quotes a noted civil rights leader as saying, "I would rather get one black woman a job as an airline stewardess than get

FIGURE 12.1   A Framework for the Social Construction of Target Groups

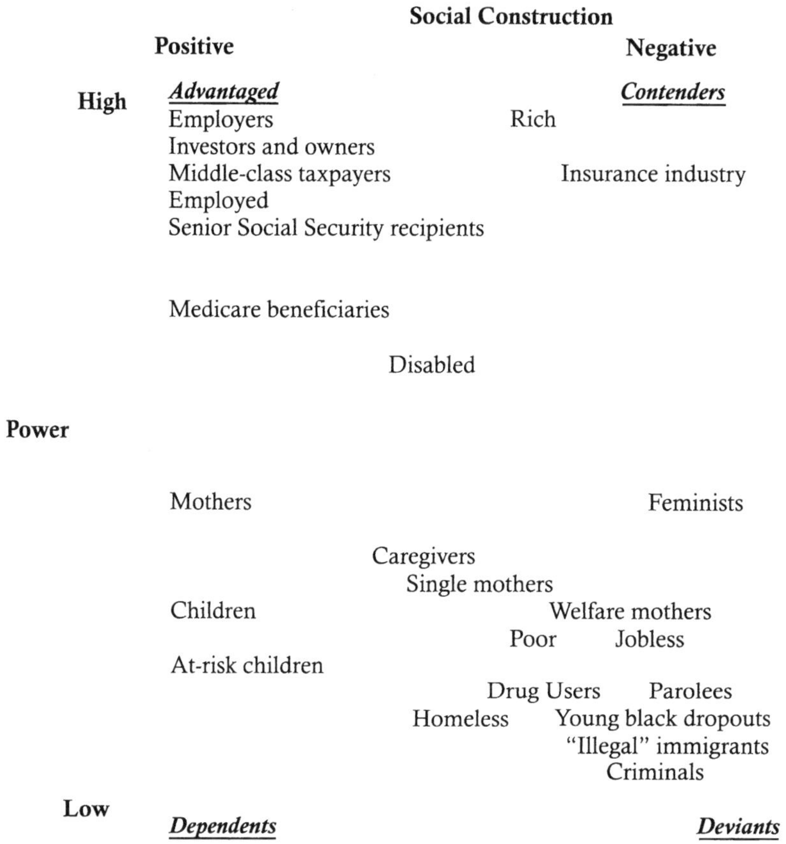

Social Construction

Positive   Negative

High   *Advantaged*   *Contenders*
        Employers   Rich
        Investors and owners
        Middle-class taxpayers   Insurance industry
        Employed
        Senior Social Security recipients

        Medicare beneficiaries

                              Disabled

Power

        Mothers   Feminists

                        Caregivers
                        Single mothers
        Children   Welfare mothers
                              Poor   Jobless
        At-risk children
                              Drug Users   Parolees
                        Homeless   Young black dropouts
                                       "Illegal" immigrants
                                              Criminals
Low
        Dependents   *Deviants*

Source: Author's compilation.

thousands of black women on welfare." Such constructions have undergone little change in nearly half a century.

As the authors of many chapters in this book show, public policies have had an important role in carving out a large segment of our population, the relatively powerless and negatively constructed, and slating these groups for burdens and bleak options. Deborah Stone (chapter 9, this volume) observes that poor mothers on welfare are distinguished from their middle- and upper-class counterparts and are placed in a double bind. Caregiving is considered a family obligation, and caregivers, mainly women, are relatively powerless. Middle-class families may be able to afford for mothers and other women caregivers to stay at home rather than working, but for poor caregivers on welfare, this is not an option. Either they ignore the ethic of care that instructs them to honor their obligations to their families, or they must break harsh laws dictating that work and economic values trump all else. Women of color are overrepresented among welfare recipients, and race is an undeniable component in the construction of dependency and deviance. Persistent color-based inequality is historically rooted in state policy. The chapter by Jennifer Hochschild and Vesla Weaver reveals the way in which state government has inscribed and legitimated skin color as a fundamental difference among citizens.

A permanent underclass exists that is subject to negative stereotyping as deviants in the media, popular culture, and in a variety of institutional settings. As Joshua Guetzkow and Bruce Western argue in chapter 11, the penal system (and the "war on drugs" policies and truth in sentencing measures that support it) has functioned to divide society's outcasts—particularly young black men with little schooling—from the commonwealth. Poor urban African American men rarely have a positive interaction with government. Instead, they are targeted as having attention-deficit syndrome in schools and segregated into special classes. If they gather in groups they tend to be identified as gang members and incarcerated. One of the shocking statistics in the Guetzkow and Western chapter is that 58 percent of African American high school dropouts will have served some prison time by the age of thirty-five. In prisons, they are deprived of opportunities for education and training, and their communication with family members and other supportive individuals outside prison is limited or forbidden. Once released from prison, they are regularly targeted by the police as suspects in crimes. As felons, they may not be able to find and keep jobs that raise them out of poverty. They may, in fact, be eligible for a whole variety of programs that might help, but such programs seldom have outreach. People stereotyped as deviants rarely apply for services from the same governmental source that regularly metes out punishments. Laws in many states prevent felons from voting, even after they have completed parole.

Dependent populations, categories of people who are sometimes sympathetically constructed but lack political power, are also marked by poverty policy. In the 1930s, welfare recipients were initially positively portrayed as sympathetic figures deserving of both pity and a helping hand. As time and policy changed, welfare recipients were racialized, and programs helping them became less popular and more coercive. Paternalistic eligibility rules now signal that poor people's problems are of their own making. The only way out of poverty is through individual effort. Such policies divert the poor from understanding and combating the systemic and structural causes of poverty. Yet, as Joe Soss and Sanford Schram illustrate (chapter 5), successfully negotiating the "welfare-to-work" policy terrain does not mean that targets escape their dependent-tending-toward-deviant image. The graduates of welfare-to-work programs and those paroled from prisons are thrown together in neighborhoods with few jobs and little social support structure. Both groups are oppressed by the overbearing monitoring of state officials.

POLICY RULES, TOOLS, AND
IMPLEMENTATION STRUCTURES

The elements of public policy design, such as rules, are fashioned differently for advantaged and dependent groups. Shep Melnick (chapter 3) tells the story of how administrative rules affecting eligibility of the disabled allowed this target group to be more positively constructed and gain better treatment by government. Rules dictated that the disabled were entitled to individualized, functional analysis of disability, rather than the application of hard and fast administrative rules. Access to the courts allowed the disabled to portray themselves more sympathetically and gain political power because administrators did not relish the type of attention such cases tended to attract. Rules were fashioned by courts and pursued by lawyers with the social construction of deservedness in mind. Melnick quotes from a legal service manual that warns against pursuing the claims of clients who are perceived to be undeserving or who are themselves mainly to blame for bad outcomes.

Paternalistic policy tools that make draconian demands affecting the personal lives of welfare recipients, and demeaning means tests that stereotype them as paupers, are elements of contemporary welfare-policy designs. Caseworkers can be quite intrusive in their treatment of clients, but the clients themselves have little agency. Whatever insufficient benefits the dependent and deviant are entitled to usually are poorly implemented. Instead of engaging in the outreach typical of policies aimed at the advantaged, social-services offices require clients to apply for program participation in person at overcrowded offices often located far from their homes.

POLICY AND OPPORTUNITY STRUCTURES
FOR MOBILIZATION

Standard pluralist theory would suggest that ill treatment by government is the kind of grievance that would lead target groups to defensive mobilization. However, the stigma associated with group membership and perpetuated in policy design and discourse very often discourages members from identifying with the group or taking on the group cause. Andrea Louise Campbell's analysis (chapter 6) shows that policy designs, through resource, engagement, and mobilization mechanisms, can have either a positive or negative effect on political participation. A "participation-policy cycle" emerges whereby programs influence the level and nature of client political participation, and that participation in turn influences policy outcomes. Campbell compares Social Security with welfare and the Head Start program. Social Security created a politically relevant group identity for seniors, who otherwise were only a demographic group. Government provided retirement income, reduced poverty, and increased free time to participate in politics. In contrast, welfare has negative effects on its clients by undermining their feelings of external political efficacy and assigning the stigma of means-tested programs. Means tests alone, however, are not sufficient to dampen participation. When counteracted by participatory policy designs that engage recipients, the means-tested Head Start program engenders positive citizenship learning and empowerment.

Public policies can be structured in ways that encourage or impede feedback, and this in turn affects the extent of political support or opposition (Meyer, Jenness, and Ingram 2005). Consider the different ways in which financial aid is provided to different groups. Advantaged groups are regularly served by tax breaks that often occur without drawing attention, objection, or countermobilization because of the opaqueness and the Byzantine complexity of the tax code. As Kimberly Morgan notes (chapter 2), the revenue loss caused by tax breaks has grown to total more than half of tax receipts, yet they remain virtually hidden, a private welfare state benefiting the advantaged, who are both powerful and positively constructed. Tax breaks are a greater drain on government budgets than welfare checks are, but direct outlays such as welfare checks are much more visible in budgetary discussions and arouse much more opposition. Participation in politics and political mobilization of the poor requires resources, and tax policy is no longer the strong redistributive force it was before 1970. Tax breaks for the wealthy are rationalized by the deservingness of the well-to-do. In political debates, employers and CEOs with high incomes are portrayed as generators of economic wealth that lifts all boats. In contrast with the poor, well-off investors and property owners have both a positive construction as entitled to special treatment as well as ample resources with which to pursue their interests.

Lawrence Jacobs (chapter 4) emphasizes cognitive processes whereby people (elites and other target groups) process information, and he discusses the ways in which this learning affects policy feedback. How target groups interpret the messages of public policy has long been a matter of concern among policy scholars. Many dependent groups are targets of policies that individualize and atomize people who have problems, so that systemic causes are ignored. Deborah Stone (1993) has written about the deleterious effects of diagnostic tools that shape and limit the discourse about dependent groups. For example, when a test by a clinical expert is necessary to identify such conditions as rape crisis syndrome or attention deficit disorder, recipients are linked with the tests related to their own particular case but not to the broader systemic forces that may make whole classes of people particularly vulnerable to these conditions. The policy message sent by clinical reasoning individualizes clients as "patients" needing treatment, rather than as part of a larger vulnerable group needing protection. Jacobs takes this line of analysis of policy discourse further. He notes that elected leaders are likely to be most sensitive to the early rather than delayed feedback of policy. Thus these leaders react to the immediate costs of policy rather than the likely delayed effects of positive and supportive target-group mobilization. Analysts must therefore attend to "on-line" dialogue, or what is being said at the time, not effects anticipated in the future. Jacobs argues that preoccupation with immediate costs led the Johnson administration to adopt an implementation design dependent on a private, employer-based insurance system for the Medicare program. The feedback effects of this policy design choice were to build a powerful constituency in favor of perpetuating the private administration of Medicare and opposed to any takeover by "big government." Although Medicare recipients gained power and a positive social construction, their numbers did not grow. The uncontrolled growth in health spending fueled by the private administration of Medicare resulted in increased opposition by business interests to the extension of Medicare to uninsured groups.

CHANGING SOCIAL CONSTRUCTION

The work Anne Schneider and I have done on linking public policy to social construction of target groups has failed to adequately discuss how social constructions can change so that negatively constructed groups can be recast in a more favorable light (deLeon 2005). Soss and Schram's (chapter 5) examination of what they call "feedback failure" goes a long way toward explaining why this occurs. Changing the social construction of those seen as deviants requires changes in the images held by publics that are not themselves targets of policy. The implicit theory of welfare reform that sharply limited benefits and forced many beneficiaries off the welfare rolls and into low-wage work was that the working poor would have a much more positive image and attract more generous public support. Yet opinion polls conducted after what is widely regarded as successful implementation of welfare reform find that welfare beneficiaries continue to be racialized and that African Americans are still stereotyped as lazy. Soss and Schram explain that what policy conveys is not necessarily consistent with what it does. The discourse associated with welfare reform fed into, rather than contradicted, widespread stereotypes of welfare recipients. The mass public focused only upon the highlights of the welfare reform debate, and what was heard was fully consistent with well-established negative social constructions of the targets of welfare. Further, the few recipients of welfare-to-work policy reform whose lives were transformed were not sufficiently numerous or salient for their experience to weigh very heavily in the court of public opinion, which continued to stigmatize welfare recipients. The chapters by Jacobs and Soss and Schram urge policy scholars to carefully examine the discourse and "on-line" framing of policy issues and the portrayal of targets to gauge the likelihood of changing social constructions, whatever the policy intent.

PUBLIC POLICY AND CITIZENSHIP

Over the past few years the link between target groups' experience and treatment by policy and their propensity to engage in political action has been established. Plainly stated, the recipients of benefits administered via fair, transparent, and respectful processes—such as the G.I. Bill, Social Security Disability Insurance, and Head Start benefits—are more likely than other similarly situated citizens to participate in politics and have a positive view of government. By contrast, where the dominant experience with government agencies is that of disrespect and capricious misuse of power, target groups tend to withdraw and believe that participation is useless and potentially dangerous.

If public policy is one of the primary ways in which less-advantaged groups in American society have traditionally gotten what they believe to be a leg up through policies such as the Homestead Act, universal public education, veterans' benefits, and the like, what does it mean for the future of American democracy if the poor further withdraw from politics? What will be the political impetus for politicians to serve their interests?

In the next chapter, Paul Pierson paints a rather forbidding overall picture of mounting political inequality and insecurity in an America with fewer compensating gains in overall fiscal and economic well-being than other industrialized democracies. The equally troubling message is that policies undercut the mechanisms and processes that are supposed to correct failing policies. At the same time, they have institutionalized the advantages of the privileged. Better understandings of the influences of policy feedback mechanisms upon the political processes of responsiveness and accountability are critical to both dealing with the problems of inequality and improving American democracy.

REFERENCES

deLeon, Peter. 1997. *Democracy and the Policy Sciences*. Albany, N.Y.: State University of New York Press.

———. 2005. "Review of *Deserving and Entitled*." *Public Administration Review* 65(September–October): 635–40.

Goodin, Robert E., Martin Rein, and Michael Moran. 2006. "The Public and Its Policies." In *The Oxford Handbook of Public Policy*, edited by Michael Moran, Martin Rein, and Robert E. Goodin. Oxford: Oxford University Press.

Ingram, Helen, and Anne Schneider. 1995. "Social Construction (Continued): Response." *American Political Science Review* 89(June): 441–6.

———. 2006. "Policy Analysis for Democracy." In *The Oxford Handbook of Public Policy*, edited by Michael Moran, Martin Rein, and Robert E. Goodin. Oxford: Oxford University Press.

Ingram, Helen, Anne Schneider, and Peter deLeon. 2007. "Social Construction and Policy Design." In *Theories of the Policy Process*, edited by Paul Sabatier. Boulder, Colo.: Westview Press.

Ingram, Helen, and Steven Rathgeb Smith, editors. 1993. *Public Policy for Democracy*. Washington: Brookings Institution.

Lasswell, Harold. 1936. *Who Gets What, When, and How?* New York: McGraw-Hill.

Lieberman, Robert C. 1995. "Social Construction (Continued)." *American Political Science Review* 89(June): 437–41.

Meyer, David, Valerie Jenness, and Helen Ingram, editors. 2005. *Routing the Opposition: Social Movements, Public Policy, and Democracy*. Minneapolis, Minn.: University of Minnesota Press.

Pierson, Paul. 1993. "When Effect Becomes Cause: Policy Feedback and Political Change." *World Politics* 45(July): 595–628.

Schneider, Anne, and Helen Ingram. 1993. "Social Constructions and Target Populations: Implications for Politics and Policy." *American Political Science Review* 87(June): 334–47.

———. 1997. *Policy Design for Democracy*. Lawrence, Kan.: University of Kansas Press.

———, editors. 2005. *Deserving and Entitled: Social Constructions and Public Policy*. Albany, N.Y.: State University of New York Press.

Stone, Deborah. 1993. "Clinical Authority in the Construction of Citizenship." In *Public Policy for Democracy*, edited by Helen Ingram and Steven R. Smith. Washington: Brookings Institution.

———. 2005. Foreword. In *Deserving and Entitled: Social Constructions and Public Policy*, edited by Anne Schneider and Helen Ingram. Albany, N.Y.: State University of New York Press.

Paul Pierson

Chapter 13

Policy, Politics, and the Rise of Inequality

The chapters in this volume make a compelling case for the benefits of a "policy-centered approach" to social analysis. Central to that case is an appreciation that policy is not just a "product" of the political process—an end result—but a central component of that process. Policies create some of the critical features that structure ongoing political contestation, including the organization and mobilization of groups and the formation of political identities and political agendas.

In the very long run, moreover, public policies can have a strong influence on the composition of the polity itself. To employ an ecological metaphor, public policy regimes help to create environmental niches that allow some actors and activities to flourish while others wither. For example, in many ways small firms operate in a much more favorable policy environment in the United States than they do in, say, Sweden (Huber and Stephens 2001). As a result, over the long run we would expect the population of small businesses operating in these different environments to diverge—as indeed they have.

Equally important, to focus on politics is to focus on substance. Much contemporary political analysis is surprisingly content-free, whether it takes the form of the highly abstract and process-oriented statistical and formal analysis common in political science or the horse-race-fixated accounts of political pundits. Yet those engaged in politics over sustained periods, especially the organized groups whose allegiances and efforts are so consequential, care enormously about the substance of governance. They recognize that what is at stake in politics is control over political authority—the capacity to make policies. Politics matters because it is a contest where some gain the authority to make decisions of fundamental significance for others. To focus on policy is thus to concentrate attention on these substantive conflicts, and to follow those conflicts (both the highly publicized and the subterranean) as they shift across the venues of American politics.

To focus on policy is also to focus on the long-term. Intent on the substantive impact of political authority, this volume's contributors pay attention not just to the big public confrontations that typically attract discussion but to features of the political environment that shift only slowly. Never dramatic enough at any particular moment to call attention to themselves, these slow-moving shifts may nonetheless have profound effects on a political system. They may themselves represent important changes that cry out for explanation, or they may constitute important sources of other shifts that are too easily attributed instead to more proximate but superficial causes.

A long view also gives us a richer sense of the contours of political action. Most of the individuals playing a prominent role in American politics participate over an extended period of time. They are engaged not in a single political episode, but in a series of encounters that may stretch over decades. This is even more the case for politically relevant organizations. Indeed, one of the principal purposes of organizations is to bring some coherence and continuity to the activities of overlapping generations of individuals.

Studying the activities of these individuals and groups over time forces us to connect seemingly separate events. By doing so, we gain an appreciation for the sophistication of much political action—as well as its characteristic limitations. Investigating activity over time draws attention to the significance of political learning. Serious long-term participants in politics gain insights and skills from their experience, and incorporate those lessons into their practices. At the same time, a long view of policy development heightens our sensitivity to the often unexpected or even perverse effects of political action. Even the most skilled and strategic political actors commonly produce results they had not anticipated. Often we will not see these effects unless we follow the story long enough to watch them unfold.

All of these advantages of a policy-centered approach to the study of politics are evident in the preceding chapters. In this brief concluding chapter I explore the macropolitics of policy development over the past quarter-century. This is one line of inquiry that is both "policy-centered" and complementary to the other contributions yet receives limited attention in the volume's individual chapters. In addition to the "micro" accounts of individual policy arenas, we can usefully think of a "macro" politics involving the dynamics of policymaking that operate over a range of issues simultaneously. Focusing on a particular arena (such as health care or welfare) allows very useful specificity. However, it also introduces potential biases (such as a tendency to interpret outcomes as primarily or exclusively determined by what is happening in that arena). Examining the broader patterns can provide a useful corrective, while retaining the focus on policy.

THE RISE OF THE ACTIVIST STATE AND THE POLITICS OF BACKLASH

Adopting this more macro perspective on policy development, one can see two fundamental trends over the past half-century—the rise of a more activist state and the emergence of a strong conservative backlash against that expansion. Between 1960 and 1980 the American state underwent a great transformation. This was no constitutional revolution. On the contrary, despite the political and social upheavals of the 1960s and early 1970s, the formal rules of American governance were quite stable. But this formal stability belied a fundamental institutional shift. In two decades, the domestic role of the American national state underwent a stunning expansion, involving big increases in spending, an explosion of regulatory activity, the extension of a "hidden welfare state" based on tax expenditures, and a "rights revolution" that established new national requirements with respect to discrimination, abortion, and a host of hot-button social issues (Pierson 2007).

For students of comparative politics (Evans, Reuschemeyer and Skocpol 1985; Lange and Reuschemeyer 2006) and American political history (Skowronek 1982) it is conventional to talk about "state building." For good reason, such transformative episodes are seen as defining developments in the life of a society. But students of contemporary American politics, having largely marginalized the study of public policy and perhaps averse to thinking of the world we inhabit in such sweeping historical terms, remain only vaguely aware that the American polity has just witnessed something similar. Moreover, the vast political and social implications of this remarkable transformation remain surprisingly underappreciated.

The rise of the activist state ushered in a profound set of changes in American politics (Melnick 2003). Many of the chapters in this volume confirm E. E. Schattschneider's (1935) old suggestion that "new policies create new politics." Here I wish to highlight just a few of the most important dynamics triggered by the remarkable growth of the American national state.

The great transformation of the American state generated new political opportunity structures. Conventional arguments about policy effects have stressed their capacity to entrench certain political arrangements. Strongly supportive constituencies grow up around these programs. These constituencies include both the ultimate beneficiaries of programs and intermediate groups that participate in providing the benefits. Other actors, perhaps initially less supportive, may gradually adapt to the new policy arrangements. As more and more elements in society come to recognize the new policies as durable, they make various individual and group-level investments on the basis of that recognition. These investments in turn help to further consolidate the new arrangements. Additional entrenchment can be produced by specific features of policies, such as the "rolling intergenerational contract" dynamic created by Social Security's "pay-as-you-go" financing.

There is considerable evidence that the expansion of the activist state generated many of the political repercussions associated with entrenchment. Consider group formation. Public policies may provide the foundation for particular patterns of collective mobilization. Policies can create major incentives to organize, and to organize in particular ways. They can also confer substantial resources on particular types of groups, including direct and indirect financial subsidies, as well as organizational infrastructure and crucial information that private actors can "piggyback" on in their efforts to generate collective action (Moe 1980). These can be especially important in addressing the high start-up costs and coordination problems that are often crucial to overcoming the formidable initial obstacles to successful collective action (Marwell and Oliver 1993).

Theda Skocpol (2007) has documented the contribution of heightened government activism in the United States to organizational formation. The "advocacy explosion" that many see as such a central part of contemporary American politics largely followed, rather than preceding, the expansion of the activist state. Moreover, the dominant organizational forms and strategic repertoires of these groups were customized to fit the opportunity structure of government activism. This customization partly reflects the vision of thoughtful entrepreneurs—but only partly. It emerges at least as much from group adaptation on the fly, as well as from differential survival rates among the groups that happened to be capable of exploiting the opportunities available.

As is demonstrated repeatedly in this volume, the expansion of the activist state also fostered the growth of strong constituencies among beneficiaries. Nowhere has this been more evident than in the major expansion of entitlement spending associated with Social Security and Medicare. The same case can be made more broadly. Where government programs provide substantial, tangible benefits, they will often generate consistent supporters as well.

Thus at least in the short to medium-run, the new policies associated with government activism generated supportive politics. Yet with the transformation of the American state came other political repercussions, less direct, less immediate, and less well understood. These less direct repercussions of expanded policy activism become particularly visible when one steps back from individual issue areas to adopt a more macro perspective. An overarching term for much of this less direct fall-out from heightened activism is "backlash." The expansion of the activist state created not only its own support structure but also, through a variety of pathways, many of the conditions for political challenges to its prominence in the decades to follow.

Recent research by political sociologists has stressed how new institutional arrangements necessarily produce exclusion as well as inclusion. This in turn can galvanize major countermobilizations. Institutions, as Marc Schneiberg and Elisabeth S. Clemens (forthcoming) write in a recent summary, "generate grievance (through political exclusion). . . . Actors who are aggrieved but not co-opted are an important source of pressure for institutional change." Some groups facing unfavorable circumstances may concede, accepting the new institutional status quo and trying to do the best they can within it. Others, however, may turn oppositional. As Clemens and James M. Cook (1999, 452) put it, "Denied the social benefits of current institutional configurations, marginal groups have fewer costs associated with deviating from those configurations." This backlash dynamic is evident in Steven Teles's (forthcoming) insightful analysis of conservative mobilization, where the emergence of energetic opposition is in large part triggered by the rise of activist government. As Kimberly Morgan (chapter 2, this volume) notes, one can see a similar process with respect to the crucial issue of taxation. Rebuffed in their direct efforts to challenge popular public spending programs, conservatives eventually identified tax cuts as the centerpiece for efforts to challenge the nagging durability of government activism.

No other aspects of the transformed American state generated grievances as intensively as the rights revolution. A range of profoundly contentious issues—many containing a strong moral component and raising fundamental matters of identity—that had previously been handled locally and in diverse ways now became national issues. Abortion, sexuality, education, welfare, crime and punishment, the relationship between church and state, and many similarly charged matters became subject to determination in Washington. The character of these issues not only made compromise difficult; it created incentives for polarizing forms of mobilization (Fiorina 2004). Few would look back with nostalgia at some of the practices tolerated or enforced in many localities prior to the rights revolution. Nonetheless, in retrospect it is apparent that a more decentralized federalism had permitted a diversity of practices that often muted the intensity of political conflict.

The transformation of the American state—the development of the distinctive policy structures of an activist government—did not only trigger a countermobilization. A policy-centered approach makes clear that the activist state was not just the target of conservative backlash but was a critical element of the new political terrain. It established important contours that both shaped the nature of that countermobilization and the strategies that successful elements of the conservative movement came to adopt. Policies, the apparatus of supportive groups and beneficiaries, and adaptations of other social actors created constraints that conservatives needed to circumvent.

As Martha Derthick and Steven Teles (2006) have detailed, for instance, efforts to undermine the strongly entrenched position of Social Security required that its powerful roots in the new American polity be taken into account. At the same time, however, specific patterns of policy intervention also create specific opportunities for countermobilization. Social Security, for instance, not only produces sources of entrenchment through the creation of committed constituencies and a formidable transition problem but also operates a "trust fund" system of finance that opens space for a discourse of looming "bankruptcy"—a feature that provides a crucial opportunity for reframing discussions about radical reform of the retirement system.

That the activist state created opportunities for successful countermobilization is equally evident in the rising role of the "hidden welfare" state based on tax subsidies. Although tax subsidies for private activity themselves are a form of activism, they are in fact the antigovernment form of government spending. They can lead upper-middle-class voters to see the private sector (for example, homeownership and mutual funds) rather than government (Social Security) as the guarantor of protection against life's economic hazards (Hacker 2002). For Republicans seeking to curb and redirect the activist state, tax expenditures possessed multiple virtues. They redirected fiscal resources to upper-income constituencies, they diminished the revenue stream available to government for other initiatives, and they did both these things in the form of tax "cuts" or breaks that were rarely perceived as instances of government largesse.

Finally, the particular form that the rise of activism took in the United States contributed to the mobilization of backlash in an indirect, long-term manner that has been poorly understood. A large component of the growth in spending during the wave of government expansion took the form of long-term promises embodied in new or greatly enhanced entitlement programs. Since the early 1970s, the government has witnessed the gradual maturation of these commitments, such that growth in public expenditure since that time has occurred largely among entitlement programs, along with rising interest payments. Higher interest payments reflected the deficits of the 1980s, themselves a result of a failure to adequately finance these maturing commitments.

The result is that since as early as 1980, politicians have increasingly played the role of bill collectors for previous promises (Pierson 2001). In the expansionist phase, politicians could make attractive policy promises while deferring most of the costs. Now, the bill has come due, and politicians must pay it, without getting much in the way of credit for the programs enacted by their predecessors. It is not an enviable position. Politicians must run faster and faster just to stand still. With few exceptions, legislated changes (that is, explicit policy choices) in entitlements over the past twenty years have been in the direction of retrenchment rather than expansion. Not surprisingly, this unending climate of austerity both weakens popular enthusiasm for social programs and can be utilized to foster more general resentment against government activity.

All of these dynamics underscore the central point of this analysis. The development of policy shapes the conduct of politics. No account of contemporary American politics can succeed without grappling with the reality of the new, activist American state. A little over a generation ago, the United States began a fairly rapid transition toward a markedly expanded federal role. Part of a broad cross-national trend, it also exhibited patterns that were uniquely American. This remarkable exercise in state building in turn contributed in fundamental ways to a remaking of the American polity. It fostered the growth of an unprecedented range of support structures for government action. Paradoxically, and over a longer time frame, it also fueled the rising hostility and growing influence of its greatest detractors.

PUBLIC POLICY AND THE CONTEMPORARY POLITICS OF INEQUALITY

It remains to connect these broad transformations in governance to the rise of inequality in the United States. Although that increase is often seen as driven by economics rather than politics, cross-national comparisons suggest that something distinctive has happened in the United States. Not only has the increase in inequality been greater here than most other countries; public policy in the United States appears to have done much less to counteract that trend than has been the case elsewhere. A closer look at policy development over the long term suggests that patterns of both government action and inaction have played a significant role.

As this volume's coeditors made clear in their introduction, a confluence of political shifts has set the context for the recent restructuring of the American social contract. First, the balance of organized interests in the economic sphere has shifted decisively in favor of employers. Second, the role of money in politics has expanded considerably (even as the distribution of economic resources has become more unequal). Third, American politics has become increasingly polarized along partisan lines, largely due to the rise of a more unified and aggressive conservative coalition. In combination, these three trends have had powerful effects on the exercise of political authority over the contours of social policy.

These broad political trends have set the context for a quarter-century of conflict between an entrenched activist state and an increasingly assertive conservative effort to redefine the role of government. As a policy-centered approach reminds us, however, the development of policy has played a central role. The much higher profile of federal policy not only served as a catalyst for conservative backlash but also was both the main target of conservative elites and a critical feature of the political terrain on which these conflicts have played out.

As the contributors to this volume demonstrate, these conflicts have had a substantial impact on the peculiar American response to rising inequality. Most obviously, the rise of a more aggressive conservatism has effectively blocked most public-sector efforts to address long-standing holes in the American system of social protection or to respond to newly emerging social risks. Where proposed interventions required expanded federal spending or regulatory activity, conservative resistance has been fierce and effective. As revealed most clearly in the stalemating of the Clinton administration's plan for health security in the early 1990s, an energized conservative coalition, increasingly critical of federal social policy initiatives, has succeeded in keeping most such initiatives off the agenda or defeating them when they arose. Since the late 1970s, social-policy initiatives that involve extensive federal spending or regulation have been rare.

By contrast, conservative desires to expand options for individualized or market-driven social provision have spurred somewhat greater policy innovation. One of the most important developments over the past few decades has been a growing recognition among conservatives that the political popularity of entrenched social programs rendered a straightforward political assault counterproductive (Teles forthcoming; Derthick and Teles 2006). Effective policy contestation required the development of new instruments that promised a response to social concerns about economic insecurity. The challenge was to find responses that employed instruments conservatives could endorse and favored constituencies that were part of their emerging coalition.

The development and advocacy of these instruments has been a major conservative project of the past twenty years. Enormous resources have been devoted to the expansion of policy incubators—organizations devoted to the exploration, refinement, and dissemination of conservative proposals for domestic policy change. Well-funded think tanks, such as the Heritage Foundation, the Cato Institute, and the American Enterprise Institute, have fashioned an organizational model that blends the traditional "analytic" quality of think tanks with a much stronger commitment to advocacy and marketing. Rather than being treated as something alien to "objective" policy analysis, political strategy has emerged as a key priority (Teles forthcoming).

In social policy, this effort has congealed around the concept of the "ownership society." Government activism is to be reconfigured around tax-subsidized, individualized accounts. Advocates stress that such programs maximize choice. Other benefits are touted as well (increased national savings for retirement accounts; increased cost-consciousness in the case of health care). At the same time, such programs clearly undercut many of the original aspirations of social policy. Even modest redistribution is eliminated. So is the pooling of risk, since the assets accumulated in individualized accounts—and the need to draw them down in the case of ill health—will vary radically (Hacker 2006). Equally significant, the structuring of these initiatives as tax breaks also concentrates their benefits on the most affluent. Not only are the well-to-do most likely to have the resources to participate, their participation receives a larger effective subsidy because of their higher marginal tax rates.

This conservative project can point to notable successes. Most dramatic was the replacement of the main income maintenance program for the able-bodied poor, Aid to Families with Dependent Children (AFDC), with a more decentralized and work-focused alternative, Temporary Assistance for Needy Families (TANF). In addition, there has been a tremendous expansion of the use of tax-subsidized, individualized savings instruments as a major policy for addressing retirement security. Finally, conservatives have explored various experiments in health-care reform, involving tax subsidies and the introduction of individualized "health savings accounts." Widespread introduction of these initiatives would entail a major reconfiguration of health policy along the contours of the "ownership society."

Yet conservative reformers have also had to confront the enormous obstacles to policy change created by a veto-ridden structure of political institutions, an increasingly polarized environment, and the entrenchment of existing policies. In just the past few years, major initiatives on public pensions and tax policy, designed to foster the new conservative vision of an "ownership society" to replace the "welfare state," degenerated into political routs that implicitly endorsed the status quo. Similar reforms for health care are still at the trial stage, but there is very little in the current climate to suggest that they have any better immediate prospects of overcoming gridlock.

One common assessment of the current setting would stress entrenchment—the conventional theme of policy-focused analyses of American politics. In this account, institutional obstacles to reform are so extensive, and organized opposition to any proposed changes so well entrenched, that neither conservatives nor progressives have much opportunity to alter the social policy landscape. Indeed, this would be a reasonably accurate portrayal of the large, intensive, and visible battles over social policy that have occurred in recent years. Reagan's major legislative agenda was blocked or severely watered down. The political parallels between Clinton's proposal for national health insurance and George W. Bush's recent push to partly privatize Social Security were evident. In both instances, tremendously ambitious reform initiatives quickly galvanized powerful opponents. Each ultimately crashed against the rocks of political institutions designed specifically to thwart such grand experiments.

Yet this assessment of a frozen policy landscape is highly misleading—in a manner that only an analysis highly attentive to the specific features of public policies is likely to identify (Hacker 2004). Social-policy arrangements can shift in meaningful ways even in the absence of dramatic episodes of policy reform. Small changes sometimes add up over time to major revisions. Modifications introduced with little fanfare or opposition may have major, often unanticipated, consequences—and these consequences may be difficult to reverse.

Perhaps most important, profound changes in social policy arrangements may occur in the absence of dramatic policy reform because of shifts in the social context within which public policies are embedded. Changes in the contours of the economy, evolving demographics, and transformations in the behavior of individuals and organizations may have substantial effects on the functioning of social policy arrangements even in the absence of major new interventions by policymakers.

Indeed, this dynamic is especially likely to occur in social contexts like the American one. Social-policy arrangements in the United States typically involve intensive public-private interplay. Government creates a structure of incentives, subsidies, and regulations. Much social provision, however, is channeled through employers, nonprofits, or arrangements constructed by individual households. Shifting circumstances may powerfully alter the opportunities and constraints on these actors, in ways that transform the actual functioning of systems of social provision. Indeed, changes of this kind have profoundly altered the character of the social contract in the United States over the past quarter-century, especially with respect to health care and retirement security (Hacker 2002, 2006).

At first glance, this process of what Hacker calls social policy "drift," anchored in the shifting activities of private actors, may appear apolitical. Substantial change has occurred despite the absence of a dramatic, widely recognized realignment of policy structures. Many of the changes have been unplanned. In the contemporary context, it is often misleading to say that policy is being "made" at all; it might be more accurate to say that policy emerges. Policymakers, happily or not, have responded after the fact to developments they did not control. Often, these responses themselves have been only weakly coordinated.

To describe these changes as apolitical, however, would be a profound mistake—the kind of mistake a policy-centered analysis is positioned to correct. The adjustments to the American structure of social provision may seem largely driven by the discrete choices of private individuals and firms. Yet these shifts also reflect conscious efforts on the part of politically mobilized actors to block competing public-sector initiatives. Conservatives may have been less than fully successful in legislating their vision of optimal social-policy structures, but they have been extremely effective in blocking efforts to update or adjust public-sector policy structures to accommodate new social realities. Moreover, in many cases they have managed to launch more modest social policy reforms that have encouraged or accelerated the private adjustments they wished to promote.

A policy-centered approach reveals that the gridlock and polarization that have characterized American policymaking over the past two decades are not politically neutral. The responses (and deliberate failures to respond), have not been random or without significance. On the contrary, they have given a definite direction to the drift of social policy over time. They advantage those adjustments in social provision that lean toward increasing reliance on the private sector. Even within the private sector, they have encouraged a shift away from more "collectivized" or "solidaristic" forms of protection against social risks (those that are organized through employers).

The drift in structures of American social provision over the past two decades has clearly been in the direction of both greater privatization and greater individualization. Planned or not, coherent or not, what is clear is that very substantial changes in the American social contract have appeared over the past quarter-century.

Any assessment of the recent social-policy record reviewed in this volume obviously must reflect the normative orientations and priorities of the analyst. Certainly from the standpoint of social inequality the American record of social-policy adjustment is an unenviable one. There have clearly been very considerable social costs associated with changes in the American social model. For the poor the evolution of labor-market structures and public policies has been fairly successful in providing jobs, but those jobs no longer seem to provide much opportunity for material advancement into the middle class. More disturbing has been the turn toward mass incarceration as an instrument of social control.

Evolving structures of social provision have also had major costs for the middle class. Even as economic insecurity has grown, protections against that insecurity have eroded for most Americans. The system of health insurance has weakened significantly, even as the potential burdens associated with health costs have soared. Retirement security is also at greater risk. Middle-income households are being asked to rely increasingly on their own savings during old age. Yet for most households those savings have not grown. Moreover, the instruments employed to foster private and individualized retirement provision have shifted considerable risk onto individual households. A clear sign of the growing strains falling on middle-class households in the United States has been a sharp rise in personal bankruptcies—and it is an equally clear sign of the times that the policy response was not to address the increasing concentration of financial risk that was driving this trend but to make it much more difficult to file for bankruptcy.

That developments in the United States have led to growing inequality and intensified individual exposure to substantial social risks is perhaps unsurprising—although the degree of change in both respects may be. What is perhaps less obvious is that there seem to be relatively few offsetting gains as a result of these changes. Adverse performance on some outcome measures is one thing if it reflects unavoidable trade-offs. Policymakers might be willing to accept some increases in inequality or exposure to risk if these changes were required in order to achieve valued collective goals. In the American case, and elsewhere, some of these goals might include greater efficiency and effective cost containment in health-care provision, higher rates of national savings, higher economic growth, or diminished long-term projections of fiscal burdens associated with government programs and population aging.

There is, however, very little evidence that any of these potential gains have appeared.

- The pursuit of cost containment in health care has been an abject failure. Indeed, what characterizes the American system over the past two decades is a simultaneous and staggering breakdown of health security *and* a cost explosion without parallel in the affluent democracies.

- National savings have not increased. Generous subsidization of private retirement savings often results not in significant new infusions but in the repackaging of savings to maximize tax avoidance. Moreover, the provision of these subsidies increases public dissaving (deficits). On balance, there appears to be very little net gain, if any.

- The rate of growth in per capita income between 1990 and 2002 was no higher in the United States than it was in the European Union fifteen (EU-15), even as the distribution of that growth was much less equitable.

- The long-term fiscal challenges have not been addressed. Although considerable progress was made in the 1990s, these gains have effectively been reversed since 2000. Essentially nothing has been done to address the greatest long-term challenge: the huge and rapidly escalating costs of the American health-care system.

In short, there seem to be few, if any, offsetting social benefits to set against the social costs of mounting inequality and expanding social risk.

To some observers, this unimpressive record might suggest that American national policymakers are simply incompetent. Instead, what the policy-centered view advanced in this volume suggests is that this record reflects the inescapability of politics. Social-policy arrangements engage powerful interests. Especially in the American context, with its multiple points of access to political decisionmaking and veto-ridden institutional arrangements, these interests have the power to make themselves heard.

In this respect, the market-oriented social-policy initiatives that attract so much current interest are no different than any other kind. One of the claims often made on behalf of such instruments is that they somehow depoliticize policymaking, creating an environment governed by individual, autonomous choice. Yet making markets is an inherently political activity. The structure of the relevant markets needs to be built. Especially in the case of social policies such as health and retirement security, where the prospects for market failure are an ongoing concern, the contours must be established by political authority.

Moreover, it is not as if political authorities can then retire from the scene, leaving a self-regulating system in place. To initiate such policies, politicians will draw on powerful interests for support. Not only will these organized interests' concerns be reflected in the initial designs but these same interests also can be expected to seek opportunities to shift arrangements to their advantage over time.

Structures of policy can be redesigned to constrain competition and oversight and maximize the flow of public subsidies. The most organized among private-sector providers and beneficiaries (typically the most affluent) have the greatest capacity to influence such arrangements. Few of these actors are focused on the most efficient or effective response to social-policy challenges. Few face much incentive to protect open, competitive markets. They do, however, have incentives to stay organized and to mobilize to reconfigure policies on the terms that are the most favorable possible to themselves. It should come as no surprise that recent reforms have done little to advance such broad public goals as health-care cost containment, long-term fiscal balance, or the limitation of economic insecurity. They have been much more effective at channeling resources to organized interests within the conservative coalition—the financial-services industry, health-care providers (such as the pharmaceutical industry), and the very affluent.

Politics also governs efforts to impose austerity—to make difficult choices that would improve the long-term financial setting of the public sector. In the United States, as elsewhere, long-term fiscal projections are alarming. Budget experts emphasize the advantages of moving as swiftly as possible to do something about these issues. Phased-in adjustments would permit more gradual (and thus less disruptive) adaptations. Equally significant, the permanent cost of adjustment would be lower because of the reduced debt service associated with diminished fiscal imbalances. The earlier an adjustment is made, the smaller the adjustment needs to be.

These are powerful economic arguments, but their resonance in the political sphere is much weaker. Imposing visible pain rarely appeals to politicians. Typically, they are motivated to obscure or defer painful choices. This dynamic has been evident in the United States over the past few decades. Although there have been occasional episodes of stringency (the 1983 Social Security amendments, and the deficit reduction agreements of 1990 and 1993), politics has often pushed in the other direction.

Most notably, and with greatest long-term consequences, the Republican coalition appears to have determined that tax reduction is a far more attractive political stance than fiscal conservatism. In the past decade especially, conservatives have placed much higher priority on the aggressive pursuit of tax cuts (heavily tilted to the most affluent) and the expansion of tax subsidies for private social provision (again, heavily tilted to the affluent). Rather than improving, long-term fiscal projections have deteriorated.[1] And again, the targeting of these transfers to the most affluent suggests that for most Americans there have been limited compensations for the decision to accumulate additional public debt. From the perspective of those seeking to reconcile improved long-run fiscal performance with sustained attention to social concerns that justified the welfare state in the first place it is hard to avoid the conclusion that enormous fiscal resources have simply been squandered.

For those eager to find a path that preserves the tremendous achievements of modern social provision, placing those arrangements on a sounder footing rather than jettisoning them, the political dynamic evident in the United States reveals some obvious problems. Certainly in the cases of retirement and, especially, health care—the two great challenges that have commanded the greatest efforts of modern welfare states—mounting political inequality and conservative strength have led to an "adjustment process" in which declines in economic security have been great but improvements in fiscal health and policy efficiency have been largely lacking.

Policy reforms rest on supporting political coalitions. Truly consequential reforms will in turn create new winners and losers. They may also shift expectations in ways that drive further changes. Policymakers cannot simply introduce a technical adjustment to recalibrate social provision and assume that it will be stable and self-regulating. Instead, they must think carefully about the dynamic consequences of their interventions. In particular they need to consider whether they are empowering political interests with a strong stake in pushing their advantage.

The striking American experience suggests that there is nothing hypothetical about this scenario. Here, the dramatic rise in economic inequality and vulnerability have been met with a series of policy initiatives that have enriched particular powerful groups but have neither counteracted those trends nor addressed the most formidable long-term social challenges facing the country. Indeed, in many ways these problems have become worse.

This record stands as a clear, if sobering, testament to the intrinsically political nature of social reform. Careful policy design and assessment must rest on sound political analysis. It is not a subject for technocratic discussion of how such interventions might function in some apolitical world—a world that exists only in fiction and the rhetoric of advocates.

NOTES

1. Long-term projections are clouded by the impending "sunset" provisions of the large tax cuts passed in 2001 and 2003. For political reasons most were scheduled to expire within the next two to seven years, and there is great uncertainty about the prospects for their extension.

REFERENCES

Campbell, Andrea Louise. 2003. *How Policies Make Citizens: Senior Political Activism and the American Welfare State.* Princeton, N.J.: Princeton University Press.
Clemens, Elisabeth S., and James M. Cook. 1999. "Politics and Institutionalism: Explaining Durability and Change." *Annual Review of Sociology* 25: 441–66.
Derthick, Martha, and Steven Teles. 2006. "From Third Rail to Presidential Commitment—And

Back? The Conservative Campaign for Social Security Privatization and the Limits of Long-Term Political Strategy." Unpublished paper. Yale University.

Evans, Peter, Dietrich Reuschemeyer, and Theda Skocpol, editors. 1985. *Bringing the State Back In.* Cambridge: Cambridge University Press.

Fiorina, Morris P. 2004. *Culture War? The Myth of a Polarized America.* New York: Longman.

Hacker, Jacob. 2002. *The Divided Welfare State.* Cambridge: Cambridge University Press.

———. 2004. "Privatizing Risk Without Privatizing the Welfare State: The Hidden Politics of Social Policy Retrenchment in the United States." *American Political Science Review* 98(2): 243–60.

———. 2006. *The Great Risk Shift.* Oxford: Oxford University Press.

Howard, Christopher. 1997. *The Hidden Welfare State.* Princeton, N.J.: Princeton University Press.

Huber, Evelyn, and John Stephens. 2001. *Development and Crisis of the Welfare State.* Chicago, Ill.: University of Chicago Press.

Lange, Matthew, and Dietrich Reuschemeyer, editors. 2006. *States and Development: Historical Antecedents of Stagnation and Advance.* London: Palgrave/Macmillan.

Marwell, Gerald, and Pamela Oliver. 1993. *The Critical Mass in Collective Action: A Micro-Social Theory.* Cambridge: Cambridge University Press.

Melnick, R. Shep. 2003. "From Tax-and-Spend to Mandate-and-Sue: Liberalism After the Great Society." In *The Great Society and the High Tide of Liberalism,* edited by Sidney Milkis and Jerome Mileur. Amherst, Mass.: University of Massachusetts Press.

Moe, Terry M. 1980. *The Organization of Interests: Incentives and the Internal Dynamics of Political Interest Groups.* Chicago, Ill.: University of Chicago Press.

Pierson, Paul. 2001. "Coping with Permanent Austerity: Welfare State Restructuring in Affluent Democracies." In *The New Politics of the Welfare State,* edited by Paul Pierson. Oxford: Oxford University Press.

———. 2007. "The Rise and Reconfiguration of Activist Goverment." In *The Transformation of American Politics: Activist Government and the Rise of Conservatism,* edited by Paul Pierson and Theda Skocpol. Princeton, N.J.: Princeton University Press.

Schattschneider, E. E. 1935. *Politics, Pressures, and the Tariff.* New York: Prentice-Hall.

Schneiberg, Marc, and Elisabeth Clemens. Forthcoming. "The Typical Tools for the Job: Research Strategies in Institutional Analysis." In *How Institutions Change,* edited by Walter W. Powell and Dan L. Jones. Chicago, Ill.: University of Chicago Press.

Skocpol, Theda. 2007. "Government Activism and the Reorganization of American Civic Democracy." In *The Transformation of American Politics,* edited by Paul Pierson and Theda Skocpol. Princeton, N.J.: Princeton University Press.

Skowronek, Stephen. 1982. *Building a New American State: The Expansion of National Administrative Capacities, 1877–1920.* Cambridge: Cambridge University Press.

Teles, Steven. Forthcoming. *The Rise of the Conservative Legal Movement.* Princeton, N.J.: Princeton University Press.

Index

Made in the USA
Middletown, DE
23 October 2020